D1116839

Philosophers, Sufis, and Caliphs

What was the relationship between government and religion in Middle Eastern and North African history? In a world of caliphs, sultans, and judges, who exercised political and religious authority? In this book, Ali Humayun Akhtar investigates debates about leadership that involved ruling circles and scholars of jurisprudence and theology. At the heart of this story is a medieval rivalry between three caliphates: the Umayyads of Cordoba, the Fatimids of Cairo, and the Abbasids of Baghdad. In a fascinating revival of Late Antique Hellenism, Aristotelian and Platonic notions of wisdom became a key component of how these caliphs debated their authority as political leaders. By tracing how these political debates impacted the theological and jurisprudential scholars (*'ulamā'*) and their own conception of communal guidance, Akhtar offers a new picture of premodern political authority and the connections between Western and Islamic civilizations. It will be of use to students and specialists of the premodern and modern Middle East and North Africa.

Ali Humayun Akhtar is an Assistant Professor at Bates College. He is also the Robert M. Kingdon Fellow at the Institute for Research in the Humanities at the University of Wisconsin-Madison. He holds a PhD in History and Middle Eastern Studies from New York University.

Philosophers, Sufis, and Caliphs

Politics and Authority from Cordoba to Cairo and Baghdad

Ali Humayun Akhtar

Bates College, Maine
University of Wisconsin-Madison

CAMBRIDGE
UNIVERSITY PRESS

CAMBRIDGE
UNIVERSITY PRESS

University Printing House, Cambridge CB2 8BS, United Kingdom

One Liberty Plaza, 20th Floor, New York, NY 10006, USA

477 Williamstown Road, Port Melbourne, VIC 3207, Australia

4843/24, 2nd Floor, Ansari Road, Daryaganj, Delhi – 110002, India

79 Anson Road, #06-04/06, Singapore 079906

Cambridge University Press is part of the University of Cambridge.

It furthers the University's mission by disseminating knowledge in the pursuit of education, learning, and research at the highest international levels of excellence.

www.cambridge.org
Information on this title: www.cambridge.org/9781107182011
DOI: 10.1017/9781316855669

© Ali Humayun Akhtar 2017

This publication is in copyright. Subject to statutory exception and to the provisions of relevant collective licensing agreements, no reproduction of any part may take place without the written permission of Cambridge University Press.

First published 2017

Printed in the United States of America by Sheridan Books, Inc.

A catalogue record for this publication is available from the British Library.

Library of Congress Cataloging-in-Publication Data
Names: Akhtar, Ali Humayun, author.
Title: Philosophers, sufis, and caliphs: politics and authority from Cordoba to Cairo and Baghdad / Ali Humayun Akhtar.
Description: Cambridge, United Kingdom: Cambridge University Press, 2017. | Includes bibliographical references and index.
Identifiers: LCCN 2017007508 | ISBN 9781107182011 (hardback)
Subjects: LCSH: Islam and politics. | Islamic Empire – Politics and government. | Caliphs. | Sultans. | Judges. | Umayyad dynasty. | Fatimites. | Abbasids. | Sufis. | Islamic philosophy. | Philosophy, Ancient – Influence.
Classification: LCC BP173.7.A4924 2017 | DDC 297.2/7209–dc23
LC record available at https://lccn.loc.gov/2017007508

ISBN 978-1-107-18201-1 Hardback

Cambridge University Press has no responsibility for the persistence or accuracy of URLs for external or third-party Internet Web sites referred to in this publication and does not guarantee that any content on such Web sites is, or will remain, accurate or appropriate.

For my parents,
Dr. Humayun Aftab Akhtar and
Ms. Yosria M. Zaki El Sabban, and
for my siblings

Contents

Part II Philosophical Sufis among Scholars (*'ulamā'*) and Their Impact on Political Culture

4 Sufi Metaphysics in the Twelfth Century 137
Sufism and Its Integration of Philosophical Doctrines 137
The Konya Manuscript of Ibn Barrajān's Major *Tafsīr* 145
The Epistemology of Sufi Metaphysics 146
Philosophical Knowledge and Esoteric Hermeneutics 149
Celestial Agency and the Mystical Ascent 157
Ibn Barrajān's Reform of Philosophy 162

5 A New Political Model and Its Sufi Dimensions 178
A Sufi Debate about Communal Leadership 178
Ibn Qasī's *Doffing of the Sandals* 182
The Platonizing Ascent to the Universals 186
A Philosophical Sufi Cosmology 193
Sufis in Politics 199

6 The Transformation of Caliphal Politics 211
The Almohads' Articulation of a New Caliphal Legitimacy 213
Mysticizing Aristotle in a Platonizing Sufi Treatise 216
Ḥayy ibn Yaqẓān's Celestial Promenade 221
An Enduring Dialectic of Political and Religious Authority 225

Conclusion 238

Bibliography 241
Index 259

Figures

Acknowledgments

This book is based on research that I conducted while teaching at three institutions: New York University, Bard College, and Bates College. It was at NYU, as a doctoral candidate and instructor under the supervision of Dr. Everett K. Rowson, where I learned how to grapple with the labyrinth of primary sources that have survived from the medieval world. I would like to express my deepest gratitude to Dr. Rowson for guiding my research through each new challenging step during my years at NYU, instilling new ideas in my research trajectory, encouraging me to pursue research from a diverse set of investigative tracks, and reminding me to "keep digging" through the rich array of textual materials available. I am also very grateful to Dr. Marion H. Katz at NYU, who encouraged me to examine and reconsider multiple theoretical frameworks in my research, and who always offered a sense of intellectual security in moments when my scholarly aspirations seemed daunting during my doctoral years. I also thank Dr. Maribel Fierro at the Spanish National Research Council (CSIC) in Madrid, whose work has opened my eyes to the richness of the interdisciplinary research undertaken in European and North African universities, and who has helped me see one of the most beautiful and rich eras of world history, al-Andalus and its legacy, through multiple investigative perspectives. I thank Dr. Tamer el-Leithy at NYU for having been an inspiration to every scholar who aspires to master the diverse genres of edited and unedited materials available in the world's archival and manuscript libraries. I also thank Dr. Arang Keshavarzian at NYU for encouraging me to analyze the interplay between politics and social movements when conducting research on the Middle East.

The trajectory of my research for this project also reflects the continued guidance of my undergraduate advisor at Cornell University, Dr. Shawkat M. Toorawa, whom I thank for believing in my abilities as an aspiring historian and educator at a time when there was a variety of intellectual, research, and career choices to pursue. I thank Dr. Ross Brann at Cornell, who encouraged my fascination with the confluence of cultures and languages in history, and who directed through patient guidance my interest in thinking about research at a doctoral level. I also thank Dr. Cynthia Robinson at Cornell, who has inspired me to think of art as a window into history and humanity to the point of helping me realize that the scholar of the humanities must aspire to turn a work of scholarship into a carefully crafted work of literature.

I am also grateful to Dr. Ahmed Ferhadi, Dr. Sibel Erol, and Dr. Mohammad Mehdi Khorrami at NYU for many years of guiding my fascination with world languages through coursework on Arabic, Turkish, and Persian literature. This language training has allowed me to expand my research on comparative politics and intellectual history, which was the basis of this book, into the realm of early modern global trade routes in my forthcoming second book.

At Bard College and Bates College, I thank all of my colleagues and students for many years of truly enriching dialogue that has helped me think in new ways about questions of methodology when conducting research on medieval and early modern history. At Bard College, I am particularly grateful to Dr. Mairaj Syed, Dr. Dina Ramadan, Dr. Jennifer Derr, and the entire faculty in the Departments of History, Middle Eastern Studies, and Latin American and Iberian Studies. At Bates College, I thank all of my colleagues in the Departments of Religious Studies, Classical and Medieval Studies, Asian Studies, and History. I am particularly grateful to Dr. Marcus Bruce, Dr. Cynthia Baker, Dr. John Strong, Dr. Thomas Tracy, and Dr. Alison Melnick. While in New England, I had the opportunity to have conversations with a number of faculty whose research methodologies inspired some of my own, and who offered feedback of inestimable value. I thank especially Dr. Kenneth Garden of Tufts University as well as Dr. Russell Hopley and Dr. Robert Morrison of Bowdoin College for sharing their investigative insights on the premodern world.

I thank the students in my survey courses and seminars at both Bard College and Bates College, where the chance to be involved in liberal arts education has been a deeply enriching and formative experience as an educator. Class discussions offered an enlightening opportunity to exchange perspectives on historical research methods in a way that has reshaped my understanding of questions of historical agency and intellectual boundaries in the study of Europe, the Middle East, and East Asia.

I also thank Dr. Susan Friedman, Director of the Institute for Research in the Humanities (IRH) at the University of Wisconsin-Madison, for cultivating an interdisciplinary intellectual environment that allowed me to continue research for my second book on global trade networks while revising and expanding this book. The time I have spent at UW-Madison as Robert M. Kingdon Fellow of Judeo-Christian Studies has been central to the progress of both books, and I thank Dr. Andre Wink, Dr. Elaine Fisher, Dr. Andreas Schwab, and Dr. Nathanael Andrade for their conversations and profound insights.

I am also grateful to the staff members of the various manuscript and archival libraries that have been central to my research, especially those of the Süleymaniye Manuscript Library of Istanbul, the Yusuf Ağa Manuscript Library of Konya, the Spanish National Research Council (CSIC) in Madrid, the Freie Universität of Berlin, the National Library and Archives of Egypt in Cairo, and the National Library and Archives of Morocco in Rabat.

At Cambridge University Press, I would like to thank Maria Marsh, William Hammell, Cassi Roberts, and Kate Gavino for taking on this book project and moving it through production with patience and multifaceted editorial expertise. Maria Marsh's editorial insights and close attention to this project has made the process of completing it a truly rewarding one. Cassi Roberts moved this book through the production process with extraordinary care. I also thank the scholars who reviewed this book for Cambridge University Press. Their careful and thorough feedback has been of utmost importance to the completion of this book.

Finally, I would like to thank each individual I have encountered in the world's spectrum of cultures, philosophies, and spiritual traditions who has inspired in me a deeper understanding of diversity, optimism, and love in the spirit of shared humanities.

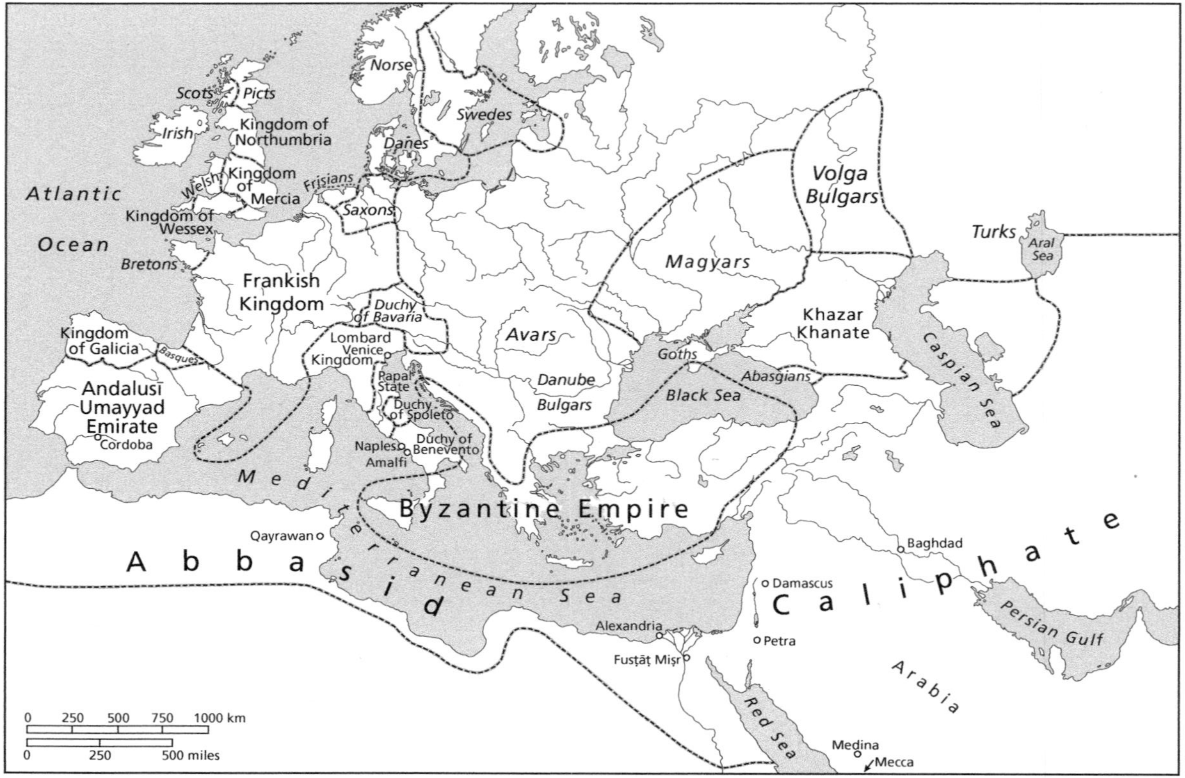

The Abbasid caliphate after the 750s following the transition of the late antique Middle East and North Africa from Eastern Roman (Byzantine) and Sassanian dominion to Umayyad ascendancy (r. 661–750).

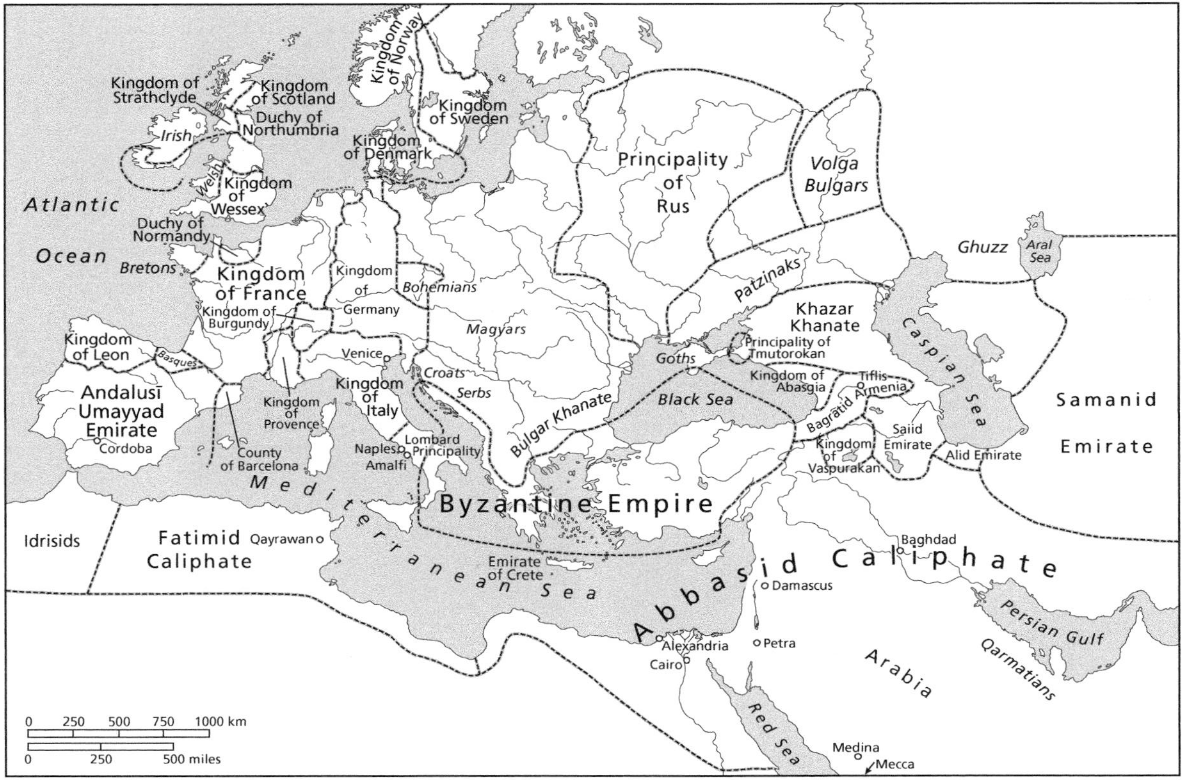

Three caliphates in competition in the 900s: the Andalusī Umayyads of Cordoba, the Fatimids of Cairo (after 969), and the Abbasids of Baghdad.

Introduction
Politics, Law, and Authority in the Abbasid and Fatimid Eras

What was the relationship between government and religion in Middle Eastern and North African history? In a world of caliphs, sultans, and judges, who exercised political and religious authority? This book investigates debates about leadership that involved ruling circles and scholars (*ʿulamāʾ*) of jurisprudence and theology from medieval Cordoba to Cairo and Baghdad. At the heart of this story is a historical rivalry between three caliphates: the Umayyads of Cordoba, the Fatimids of Cairo, and the Abbasids of Baghdad. In a fascinating revival of late antique Hellenism, Aristotelian and Platonic notions of wisdom became a key component of how caliphs articulated their authority as political leaders. By tracing how these political debates impacted the scholars (*ʿulamāʾ*) and their own conception of communal guidance, this book offers a new picture of two key phenomena central to world history: the interplay between ruling political authority and scholarly religious authority that distinguished the Middle East and North Africa from medieval Europe, and the enduring legacy of Aristotelian-Neoplatonic political theory, psychology, and ethics in the Middle East and North Africa prior to the European Renaissance (ca. 1300s-1600s).

The Judiciary and Islamic Intellectual Culture in the Early Centuries

The scholars (*ʿulamāʾ*) and their changing relationship with both the wider populace and the ruling circles of caliphs and courtiers are at the center of this book's two main questions: First, in what ways did Hellenistic thought of the late antique Middle East find a place in the politics, theology, and ethics of the Islamic period? Second, what was the relationship between models of political and religious authority in the early Islamic-era Middle East, where urban scholars (*ʿulamāʾ*) and not ruling circles dominated religious authority? The scholars were a broad group who overlapped with other influential figures in the cities of

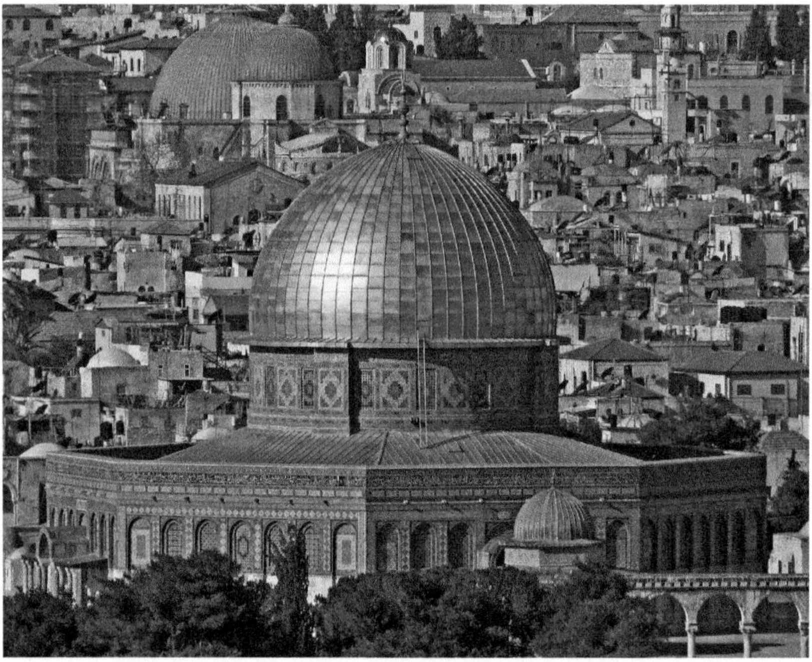

Figure I.1. Dome of the Rock in Jerusalem, built in the late 600s in a design at the intersection of Eastern Roman (Byzantine), Arabian, and Islamic visual cultures.

the Middle East and North Africa. Their social influence and expertise in a growing set of scripture-related sciences – such as scriptural exegesis, *ḥadīth* science, jurisprudence (*fiqh*) including commercial law, language theory, ethics, and speculative theology (*kalām*) – meant that their legacies intertwined with those of the most famous tradespeople, astronomers, Aristotelian logicians, and saintly mystics. In the medieval or classical Islamic era prior to the arrival of the early modern Ottomans, judges Ibn Rushd (Averroes 595 A.H./1198 C.E.) in Almohad Cordoba and al-Ghazālī (d. 505/1111) in Abbasid-Seljuk Baghdad represented examples of the more politically influential and polymathic figures within the wider urban scholarly networks.

Ibn Rushd was memorialized in Renaissance-era Europe as the Aristotelian philosopher Averroes who inspired the rise of Latin Averroism. His writings on philosophy and religion, despite emerging from an Islamic intellectual milieu, influenced the writings of the monumental Catholic philosopher and theologian San Tommaso d'Aquino of Sicily (St. Thomas Aquinas d. 1274). In his own historical context, however, Ibn Rushd was one of the scholars of the Mālikī school of jurisprudence in Sunnī Islam, the chief judge of Almohad Cordoba, a Graeco-Arabic philosopher (*faylasūf*), a physician, and an influential scientist in the history of astronomy, physics, medicine, and mathematics.[1] al-Ghazālī, likewise remembered in Europe as the philosopher Algazel, was in his own historical context one of the scholars of the Shāfiʿī school of jurisprudence, a central figure in the introduction of Aristotelian-Avicennan modal logic in both jurisprudence and speculative theology (Ashʿarism), and notably for Part II of this book, an early philosophical mystic (Sufi metaphysician).[2] As administrative judges and polymathic scholars, both Ibn Rushd and al-Ghazālī represented a phenomenon found in both the Abbasid and the early modern Ottoman eras, in which scholars played an increasingly influential role in multiple aspects of the social, political, economic, and intellectual life of the cities of the Middle East and North Africa.

The history of scholars such as Ibn Rushd and al-Ghazālī offers a lens for investigating the elusive and changing relationship between medieval political authority and religious authority precisely because the scholars' diverse activities extended into the realms of both governing administrative circles and the general urban populace. This fluid relationship between ruling circles and scholars, and the sometimes contentious dialogues they had about communal leadership, has been studied largely in the context of the judiciary.

In the early centuries of Islamic history, particularly after the rise of the Umayyad caliphate in 661 in formerly Byzantine (Eastern Roman) Damascus, the scholars of Islam rose to a powerful leadership position in the urban societies of the Middle East. In a trend analogous to the rise of rabbis in rabbinic Judaism in the ancient Middle East, the scholars developed a reputation in the eyes of local Muslims and urban ruling circles for their expertise in the application of particular modes of knowledge, including Islamic ethics. This expertise in the ability to apply sound reasoning in scripture-related ethical, legal, and theological matters became the basis of a degree of religious authority that ultimately demarcated the changing contours of the ruling circles' own authority.[3] The scholars did not interpret the claims to a caliphate made by the Umayyad dynasty (r. 661–750 in Damascus) or the following Abbasid dynasty (r. 750–1258 in Baghdad, r. 1261–1517 in Cairo) as a claim to being the final or even primary authority on juridical and theological affairs. Rather, they recognized these caliphs as politically and religiously uniting figures in a manner that might be compared to the way Western Europeans viewed the Holy Roman Emperor, who was seen as a ruler among rulers with the privilege of representing the political unity of the Roman Catholic world west of Greek Orthodox centers. The caliph, whose political power was counterbalanced by the power of ministers (viziers) and regional military governors (sultans, emirs), stood officially at the head of a hierarchy of these political administrators and inherited the privilege of offering an investiture of authority to local governing circles, from the emirs of Cordoba to the sultans of Persia and India.[4] There were aspects of continuity in this political framework with the first caliphate in Medina (r. 632–660). The first four caliphs (Abū Bakr, ʿUmar, ʿUthmān, ʿAlī), who were among the Companions (*ṣaḥāba*) of the Prophet Muḥammad (d. 11/632) and who therefore knew him personally, governed in consultation with various individuals recognized for their knowledge of legal matters and various customs, including the practices (*sunan*) of the Prophet.[5] The Prophet's wife ʿĀʾisha is notable in this regard as a major authority on these early practices. The growing body of scholars grew partly out of these early circles of learned figures, particularly those with formal knowledge of the traditions of the Prophet (*ḥadīth*). The faith of the general populace in these traditions meant that the scholars of Islam came to exercise significant religious authority during the caliphal eras of the Umayyads in Damascus, the Abbasids in Baghdad, and the Andalusī Umayyads of Cordoba. From an administrative perspective, with the expansion of the judiciary as a formal system of administrative courts oriented around the scholars' expanding jurisprudential sciences, the judiciary's institutions increasingly became a historical site of negotiation or dialogue between ruling circles and scholars about communal leadership. What made the judiciary a somewhat contested site of authority, one in which ruling political authority and scholarly religious authority were often counterbalancing forces, was the fact that individual scholars reacted to its historical development in different ways, particularly in the earliest centuries.

Most early specialists of jurisprudence within the growing body of scholars earned their livelihood from other skills, numbering among merchants, copiers of manuscripts, textile manufacturers, and tradespeople in a variety of occupations illustrative of their deep ties with local communities in the cities and towns of the Middle East and North Africa.[6] That is, the scholars' growing expertise in fields such as lexicography and Islamic ethics was not an inherently salaried pursuit. In terms of harmonizing paid careers with polymathic intellectual pursuits, the financial situation of the early scholars paralleled that of the early astronomers and philosophers. Some of the most influential figures in the history of medicine and surgery were also philosophers and astronomers, which meant that many astronomers saw patients when not reading Aristotelian-Neoplatonic writings on the nature of the cosmos.[7] In the case of the scholars' harmonization of paid careers and intellectual pursuits, the push to professionalize the geographically wide networks of scholars as full-time paid jurists and judges in a growing administrative system of courts was partly the aspiration of centralizing ruling circles. Ruling circles may have drawn on a mix of early Islamic and pre-Islamic administrative practices in this process. As far as how scholars reacted to and participated in the administrative development of the judiciary, some scholars resisted appointments to administrative positions as judges, protective of what they perceived as the independence of their knowledge and authority.[8] Other scholars, however, were more willing to take on official judicial appointments, even in the early centuries.[9]

Significantly, even after the proliferation of administrative courts of justice and later theological colleges, which came to be funded largely by charitable endowments (*awqāf*), the scholars largely held onto their intellectual dominance in the justice system because of the epistemic authority they held at a popular level.[10] What supports this conclusion is the vast surviving body of non-binding legal opinions (*fatāwā*) from the writings of early scholars, which are illustrative of how scholars were available locally to offer a variety of answers to questions dealing with the most mundane of family matters and the mediation of neighborhood disputes.[11] The general populace's informal accessibility to the scholars, who issued these non-binding juridical opinions in their capacity as specialists of jurisprudence, continued to develop hand in hand with the scholars' more formal presence in these administrative courts as both judges and advisers to judges. Court-appointed judges, who were typically scholars themselves, often drew directly on the growing body of non-binding legal opinions that were specific to what became the most influential schools of jurisprudence in early Sunnī circles: the Ḥanafī, Shāfiʿī, Mālikī, and Ḥanbalī schools of thought, and for a long period particularly in al-Andalus, the Awzāʿī and Ẓāhirī schools of thought. In some cities and periods, these judges drew directly on the opinion of a sitting juris consul (*muftī*) for a specialized legal matter.

To be sure, the scholars' role in the judiciary did not necessarily limit the rulers' ability to mete out justice directly. On the one hand, the scholars' epistemic authority in many cases dictated how even a caliph who attempted to impose an unpopular legal ruling against the wishes of the scholars risked running afoul with urban Muslim populations who looked to those scholars as ethical mediators of local disputes. On the other hand, in the historical development of the judiciary, the scholars and their opinions did not dominate all aspects of these courts given key limitations of jurisdiction in the governance of public space, security, and order. The *maẓālim* courts and the jurisdiction of market inspectors (*muḥtasib*) in public space offer illustrative examples.

Specifically, beyond the early limitations of interference in the Christian and Jewish clergy's internal communal affairs, the Muslim scholars' religious authority in the judiciary was additionally limited or perhaps counterbalanced by a court structure known as the *maẓālim*. The *maẓālim* courts were a type of court system in which rulers and not scholars administered justice directly. The jurisdiction of a ruling figure in these courts had theoretical parallels with the way the market inspectors, who were political administrators, oversaw financial and social practices in the public marketplaces. On the one hand, the *maẓālim* courts and the role of the market inspectors illustrate the extent to which some legal jurisdictions were shaped directly by ruling circles. On the other hand, the respective roles of a ruler in the *maẓālim* courts and a market inspector became partly embedded in the way the scholars themselves theorized, or more likely accommodated retroactively, the historical role of governing circles in administering justice and maintaining security and order in a slowly expanding public sphere.[12] Notably, this scholarly theorization of the role of ruling circles in maintaining security and order occurred long before the bureaucratic nation-state made deep inroads of direct governance into a vastly expanded public sphere. In this context of the scholars' theorization of ruling governance in empire, it is notable that the scholars also identified and recognized aspects of other legal systems that already existed in the central lands of the Middle East. These legal systems include the laws and customs of the previously mentioned Christian and Jewish clergy, who held onto semiautonomous legal jurisdictions within their own Middle Eastern communities.[13] In sum, the image of these distinctions in legal systems and legal jurisdictions in the medieval Middle East, from courts with a scholarly *muftī* and the ruling *maẓālim* courts to the semi-independent legal realm of the Christian clergy, offers a picture of Muslim scholars who constituted a significant part of premodern religious authority, but whose authority and power was contested or perhaps counterbalanced within the judiciary by ruling political authority and non-Muslim religious authority.

Against the backdrop of this historical development of the judiciary and the rise of the scholars, what deserves more attention in current research is how this interplay between the rulers' political authority and the Muslim scholars' religious authority continued to develop not only inside, but also outside the judiciary's institutions. In the current study, the multifaceted realm of Islamic intellectual culture, and specifically written debates on philosophy and theology, is of particular concern.[14] Alongside the vast corpus of surviving writings on jurisprudence, legal theory, language theory, ethics, and other fields in the expanding scholarly sciences, the scholars' writings on philosophy and theology have also survived. These latter works offer overlooked evidence of the way models of ruling political leadership and scholarly religious leadership developed in tandem within a larger dialogue over the intellectual underpinnings of communal guidance. By the tenth century, distinct trends in Graeco-Arabic philosophical doctrines were becoming an increasingly common and openly acknowledged part of how ruling circles and scholars debated and articulated conceptions of sound knowledge, communal guidance, and leadership. One controversial example of an influential political model that drew on Graeco-Arabic theories of cosmology is the tenth-century Fatimid caliphate, which was founded by political reformers within a subgroup of Ismāʿīlī Shiism. As discussed in the next section of this introduction, by the time the Fatimids founded Cairo in the late tenth century on the site of Fusṭāṭ, Fatimid ruling circles had begun to project to their neighbors in Abbasid Baghdad and Cordoba a unique representation of the Ismāʿīlī Shiite caliph as a semi-messianic (*mahdī*) Platonizing guide to salvation. The Fatimids thus challenged not only the ruling political authority of the Abbasid caliphs in Baghdad, but also the scholarly religious authority of the networks of predominantly Sunnī scholars and rising Imāmī (Twelver) Shiite scholars.

The Fatimid Ismāʿīlī theologians' embrace of Graeco-Arabic cosmological doctrines in their conceptions of communal guidance was not an isolated phenomenon. In the same early centuries of the Islamic-era Middle East, although the Sunnī scholars rejected the Fatimid caliphate's Platonizing conception of political and religious leadership, the scholars had already been in the process of expanding their sciences and conceptions of scholarly religious authority in ways that engaged the Aristotelian-Neoplatonic theories of the Graeco-Arabic philosophers. Specifically, many scholars of the Qur'an and *ḥadīth* who studied sciences such as lexicography were also interested in the theological value of Graeco-Arabic philosophy's analysis in logical reasoning, doctrines in psychology on the soul and the intellect, and theories of cosmology about the underlying elements of the world and the agency of God in it. That is, from Cordoba to Baghdad, the early Sunnī scholars were part of an intersection of diverse intellectual networks that included, most notably for this book, the following: dedicated *ḥadīth* specialists among the scholars (*ʿulamāʾ*), writers of Arabic-language commentaries on Aristotle (*Arisṭūṭālīs*) and Plato (*Aflāṭūn*) among the Baghdad Peripatetics (*mashshāʾiyyūn*), and writers of a specifically Islamic metaphysics among the speculative theologians (*mutakallimūn*) interested in both *ḥadīth* and Graeco-Arabic philosophy, each group intermingling with the next and influencing each other's works. In the case of the Cordovan scholars Ibn Masarra (d. 319/931) and Ibn Ḥazm (d. 456/1064), discussed in Chapters 1 and 2, their writings illustrate how the polymathic learning of a scholar who studied *ḥadīth* in the tenth and eleventh centuries often included an education in Aristotelian-Neoplatonic doctrines related to scriptural topics, from discussions of human intellect and sense perception to the underlying mechanisms of causality. That is, the example of early Sunnī scholars interested in philosophy shows that in addition to studying scriptural texts, jurisprudence, ethics, and other expanding Islamic sciences, a scholar in early Sunnism might also engage the tools of Aristotelian logical reasoning or Neoplatonic conceptions of the soul and intellect in order to investigate more deeply the various scriptural references to the world's natural phenomena, the afterlife, and what lies beyond the visible realm both within and beyond the human mind.

With a focus on these changing modes of knowledge and authority that were part of both ruling and scholarly conceptions of communal leadership, the heart of this book offers an investigation of the following two-part hypothesis: First, in the multi-religious, scripture-valuing urban societies of the medieval Middle East and North Africa, where Graeco-Arabic philosophical doctrines were in various levels of circulation among the general populace of urban Muslim, Christian, and Jewish communities, debates within ruling circles and scholarly networks about sound leadership of the growing Muslim populace played out not only in a negotiation over the expanding judiciary, but also in a theological dialogue about Graeco-Arabic psychological and cosmological doctrines that had widely recognized implications for conceptions of personal virtue and communal ethics. Second, the joint participation of ruling circles and the scholars in this dialogue, which occurred through both oral and textual mechanisms such as the patronage of books, was an intertwined and contested activity illustrative of how the ruling political leadership and scholarly religious leadership shaped each other's historical development in a dialectic of authority that constituted neither a ruling political orthodoxy nor a scholarly clerical orthodoxy. The parallel rise of philosopher-governors among the caliphs together with philosophical theologians and philosophical Sufis among the scholars offers a window into this interaction of political and religious leadership.

Given this overview of the judiciary as a site of the rulers' and scholars' dialogue over leadership, and against the backdrop of an Islamic intellectual culture that was an additional site of ruling and scholarly debates about leadership, the remainder of this historical introduction will turn more closely to the following questions: Why did specific Graeco-Arabic doctrines in logical reasoning, psychology, and cosmology become part

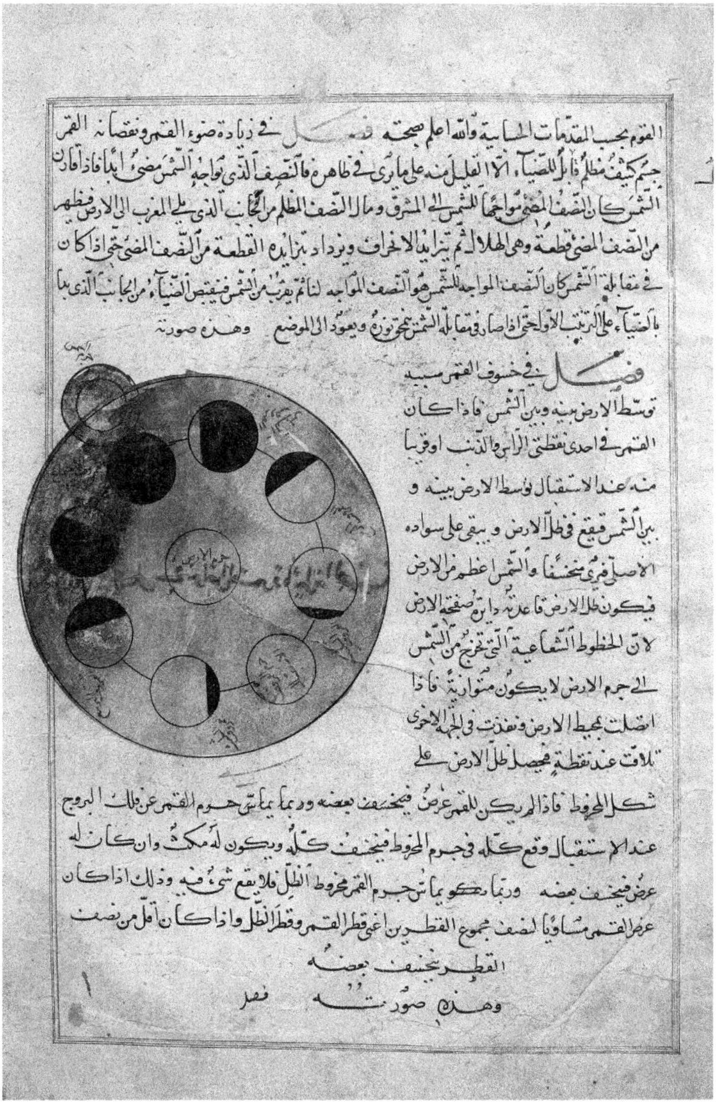

Figure I.2. Phases of the moon analyzed in a fourteenth-century Arabic manuscript.

of the ways that early Abbasid-era Sunnī-majority scholars and Muslim ruling circles articulated theories about the authority to guide and lead the early community? A key point that runs through the rest of this introduction is that among Abbasid-era rulers and scholars, conceptions of sound knowledge and leadership engaged not only sacred text, but also the enduring legacy of late antique Hellenistic cosmology, which permeated the popular material and visual culture of the early Islamic-era Middle East.

The Scholars (*ʿulamāʾ*) and the Graeco-Arabic Philosophers

The scholars (*ʿulamāʾ*) were analyzed in the previous section as an urban social network with influential scripture-related knowledge in sciences such as jurisprudence, legal theory, language theory, and ethics. Coinciding with the bibliophile Abbasid caliphs' support for the translation of Hellenistic philosophy and science in Baghdad, and in a move reminiscent of the Middle East's late antique Christian clergy and Jewish rabbis' activities, some of the Muslim scholars began to engage Aristotelian-Neoplatonic philosophy in its Graeco-Arabic form when debating two questions: What did it mean to be one of the Muslim scholars, and what modes of knowledge were relevant and sound when providing spiritual and theological guidance to the faithful Muslim populace? In the eyes of large swaths of early scholars in Sunnism, it was not inherently problematic to draw on the curriculum of late antique Aristotelian-Neoplatonic philosophy and science in the investigation of scripture-oriented theological questions about the cosmos, God's agency in that cosmos, and the mechanisms of the human intellect and soul as referenced in scripture. The study of particular sciences in the Graeco-Arabic philosophical curriculum was of particular interest to early scholars because it included not only the widely practiced medical sciences, but also natural sciences such as astronomy, which had perhaps the clearest religious significance both for ritual and theological matters. From the perspective of ritual, the nature of the daily prayer and the fasting month of Ramadan encouraged a precise awareness of solar patterns, lunar movement, and geographical direction. From the perspective of scriptural exegesis and theology, astronomy offered the possibility of exploring further the omnipresent astronomical references found throughout the Qur'an that described the nature of the cosmos and the agency of God in it. These questions were at the heart of the early Muʿtazilī and Ashʿarī speculative theologians' (*mutakallimūn*) investigations of the nature and underlying elements of the created cosmos as experienced by mankind and as described in scripture.[15] The fact that scholars of *ḥadīth* began to participate in these discussions, and the fact that both *ḥadīth* scholars and specialists in speculative theology began to engage the writings of the Baghdad Peripatetics, meant that for many scholars, aspects of the late antique Aristotelian-Neoplatonic curriculum of philosophy were key to what it meant to be one of the scholars of Islam by the tenth and eleventh centuries.[16] To be sure, these developments were debated internally among the scholars, and Chapters 1 and 2 highlight how these debates even erupted politically in the tenth century. However, by the time the Timurids and Ottomans rose to power at the end of the European medieval era, the scholars of Islam had come to incorporate into the Islamic sciences a wide variety of disciplines transmitted in Arabic and Persian from the late antique philosophical curriculum. In what illustrates the longevity of these developments, fourteenth-century scholar Niẓām al-Dīn al-Nīsabūrī even declared the study of astronomy morally recommended (*mandūb*) as a kind of religious virtue, while the most influential jurisprudential college in fifteenth-century Timurid Samarkand incorporated an observatory to enrich the Islamic sciences' curriculum.[17]

In an additional avenue for an early scholarly bridge between Graeco-Arabic philosophy and Islamic theological writing, the early philosophers among the Baghdad Peripatetics also described the ancient philosophical tradition as one with roots in the wisdom of prophetic figures such as Luqmān and Idrīs, the latter whom some early philosophers identified with the ancient sage Hermes.[18] The identification of Hermes with the prophet Idrīs became commonplace by the ninth century in what further contextualizes the various angles of early scholarly interest in Graeco-Arabic philosophy. In late antique Hellenistic philosophical writing, Hermes appears to have been a marginal figure in contrast with the towering legacies of philosophers like Aristotle, Socrates, and Plato. However, early Graeco-Arabic philosophers emphasized the description of Hermes as having achieved an intellectual ascent to the higher world, a goal that was of paramount importance to mystical piety in early Islamic mysticism. In the lens of Aristotelian-Neoplatonic and specifically Plotinian cosmology and psychology, which was central to the writings of the Baghdad Peripatetics, Hermes' intellectual ascent was understood as the ascent of the human soul toward a greater Universal Soul, of which the Neoplatonic human soul was a part. Plotinus (d. 270), who was born in Graeco-Roman Egypt and who was one of the most influential Platonic philosophers after Plato and Aristotle, understood the human intellect and soul to be connected to a greater Universal Intellect and Universal Soul that were spaceless and outside of time. In late antique Plotinian psychology and cosmology, the underlying principles of the cosmos included One, Intellect, and Soul. al-Fārābī interpreted this cosmology according to Ptolemaic astronomy in a revised theory on the celestial emanation of these principles through the world's ensouled cognizant spinning planets, identified by some

Graeco-Arabic philosophers as planets with angels.[19] This emanation, according to Neoplatonic cosmology, proceeds logically down to the sublunary world of man. From this perspective, Hermes's intellectual ascent was the human soul's rediscovery of this primordial spiritual realm. The early philosophical emphasis on Hermes as having achieved an intellectual ascent to the higher world encouraged the claim among some particularly influential early Graeco-Arabic philosophers that the ancient Hermes, identified increasingly with the prophet Idrīs, was the most accomplished of the ancient sages. This picture of Hermes-Idrīs was one of the various links that bridged Graeco-Arabic philosophical writing with both theological and mystical writing among the early scholars of Islam. Two influential figures in transmitting this early understanding of Hermes-Idrīs more widely are of particular significance, as their legacies illustrate the process through which the intersection of Graeco-Arabic philosophy and theological writing became more widespread. The first is the philosophical Sufi Shihāb al-Dīn Yaḥyā al-Suhrawardī (d. ca. 1190–2), and the second is the group of early anonymous writers of the highly influential and widely circulated *Epistles of the Pure Brethren.*[20]

The first figure, Shihāb al-Dīn Yaḥyā al-Suhrawardī, was the founder of a school of Sufi metaphysics that brought together philosophically oriented theological writing with theories on mystical experience. His school of thought, known as Illuminationism (*Ḥikmat al-Ishrāq*), offered a Neoplatonic (Neoplatonic-Avicennan) critique of aspects of Aristotelian (Aristotelian-Avicennan) formal and material logic.[21] al-Suhrawardī's legacy represents the culmination of a process, highlighted in Part II of this book, in which scholars who were interested in Islamic mysticism increasingly and deliberately drew on Neoplatonic-Avicennan philosophical doctrines and, in some cases, represented figures like Hermes, Plato, and the ancient Hellenistic philosophers as pre-Islamic proto-Sufi figures.[22] The second group, the Brethren of Purity, was an anonymous philosophical coterie in early Abbasid Iraq who wrote and transmitted the *Epistles of the Pure Brethren*. The *Epistles* were a set of popularly circulated philosophical works that were influential in the development of Platonizing theological writing in both Sunnism and Shiism, particularly among Sunnī mystics and Ismāʿīli Shiite theologians. The wide scholarly and popular appeal of the *Epistles of the Pure Brethren* is well documented in early Islamic history, and while later Ismāʿīlī theologians took a particular interest in their writings and actively adopted their legacy, the Brethren's original theological affiliation remains uncertain given their eclectic interests and intentional anonymity. Though some of their strongest critics were found in Sunnī scholarly circles, the writings were in fact absorbed very quickly by both early Sunnī and Ismāʿīlī Shiite theological circles, both having picked and chosen which sections they found sound and valuable. Current research has left the question open of the Brethren of Purity's original theological affiliation in what illustrates how the *Epistles*' eclectic mix of Graeco-Arabic philosophy, Islamic theology, and mysticism in their diverse discussions of the mind and the cosmos had wide appeal in early Islamic history.[23] The legacies of al-Suhrawardī and the Pure Brethren together underline the point that in sum, from the perspective of the predominantly Sunnī scholars interested in Graeco-Arabic philosophy's relevance to their own education and conception of communal guidance, multiple avenues existed for a theological engagement with philosophical doctrines in psychology and cosmology.

By the twelfth century, against this backdrop of various links connecting Graeco-Arabic philosophy and Islamic theological writing, two intertwining trends emerged outside the realm of jurisprudence in the absorption of Graeco-Arabic philosophy into the scholarly sciences. The first was the incorporation of Aristotelian-Avicennan logic into Islamic theology's methodology, a development that paralleled the use of Aristotelian-Avicennan logic in Islamic jurisprudence. The second was the looser incorporation of conclusions in Neoplatonic-Avicennan psychology and cosmology into Islamic mystical writing, resulting in the rise of a more philosophically oriented Sufi metaphysics akin to the writings of Shihāb al-Dīn al-Suhrawardī. What follows is a look at both scholarly trends, which became increasingly intertwined, and the enduring critique leveled by some scholars against both developments.

Scholars as Philosophical Theologians and Philosophical Sufis

From the perspective of the theological dimensions of a scholar's polymathic knowledge and guidance of the general Muslim populace, later forms of speculative theology in Sunnism after the eleventh century increasingly intersected with Graeco-Arabic philosophy in the formulation of dedicated philosophical theologies. This development was centered not only in the Middle East and North Africa, but also in Central Asia. That is, the scholars' scripture-based understanding of the mechanisms of the world, God's agency, and the process of deepening one's spirituality increasingly absorbed and reinterpreted doctrines of Graeco-Arabic philosophy in Aristotelian logical reasoning, Neoplatonic conceptions of the mind, and Neoplatonic understandings of the body and soul. In the case of what became the predominant Ashʿarī school of theology that emerged from the earlier Muʿtazilī approach, later Ashʿarism after the twelfth century became increasingly oriented around Aristotelian

(Aristotelian-Avicennan) methods of logical reasoning with additional engagement of select aspects of Neoplatonic (Neoplatonic-Avicennan) psychology and cosmology.[24] On the one hand, the picture of an increasingly philosophical dimension of scholarly theological knowledge is not the picture of scholars encouraging the general Muslim populace to draw on Aristotelian (Aristotelian-Avicennan) logical reasoning in the formulation of basic creedal beliefs. On the other hand, evidence suggests that large segments of the urban Muslim populace came to understand the scholars' original role of mediating disputes, offering guidance in ethics, and clarifying doctrinal questions, as a role increasingly connected to logic-oriented (*manṭiq*) reasoning in the tradition of Aristotle and Avicenna. What supports this picture is a combination of the following: the wide circulation of scholarly texts that include logical treatises and short creedal works with theoretically complex conclusions, the enduringly large social networks of urban scholars even after the rise of colleges, the public dimension of the later scholars' occupational activities as increasingly full-time paid professional scholars educated in publicly funded legal-theological colleges of prominence, and the text-oriented careers of much of the urban general populace.[25] The general urban populace in the medieval Middle East and North Africa included teachers, civil servants, accountants, hobbyist scientists, friends of scholars, and writers of *belle-lettres*. The most recent analyses of Middle Eastern social history and Arabic writerly culture show that the general urban populace in the ninth and tenth centuries was educated in a manner that cultivated a strong value for the practical importance of books, reading, and various forms of written and oral knowledge in an intellectual milieu from which the scholars themselves emerged.[26]

In contrast with this philosophical turn in Islamic theological writing, and against the backdrop of Middle Eastern Christian Christological debates that had grown highly philosophical in both the late antique and early Islamic eras, some Muslim scholars unsurprisingly articulated concerns about the integration of Aristotelian-Neoplatonic theories into an otherwise simple and straightforward doctrinal system oriented around the basic belief in "No God but God" Who created the cosmos. Scholars asked whether the average individual's sacred belief system might misunderstand basic theological precepts if complex theoretical discussions were taught in the context of scriptural hermeneutics, creedal belief, and spiritual reflection. Examples of these more complex theological discussions that became increasingly philosophical include theories on the relationship between divine agency (*qudra*) and divine knowledge, the connection between divine knowledge and the divine attributes (*ṣifāt*), the relationship of the attributes with the Beautiful Names (*al-asmā' al-ḥusnā*), and other fine points of doctrinal belief drawing on scriptural references.[27] Among the scholars, the early critics of speculative theology in either its simpler or more philosophical forms were a diverse group. They included the *ḥadīth*-compiler Ibn Ḥanbal (d. 241/855), the defender of the Aristotelian-Neoplatonic corpus and Cordovan judge Ibn Rushd (Averroes d. 595/1198), and even the later Platonizing Sufi metaphysician Ibn ʿArabī (d. 638/1240), all of whom articulated some criticism over the potential misguidance of the general populace following the proliferation of more complex and often contested theoretical approaches to theological ideas.[28] In this concern, however, these scholars moved against the prevailing tide of history that saw the Sunnī scholarly discipline of theology, particularly later Ashʿarī theology, take on more philosophical approaches to articulating doctrinal beliefs, with conclusions that were ultimately transmitted to the general populace through various intertwining channels such as al-Ghazālī's treatises. By the thirteenth century, Sunnī scholars increasingly tended toward conclusions in psychological and cosmological doctrines found in the philosophical neo-Ashʿarī and Māturīdī schools of theology, which showed continuity with trends in the early and once prominent eleventh-century Andalusī Ẓāhirī school discussed in Chapter 2.[29] Ibn Ḥazm, who systematized a local Andalusī form of Ẓāhirī theological writing, formulated a pioneering epistemology in this regard. Several decades before al-Ghazālī articulated his logic-oriented nominalist critique of Neoplatonism in later Ashʿarī theology, Ibn Ḥazm called for the absorption of Aristotelian logic in Islamic theological writing to the exclusion of Neoplatonic cosmological conclusions.

Even after this widespread intersection of Graeco-Arabic philosophy and Islamic theology in Sunnism, however, the question of whether this development was epistemically sound continued to be discussed by influential scholars well into the Ottoman period. Ibn Taymiyya (d. 728/1328), who lived in the last decades of the Abbasid-Mamlūk period as the Ottomans were coming to power, was famous among the later critics. Had even the most judicious philosophical theologians absorbed philosophy into Islamic thought too uncritically? Were the revised applications of Aristotelian-Avicennan logic really able to avoid Neoplatonic-Avicennan conclusions in Plotinian cosmology and psychology? Despite his admiration for aspects of philosophy's logical tools, Ibn Taymiyya's fourteenth-century position on the place of Graeco-Arabic philosophy in Islamic theology echoed significant aspects of Ibn Ḥazm's pre-Ghazālian nominalist critique of Neoplatonism discussed in Chapter 2. Ibn Taymiyya broke with Ibn Ḥazm and al-Ghazālī, however, as these earlier scholars embraced a reformed approach to Graeco-Arabic philosophy as part of Islamic theology.[30] In systematizing this project, both Ibn Ḥazm and al-Ghazālī built on the work of some early Graeco-Arabic philosophers who already questioned a wholesale acceptance of the Aristotelian-Neoplatonic corpus into an Islamic theological worldview. al-Kindī (d. 260/873), whom al-Fārābī (d. 235/850) and Avicenna (d. 428/1037) represented as more a theologian than a true Peripatetic philosopher, offers an illustrative example. al-Kindī was influential among later philosophers such as al-ʿĀmirī (d. 381/992) and objected to the philosophical doctrine on the pre-eternity of the world.[31] In formulating a philosophical argument for the divine creation of the world out of nothing (*ex nihilo*) in time, which would break with Aristotelian-Neoplatonic doctrine and agree with scriptural cosmology's references to God's creation of the world *ex nihilo*, even al-Kindī did not need to create a philosophical solution from scratch. Christian philosophers and philosophical theologians of the late antique Middle East, who were writing in Aramaic and Arabic in the early Islamic-era Middle East, were long at work formulating philosophical positions that were in agreement with the cosmological tenets of biblical texts. For example, al-Kindī had at his disposal the logical arguments of pre-Islamic Christian philosophers such as John Philoponus, and he was likewise in conversation with contemporary Muslim speculative theologians such as the Muʿtazilīs and their early Ashʿarī successors who were already at work extracting a system of metaphysics of the world from the scriptural text.[32] Ibn Ḥazm's philosophical theology, discussed in Chapter 2, represents one example of the way al-Kindī's synthesis of Graeco-Arabic philosophy and Islamic theology anticipated or found an audience among the growing numbers of philosophically minded Muslim scholars who simultaneously studied Aristotelian logic for both jurisprudence and theology and also questioned key conclusions in Neoplatonic psychology and cosmology. Where Platonizing trends in psychology and cosmology found an additional place in scholarly writing was in the language of Sufi metaphysics, which came to intersect very strongly with Islamic theology after the twelfth century.

Sufi metaphysics, like philosophical theology, was likewise formulated and transmitted within the circles of the scholars, specifically among mystics like the Ḥanafī scholar Abū Bakr al-Kalābādhī (d. ca 380/990) and the Shāfiʿī scholar Abū ʿAbd al-Raḥmān al-Sulamī (d. 412/1021).[33] Remarkably, the figure in Sunnism popularly associated with a more enduring absorption of Aristotelian (Aristotelian-Avicennan) logic into scholarly jurisprudence and theology was the same figure associated with the more widespread absorption of Sufi metaphysics into the scholarly sciences – namely, al-Ghazālī (d. 505/1111). In the decades and centuries following the popularization of mysticism in ninth-century Iraq, scholars who were interested in an experiential dimension of theological truths began to articulate theories of metaphysics that amounted to what might be called today a kind of mystical theology.[34] al-Ghazālī's short *Niche of the Lights* foreshadowed the extent to which works of Sufi metaphysics written by scholars were to become increasingly oriented around Neoplatonic-Avicennan conceptions of psychology and cosmology.[35] These works, whether short mystical treatises or longer volumes of metaphysics, were not oriented around the Baghdad Peripatetics' harmonizing of Aristotle with Plato, nor were they oriented around the philosophical theologians' attempt to formulate a systematic scripture-based logic-oriented representation of the world's mechanisms and God's agency. Rather, among the more primary goals of these mystical treatises and volumes was to articulate to mystical aspirants how to attain, through spiritual contemplation and ritual, a form of experiential knowledge (*ma'rifa*, *kashf*, *dhawq*) of the spiritual realm, and additionally how to articulate one's mystical experience scrupulously. Given this distinction between the Sufis' intellectual goals and those of the Baghdad Peripatetics and philosophical theologians, the interest in Graeco-Arabic philosophy among Sufi metaphysics seems, at first glance, perplexing. What makes this interest in philosophy among Sufi metaphysicians confusing is the history of Sufis criticizing the philosophers' deductive methodology and championing a more inductive and mystical epistemology, a criticism matched by the philosophers' own representation of some Sufis and theologians as pseudo-philosophers.[36]

There are two possible explanations why these Sufi metaphysicians took on an explicit interest in Neoplatonic (Neoplatonic-Avicennan) or rather Platonizing conceptions of the mind, body, soul, and universe to an extent that employed select aspects of Neoplatonic language and imagery. First, these Sufis interested in Neoplatonic-Avicennan conceptions of the mind, such as al-Ghazālī himself, often numbered among the same scholars who were writing works of Aristotelian-Avicennan logic-oriented philosophical theology. Second, as mentioned, Sufis made their own claim on Hellenistic philosophy through an alternative genealogy in which the Sufis and not the Peripatetic philosophers inherited the knowledge of ancient philosophers like Socrates and Hermes, or rather Hermes-Idrīs.[37] The previously mentioned founder of Illuminationism, Shihāb al-Dīn Yaḥyā al-Suhrawardī (d. ca. 1190–2), provides an illustrative example of a Sufi whose mystical metaphysics offered a Neoplatonic-Avicennan critique of aspects of formal and material Aristotelian-Avicennan logic.[38] In the case of philosophically oriented Sufis like him, who increasingly emerged from the circles of the scholars, they often identified their Sufi metaphysics neither as the scholarly discipline of "speculative theology" nor the contemporary study of Graeco-Arabic "philosophy" (*falsafa*), but rather "wisdom" (*ḥikma*). In what makes the exact meaning of the term *ḥikma* dependent on time and place, philosophers like al-Fārābī (d. 235/850), Ibn Sīna (d. 428/1037), and Ibn Rushd (d. 595/1198) used the term "wisdom" (*ḥikma*) interchangeably with the term "philosophy" (*falsafa*) of the Peripatetic (*mashshāʾī*) Aristotelian-Neoplatonic commentary tradition.[39] For many Sufis, the term *ḥikma* became synonymous with Sufi metaphysics, with pre-Islamic philosophers such as Empedocles represented in later Sufi texts as influences on early mystics like Dhū l-Nūn al-Misrī (d. 245/859) and his student Sahl al-Tustarī (d. 238/896).[40] As seen in Chapter 4, for example, the scholar and Sufi Ibn Barrajān (d. 536/1141) of Seville represented *ḥikma* as his own mystical approach to cosmological conclusions attained erroneously by the philosophers. Ibn Barrajān's use of *ḥikma* in this way very closely anticipated Ibn ʿArabī's (d. 638/1240) critical assessment of Ibn Rushd's (Averroes d. 595/1198) deductive methodology and likewise echoed the writings of his Cordovan predecessor Ibn Masarra (d. 319/931). As discussed in Chapter 1, Ibn Masarra claimed the philosophers (*falāsifa*) arrived successfully at key theological truths when discussing the Universal Intellect and Soul while simultaneously criticizing the philosophers' use of imprecise language.

Despite the fact that Sufi metaphysics developed among mystics within scholarly circles, some scholars offered enduring critiques of the mystics and Sufi metaphysics in the twelfth and thirteenth centuries. Significantly, these criticisms were often less centrally oriented around their approach to philosophical doctrines and more oriented around their use of esoteric scriptural hermeneutics. Scholars pointed to the potential dangers of how the mystics, much like the Ismāʿīlīs, integrated interpretations of theological beliefs and ritual in an "interior" (*bāṭin*) category of scriptural meaning that in some cases departed significantly from the corresponding "exterior" (*ẓāhir*) level of meaning.[41] Though mystics pointed to the parallel importance of these interior and exterior meanings, critics highlighted controversial cases where "interior" meanings appeared to compromise traditional creedal doctrines and ritual obligations. The resulting controversy was the Islamic version of an antinomianism (*ibāḥiyya*) debate, which saw some critics misrepresent mystical approaches to esoteric scriptural hermeneutics.[42] From the critics' perspective, the discovery of deeper meanings of theological belief and ritual was not itself problematic, as it was commonplace in Qur'an commentary. Where criticism emerged was in cases when the

Figure I.3. Socrates (Sūqrāṭ) discussing philosophy with students, as represented in a thirteenth-century Arabic miniature.

distinction between "interior" meanings and "exterior" meanings was so great that the resulting dichotomy resembled the esoteric hermeneutics of the Ismāʿīlī Shiite theologians. That is, Sufi metaphysics, despite being systematized within Sunnī scholarly circles, had become entangled in the writings of critics with the controversy over Ismāʿīlī theology because of a shared history of interest in esoteric scriptural hermeneutics. In what brings the political dimensions of this controversy into clearer focus, esoteric scriptural hermeneutics formed the basis of the Fatimid Ismāʿīlī movement's claim to the caliphate in tenth-century North Africa, which explains the rise of the epithet "esotericists" (*bāṭiniyya*) to describe the Fatimid caliphate and the Ismāʿīlīs more broadly. By the fourteenth century, the scholar Ibn Taymiyya applied the Ismāʿīlī epithet "esotericists" to both the philosophers and the Sufis in a critique that included special criticism of al-Ghazālī, whom medieval and modern historians identify as a key figure in the rise among the scholars of philosophical theology and philosophically oriented Sufi metaphysics. Ironically, al-Ghazālī was the author of the *Scandals of the Esotericists*, a work written under political patronage that praised the Abbasid caliphate and criticized the rivaling Fatimid caliphate. That this work included its own criticism of the Fatimid caliphate's political use of Graeco-Arabic philosophy, and that it was written under a caliphate in Baghdad that once sponsored the translation of Hellenistic works into Arabic, reflects the extent to which scholarly debates about philosophy's value in communal guidance and leadership were heavily impacted by caliphal politics.

Caliphs as Bibliophile Patrons of Philosophy and Platonizing Guides

As discussed in the last section, the intellectual milieu of the multireligious Hellenistic Middle East contextualizes the way early Sunnī scholars found a place for Graeco-Arabic philosophy in conceptions of their own knowledge and role as communal guides. From the perspective of politics and its impact on religion, this development was also a function of the rise of caliphal courts in Damascus and Cairo that financially supported the translation and transmission of Graeco-Arabic philosophy and science.[43] The rise of what might be called philosophical caliphs occurred especially in the Abbasid caliphate of Baghdad and the rivaling Fatimid Ismāʿīlī caliphate of Cairo, even as their respective approaches contrasted significantly. The early decades of the Abbasid period (r. 750–1258 in Baghdad, r. 1261–1517 in Cairo) saw the rise of a caliph, namely al-Maʾmūn (r. 813–833), who claimed to have spoken with Aristotle in a famously recounted dream.[44] This period saw the politically backed and socially supported absorption of late antique Hellenistic thought in early Islamic intellectual and visual culture, an absorption that was part of a wider Greek-Arabic, Aramaic-Arabic, and Pahlavi-Arabic translation movement centered in Baghdad. In continuity with the pre-Islamic Sassanian monarchs who welcomed philosophers and physicians fleeing the Byzantine (Eastern Roman) empire for the Persian city of Gundishapur, the Abbasid caliphs of Baghdad likewise cultivated a model of authority akin to a kind of bibliophile philosopher-governor. The rise of the Abbasids' neighbors in tenth-century Cairo, the rivaling Fatimid caliphate (r. 909–1171), also saw the absorption of Graeco-Arabic philosophy into ruling political culture, but the model of authority the Fatimids projected was a controversial one in the eyes of the predominantly Sunnī scholarly networks. In contrast with the Abbasid model, where the caliph was an administrative and imperial uniting figure, the Fatimids conceived of their caliph as a semi-messianic (*mahdī*) Platonizing guide, complete with an elusive political lore that stirred vivid imaginations around the Islamic world for centuries.

As mentioned, the Fatimid caliphate (r. 909–1171) emerged in North Africa from a movement not in the predominantly Sunnī manifestation of Islam, but in a subset of early Shiism, specifically early Ismāʿīlism. The early history of the Ismāʿīlī movement in the ninth century is vague because of the loss of early texts, and it is largely known based on representations of its origins written both by later Ismāʿīlī theologians and by critics of Ismāʿīlism. By the formative ninth century, the other main subset of Shiism, the Imāmī (Twelver) form of Shiism dominant in present-day Iran, had already adopted a politically conciliatory position within the Sunnī political and religious establishment of the Abbasid caliphate. Twelver Shiism's political position was so conciliatory in recognizing the Sunnī Abbasid caliphate that the reigning "protectorate" dynasty of military emirs in Abbasid Baghdad who ruled coterminously with the caliph was an Imāmī Shiite military dynasty – namely, the Būyid or Buwayhid emirs (r. 945–1055).[45] While the successor Seljuk sultans of Baghdad (r. 1055–1258) represented themselves as restorers of Sunnī authority within the Abbasid caliphate during the sultanate of Toghril (r. 1040–1063), the Būyids' earlier military reign throughout Iraq and Iran had already been partially accommodated in political theory by the Sunnī scholarly establishment of Iraq.[46] The arrangement of a reigning emir or sultan in Baghdad who ruled concomitantly with a caliph in Baghdad became embedded in the later Sunnī scholars' formally elaborated distinctions between the nature of the caliph's leadership and the sultan's or emir's leadership. These theories were articulated formally by figures such as the jurist and political theorist al-Māwardī (d. 450/1058) and the polymath scholar al-Ghazālī (d. 505/1111), chief judge under the coterminous rule of the Abbasid caliphs and Seljuk sultans.

What made the rise of a rival Fatimid Ismāʿīlī Shiite caliphate much more alarming to the predominantly Sunnī scholars than the rise of an Imāmī Shiite emirate in the Abbasid heartland was the fact that the Fatimids rejected the entire Abbasid imperial framework. A rejection of the Abbasid caliphate was not simply the rejection of the caliph. Because the caliph stood atop a decentralized imperial hierarchy of political authority, a rejection of the Abbasid caliph implied a rejection of the governing authority of reigning sultans and emirs from Cordoba to Baghdad, as well as a dismissal of the religious authority of the networks of influential Sunnī and Imāmī Shiite scholars who recognized the political legitimacy of the prevailing Abbasid political system. The declaration of a rival caliphate in 909 by the Fatimid Ismāʿīlīs challenged the authority of all of these groups.[47] This rejection of the legitimacy of what amounted to the prevailing imperial commonwealth of Islam based in Baghdad had its roots in some ninth- and tenth-century Ismāʿīlī Shiite theological circles that theorized significant political change. While early Ismāʿīlī Shiite writers did not have a uniform approach or conception of what ideal models of religious and political authority looked like, some writers appear to have theorized a politically revolutionary approach that contrasted with Imāmī Shiism's more politically conciliatory approach. How the Platonizing philosophical underpinnings of this Ismāʿīlī political theology took shape is a particularly elusive story.

Ismāʿīlī theologians in the ninth century had begun to develop a reputation found in Sunnī representations of Ismāʿīlism for synthesizing Shiite theories of a coming semi-messianic leader (*mahdī*) with Graeco-Arabic doctrines in psychology related to inspired knowledge and celestial intelligence. This Platonizing representation of Ismāʿīlī theology, epitomized in al-Ghazālī's writings examined in Chapter 3, had a genuine basis in the writings of early Ismāʿīlī theologians. Specifically, some early philosophically oriented Ismāʿīlī writers active in Persia and Central Asia, including Muḥammad b. Aḥmad al-Nasafī (d. 332/942), were interested in explaining Ismāʿīlī theology and conceptions of salvation using the analysis of contemporary Neoplatonic psychology and cosmology.[48] Al-Nasafī agreed with Graeco-Arabic forms of Plotinian (Neoplatonic) cosmology. According to this cosmology, human souls were connected to a greater Universal Soul, and human intellects were likewise connected to a greater Universal Intellect, which philosophers like al-Fārābī (d. 235/850) understood to be spaceless and outside of time in agreement with Plotinus (d. 270). As previously discussed in the context of the scholars' encounter with philosophy, the late antique synthesis of Aristotelian and Platonic commentary traditions found in Plotinus's legacy posited that the underlying principles of existence included One, Intellect, and Soul. Drawing it seems on the Baghdad Peripatetics who emerged from the Greek-Arabic, Aramaic-Arabic, and Pahlavi-Arabic translation movement under the early Abbasid caliphate, al-Nasafī understood the human soul to be an element that somehow linked man in the corporeal world with the Plotinian Universal Soul outside of time and space. In line with aspects of Plotinian soteriology, al-Nasafī and later Ismāʿīlī theologians such as al-Kirmānī (d. 411/1020) characterized the process of perfecting the soul as part of man's spiritual ascent toward ultimate enlightenment and eventually salvation. According to these theories, this spiritual ascent was enabled through the medium of intellect, and in a way that had implications for religious authority, Ismāʿīlī theologians came to represent Ismāʿīlī spiritual guides and teachers as facilitating this process of a philosophical intellectual ascent.

During the early reign of the Fatimid caliph al-Muʿizz (r. 953–975), the Fatimids ultimately adopted, in part through the patronage of Ismāʿīlī theological books, this early ninth-century Ismāʿīlī synthesis of Neoplatonic psychology and Ismāʿīlī conceptualizations of leadership and salvation.[49] While these theories were originally formulated by figures like al-Nasafī (d. 332/942) who were not officially connected to the Fatimid movement, others like al-Kirmānī (d. 411/1020) were formally aligned with the Fatimids. Given the Abbasid-era Sunnī scholars' geographical proximity to the early philosophical Persian Ismāʿīlīs of al-Nasafī's (d. 332/942) circle, Sunnī scholars may not have had to wait for Fatimid caliph al-Muʿizz (r. 953–975) to adopt these more Neoplatonic Ismāʿīlī concepts of leadership in order to develop an early stereotype of Ismāʿīlī theology as a Platonizing one. In fact, from a Sunnī scholarly perspective, the idea of ruling circles drawing on select aspects of Hellenistic thought in ruling political culture was a familiar one, even if the Fatimids' addition of semi-messianic overtones was less familiar. As mentioned, from at least as far back as the bibliophile Sunnī Abbasid caliphs such as al-Maʾmūn (r. 813–833), the caliph associated with the dream about Aristotle, Sunnī scholars from the era of the politically backed Greek-Arabic translation movement were already familiar with the idea that a ruling political administration could draw on Graeco-Arabic philosophy in the formation of political culture and articulation of political leadership. However, it was particularly the messianic dimension of the Fatimids' conception of a philosophical caliph that attracted special criticism in its representation of the caliph as claiming more religious authority than any of the previous caliphs of Baghdad, Damascus, or Medina. The Fatimid conception of the caliph was even the source of the Qarmaṭī Ismāʿīlīs' unwillingness to join the Fatimid Ismāʿīlī movement. Still, the more basic notion of the caliph as a philosopher-governor was not a new one, as it had a place in both Abbasid and Fatimid political culture despite the distinctions in approach. What is particularly significant in this concept's tandem development in Abbasid and Fatimid political culture, however, is how one came to impact the other. Specifically, the Fatimids' model of a Platonizing Ismāʿīlī caliphate seems to have had an impact on how the Abbasid caliphate revised and backpedaled its political connection with Graeco-Arabic philosophy.

While the early Abbasid caliphate in the era of Maʾmūn (r. 813–833) was originally a source of patronage of a wide spectrum of Graeco-Arabic philosophical books and ideas, a pattern that made the caliphate a bibliophile center of global knowledge, the later Abbasid caliphate in the era of al-Mustaẓhir (r. 1094–1118) moved toward sifting out problematic political and theological manifestations of Graeco-Arabic philosophy. At the center of the Abbasid caliphate's critique, which can be located in the realm of a new set of court-commissioned books, was a disapproving representation of the Ismāʿīlīs' conception of the Ismāʿīlī caliph and his inner circles as Platonizing guides who claimed to facilitate a kind of spiritual enlightenment among the general populace. More specifically, in response to both the Fatimid Ismāʿīlīs and the breakoff Nizārī Ismāʿīlīs led by Ḥasan-i Ṣabbāḥ (d. 518/1124) of the famous *Ḥashīshiyya*, the court of the Abbasid caliph al-Mustaẓhir (r. 1094–1118) commissioned chief judge al-Ghazālī to write a short theological treatise called the *Scandals of the Esotericists* that criticized Ismāʿīlī politics and theology.[50] The treatise condemned in particular the way the Ismāʿīlīs used philosophical doctrines in psychology and cosmology as the basis of a claim to communal leadership and guidance.[51] Interestingly, as Chapter 3 discusses, three of the doctrines in cosmology that al-Ghazālī criticized in Ismāʿīlī philosophical theology were the same three that he selected for special condemnation against the Graeco-Arabic philosophers in the form of a *fatwā* in the *Incoherence of the Philosophers*. These doctrines were specifically the philosophical notion of the pre-eternity of the world, the nature of God's knowledge of the universals and particulars, and the nature of human resurrection in terms of body and soul.[52] The *Incoherence*, in turn, played an important role in laying out more enduring contours of Sunnī scholarly distinctions between theologically sound and unsound absorptions of Graeco-Arabic philosophical doctrines. Scholarly works like the *Scandals of the Esotericists* and the *Incoherence of the Philosophers* shaped the parallel development of an Aristotelian-Avicennan logic-oriented form of Islamic theology (later Ashʿarism) and a more loosely Platonizing form of Islamic mysticism (Sufi metaphysics), both of which became central dimensions of what it meant to be a Sunnī scholarly guide of the community after the eleventh century. One of the key arguments of Part I of this book is that earlier sets of writings in al-Andalus, especially those of Ibn Ḥazm (d. 456/1064), anticipated al-Ghazālī's call for a more systematic reassessment of Aristotelian logic and Neoplatonic doctrines in psychology and cosmology in a way that similarly responded to the controversial rise of the Fatimids as a semi-messianic Platonizing political movement.

The examples of Ibn Ḥazm (d. 456/1064) and al-Ghazālī (d. 505/1111) criticizing the Fatimids' Platonizing political theology within their respective investigations of Neoplatonic cosmology's role in the Sunnī scholarly sciences points to a key pattern illustrated in this book: Just as the Abbasid–Fatimid rivalry in political models had an impact on Abbasid conceptions of ruling political authority, it likewise had an impact on how the predominantly Sunnī networks of scholars articulated the contours of their own scholarly knowledge and religious authority as communal guides. In particular, the Abbasid–Fatimid political rivalry helped shape a tenth- and eleventh-century scholarly conversation about which aspects of Graeco-Arabic philosophical knowledge were relevant parts of what it meant to be a theological guide of the Muslims within the general multi-religious populace. As Part I shows, the impact of this conversation on the scholars was twofold. First, Sunnī scholars cultivated a lasting place for Aristotelian logic to the exclusion of specific Neoplatonic conclusions in the most influential methodologies of Islamic theology. Second, the scholars cultivated an enduring space in Sufi metaphysics for revised interpretations of Neoplatonic doctrines in psychology and cosmology. That is, the history of the scholars embracing Aristotelian-Avicennan logic-oriented forms of philosophical theology and more loosely Platonizing forms of Sufi metaphysics in their debates about what it meant to be a Sunnī scholarly guide of the community's belief, which was discussed in the first part of this introduction, was shaped partly by the political contingencies of this Abbasid-Fatimid rivalry and its competing philosophical conceptions of political leadership. This dialectical relationship between conceptions of ruling political authority and scholarly religious authority can be located in two key textual phenomena traced in this book. First, scholarly theological debates about the contours of sound belief and ritual were often articulated in writing with an explicit awareness of how specific positions were used controversially in contemporary politics, especially in Fatimid politics. Second, the texts in which these ideas were elaborated were often entangled with ruling attempts to sponsor or alternatively marginalize specific groups of scholars and works. At the highest level of the Abbasid-Fatimid rivalry, this attempt to sponsor specific scholarly circles developed into competing patterns of patronage for the Sunnī theological-juridical colleges of Iraq and the originally Ismāʿīlī al-Azhar college of Cairo. Ironically, scholarly circles maintained a degree of intellectual independence despite this patronage, though the scholars' conception of their own role as communal guides developed in dialogue with continuing political developments.

A Fluid Dialectic of Authority between Rulers and Scholars

In sum, the historical picture of authority illustrated in this book is still the familiar image of scholarly networks constituting the core of religious authority in the medieval Middle East and North Africa, whose authority in jurisprudence was extensive yet limited by the legal jurisdiction of political ruling circles and the communal boundaries of Jewish and Christian communities. What is new in this book's analysis is an illustration of how the knowledge and epistemology that undergirded the scholars' own communal leadership as doctrinal guides changed in response to the ideological underpinnings of various political models of leadership, which scholars debated and deemed either legitimate or illegitimate conceptions of political leadership. The trajectory of the rulers' and scholars' respective embrace of Graeco-Arabic philosophy in political culture and the scholarly sciences, and the scholars' growing distinction between the value of Aristotelian-Avicennan logic and shortcomings of Neoplatonic-Avicennan psychology and cosmology, represent one of the most significant consequences of this dialogue of authority, one that ultimately impacted Latin Europe's nominalist critique of Neoplatonism and the discussions of the Scientific Revolution.

At the center of the analysis of politics and religion in this book, in sum, is evidence in Arabic from philosophical treatises, works of heresiography, bio-bibliographical dictionaries, court chronicles, and mystical exegesis that have rarely been seen by Western audiences. The Arabic manuscripts from the archival libraries of present-day Turkey in particular have not been widely read even in the original Arabic, as the manuscripts have only recently begun to be edited after centuries of remaining in Ottoman libraries alongside a variety of unpublished Andalusian manuscripts. These manuscripts arrived in Anatolia with the slow exodus of both Muslim and Jewish Andalusī intellectual circles before the transfer of the last Andalusī domain, Nasrid Granada, to the Crowns of Castile and Aragon in 1492. Drawing on this evidence, this book begins with an analysis of how the rise of the Fatimid caliphate, which rivaled the Andalusī Umayyad caliphate in Cordoba and the Abbasid caliphate in Baghdad, brought about a complex negotiation over religious leadership and political power in the tenth-century Middle East and North Africa.

Notes

1 In contrast with the predominantly philosophical legacies of Averroes and al-Ghazālī during the Latin-Arabic translation movement in Catholic Toledo, Ibn Rushd's juridical legacy as a judge and legal theorist loomed large in his own historical context of Almohad-era al-Andalus. At the same time, there were parallels in the political culture of patronage that fostered philosophical writing between the Almohad era of al-Andalus and the coterminous Castilian and Nasrid eras that followed. The respective works of Richard Taylor and Maribel Fierro have highlighted the multiple historical contexts in which the legacy of Averroes and the Andalusī philosophers developed. Richard Taylor, "Arabic/Islamic Philosophy in Thomas Acquinas's Conception of the Beatific Vision in IV Sent. D. 4 49, Q. 2. A. 1," *The Thomist* 76 (2012): 509–50; idem,

"Ibn Rushd/Averroes and 'Islamic' Rationalism," in *Medieval Encounters. Jewish, Christian and Muslim Culture in Confluence and Dialogue* 15 (2009): 125–35. Maribel Fierro, "The Legal Policies of the Almohad Caliphs and Ibn Rushd's *Bidāyat al-Mujtahid*," *Journal of Islamic Studies* 10 (1999): 226–48; idem, "Alfonso the Wise: The Last Almohad Caliph?" *Medieval Encounters* 15 (2009): 175–98. A picture of the political, religious, and intellectual context of the transmission of Graeco-Arabic philosophy into Latin in centers such as Toledo can be seen in Charles Burnett's study of Iohannes Hispanus. An Arabic-Latin translator and dean at the cathedral of Toledo in the late twelfth century, Hispanus came most likely from an originally Andalusī Christian (Mozarab) family. Charles Burnett, "Magister Iohannes Hispanus: Towards the Identity of a Toledan Translator," in *Comprendre et maîtriser la nature au Moyen Age. Mélanges d'histoire des sciences offerts à Guy Beaujouan* (Geneva/ Paris: Librairie Droz/Librairie Champion, 1994), pp. 425–36.

2 As in the case of Ibn Rushd's career as chief judge under the Almohads in Cordoba, al-Ghazālī's career as chief judge under the Abbasid caliphs and Seljuk sultans in Baghdad was similarly illustrative of a historical context distinct from the politics of Europe that shaped the Latin reception of al-Ghazālī's philosophical writings. Kenneth Garden's analysis of this political context in Baghdad offers a valuable starting point for considering this comparison. Kenneth Garden, *The First Islamic Reviver* (New York: Oxford University Press, 2013), pp. 17–29.

3 Various studies on the history of scholars' religious authority and its relationship with ruling political authority offer a useful starting point for understanding the connections between politics and religion in the medieval Middle East more broadly. Ira M. Lapidus, "The Separation of State and Religion in the Development of Early Islamic Society," *International Journal of Middle Eastern Studies* 6 (1975): 363–85; Jonathan Berkey, *The Formation of Islam: Religion and Society in the Near East, 600–1800* (New York: Cambridge University Press, 2003), pp. 111–76; Michael Cook, "Activism and Quietism in Islam: The Case of the Early Murji'a," in *Islam and Power*, eds. Alexander S. Cudsi and Ali E. H. Dessouki (London: Croom Helm, 1981), pp. 15–23. Christopher Melchert, "Religious Policies of the Caliphs from al-Mutawakkil to al-Muqtadir, AH 232–295/AD 847–908," *Islamic Law and Society* 3 (1996): 316–42.

4 The public dimension of this caliphal role can be identified in the shared coinage of the various regions of the caliphate and in the Friday sermon that mentioned the caliph's name. Hugh Kennedy offers a picture of the early Abbasid caliphate in terms of a "commonwealth" linked by these political elements. A particularly useful overview can be found in "The Structure of Politics in the Muslim Commonwealth," in Hugh Kennedy, *The Prophet and the Age of the Caliphates: The Islamic Near East from the 6th to the 11th Century* (London: Longman, 1986), pp. 200–11.

5 For an overview of the rise of scholars and the judiciary, including the role of scholars as both local mediators and administrative judges, see "The Formative Period," in Wael Hallaq, *Sharīʿa: Theory, Practice, Transformations* (Cambridge: Cambridge University Press, 2009), pp. 27–72. See also Jonathan Brockopp, "The Formation of Islamic Law: The Egyptian School, 750–900," Annales Islamologiques 45 (2011): 123–140.

6 The case of Abū Ḥanīfa as a manufacturer of a type of silk fabric (*khazz*) is illustrative of this phenomenon. *Encyclopaedia of Islam*, 3rd ed., s.v. "Abū Ḥanīfa" (by Hiroyuki Yanagihashi).

7 One medieval account on al-Andalus represents figures prior to the eleventh century who were interested in Graeco-Arabic philosophy as having numbered largely among the physicians of their time. Josef Puig Montada, "Philosophy in Andalusia: Ibn Bājja and Ibn Ṭufayl," in *The Cambridge Companion to Arabic Philosophy*, eds. Peter Adamson and Richard Taylor (Cambridge: Cambridge University Press, 2005), p. 155ff. The case of the Christian philosopher-physician and logician Sergius of Reshʿaynā (d. 536) in the pre-Islamic Middle East highlights the continuity of this late antique framework in the early centuries of Islam.

8 Studies by Christopher Melcher and Wael Hallaq help illustrate this point. Melchert has offered an illustrative picture of how the rise of scholarly schools of thought in jurisprudence constituted an intellectual development that depended less on political patronage and more on the transmission of scholarly sciences from teachers to students. Still, Melchert highlights how the history of political patronage may help explain the disappearance of the originally prominent Ẓāhirī school of jurisprudence, which continues to be studied in modern scholarly circles. In a similar context, Hallaq has pointed out that in much of early Islamic history, the scholars did not see the attainment of an official judgeship as a necessary part of a successful legal career. Christopher Melchert, *The Formation of the Sunnī Schools of Law* (Brill: Leiden, 1997). Wael Hallaq, *Authority, Continuity, and Change in Islamic Law* (Cambridge: Cambridge University Press, 2004), pp. 168–89.

9 Muhammad Qasim Zaman's discussion of scholars who were more willing to take those positions in particular periods can be compared with Hallaq's analysis in note 8. Their respective findings point, ultimately, to a diversity of medieval scholarly opinions about judgeship appointments in different times and places. Muhammad Qasim Zaman, "The Caliphs, the *ʿUlamāʾ*, and the Law: Defining the Role and Function of the Caliph in the Early ʿAbbāsid Period," *Islamic Law and Society* 4 (1997): 1–36.

10 This widespread religious authority of the scholars can be contextualized alongside the rise of intellectual, social, and commercial networks that connected scholars and scholarly families from Iberia to Central and South Asia. Several studies offer a picture of the scholars as constituting much of premodern Islamic religious authority precisely because of the lasting intellectual or epistemic authority they commanded even after they began to take on administrative positions. Michael Chamberlain, *Knowledge and Social Practice in Medieval Damascus, 1190–1135* (Cambridge: Cambridge University Press, 1994), pp. 69–90, 111–76; Hallaq, *Authority, Continuity, and Change in Islamic Law*, pp. 168–74; Muhammad Qasim Zaman, *Religion and Politics under the Early ʿAbbāsids: The Emergence of the Proto-Sunnī Elite* (Leiden: Brill, 1997), pp. 119–66.

11 Devin Stewart has offered an analysis of the authority to issue these opinions in later centuries. Devin Stewart, "The Doctorate of Islamic Law in Mamlūk Egypt and Syria," in *Law and Education in Medieval Islam Studies in Memory of Professor George Makdisi*, eds. Joseph. Lowry, Devin J. Stewart, and Shawkat M. Toorawa (Cambridge: The E. J. W. Gibb Memorial Trust, 2004), pp. 45–90. For the early centuries, see "Law and Society" in Hallaq, *Sharīʿa*, pp. 159–96. Joseph Lowry's analysis of al-Shāfiʿī's ninth-century

work on legal theory offers a window into the toolbox scholars developed in the early centuries for the formation and articulation of these opinions. Joseph E. Lowry, *Early Islamic Legal Theory: The Risāla of Muḥammad Ibn Idrīs Al-Shāfiʿī* (Leiden: Brill, 2007).

12 A succinct picture of these *maẓālim* courts and their place in Islamic legal theory, with particular focus on the story of the scholars' historical accommodation of the rulers' judicial authority, can be found in the following: Linda T. Darling, *A History of Social Justice and Political Power in the Middle East: The Circle of Justice from Mesopotamia to Globalization* (London: Routledge, 2012), pp. 79–80. The reference to the modern expansion of public spaces here draws on the contrast, highlighted in a variety of works, between the public sphere in the modern and premodern Middle East. The mosque and the marketplace are examples of public spaces in the medieval era where it was within the legal jurisdiction of figures such as market inspectors to regulate defined ethical boundaries of social behavior and financial exchange. There were also semi-public spaces such as graveyards where the market inspectors' jurisdiction to regulate social behavior, such as mourning practices, was more complex. These public and semi-public spaces contrast with the large swaths of what might be thought of as semi-private spaces in these medieval cities, including the often discussed domestic courtyards and alleyways that led to the market streets. In practice, the boundaries of public, semi-public, private, and semi-private spaces in premodern cities has been as much a topic of debate among modern reformers of the public sphere as it is currently a topic of debate among historians seeking to revise the twentieth-century historiography of the often over-generalized "medieval Islamic city." For an overview of this twentieth-century historiography and for some examples of recent reconceptualizations of this history, see Masashi Haneda and Tōru Miura (eds.), *Islamic Urban Studies: Historical Review and Perspectives* (London: Kegan Paul International, 1994). On the market inspectors, see Roy Mottahedeh and Kristen Stilt, "Public and Private as Viewed Through the Work of the *Muḥtasib*," *Social Research* 70 (2003): 735–48; Yaron Klein, "Between Public and Private: An Examination of *ḥisba* Literature," *Harvard Middle Eastern and Islamic Review* 7 (2006): 41–62.

13 The continued prominence of originally late antique Christian and Jewish clerical and semi-clerical figures within early Islamic-era Christian and Jewish communities was due partly to historical distinctions in legal status and legal jurisdiction according to membership in one of the many semiautonomous religious communities of these cities. This legal framework, which echoed aspects of pre-Islamic Sassanian Iranian administration and the political administration of Medina during the lifetime of the Prophet, had a notably enduring legacy in the later Ottoman history of legal dualism and legal pluralism. During the rise of late Ottoman nationalism in nineteenth-century Istanbul and other eastern Mediterranean Ottoman cities, in the decades leading up to the fragmentation of the empire, a later form of this legal pluralism became entangled with debates about extraterritoriality. Dating back especially to the medieval era of trade with the Venetian empire, non-Muslim communities, particularly merchants and diplomats, had attained legal exceptions and legal privileges as go-betweens connecting Ottoman lands

with European powers. Michelle Campos has highlighted how in the modern period, with the growth of local resident communities with foreign citizenship, the existence of multiple legal statuses formed part of the centrifugal forces that clashed with the centripetal aspirations of Ottoman nationalism. Paradoxically, Ottoman nationalism was the project of some of the very same Muslim, Christian, and Jewish figures who were part of what had become a transnational and legally dualistic, or perhaps fragmented, civic framework. Michelle Campos, *Muslims, Christians, and Jews in Late Ottoman Palestine* (Stanford, CA: Stanford University Press, 2007).

14 Shawkat Toorawa's analysis of Arabic writerly culture in the Abbasid era traces early developments in the production and circulation of a vast body of medieval Arabic texts. The wide circulation of these writings contextualizes one key point illustrated in the current study: Debates among scholars assessing theories of knowledge and defining the custodians of that knowledge were written and transmitted in an urban context in which textual concepts had wide readership and where textual ideas were transmitted in both written and oral forms. Shawkat M. Toorawa, *Ibn Abī Ṭāhir Ṭayfūr and Arabic Writerly Culture: A Ninth-Century Bookman in Baghdad* (London: RoutledgeCurzon, 2005), pp. 1–24.

15 Richard Frank's analysis of the beginnings of speculative theology remains a key starting point for an investigation of how early speculative theologians were active at the elusive intersection of early scholarly circles and the world of early Graeco-Arabic philosophers in Iraq. Richard Frank, *The Metaphysics of Created Being According to Abû l-Hudhayl al-ʿAllâf: A Philosophical Study of the Earliest Kalâm* (Istanbul: Nederlands Historisch-Archaeologisch Instituut in het Nabije Oosten, 1966).

16 Christopher Melchert and Ahmet Karamustafa have each examined some of the contours of this debate among early *ḥadīth* scholars about the soundness of speculative theology. In the case of early mystics among the scholars, this debate was additionally entangled with sound approaches to articulating mystical thought. Christopher Melchert, *The Formation of the Sunni Schools of Law* (Brill: Leiden, 1997), pp. 68–86. Ahmed Karamustafa, *Sufism: The Formative Period* (Edinburgh: Edinburgh University Press, 2007), pp. 83–113.

17 An illustrative example of the inclusion of astronomy as part of the educational curriculum of Islamic scholars is found in Robert Morrison's analysis of Niẓām al-Dīn al-Nīsabūrī's fourteenth-century writings, which include views on *falsafa* more broadly. Robert G. Morrison, *Islam and Science: The Intellectual Career of Nīẓām Al-Dīn Al-Nīsābūrī* (London: Routledge, 2007), pp. 20–36.

18 On this early debate about the identification of Hermes with Idrīs, and the representation of Hermes as a philosopher and mystic, see Kevin Thomas van Bladel, *The Arabic Hermes: From Pagan Sage to Prophet of Science* (New York: Oxford University Press, 2009), pp. 166–8.

19 David Reisman offers a succinct overview and analysis of al-Fārābī's thought. David Reisman, "al-Fārābī and the Philosophical Curriculum," *The Cambridge Companion to Arabic Philosophy*, eds. Peter Adamson and Richard Taylor (Cambridge: Cambridge University Press, 2005), pp. 52–71.

20 Van Bladel, *The Arabic Hermes*, pp. 222–6.

21 For two brief overviews on his thought, see John Walbridge, "Suhrawardī and Illuminationism," in *The Cambridge Companion to Arabic Philosophy*, eds. Peter Adamson and Richard Taylor (Cambridge: Cambridge University Press, 2005), pp. 201–23. Hossein Ziai, "The Illuminationist Tradition," in *History of Islamic Philosophy*, eds. Seyyed Hossein Nasr and Oliver Leaman (London: Routledge, 1996), pp. 465–96.

22 Among these later Sufis, particularly after the eras of al-Suhrawardī and Ibn ʿArabī, the representation of Socrates and Plato as proto-Sufi figures loomed increasingly large. One example of this kind of representation is found in the chief minister Ibn al-Khaṭīb's politically commissioned work on Sufism, *Rawḍat al-Taʿrīf bi-l-Ḥubb al-Sharīf*. Ali Humayun Akhtar, "The Political Controversy over Graeco-Arabic Philosophy and Sufism in Nasrid Government: The Case of Ibn al-Khaṭīb in al-Andalus," *International Journal of Middle Eastern Studies* 47 (2015): 323–42.

23 Abbas Hamdani summarized the state of early research on the texts in a quote that remains illustrative of the inherently multidisciplinary and eclectic nature of the writings: "Having taken their stand on the date of composition of the *Rasāʾil*, scholars have argued whether its authors were Sunnis or Shiis; if Sunnis, whether they were Mutʿazilī or Sufi; if Shiis, whether they were Zaydī, Ithnā-ʿAsharī, Fatimid or Qarmatian." Abbas Hamdani, "The Arrangement of the *Rasāʾil Ikhwān al-Ṣafāʾ* and the Problem of Interpolations," *Journal of Semitic Studies* 29 (1984): 97–110. See also Maribel Fierro, "Bāṭinism in al-Andalus: Maslama b. Qāsim al-Qurṭubī (d. 353/964), author of the *Rutbat al-ḥakīm* and the *Ghāyat al-ḥakīm (Picatrix)*," *Studia Islamica* 84 (1996): 87–112.

24 Studies by Robert Wisnovsky and Yahya Michot offer useful starting points for examining the Avicennan turn of later Islamic theology. Yahya Michot, "L'avicennisation de la *sunna*, du ṣabéisme au leurre de la Ḥanīfiyya: À propos du Livre des religions et des sectes, II d'al-Shahrastânî," *Bulletin de Philosophie Médiévale* 35 (1993): 113–20; Robert Wisnovsky, "One Aspect of the Avicennian Turn in Sunnī Theology," *Arabic Sciences and Philosophy* 14 (2004): 65–100.

25 Historical context for the rise of college is offered in the following interdisciplinary volume: Joseph E. Lowry, Devin J. Stewart, and Shawkat M. Toorawa (eds.), *Law and Education in Medieval Islam: Studies in Memory of Professor George Makdisi* (Cambridge: E. J. W. Gibb Memorial Trust, 2004). Tony Street has provided an overview of one of the most widely circulating later primers of Aristotelian-Avicennan logic that became a key text in scholarly education. Tony Street, "Logic," in *The Cambridge Companion to Arabic Philosophy*, eds. Peter Adamson and Richard Taylor (Cambridge: Cambridge University Press, 2005), 247–65. Roy Mottahedeh's novel on mid-twentieth-century Iran offers an illustrative literary representation, albeit in an extremely different political and social context, of the way Aristotelian-Avicennan logical reasoning was taught by Imāmī Shiite scholars to the youth among scholarly families who were part of the fabric of local neighborhoods. In the parallel historical analysis that runs through the novel, Mottehedeh points to the historical background of this paradigm in what we know was the predominantly

Sunnī scholarly world of the medieval Middle East. Roy P. Mottahedeh, *The Mantle of the Prophet: Religion and Politics in Iran* (New York: Simon and Schuster, 1985).

26 Toorawa, *Ibn Abī Ṭāhir Ṭayfūr and Arabic Writerly Culture*, pp. 1–24. Alexander Knysh's analysis of the scholarly response to philosophically oriented forms of Sufi metaphysics throughout the late medieval Islamic world offers examples illustrative of how theological doctrinal debates were not isolated monastic or bibliophile affairs. Rather, these debates were embedded into the social fabric of Middle Eastern and North African urban intellectual life. Alexander Knysh, *Ibn ʿArabī in the Later Islamic Tradition* (Albany: State University of New York Press, 2007). A picture of the place of scholars in urban and rural social life emerges in the works of Vincent Cornell on North African Sufism. Vincent Cornell, *Realm of the Saint: Power and Authority in Moroccan Sufism* (Austin: University of Texas Press, 1998), pp. 3–31; idem, "Faqīh versus Faqīr in Marinid Morocco: Epistemological Dimensions of a Polemic," in *Islamic Mysticism Contested*, eds. Frederick de Jong and Bernd Radtke (Brill: Leiden, 1999), 207–24.

27 The breadth of analysis in Daniel Gimaret's classic work on the Names of God in Islam is illustrative of the depth of the theoretical discussions and debates that emerged within medieval scholarly circles about scriptural concepts and precepts. These concepts include the scriptural reference to the importance of calling upon God by His Beautiful Names. Daniel Gimaret, *Les noms divins en Islam: Exégèse lexicographique et théologique* (Paris: Editions du Cerf, 2007).

28 Ibn Rushd pushed his argument very far in calling for a strict separation between a scholar's philosophical understanding of theology from the general populace's non-philosophical understanding. For him, al-Ghazālī was a theologian worthy of criticism because of the eclectic methods of al-Ghazālī's interest in philosophical theology and Sufism. Interestingly, Ibn Rushd's critique agreed with key aspects of Ibn Taymiyya's analysis of al-Ghazālī, even though Ibn Rushd and Ibn Taymiyya differed on the role of Aristotelian logic in Islamic theology. What follows are two interesting quotes from Ibn Rushd's discussion in which he criticizes the speculative theologians' mix of philosophical and theological methods: "Revelation must be affirmed on its manifest level and not be explained to the masses in a mix of [revelation] and philosophy, because [this mixed] explanation is an explanation of the results of philosophy for [the masses] without their having a proof for it." Ibn Rushd, *Kashf ʿan Manāhij al-Adilla fī ʿAqāʾid al-Milla*, ed. M. A. al-Jabrī (Beirut: Markaz Dirāsāt al-Waḥda al- ʿArabiyya, 1998), p. 154. In the *Decisive Criterion*, he describes al-Ghazālī as "a philosopher with the philosophers, an Ashʿarī with the Ashʿarīs, and a Sufi with the Sufis," whose use of the syllogism makes his work "more meritorious" than other theologians and Sufis. Ibn Rushd, *Faṣl al-Maqāl Fī Mā Bayn al-Ḥikma wa-l-Sharīʿa min al-Ittiṣāl*, ed. M. Amara (Cairo: Dār al-Maʿārif), p. 51.

29 In the Shāfiʿī scholar Sayf al-Dīn al-Āmidī's (d. 631/1233) relatively late analysis of comparative positions in jurisprudence, he includes references to Muʿtazilī positions that appear to the modern reader as striking inclusions. While Muʿtazilī theology has been the subject of much research and

came to be an enduring part of later Shiism, Muʿtazilī jurisprudence is less commonly referenced among historians of early Sunnism, which makes al-Āmidī's inclusion of it in comparative jurisprudential positions illustrative of the extent to which Sunnī jurisprudence and theology was in flux. The disappearance of Ẓāhirī jurisprudence and theology from conceptions of Sunnī history is similarly striking. Bernard G. Weiss, *The Search for God's Law: Islamic Jurisprudence in the Writings of Sayf Al-Dīn Al-Āmidī* (Salt Lake City: University of Utah Press, 1991).

30 While Ibn Taymiyya did not dispute the inherent value of deductive reasoning and the syllogistic sciences, his criticisms of the applications of logic in Islamic theology reflect an argument that the philosophers themselves made – namely, that the separation of Aristotelian-Avicennan logic from Neoplatonic-Avicennan conclusions in psychology and cosmology can be difficult. Wael Hallaq has offered an analytical overview of Ibn Taymiyya's critique of the logicians. Wael Hallaq, *Ibn Taymiyya against the Logicians* (Oxford: Clarendon Press, 1993), pp. xlv–xlviiii.

31 Everett Rowson's study of the tenth-century philosophy of al-ʿĀmirī leaves readers with an understanding of the various ways in which early Graeco-Arabic philosophy intersected with Islamic theology in approaches that also engaged Sufism. al-ʿĀmirī's approach, like that of al-Kindī, is more eclectic than the more famous models of al-Fārābī and Ibn Sīna. This analysis offers important context for a point made in the current study, which is that early scholars had a variety early philosophical models to draw on in the formation of a more philosophical theology and philosophically oriented mystical theology. Everett K. Rowson, *A Muslim Philosopher on the Soul and Its Fate: Al-ʿĀmirī's Kitāb al-Amad ʿAlā l-Abad* (New Haven, CT: American Oriental Society, 1988).

32 Peter Adamson compares John Philoponus and al-Kindi's respective arguments for the creation of the world *ex nihilo*. al-Kindi's arguments appear in various sections of his *Oneness* and *On First Philosophy*, available in edited form in *Rasāʾil al-Kindī al-Falsafiyya*. Peter Adamson, *al-Kindī* (New York: Oxford University Press, 2006), pp. 75–98.

33 See Chapter 1, note 29.

34 In the discussion of Islamic theology, while the English word theology is normally used as a specific translation for speculative theology as distinct from philosophy (*falsafa*), Sufi works of metaphysics became increasingly theological and philosophical in the early centuries to a point that makes the modern English term mystical theology a useful description and synonym for Sufi metaphysics. The term Sufis themselves often used was wisdom (*ḥikma*), which was also used by the philosophers together with philosophy and which became a distinct science in the later curricula of the Ottoman academies where philosophical *ḥikma* was taught. Sufi writers of philosophically oriented works of Sufi metaphysics, even if they were scholars, did not describe their treatises as speculative theology or philosophy in a phenomenon illustrative of how these works were often not aimed at providing a comprehensive theory of metaphysics. Even with the use of Neoplatonic-Avicennan doctrines, the goal of Sufi metaphysicians in many cases appears to have been more closely oriented around a method, in ritual and thought, of bringing about

mystical experience and articulating that experience in writing. In this regard, it is unsurprising that the most famous philosophical Sufis contrasted their mystical method with that of the philosophers. In the case of the philosophically oriented Neoplatonic-Avicennan Sufi al-Suhrawardī, he explicitly distinguished himself from the Peripatetics, including the Baghdad Peripatetics among the philosophers, on the basis of methodology. He simultaneously celebrated Hermes as a more authoritative figure than Aristotle, and presented himself as a follower of Plato, but he criticized the Aristotelian-Avicennan approach of the Baghdad Peripatetics. Van Bladel offers useful context for the example of al-Suhrawardī. Van Bladel, *The Arabic Hermes*, pp. 222–6. Ibn Barrajān (d. 536/1141) discussed in Chapter 6 of the current study, similarly distinguished Sufi *ḥikma* from *falsafa*, and he may have drawn on early tenth-century examples seen in Chapter 1. Ibn Masarra (d. 319/931), a scholar and follower of Sahl al-Tustarī, distinguished between the philosophers and the sages (*ḥukamāʾ*).

35 The precise nature of al-Ghazālī's engagement with Graeco-Arabic philosophy in his theology as an Ashʿarī theologian and in his mysticism as a Sufi has been the subject of debate for several decades. The introduction of Chapter 3 examines a recent trend in emphasizing al-Ghazālī's engagement with Neoplatonic psychology and cosmology in both his theology and mysticism. The respective works of Michael Marmura and Richard Frank offer a useful starting point for examining the early positions in this debate. Michael Marmura, "al-Ghazālī's Chapter on Divine Power in the *Iqtiṣād*," *Arabic Sciences and Philosophy* 4 (1994): 279–315; Richard Frank, *Creation and the Cosmic System: Al-Ghazālī and Avicenna* (Heidelberg: Carl Winter-Universitätsverlag, 1992). See also Frank Griffel, "Al-Ghazālī's Concept of Prophecy: The Introduction of Avicennan Psychology into Ashʿarite Theology," *Arabic Sciences and Philosophy* 14 (2004): 101–44; Alexander Treiger, "Monism and Monotheism in al-Ghazālī's *Mishkāt al-Anwār*," *Journal of Qur'anic Studies* 9 (2007): 1–27.

36 The previously mentioned case of al-Fārābī's critique of al-Kindī as well as Ibn Rushd's critique of al-Ghazālī's eclecticism are relevant examples in this context. From the perspective of philosophically oriented Sufi critiques of *falsafa*, Ibn ʿArabī's comments on Ibn Rushd echo aspects of al-Suhrawardī's comments on the Peripatetics. See n. 38.

37 See n. 26.

38 Walbridge, "Suhrawardī and Illuminationism," pp. 201–23. Ziai, "The Illuminationist Tradition," pp. 465–96.

39 Dimitri Gutas has shown how Ibn Sīna's reference to a work on Eastern wisdom (*al-ḥikma al-mashriqiyya*) is in fact a reference to a work on Peripatetic philosophy, in contrast with the conclusions of earlier scholarship that argued for a Sufi side of Ibn Sīna's work based on this reference. Still, as Chapter 6 points out, Ibn Sīna did have at least some interest in what contemporary Sufis had to say, and the Almohad courtier Ibn Ṭufayl's deliberate mysticizing of Ibn Sīna's (Avicenna) corpus in his novel *Alive, Son of Awake* appears to have been motivated by an interest in this aspect of Ibn Sīna's work. Ibn Ṭufayl's representation of Ibn Sīna closely parallels the engagement of contemporary Platonizing Sufis with Ibn Sīna's writing on psychology and cosmology. Dimitri Gutas, "The Study of Arabic Philosophy in the Twentieth

Century," *British Journal of Middle Eastern Studies* 29 (2002): 5–15; idem, "Ibn Ṭufayl on Ibn Sīna's Eastern Philosophy," *Oriens* 34 (1994): 359–85.

40 See Chapter 1, n. 44.

41 Mahmoud Ayoub has contextualized some of these debates in a larger analysis of the various genres and approaches to Qur'an commentary that developed historically. Mahmoud Ayoub, *The Qur'an and Its Interpreters* (Albany: State University of New York Press, 1983), pp. 16–40.

42 The notion of esoteric knowledge (*ʿilm al-bāṭin*), found in early Sunnism (especially Sufism) and early Shiism (especially Ismāʿīlism), implied a binary relationship between esoteric and exoteric knowledge (*ʿilm al-ẓāhir*). According to early critics, one of the dangers of this binary was that a Sufi or Ismāʿīlī writer could erroneously associate scripturally ordained rituals and practices with the category of exoteric knowledge (*ʿilm al-ẓāhir*) and, thus, conceive of the possibility of bypassing both textual meaning and prescribed ritual piety in the pursuit of this esoteric knowledge (*ʿilm al-bāṭin*). A further danger was that everything prohibited in moral and ritual practice could be understood as permissible, and that therefore the entire moral legal framework would be flouted. The concern over this erroneous release from one's moral and ritual obligations, or antinomianism (*ibāḥiyya*), became the subject of many discussions in later Islamic history about Sufis, whether Sunnī or Shiite, and Ismāʿīlīs. However, in reality, many of the most well-known medieval writers of both Sufi metaphysics and Ismāʿīlī theology were careful to emphasize the necessity and importance of the scripturally ordained moral and ritual obligations (*sharʿ*). For example, the dual importance of both exterior and interior meanings of scriptural text and understandings of ritual is fundamental to the Sufi writings of Ibn al-ʿArīf (d. 536/1141), a contemporary of Ibn Qasī (d. 546/1151) discussed in Chapter 5. Ibn al-ʿArīf's *Maḥāsin al-Majālis* is dedicated in part to a mystical understanding of additional interior meanings of ritual practices in order to understand the exterior with greater depth. Ibn al-ʿArīf, *Maḥāsin al-Majālis*, ed. Miguel Asín Palacios (Paris: Paul Geuthner, 1933). Sufis such as al-Kharrāz were similarly critical of an approach to understanding esoteric knowledge that would sideline the jurisprudential sciences as a lesser exoteric knowledge. Ahmet Karamustafa has highlighted figures such as Ibn al-Jawzī who were nonetheless critical of the Sufi distinction between *ʿilm al-bāṭin* and *ʿilm al-ẓāhir*. Ibn al-Jawzī's criticism was based on these previously mentioned concerns about the preservation of the moral and legal framework, which were systematized by Islamic jurisprudence and informed ultimately by scripture. Ahmet Karamustafa, *Sufism: The Formative Period* (Edinburgh: Edinburgh University Press, 2007), p. 158. Writing against *ibāḥiyya* approaches was often part of a polemical genre of writing. See Garden, *The First Islamic Reviver*, pp. 133–5.

43 The political intersection of Umayyad- and Abbasid-era forms of political culture with those of late antique Hellenistic and Persian political legitimacy is contextualized succinctly in the following two studies: Ira M. Lapidus, *A History of Islamic Societies* (Cambridge: Cambridge University Press, 2002), pp. 67–80; Hugh Kennedy, "From Polis to Medina: Urban Change in Late Antique and Early Islamic Syria," *Past and Present* 106 (1985): 3–27.

44 George Saliba and Dimitri Gutas have each contextualized this dream in respective analyses of the motivations in early Islamic history for the translation of philosophical and scientific works into Arabic. George Saliba, *Islamic Science and the Making of the European Renaissance* (Cambridge, MA: MIT Press, 2007), pp. 1–26; Dimitri Gutas, *Greek Thought, Arabic Culture: The Graeco-Arabic Translation Movement in Baghdad and Early ʿAbbāsid Society (2nd–4th/8th -10th centuries)* (London: Routledge, 1998), pp. 95–106.

45 Joel Kraemer's classic work on the Būyid era highlights how the theoretical friction of Imāmī Shiite military rule in a Sunnī caliphate was counterbalanced by an enduring arrangement that saw something of an alignment of interests between Sunnī and Imāmī Shiite authority in Iraq that together rivaled the rising authority of the Fatimid Ismāʿīlī caliphate. Joel L. Kraemer, *Humanism in the Renaissance of Islam: The Cultural Revival During the Buyid Age* (Leiden: Brill, 1986).

46 Omid Safi has offered an analysis of the transition period within a larger study of changing political ideologies and structures of authority. Omid Safi, *The Politics of Knowledge in Premodern Islam: Negotiating Ideology and Religious Inquiry* (Chapel Hill: University of North Carolina Press, 2006).

47 Chapter 3 of the current study offers an in-depth analysis of al-Ghazālī's representation of the theological underpinnings of the early Ismāʿīlī political movements (Fatimids, Nizārīs) in a court-commissioned text that he wrote as chief judge under the Abbasids. The respective works of Heinz Halm and Paul Walker on the Fatimids offer key starting points for considering how medieval critics of the Fatimids understood the rise of the Fatimid caliphate as not only a political challenge, but also an ideological one. Heinz Halm, *The Empire of the Mahdi: The Rise of the Fatimids* (Leiden: Brill, 1996); Paul Walker, *Exploring an Islamic Empire: Fatimid History and Its Sources* (London: I. B. Tauris, 2002).

48 The respective works of Paul Walker and Farhad Daftary have traced how Ismāʿīlī writers increasingly integrated Neoplatonic doctrines into Ismāʿīlī theology beginning in at least the early tenth century. Paul Walker, *Early Philosophical Shiism: The Ismāʿīlī Falsafa of Abū Yaʿqūb al-Sijistānī* (Cambridge: Cambridge University Press, 1993), pp. 3–67; Farhad Daftary, *The Ismāʿīlīs: Their History and Doctrines* (Cambridge: Cambridge University Press, 1992), pp. 144–255.

49 Paul Walker, *Ḥamīd al-Dīn al-Kirmānī: Ismāʿīlī Thought in the Age of al-Ḥakīm* (New York: I. B. Tauris, 1999), pp. 25–30; idem, *Early Philosophical Shiism*, pp. 10–24; Farhad Daftary, *Ismāʿīlī Literature: A Bibliography of Sources and Studies*, (New York: I. B. Tauris 2004), pp. 20–36; Wilfred Madelung, "Das Imamat in der fruhen ismailitischen Lehre,' *Der Islam* 37 (1961): 43–135.

50 On the term *Ḥashīshiyya* and the etymology of the European term *assassins*, see Chapter 3, note 1.

51 Drawing on passages from both *al-Munqidh min al-Ḍalāl* and *Faḍāʾiḥ al-Bāṭiniyya*, Frank Griffel has pointed out that while the text was commissioned by the caliph's court, it may have drawn on an earlier Persian text that al-Ghazālī had previously written. Griffel, Frank Griffel, *al-Ghazālī's Philosophical Theology* (New York: Oxford University Press, 2009), p. 36ff.

52 al-Ghazālī's discussion of causality in the *Scandals of the Esotericists* synthesizes some of his most important criticisms of Graeco-Arabic cosmological doctrines found in his *Incoherence of the Philosophers.* Michael Marmura, "al-Ghazālī on Bodily Resurrection and Causality in the *Tahāfut* and *Iqtiṣād*," *Aligarh Journal of Islamic Thought* 2 (1989): 46–58; Blake D. Dutton, "Al-Ghazālī on Possibility and the Critique of Causality," *Medieval Philosophy and Theology* 10 (2001): 23–46; Taneli Kukkonen, "Possible Worlds in the *Tahāfut al-Falāsifa:* Al-Ghazālī on Creation and Contingency," *Journal of the History of Philosophy* 38 (2000): 470–502.

Part I

Philosophical Caliphs and Their Impact on the Scholars (*ʿulamāʾ*)

1 Rival Caliphs in Baghdad and Cairo

The Iberian Peninsula in the tenth century was largely part of the political domain of the Andalusī Umayyad emirate, based in Cordoba, which was the westernmost urban center of the Abbasid caliphate. Andalusī Cordoba boasted one of the largest urban populations of the Mediterranean basin, including Muslims, Christians, and Jews who were often multilingual in an Iberian dialect of Arabic and an Arabic-influenced Romance language. The emirs of Cordoba cultivated a philosophical court culture that echoed political culture in Baghdad, which saw the caliphal patronage of the influential Greek-Arabic, Aramaic-Arabic, and Pahlavi-Arabic translation movement. In the early tenth century, both the Andalusī emirate and the Abbasid caliphate were challenged by the rising Fatimid political movement of North Africa, which claimed a rival caliphate in 909 that likewise integrated Graeco-Arabic philosophy into its own conceptions of leadership. Against this backdrop, a political and religious controversy emerged in al-Andalus over one of the early Sunnī scholars (*ʿulamāʾ*) named Ibn Masarra (d. 319/931). Ibn Masarra's surviving works drew on two modes of thought found in Abbasid Iraq: Aristotelian-Neoplatonic philosophy (*falsafa*) of the Graeco-Arabic philosophers (*falāsifa*) and Islamic mysticism of the circles around Sahl al-Tustarī (d. 238/896). Ibn Masarra's legacy offered a new understanding of the scholars as both philosophical theologians and mystics. His surviving writings, together with the posthumous scholarly debate over them, provides historians a lens into how the Fatimid–Abbasid political rivalry impacted the way early scholars debated the contours of their own knowledge and religious authority.

The Abbasids and Fatimids in Context

The rise of the Abbasid caliphate in Baghdad, founded in 749, is remembered in history as the culmination of the transformation of the late antique Middle East, divided between Eastern Roman (Byzantine) and Sassanian dominance, into a single global polity. Like its Umayyad

Figure 1.1. The mosque and university of al-Azhar in Cairo, completed in 972 during the reign of the Fatimid caliph al-Muʿizz (r. 953–975).

predecessor based in Damascus, the Abbasid caliphate stretched from the western Mediterranean to the Indian Ocean, and north through the Caspian Sea and the present-day Russian Volga River. Drawing on new Arabic-language and Islamic cultural dimensions at the court, which intersected with late antique Hellenistic and Persian forms of political culture, the Abbasid caliphate was multifaceted and global in its claims to legitimacy.[1] In terms of political and religious authority, however, the caliphate was not as centralized as the notion of a caliphal empire suggests. Politically, an array of military dynasties headed by sultans and emirs carved out independent regions of semiautonomous power throughout the eighth and ninth centuries.[2] The Andalusī Umayyad emirs of al-Andalus, who claimed descent from the pre-Abbasid Umayyad caliphs of Damascus, were one such military dynasty.[3] In terms of religious authority, networks of local scholars throughout the caliphate's cities and towns came to earn significant respect in local Muslim communities for their role as mediators of disputes and for their knowledge in the realm of Islamic ethics and faith-related questions.[4] What distinguished the office of the caliph in Baghdad from the military dynasties and networks of scholars was the caliph's historical role as the symbolic guarantor of the political and religious cohesion of the Islamic imperial polity, a role reflected in the shared coinage of the various provincial dynasties and the Friday congregations that identified the caliph as commander of the faithful.[5]

The caliph in Baghdad was also distinguished as a major patron of philosophical and scientific works, in continuity with the intellectual dimensions of late antique political culture in Eastern Roman (Byzantine) and Persian centers such as Constantinople, Ctesiphon, and Gundishapur. The pre-Islamic Hellenistic philosophers' and Islamic-era Graeco-Arabic philosophers' understanding of philosophy as having origins in ancient Mesopotamia found widespread appeal among early Muslims, who identified the ancient sage Hermes with the scriptural prophet Idrīs.[6] The image in the extant sources of philosophy's development in early Abbasid Iraq, especially in Basra and Baghdad, is one of bustling intellectual activity that included developments in the creative intersection of Graeco-Arabic philosophy and the Islamic sciences, especially Islamic theology. By the tenth century, these developments represented the culmination of two centuries of vigorous translation activity sponsored by the early Abbasid caliphs and general populace.[7] Like the Abbasid caliphs, the Andalusī Umayyad emirs in the Abbasids' western periphery of al-Andalus were patrons of philosophical and scientific works, cultivating Cordoba as a regional capital on the model of Baghdad. The emir and later caliph ʿAbd al-Raḥmān III (r. 912–961) is particularly notable for having commissioned the translation of philosophical and medical texts into Arabic.[8]

In the early tenth century, this entire political and intellectual framework from Cordoba to Baghdad was fractured by a major political event that shook both Andalusī Umayyad al-Andalus and Abbasid Iraq. In 909, in the coastal city of Mahdiyya near Tunis, a dynasty called the Fatimids that adhered to the Ismāʿīlī branch of Shiism declared a rival caliphate. The new caliphate challenged not only the political authority of the Abbasid caliphs, but also the religious authority of the predominantly Sunnī scholarly networks.[9] Among these scholars, the Fatimid caliphate came to be associated with the term esotericists (*bāṭiniyya*), an epithet applied to the Ismāʿīlī branch of Shiism because of the Ismāʿīlī theologians' predilection for interpreting both scripture and worldly phenomena esoterically, that is, by looking for exterior (*ẓāhir*) and interior (*bāṭin*) hermeneutical meanings and worldly realities. This esotericism, which had parallels among Sunnī authors of philosophical and mystical works, played a formative role in the early tenth-century articulation of a specifically Platonizing form of Ismāʿīlī theology that was adopted by the Fatimids.[10] The Fatimid caliphate's conceptions of ruling political authority drew specifically on the writings of various tenth-century figures

Figure 1.2. Top of an entry portal in Cairo's Moonlit Mosque (Jāmiʿ al-Aqmar), featuring a concentric three-ring pierced medallion with the names Muhammad and Ali in the center, surrounded by a Qur'anic verse in the middle ring.

in Persian Ismāʿīlī theology who articulated the theory of a Platonizing messianic (*mahdī*) ruler, one who would challenge the prevailing political establishment. According to this theory, the soul of the ideal ruler would attain a level of excellence by having ascended spiritually to the realm of the timeless and immaterial Universal Soul, of which all human souls were a part, according to the cosmological theories of late antique and early Islamic-era Plotinian cosmology.[11] One of the key contentions of this chapter is that against the backdrop of the rise of the Fatimid caliphate and the controversy over the Ismāʿīlī "esotericists," scholars within the majority-Sunnī schools of jurisprudence began to reexamine the theological dimensions of their own authority as communal guides. Specifically, they questioned the legacies of early Sunnī scholars among their predecessors who had drawn either on the doctrines of the Graeco-Arabic philosophers in Aristotelian-Neoplatonic psychology or on the methods of the early mystics in the use of an esoteric scriptural hermeneutic for theological writing. A look at the history of both philosophy and mysticism in al-Andalus will help contextualize the controversy of scholar Ibn Masarra in particular.

Graeco-Arabic Philosophy and Islamic Mysticism

In the introduction of his philosophical allegory *Alive the Son of Awake*, an Almohad-era philosopher and courtier named Ibn Ṭufayl (d. 580/1185) asserted that books on Graeco-Arabic philosophy *(falsafa)* were "rarer than red sulphur" in al-Andalus, suggesting that philosophy was slower in its development in al-Andalus than in Abbasid Iraq.[12] The renowned historian and geographer Ibn Saʿīd al-Maghribī (d. 685/1286) offered a similar picture of philosophy in al-Andalus in his portrait of the intellectual pursuits of the scholars. In a representation that appears almost fictional in comparison with the philosophical world of Baghdad, he wrote that "All of the branches of learning are subjects of importance to them, with the exception of philosophy and astronomy. Both of these are of great interest to the elite, but no work on these topics can be undertaken openly out of fear of the general populace."[13] He indicated, furthermore, that anyone associated with philosophy or astronomy, whether as a teacher or student of these subjects, could be labeled a "heretic" *(zindīq)* by the general populace. "The ruler might put him to death just to build favor among the common folk, and in many cases their kings have given orders that books on these subjects be burned if discovered."[14] If true, this unusual image would stand in striking contrast with the image of Graeco-Arabic philosophy in Abbasid Iraq discussed earlier.

Ibn Ṭufayl and Ibn Saʿīd al-Maghribī's representation of a limited transmission of Graeco-Arabic philosophy *(falsafa)* in al-Andalus has endured in modern historical writing, and it has been strengthened by two common assumptions about al-Andalus' early centuries.[15] The first is that a strong Andalusī Mālikī religious establishment was able to stifle the transmission and development of various sciences thriving in the

Islamic East, especially philosophy and speculative theology.[16] The second is that al-Andalus, as a geographic periphery of the Islamic world, only diffusely absorbed intellectual developments from Abbasid Iraq.[17] Both points are supported by various non-Andalusī medieval sources. For example, the geographer al-Muqaddasī (d. 381/991) depicted al-Andalus as a land where the Mālikī establishment excluded various dynamic modes of thought.[18] Recent studies since the late twentieth century have broken down this image of early al-Andalus as an intellectual periphery. Historians, including José María Forneas, Maribel Fierro, Manuela Marín, and Abdel Magid Turki, have shown that this image belies the diversity in theology and ritual practices among early Mālikī scholarly circles in al-Andalus. Specifically, these historians have shown that on the one hand, there were indeed politically influential circles of Mālikī scholars who were resistant to dynamic modes of knowledge transmitted from Iraq and North Africa.[19] On the other hand, scholars in al-Andalus by the tenth and eleventh centuries had absorbed legal theory (*uṣūl al-fiqh*),[20] Ashʿarī theology,[21] ascetic piety,[22] and in some cases mysticism as Islamic sciences.[23]

In the case of philosophy, one of the continuing difficulties in critiquing Ibn Ṭufayl and Ibn Saʿīd al-Maghribī's representation of al-Andalus as peripheral in the history of Peripatetic philosophy is that the earliest bio-bibliographical sources on al-Andalus do not make many explicit references to the Arabic term *falsafa*. Four of the most important early sources on the intellectual and scholarly life of al-Andalus, namely the bio-bibliographical dictionaries of al-Khushanī (d. ca. 371/981), Ibn al-Faraḍī (d. 403/1013), Ibn Bashkuwāl (d. 578/1183), and Ibn al-ʿAbbār (d. 658/1260), speak neither of circles of philosophers (*falāsifa*) in al-Andalus nor of the patronage of philosophy (*falsafa*).[24] However, a fifth source, Ibn Ḥazm's (d. 456–1064) *Book on the Approximation of Logic*, sheds important light on intellectual debates about philosophy in a way that indicates it was transmitted and discussed in early Andalusī history. Ibn Ḥazm's representation of philosophy in al-Andalus divides Andalusī society into four groups with respect to attitudes toward Aristotelian logic (*manṭiq*) in particular. He claims that the first considers it blasphemous, the second shows hostility toward it out of ignorance, the third dabbles in it and spreads unsound ideas, and the fourth makes profitable use of it.[25] Significantly, he characterizes the second group as the largest. In other words, despite the distinction between Ibn Ḥazm's emphasis on logic and Ibn Saʿīd al-Maghribī's emphasis on astronomy in their respective representations of the place of philosophy in al-Andalus, there is some agreement in the sources that these sciences were indeed in circulation.[26] A particularly important window into the scholarly and political dimensions of these controversies is found in the surviving works of an influential scholar in tenth-century Cordoba named Ibn Masarra.

Early sources on al-Andalus indicate that a scholarly debate developed over the writings of a certain Cordovan scholar named Ibn Masarra (d. 319/931), who was a contemporary of the Cordovan Mālikī scholar Qāsim b. Aṣbagh (d. 340/951). The two scholars even shared three teachers, including Ibn Masarra's father and the influential *ḥadīth* scholar Ibn Waḍḍāḥ (d. 287/900).[27] In line with the circulation of philosophical and mystical doctrines in contemporary Iraq, where Ibn Masarra and other Andalusī scholars had traveled, Ibn Masarra incorporated aspects of Neoplatonic psychology and cosmology into his Platonizing theological writings, which were built on his use of an esoteric scriptural hermeneutic.[28] He also taught ascetic doctrines to students who studied with him in the mountains outside Cordoba. Ibn Masarra appears, in other words, to have synthesized the intellectual trends of contemporary Abbasid Iraq's philosophers, mystics, and scholarly ascetics, and his surviving writings unsurprisingly make reference to both the philosophers (*falāsifa*) and the mystic Sahl al-Tustarī (d. 238/896) among the "people of interior knowledge" (*ahl al-ʿilm bi-l-bāṭin*). That is, Ibn Masarra ascribed his method not to the esoteric hermeneutics of the Platonizing Ismāʿīlī theologians mentioned earlier, but to the mystical circles of Iraq who often numbered among early Sunnī scholarly circles.[29] Evidence in biographical dictionaries indicates that while many scholars studied with Ibn Masarra, other scholars distanced themselves from Ibn Masarra's work. This evidence, discussed in further detail later, points not simply to a scholarly debate about philosophy and the mystics' esoteric hermeneutics, but more specifically one that was shaped by the contemporary controversy over the rising Fatimid caliphate's Platonizing cosmology and Ismāʿīlī esoteric hermeneutic. Critically, this cosmology and hermeneutic, which explains the epithet "esotericists" in criticism of the Ismāʿīlīs, undergirded the Fatimids' claim to a new semi-messianic caliphate.[30] A closer look at the sources illustrates this impact of Fatimid politics on the scholarly reception of Ibn Masarra's writings.

When Ibn Masarra was active as a scholar among the circles of predominantly Mālikī scholars in al-Andalus, the Fatimid caliphate was just beginning to rise in power prior to its move to Cairo, and the local Andalusī Umayyad emirate still paid homage to the distant Abbasid caliph's ruling political authority.[31] By the mid-tenth century, during the height of political competition between the Fatimid caliphate and the newly declared Andalusī Umayyad caliphate, Ibn Masarra's books became the subject of a series of scholarly refutations that have not survived but that indicate just how geographically widespread the controversy over Ibn Masarra had become. According to the bio-bibliographer and scholar Ibn al-Faraḍī, Ibn Masarra's texts were refuted in writing by, among others, a tenth-century judge named Ibn al-Ḥabbāb and a contemporary scholar named Muḥammad b. Yabqā b. Zarb, both of whom penned a written critique of Ibn Masarra's work.[32] Ibn al-Faraḍī reports that two influential mystics of the Islamic East, the mystics Abū Saʿīd b. al-Aʿrābi (d. 341/952) and Aḥmad b. Muḥammad b. Sālim al-Tustarī (d. 356/967), also refuted the doctrines of Ibn Masarra.[33] While these refutations have not survived, the bibliographical sources illustrate an evolution over time of critiques and representations of Ibn Masarra in a pattern that points to a controversy over Ibn Masarra's synthesis of *falsafa* and Islamic theology. Specifically, while the early sources represent Ibn Masarra as a traditional Muslim scholar closely connected to the circles of Qāsim b. Aṣbagh (d. 340/951),[34] later sources represent him variously as a philosopher (*faylasūf*)[35] and a Sufi.[36] His own extant writings indicate that he saw himself as one of the *ʿulamāʾ* (scholars) and *ḥukamāʾ* (sages), the latter term having a philosophical orientation in his writings.[37]

The fact that Ibn Masarra was later remembered as a philosopher and a Sufi indicates that two central aspects of his surviving writings piqued the interest of followers and critics: his references to and intellectual engagement with both the Graeco-Arabic philosophers and mystics of Iraq. Specifically, in both of his surviving treatises examined later in this chapter, Ibn Masarra represented himself as a scholar interested in the writings of the philosophers and their doctrines on the nature of the human intellect and soul, including the human connection with the Plotinian Universal Intellect and Universal Soul. The characterization of Ibn Masarra as a philosopher has its roots at least as early as Ṣāʿid al-Andalusī's (d. 462/1070) eleventh-century representation of Ibn Masarra as a follower of pseudo-Empedocles.[38] Upon examination of Ibn Masarra's works within a larger investigation of pseudo-Empedocles and the thought of al-ʿĀmirī (d. 381/992), Everett Rowson has demonstrated a point that substantiates what Samuel Miklós Stern surmised before the texts were available. Specifically, the tradition of pseudo-Empedocles is not identifiable in the works of Ibn Masarra as Miguel Asín Palacios once presumed based on Ṣāʿid al-Andalusī's description of him.[39] At the same time, like al-ʿĀmirī, Ibn Masarra fits in the broader history of *falsafa*, specifically in the history of early scholars who synthesized Aristotelian-Neoplatonic doctrines with Islamic theological writing and aspects of mysticism. His engagement with Islamic mysticism was in his use of an esoteric scriptural hermeneutic to articulate doctrines of Plotinian psychology and cosmology, even attributing his hermeneutical method directly to Sahl al-Tustarī among the "people of interior knowledge" (*ahl al-ʿilm bi-l-bāṭin*).[40]

One of the key reasons to read Ibn Masarra's identification of Sahl al-Tustarī among the "people of interior knowledge" (*ahl ʿilm bi-l-bāṭin*) as a specific reference to the early mystics of Iraq is the way other Andalusī scholars used the phrase "interior knowledge" (*ʿilm al-bāṭin*) in the tenth century. A closer look at the bio-bibliographical work of Ibn al-Faraḍī demonstrates a point that recent research on Ibn Masarra has overlooked. Specifically, in direct continuity with Ibn Masarra's language, Ibn al-Faraḍī used the terms *ʿilm al-bāṭin* and *al-ʿilm al-bāṭinī* to refer not to the Ismāʿīlīs, but to the knowledge of tenth-century scholars (*ʿulamāʾ*) contemporary with Ibn Masarra who studied with the famous mystic and scholar Abū Saʿīd b. al-Aʿrābī of Iraq. In his bio-bibliographical work, Ibn al-Faraḍī described the scholar Muḥammad b. Fatḥ of Guadalajara as having written work on interior knowledge, which he learned from famous mystic Abū Saʿīd b. al-Aʿrābī.[41] Ibn al-Faraḍī also mentions Muḥammad b. Aṣbagh b. Labīb as a scholar who studied under the same Abū Saʿīd b. al-Aʿrābī, returning to al-Andalus from his studies in the Islamic East and transmitting knowledge about the schools of thought of "interior knowledge" (*al-ʿilm al-bāṭinī*).[42] In sum, interior or esoteric knowledge in these cases, in agreement with Ibn Masarra's reference to the Iraqi mystic Sahl al-Tustarī as one of the "people of interior knowledge" (*ahl ʿilm al-bāṭin*), reflects the very early historical use of the term by Sunnī writers to refer to the early mystics among the scholars. This use of the term is also evident in the early Sufi compendia. Among the circles of mystics in the lifetime of al-Kharrāz (d. ca. 286/899) and the more famous al-Junayd (d. 298/910), the term interior knowledge (*ʿilm al-bāṭin*) is evocative of what the scholars identified and sought to witness of the epistemic and phenomenological "unseen" referenced in scripture.[43] In the case of Sahl al-Tustarī, the discovery and witnessing of this "unseen" was part of the knowledge of "wisdom," just as it was for the Sufi metaphysicians of the twelfth and thirteenth centuries. What points to the impact of politics on scholarly conceptions of sound knowledge and sound guidance is how later references to Ibn Masarra's interest in esoteric scriptural hermeneutics blend with polemical representations of the Fatimids as the "esotericists." This image of scholarly opinions on both philosophy and the mystics' esoteric scriptural hermeneutics becoming entangled with the controversy over the Fatimids' Platonizing scriptural esotericism is particularly clear in the writings of Ṣāʿid al-Andalusī (d. 462/1070) and al-Qifṭī (d. 646/1248).

More specifically, in contrast with Ibn al-Faraḍī's tenth-century use of the terms *bāṭin* and *bāṭinī* in a characterization of knowledge and scholarly sciences associated with the mystics, the later scholar Ṣāʿid al-Andalusī characterized Ibn Masarra as an "esotericist philosopher" during the peak of the controversy over the Fatimid "esotericists." al-Qifṭī, like Ṣāʿid al-Andalusī, indicated that Ibn Masarra was among a group of the *bāṭiniyya* who followed Empedocles' doctrines.[44] In a similar entanglement of esoteric scriptural hermeneutics in Sunnism with anti-Fatimid polemics, al-Dhahabī's work makes reference to the eleventh-century scholar al-Ṭalamankī and his written refutation of Ibn Masarra as a refutation of the esotericists more broadly.[45] This later entanglement of the mystics' esoteric scriptural hermeneutics with that of the Fatimids manifests most clearly in the fourteenth-century writings of Ibn Taymiyya, which lumps the philosophers and Sufis together with the Ismāʿīlīs as three different types of "esotericists." Ṣāʿid al-Andalusī and al-Qifṭī's use of the term esotericist reflects a climate beginning in the tenth century of growing scholarly and political concern over the perceived or potential influence of the Fatimids, and specifically of proselytizing Fatimid Ismāʿīlī teachers, on political and religious trends in neighboring al-Andalus and Iraq.

In its most dramatic manifestation in al-Andalus, this political climate of suspicion of Fatimid influence saw the caliph ʿAbd al-Raḥmān III condemn the legacy of the rebel ʿUmar b. Ḥafsūn (d. 304/917) for Fatimid-leaning *tashayyuʿ*. ʿUmar b. Ḥafsūn was a political separatist who rebelled against Andalusī Umayyad rule when Ibn Masarra was still alive.[46] The case of ʿUmar b. Ḥafsūn represented the possibility that local political factions in the tenth century could and did ally themselves with the neighboring Fatimids, just as North African tribes had changed allegiances between the Andalusī Umayyads and Fatimids. ʿAbd al-Raḥmān's public condemnation of ʿUmar b. Ḥafsūn, like his condemnation of the Fatimid neighbors, contextualizes more precisely the political climate in which scholarly debates about Ibn Masarra's "esotericism" were taking shape. al-Ghazālī's *Scandals of the Esotericists*, which represents in detail the process of attempting to win adherents to the Fatimid cause, offers the clearest textual picture of how scholarly debates about philosophical doctrines and esoteric scriptural hermeneutics became entangled with the controversy over the Fatimids.

Ibn Masarra's own surviving writings offer earlier evidence of how this scholarly dialogue was taking shape during his own lifetime, when scholars in al-Andalus were beginning to ask in a political context whether Graeco-Arabic philosophy and the mystics' esoteric scriptural hermeneutic were sound epistemic aspects of the scholarly sciences. That is, his writings offer a window into a question that the scholars of the Islamic world began to reexamine with the rise of the Fatimids' Platonizing "esotericist" caliphate: Should doctrines in Graeco-Arabic cosmology and psychology have been integrated into theological writing following the lead of Ibn Masarra, and was Ibn Masarra and Sahl al-Tustarī's use of an esoteric scriptural hermeneutic valid given its similarity with Ismāʿīlī esoteric hermeneutics? These questions were part of the larger question asking what forms of knowledge were part of the Sunnī scholars' role as a communal guide in questions of belief, and which forms of knowledge ought to be excluded. That two of Ibn Masarra's works are extant allows historians the opportunity to trace how in tenth-century al-Andalus, long before the rise of al-Ghazālī's philosophical theology and Sufi metaphysics, one of the most influential and controversial scholars of the tenth century answered these questions even before the Fatimid movement was in full force.

Ibn Masarra's surviving works show that as a scholar, he was willing to blur the boundaries between scholars, on the one hand, and the philosophers and mystics, on the other hand, in an era when Graeco-Arabic philosophy and esoteric scriptural hermeneutics were just beginning to become entangled with representations of Ismāʿīlism as a philosophically oriented "esotericist" political movement. One of Ibn Masarra's extant works, *Epistle on Contemplation* (*Risālat al-Iʿtibār*), identifies a special mode of contemplative thought (*iʿtibār*) as a fundamental tool for understanding the nature of the world and its relationship with God.[47] The other work, *Book on the Special Qualities of the Letters* (*Kitāb Khawāṣṣ al-Ḥurūf*), explains the importance of applying this same tool of contemplation (*iʿtibār*) to scripture in order to extract its interior (*bāṭin*) meanings.[48] Both texts present the harmony of scripture and Graeco-Arabic philosophical doctrines in cosmology, with scripture represented as providing a more accurate and clearer elaboration of knowledge than philosophy taken in isolation of prophecy.[49] Most importantly, the texts indicate that despite later representations of Ibn Masarra as a philosopher (*faylasūf*) or Sufi, his own writings indicate that he saw himself as one of the scholars, willing to embrace philosophy and the mystics' esoteric scriptural hermeneutic as part of theological writing.[50]

Ibn Masarra's *Book on the Properties of the Letters*

In writing his *Book on the Properties of the [Qur'anic] Letters*, Ibn Masarra pushed the boundaries of what it meant to be a scholar. The work synthesizes doctrines in Graeco-Arabic psychology and cosmology with hermeneutical methods popular among the mystics in the elaboration of a kind of philosophical theology that was new in al-Andalus. The overall framework of Ibn Masarra's intellectual project in his *Book on the*

Properties of the [Qur'anic] Letters argues that the scripturally commanded act of speculative inquiry encompasses contemplation (*iʿtibār*) of both scripture and the world. In the contemplation of scripture, Ibn Masarra wrote specifically about how the Names of God mentioned in scripture, coupled with the individual scriptural letters that make up the text, together offer a contemplative gateway into an understanding of the exterior and interior dimensions of both scripture and the world. In the articulation of these interior dimensions, Ibn Masarra elaborates a Platonizing cosmology oriented around doctrines that he explicitly indicates to be in agreement with those of the Graeco-Arabic philosophers. Surprisingly, despite the biographical dictionaries' reticence in using the terms philosophy (*falsafa*) or philosophers (*falāsifa*), Ibn Masarra makes direct reference to both the philosophers (*falāsifa*) and the mystics of Iraq (*ahl al-ʿilm bi-l- bāṭin*), including the mystic Sahl al-Tustarī specifically. By doing so, he articulates an interest in pushing the boundaries of the scholars' sciences some 150 years before al-Ghazālī wrote works of philosophical theology and Sufi metaphysics, which ultimately circulated in al-Andalus among scholars such as Ibn ʿArabī who drew on both al-Ghazālī's and Ibn Masarra's works.

The three central claims of Ibn Masarra's method can be summarized in the following way: First, the scriptural text contains multiple layers of meaning, with the Names of God found in the text and the letters that make up the text constituting critical gateways into the most subtle layers of interior (*bāṭin*) meaning. Second, the "the people of interior knowledge" (*ahl ʿilm bi-l- bāṭin*), such as the mystic Sahl al-Tustarī, are among those outside the prophets who are most adept in grasping the interior or esoteric levels of scriptural meaning. Third, interior knowledge (*ʿilm al-bāṭin*) offers metaphysical information about the phenomenal world that agrees with the cosmology of the Graeco-Arabic philosophers (*falāsifa*), whose neglect of scriptural evidence led them to use erroneous language in their otherwise sound understanding of the world's metaphysics.

The cornerstone of the entire theory of knowledge that Ibn Masarra elaborates in his work is *fikra* (thought). In his interpretation of the notion of the term thought in the Qur'anic verse – "And We revealed to you the reminder, that you may make clear to the people what we sent down to them, and so that they may give thought" – [51] he understands "thought" as broad speculative inquiry resembling inductive reasoning.

> "Thought" here [in this verse] is contemplation of what appeared of His created things, inquiry and reflection through them upon His Oneness, the discouragement from doing wrong, the warning of His authority, the encouragement to do good, the remembrance of what He possesses of divine favor, and [reflection] upon the praising of Him in His Names and Attributes.[52]

In line with the scriptural injunction to think, Ibn Masarra calls for speculative inquiry into the nature of the world as a world of created existence that was brought into being by God, Whose oneness, awe-inspiring nature, and exhortation to virtue become apparent to the inquisitive upon examination of these created beings in their totality. For Ibn Masarra, this process of thinking is as much a process of scripturally mandated contemplation (*iʿtibār*) and speculative inquiry into the world of created existences as it is reflection on God's commands to do good and to praise God through the Most Beautiful Names revealed in scripture.[53]

The Names of God elaborated in scripture are critical in his discussion because they collectively constitute one of the two main aspects of scripture that he identifies as gateways to interior or esoteric levels of knowledge about both scripture and the world. The other gateway is found in the individual scriptural letters, which he believes offer knowledge of the deeper levels of the world's phenomenal reality. At those deeper levels, Ibn Masarra identifies a Platonizing cosmology that agrees with key aspects of the contemporary Graeco-Arabic philosophers' cosmological theories.

Neoplatonic Intellect and Soul in the Scriptural Cosmos

One of Ibn Masarra's central methodological goals in this work is to explain how the divine Names, as they emerge from scriptural discussion of God's agency in the world, can reveal knowledge of the world's created cosmology. In pursuing this goal, he presents the Names of God as the vehicle to discovering cosmological doctrines in agreement with the doctrines of the Graeco-Arabic philosophers. One illustrative example of his method is his discussion of the *basmala*, that is, the phrase "In the Name of God, the Beneficent, the Merciful," which opens the individual chapters of the Qur'an. From the *basmala* of the Qur'an's first chapter, he identifies three Names of God: the name of divinity (God), the name the Beneficent, and the name the Merciful. From these three names, he derives key pieces of information about God's agency in the world.[54] Specifically, he speaks of the Names as offering knowledge of God's effusion of mercy, knowledge of God's attribute of the divine breath that gives life, knowledge of God's vision, and knowledge of the ascension of souls at the end of life. Ibn Masarra wants his reader to grasp intellectually that in the scriptural text, specifically in the Names of God found in the text, specific subtly articulated pieces of knowledge are found about God's agency as creator of the world, information that he ultimately explains can be witnessed at the level of the phenomenal world's manifest (*ẓāhir*) and hidden (*bāṭin*) realities.

Critically, in his wider presentation of how the Names lead to knowledge of the cosmos, he makes explicit reference to the Greek and Graeco-Arabic philosophers (*falāsifa*) and engages key concepts in Neoplatonic cosmology such as the Universal Intellect and Universal Soul.[55] This explicit interest in Graeco-Arabic philosophy appears most clearly in the following passage from the text, in which Ibn Masarra explains that grasping the connection between knowledge of the Names and knowledge of God's creative agency leads to an understanding, sought by the philosophers, of the order of the cosmos.

From [the Name] the Merciful is derived [the information] that God is the One Who fashions (*muṣawwir*), the One Who witnesses (*shāhid*), the One Who gives life (*muḥyī*).... Likewise from [the Name of] divinity together with [the Name] the Merciful and with [the Name] the Beneficent, comes the knowledge that the Universal Intellect (*al-ʿaql al-kullī*) is flooded in the Universal Soul (*al-nafs al-kulliyya*), and that the Universal Soul is flooded in the body of the world according to the method of the philosophers (*falāsifa*) and the ancients of the nations who went astray, [that is,] the people of the earlier periods who approached knowledge of divine Oneness without [reliance on] prophecy. [The philosophers'] knowledge in this was in agreement with the Names [derived from scripture], however prophecy expounded it with a more precise explanation and clearer demonstration.[56]

His mention of the philosophers (*falāsifa*), a reference to both the ancient Hellenistic philosophers and the contemporary Graeco-Arabic philosophers, and his reference to the doctrines of Universal Soul and Universal Intellect in his larger discussion of the Names, are striking.[57] On the one hand, it is not necessarily surprising that Ibn Masarra engages a form of Platonizing cosmology given his previous comments that the Names provide further knowledge about God as the Creator of the world. On the other hand, the presentation of specific doctrines of the philosophers as well as an explicit reference to the philosophers by name is surprising in the context of one of the last section's conclusions, namely that explicit references to the contemporary Graeco-Arabic philosophers were difficult to find in tenth-century sources on the scholars in al-Andalus. Ibn Masarra's unique and early reference to them here in this early tenth-century text calls to mind the twelfth-century philosopher and courtier Ibn Ṭufayl's misleading comment that books on philosophy were "rarer than red sulphur" in the early centuries of al-Andalus. Ibn Ṭufayl's comments, when reconsidered in light of Ibn Masarra's reference to Neoplatonic doctrines and the philosophers, likely meant that certain types of philosophical works were in wide circulation but became relegated to less open channels of transmission following controversy, perhaps in light of controversial astrological and alchemical writings.[58] Likewise, a reconsideration of the eleventh-century biographer Ibn al-Faraḍī's lack of explicit reference to Graeco-Arabic philosophy circulating among the scholars, coupled with his use of the term *mut'azila* as a vague referent to a mix of speculative methods in describing Ibn Masarra's father, points to the likelihood that Mut'azilī and Graeco-Arabic doctrines were transmitted with contested reception by a common audience of speculative theologians like Ibn Masarra and his students. This reception parallels the intertwined interest in philosophy and speculative theology among of al-Kindī's ninth- and tenth-century students in Iraq.[59]

In effect, long before the posthumous book-burning of Ibn Masarra's works, Ibn Masarra made an important overture to the knowledge of the Graeco-Arabic philosophers as knowledge that fellow scholars in the predominantly Mālikī circles of Cordoba should identify as part of the scholarly sciences. His reference to the Universal Soul and Universal Intellect should be interpreted as an effort to highlight the fact that the ancient and contemporary philosophers presented a set of unified and coherent principles explaining God's causality in the world that agree in large part with prophecy, even if the philosophers' flawed elaboration of philosophy would be "more precise" if oriented more closely around the scriptural text.[60] The method he suggests for integrating this philosophical knowledge into the scholarly sciences is this speculative approach of applying contemplation (*i'tibār*) to both scripture and the world simultaneously in order to discover not only their apparent realities, but also their hidden or interior realities. In the examples given earlier, his application of contemplation to scripture and the world was oriented around scripture's references to the Names. He interpreted these Names as being indicative of patterns of agency that he believed the philosophers identified in their own language using Neoplatonic cosmological concepts such of Universal Intellect and Universal Soul. Below, in his move from the Names in scripture to the letters of scripture, Ibn Masarra identifies more clearly this contemplation of scripture and the world as part of an explicitly "esoteric" (*bāṭinī*) scriptural hermeneutic that offers further philosophically oriented knowledge of an "unseen" (*ghayb*) cosmology of the world behind its "visible" (*shahāda*) phenomena.

Mysticism in Iraq and the Rise of Esoteric Hermeneutics

In the previous section, Ibn Masarra was seen arguing that the Names of God in scripture offered a window into an understanding of God's agency, an understanding that he believed agreed with the philosophers' interpretation of causality using doctrines such as Universal Soul and Universal Intellect. As mentioned, Soul and Intellect were fundamental building blocks of Aristotelian-Neoplatonic Plotinian cosmology. Below, in Ibn Masarra's discussion of the individual scriptural letters found at the beginning of several chapters of the Qur'an, he builds on his agreement with the philosophers' doctrines in psychology and cosmology. Specifically, in explaining "contemplation" of scripture's individual letters, he identifies his reading of scripture more explicitly as an esoteric hermeneutic that draws on the mystics' exegetical methods. Critically, in this discussion of the letters, he is even more explicit about his project of encouraging fellow scholars to be receptive of the philosophers' doctrines. He builds his argument by appealing to the essentially Islamic and scholarly nature of esoteric scriptural hermeneutics, which is where he ultimately locates his philosophical doctrines.

> Then come the letters of the Qur'an that are in the beginnings of the chapters, such as "*Alif Lām Mīm*,"[61] "*Alif Lām Ra*,"[62] "*Alif Lām Mīm Ṣād*,"[63] "*Kāf Ha Ya ʿAin Ṣād*,"[64] "*Ṭa Sīn Mīm*,"[65] and likewise among the Mothers of the Qur'an. The scholars (*ʿulamā'*) have differed in their interpretation, but their differences were not out of ignorance of them nor can one suggest that that they are not knowledgeable of them. Indeed, the scholars are closer than everyone in knowledge of God Most High and of His Book, and they are the rightful custodians of this knowledge out of their closeness to prophecy and to the model community. They, God have mercy on them, elaborated [knowledge] to the people according to the extent to which [their] understanding could grasp, since matters must reach everyone. For that reason, their [scholarly] differences increased and agreement became impossible in the exterior level (*ẓāhir*) of the word, while they agreed on the interior level of it.[66]

Ibn Masarra makes several key points in his discussion about the letters that reflect his interest in philosophy and the mystics' exegetical methods. The most important point is that he represents esoteric scriptural hermeneutics to be a historically accepted hermeneutical method among scholars articulating theological doctrines.[67] To make his argument, he paints a sanguine picture of interior knowledge of scripture as a layer of scriptural meaning on which scholarly opinions converged, in contrast with the scholars' difference of opinion over the literal or exterior reading of scripture. In other words, he takes almost the exact opposite position of Ibn Ḥazm's approach discussed in the next chapter, who rejected esoteric hermeneutics and even attempted to reform linguistic theories on metaphorical (*majāz*) readings of words.[68] Ibn Masarra explains that the difference of opinion over the exterior layer of scriptural meaning corresponds naturally to the diverse ways the scholars communicate scriptural meaning to a general populace of disparate intellectual abilities. True consensus in scholarly interpretation of scripture, he argues, is found at the level of the "interior" meanings.

Contrary to his representation of the scholars, Ibn Masarra's attempt to fit an esoteric scriptural hermeneutic into the Islamic sciences of the scholars would have been seen by these scholars as problematic for several reasons. Most important among these reasons is that in his presentation of his theory of cosmology, he appeals to a specific group that is neither identical with the scholars nor a specific subset of the scholars, though they sometimes overlapped with the scholars. Specifically, he draws on the findings of the "people of interior knowledge" (*ahl ʿilm al-bāṭin*), whom he identifies as Iraq's mystics through his reference to Sahl al-Tustarī. This reference conforms with the bio-bibliographer Ibn al-Faraḍī's previously mentioned references to contemporaries of Ibn Masarra who studied *ʿilm al-bāṭin* from the Sufi Abū Saʿīd Ibn al-Aʿrābī.[69] Ibn Masarra appears to think that the mystics' use of an esoteric scriptural hermeneutic would make it more acceptable to the scholars, which is an argument that might have been appealing specifically to fellow scholars also interested in mysticism. In anticipation of the later philosophically oriented Sufi metaphysicians of al-Andalus who quote Ibn Masarra and Sahl al-Tustarī as foundational figures of their tradition, Ibn Masarra's interest in Sahl al-Tustarī's mystical exegesis was for its synthesis of an esoteric scriptural hermeneutic and cosmological discussion:

> The people of interior knowledge (*ahl al-ʿilm bi-l-bāṭin*) assert that the letters that are in the beginnings of the Qur'anic chapters are the basis of all things, and that from them God made His knowledge and the prophets appear. Sahl b. ʿAbdullāh al-Tustarī said, "The letters are the primordial dust, the origin of all things at the beginning of their separation. From [the letters], the [creative] command (*amr*) was structured and the dominion [of the world] appeared."[70]

Ibn Masarra validates his use of an esoteric scriptural hermeneutic using an appeal to the "people of interior knowledge" and their cosmological doctrines, and he identifies them as the mystics of Iraq through his reference to Sahl al-Tustarī. That is, in a remarkable and eclectic mix of methods, Ibn Masarra appeals to the mystics of Iraq to help justify to the local scholars of al-Andalus what will emerge as a theory of cosmology drawing on Neoplatonic psychology.[71] In this short introduction to his cosmology, and drawing on a passage in Sahl al-Tustarī's writings that has not survived in its original context, Ibn Masarra offers his most important doctrine: the world as text. According to this doctrine, the letters of scripture are understood to have ontological value as the basis of the world's existence. This doctrine follows from the conclusion that since the letters of scripture reflect God's speech, and since God's speech was understood to be part of God's creative agency according to the speculative theologians, then the manifestation of the world is simultaneously the manifestation of the letters in a world of signs.

The world in its entirety is a book, its letters are His speech, and the perspicacious read it with the eyes of sincere thought according to [the capacities of] their eyes and the effort of their contemplation (*iʿtibār*). The eyes of their hearts turn in the [truly] manifest (*ẓāhir*) yet veiled wonders that are exposed [and made manifest] to the one who looks, but that are [otherwise hidden and] veiled from the one who is distracted.[72]

Ibn Masarra's discussion, from one of the opening passages of his work *Risālat al-Iʿtibār*, captures the heart of his esoteric scriptural hermeneutic and the space it makes for philosophical cosmology, which he will further elaborate in the remainder of the *Kitāb Khawāṣṣ al-Ḥurūf*. Just as scripture is read for exterior and interior meanings, so the phenomenal world can be "read" to expand interior knowledge about the world's manifest wonders. It is for this reason that letters are for Sahl al-Tustarī and Ibn Masarra "the primordial dust of creation." Ibn Masarra's own theory of cosmology, which begins with Sahl al-Tustarī's reference to the letters as the "primordial dust of creation," engages philosophy explicitly and includes references to the philosophers by name.

A Platonizing Theological Metaphysics

In the development of a nascent philosophical theology for the scholars (*ʿulamāʾ*), Ibn Masarra explains that worldly phenomena are themselves ontologically divisible into exterior and interior realities in a way that is analogous with scripture. He presents the letters of scripture as, literally, the ontological basis of the world, given that the text of the world and revelation are the products of God's creative command and speech. It for this reason that the letters of the scriptural text are literally "the primordial dust of creation" that brings to mind the similar language of the *Epistles of the Pure Brethren*.[73] In Ibn Masarra's further elaboration below of this knowledge, he indicates that contemplation (*iʿtibār*) of scriptural text and the world as text brings the contemplative individual to perceive God's creative agency, or the creative "command" (*amr*) in the world. He connects this command, significantly, to specific cosmological truths. Specifically, Ibn Masarra indicates that perception of the command at the interior level of the world's realities, what the Sufi metaphysicians in later eras of al-Andalus called the hidden realities of the world (*bāwāṭin al-ashyā'*), constitutes perception of the unfolding of the world according to God's command. The foundation of this process, according to Ibn Masarra, is the letter *Alif*, which is "His absolute Will in His creation ... the foundation of things, their starting point, their ending point, their cause, and their purpose."[74] Ascribing this knowledge of the cosmological significance of the letters to the scholars, he indicates that "one of the scholars says that the *Alif* is a paradigm of the [process of] bringing into existence, the locus of the emergence of justice, the first decree, and the movement of being (*kawn*) in the unseen (*ghayb*).[75] Critically, he simultaneously ascribes this knowledge to the scholars and to the previously mentioned mystics of Iraq ("people of interior knowledge"), specifically Sahl al-Tustarī.

> Sahl b. ʿAbdullāh al Tustarī said that all of the created things occurred from the *Kāf* and the *Nūn* [of the creative command *Kun*], and that the *Ṣād* is the [space or] locality in which the created things appear. The origins of things from which the created things were created are the air, primordial dust, wind, the atmosphere, water, fire, light, darkness, and clay, and they all fall under Being. Above all of what we mentioned are four things: the Pen, the Well-Preserved Tablet, the command "Be!" and *Ṣād*. These [together] are fourteen signs, the origin of all things, and with their letters, God divided the world in its parts.[76]

Drawing on knowledge he associates with both scholars and Sufis, Ibn Masarra asserts that the interior knowledge embedded in the letters provides detailed cosmological information about the unfolding of the unseen (*ghayb*) as an unfolding of worldly existence following God's command. He indicates that the letters are the basis of the world's existence as they proceed from God's speech and his creative command, referenced in scripture: "Be!" (*Kun*). In elaborating the results of this creative command, Ibn Masarra lays out the four key elements of his cosmology that all draw on scriptural references and language: (1) the divine command for creation (*Kun*, the command "Be!"), (2) the Well-Preserved Tablet, (3) the Pen, and (4) space or locality (*Ṣād*). He states that these four elements are "above" or have a higher ontological value than the rest of the created things of the world discussed in the passage. He explains in a closely related passage that the world is a result of God ordering the Pen to write His knowledge onto the Well-Preserved Tablet, a point that helps clarify the notion that the letters that constitute scripture are also the letters that constitute all of created existence. In this way, created existence can be "read" at the level of the phenomenal world's "unseen" (*ghayb*) realities, which can be identified through the application of an esoteric hermeneutic to the world in order to discover God's knowledge and creative agency.[77]

From a philosophical perspective, the Well-preserved Tablet, the Pen, and *Ṣād* as locality are the three most important elements in his discussion. In the preceding discussion, he indicated that they are somehow "above" or characterized by some higher or more primary ontological value than the rest of the created things of the world, and existence unfolds from them almost as tools of God's command. At this point, given Ibn Masarra's philosophical predilections, it is not surprising to find that in the passages that follow, Ibn Masarra treats these elements (Tablet, Pen, *Ṣād*) as carrying the ontological value of contemporary Neoplatonic cosmological notions, specifically Universal Intellect, Universal Soul, and locality.[78]

Specifically, in his commentary on the letters *Alif Lām Mīm Ṣād*, Ibn Masarra brings together knowledge of the Names of God, knowledge of the esoteric meanings of the letters, cosmological knowledge, and critically, specific philosophical vocabulary about the Universal Intellect and Soul. He makes this connection to the philosophers in his derivation of four divine Names from the letters *Alif Lām Mīm Ṣād*: (1) the divine self-reference (I) (2) the name of divinity (God), (3) the name The King, and (4) the name The Creator.[79] As he unpacks these four names, he identifies attributes that encompass meanings of agency and knowledge that the Graeco-Arabic philosophers were able to discover in broad terms using flawed philosophical language.

> The philosophers (*falāsifa*) have written about these attributes but not in these words.... [The philosophers] said that existence comprises four levels. There is the essence of God (Most High and Holy be His Names), and He is the clarifier of all things. Then there is the Universal Intellect (*al-ʿaql al-kullī*), and this is that which they called the formal paradigm (*mithāl*) abstracted from matter (*al-hayūla*), and it brings together the divine virtues. Then there is the Greater Soul (*al-nafs al-kubrā*), which is engrossed in matter, meaning the body, and it sustains the body of the world. According to this engrossed Soul, the King undertook and made subservient the spheres and carried out all [of existence]. [The Greater Soul] brings together, according to [the philosophers], the attributes of dominion and management. Below it in level is Nature, and it is engrossed in the body acting on it, and according to it occurs the [process of] fashioning and all of the [world's] actions [or agency].[80]

Ibn Masarra explicitly locates Neoplatonic conceptions of psychology and cosmology in what he has characterized as the interior level of the world, which he also characterizes as the unseen (*ghayb*) level of the world. In this framework, he simultaneously uses Sahl al-Tustarī's interpretation of these scriptural terms to explain cosmological phenomena and the philosophers' use of specific concepts in Plotinian cosmology and psychology.[81] As seen in the previous section of this chapter, Ibn

Masarra came to a similar conclusion in his interpretation of the meanings of the Names of God in terms of God's agency and knowledge. Bringing that discussion together with the current one, one can summarize Ibn Masarra's position on philosophy in the following way: Ibn Masarra believed that the philosophers arrived at the notion that God is transcendent, all-knowing, encompassing of the world, and the creator of the world through certain philosophical classifications of existence, including Universal Intellect and Universal Soul. As discussed in the next chapter, scholarly critics of these doctrines in Neoplatonic psychology and cosmology found their implications to be at odds with the scriptural conception of God's creation of the world out of nothing in time (*ex nihilo*), God's pre-eternal omnipotent agency, and God's omniscient knowledge.

In the context of these critics, especially the later Cordovan Ibn Ḥazm and his nominalist critique of Neoplatonic cosmology and psychology, Ibn Masarra's use of the philosophical categories of Universal Intellect and Soul is striking. On the one hand, Ibn Masarra does not identify his cosmology precisely with the theories of the Graeco-Arabic philosophers, arguing that the philosophers erred in their neglect of prophecy. On the other hand, he suggests that knowledge derived from an application of esoteric exegesis to the Names, scriptural letters, and worldly phenomena correlate directly with the philosophers' cosmological doctrines.[82] To resolve this apparent paradox, one can consider the following possibility: Given Ibn Masarra's assertion that the philosophers discovered key truths about God and the world and explained them using improper terminology in their neglect of scripture, Ibn Masarra may not have intended to identify the full ontological value of the Tablet and Pen with the Plotinian Universal Soul and Universal Intellect. That is, he appears to understand the Pen and Tablet as tools of God's creative agency and not simply parts of a timeless logical emanation of causality from the One in the world of Plotinian cosmology. Still, in anticipation of later Sufi metaphysicians, he finds the cosmological concepts of the philosophers useful and assimilates their explanatory value in his own Platonizing representation of the world, which draws on both scriptural and philosophical language.[83] Below, he edges slightly closer to blurring the ontological value of the Graeco-Arabic philosophers' cosmological principles with the principles of his own scripture-based Platonizing cosmology, offering a theory that Ibn Ḥazm directly criticized in Ibn Masarra's work.[84]

All that is found below the sphere of the moon comprise three things: body (*jism*), spirit (*rūḥ*), and soul (*nafs*). From the body comes the earth and what is on it, including water. The spirit encompassing it is the air, and it is [also] their [space or] locality (*makān*). The soul is the faculty that passes to it in the air from the sphere [of the moon].... After that are the luminous spiritual things that recite a measured chant of remembrance (*dhikr*). This remembrance is the Universal Intellect with which God particularized the Greater Soul, which is in the encompassing pedestal (*kursī*). From it [that is, the Universal Intellect], God apportioned all who are in the skies and earths their lot, from the angels and *jinn* to the people, so that they think with it [the Universal Intellect] and know their Creator.[85]

His cosmology emerges as a cross between a Platonizing philosophical theology and an early Platonizing Sufi metaphysics with allusions to the use of *dhikr* in mystical piety. Drawing explicitly on Neoplatonic theories in psychology and cosmology and connecting them directly to scriptural concepts, Ibn Masarra understands the philosophers' Greater Soul or Universal Soul as scripture's Throne, and identifies the philosophers' Universal Intellect as the agent with which God connects the Greater Soul or Throne with particular souls. In this way, he characterizes what is below the sphere of the moon in terms of Soul, Spirit, and Body, and he describes the sublunary soul as the individual's intellectual faculty. He even explicitly identifies the philosophers' interpretation of the Universal Intellect as having sound explanatory power in elaborating human cognition of the world and God.

This multifaceted overture to Neoplatonic psychology in a unique metaphysics articulated using a mysticism-influenced esoteric scriptural hermeneutic introduces a critical question: Given Ibn Masarra's attempt to represent philosophy and esoteric knowledge as part of the sciences of the scholars in a framework that embraces Neoplatonic cosmology and mysticism, what are the full implications of Ibn Masarra's epistemology for his understanding of the scholars' religious authority as communal guides in belief? That is, is Ibn Masarra simply attempting to open the gates of the scholars' sciences more widely to other forms of knowledge like Graeco-Arabic philosophy and mysticism? Are there broader implications in this approach, such as the blending of the scholars' role as communal guides with the role of mystics as Sahl-like and Hermes-like teachers of spiritual and intellectual ascent? Knowing the answer to this question will help lay out in more precise detail why Ibn Masarra's epistemology stirred scholarly debate, and how this debate ultimately became entangled with the politics of Andalusī Umayyad-Fatimid competition.

Philosophy's Place in the Changing Authority of the Scholars

Ibn Masarra's engagement with philosophical doctrines and esoteric scriptural hermeneutics was central to the way he wanted the scholars

(*ʿulamāʾ*) to open the door of the Islamic sciences more widely to new modes of knowledge, especially Graeco-Arabic philosophy and the mysticism of Iraq. As mentioned, there were early scholarly debates in al-Andalus about the soundness and utility of more controversial philosophical sciences, such as alchemy and astrology, that drew on esoteric scriptural hermeneutics even before Ibn Masarra wrote. Against this backdrop, evidence of a debate about Ibn Masarra is not necessarily surprising. However, the level of contention over his writings, which grew after his death, is puzzling. One possible and specific explanation for why the debate over Ibn Masarra's work erupted posthumously into an array of scholarly refutations, an unusual book-burning spectacle, and an official ruling condemnation, was the fact that his Platonizing cosmology reshaped conceptions of the scholars' knowledge and authority in a manner that too closely resembled the popular image of the Fatimids' proselytizing Ismāʿīlī theologians. Ismāʿīlī teachers were known to be working somewhat successfully to bring people throughout the Abbasid caliphate to the new Fatimid political cause.[86] al-Ghazālī's representation of this proselytization campaign in Iraq, discussed in Chapter 3, is indicative of the concerns about Ismāʿīlī Shiism that existed on both sides of Fatimid North Africa among the Andalusī Umayyad and Abbasid ruling circles and among the traveling networks of predominantly Sunnī and, in proportionately small numbers, Imāmī Shiite scholars.

In what points more closely to a specific aspect of Ibn Masarra's writing that synthesizes his Platonizing conceptions of scholarly knowledge with the mystics' notion of the scholar as a kind of Hermetic guide, Ibn Masarra brings together an analysis of the authority of the scholars and a more elusive group: the "sages" (*ḥukamāʾ*). Critically, he places the "sages" at the same level of the scholars in a hierarchy that he believes runs parallel with a hierarchy he identifies in the divine attributes.

> The lowest of the attributes of man is the level of the producers.... Above this in level one sees the kings and those around them from among [people] of the courtly kingdom.... Then one sees another level above that, which is the divine level that informs prophecy and those who [preserve and] shelter it among the scholars (*ʿulamāʾ*) and sages (*ḥukamāʾ*).[87]

Ibn Masarra makes a significant reference to an elusive group, namely the "sages" (*ḥukamāʾ*), in his discussion of the knowledge and authority of scholars. He uses the term *ḥukamāʾ* in notable distinction from his earlier reference to the Graeco-Arabic philosophers as the "philosophers" (*falāsifa*), whom he criticized. Unlike the Graeco-Arabic philosophers' own use of the terms interchangeably, his use of the term sages as a group distinct from the "philosophers" anticipates a distinction found in the writings of the later Platonizing Sufi metaphysicians of al-Andalus. According to these Sufis' claim on the pre-Islamic philosophical tradition, the true inheritors of the knowledge of Hermes, Empedocles, Aristotle, Socrates, and Plato were not the Peripatetic Graeco-Arabic philosophers, but the philosophically oriented Sufi metaphysicians, including the Platonizing critic of Peripatetic philosophy al-Suhrawardī. In Ibn Masarra's fusion of the sages with the scholars, he attempts optimistically to introduce his Platonizing cosmology and the mystics' esoteric scriptural hermeneutic into the theological dimensions of the local predominantly Mālikī scholars' learning. These sciences already included jurisprudence, language theory, and other areas of study brought from centers further east, especially Baghdad. Having traveled to Iraq, according to evidence in the bio-bibliographical dictionaries, Ibn Masarra may have sought to infuse Andalusī scholarly circles additionally with select aspects of the methods of the Baghdad Peripatetics and the mystics. In doing so, Ibn Masarra imagined the scholars being able to teach contemplative intellectual ascents in emulation of Sahl al-Tustarī, and likewise being able to articulate their flashes of mystical knowledge in emulation of the philosophers' representation of Hermes-Idrīs. This reading of Ibn Masarra's goals would agree with the later Platonizing Sufis' representation of Ibn Masarra and Sahl al-Tustarī as pivotal figures in the rise of Sufi metaphysics in al-Andalus, and it would also agree with the biographical image of Ibn Masarra as having taught Sahl-like ascetic ritual piety to students in the mountains outside Cordoba.

In bringing philosophy, mysticism, and the scholarly sciences closer together in his conception of Platonizing scholarly sages (*ḥukamā'*), Ibn Masarra was likely describing himself. The large number of followers he had among the tenth-century scholars and later twelfth-century Sufi metaphysicians points to the widespread acceptance of his project of blending the scholars with the philosophers and mystics. In the late tenth and eleventh centuries, however, the climax of the controversy over the Fatimid "Esotericists" and their itinerant theologians pushed Ibn Masarra's writings to the center of scholarly and political contention. As the next chapter shows, Ibn Ḥazm picked this debate up in his critique of Ibn Masarra's writings, arguing in anticipation of al-Ghazālī's work for an alternative philosophical theology drawing more narrowly on Aristotelian logic to the exclusion of Ibn Masarra's and the Fatimids' Neoplatonic conclusions in psychology and cosmology. Ibn Ḥazm's influential approach, which was formulated in a political context that he explicitly identified, offered an early integration of Graeco-Arabic philosophy into the knowledge and authority of the Sunnī scholars in anticipation of one aspect of al-Ghazālī's enduring multifaceted conception of the scholars – namely, the scholars as logicians.

Notes

1 Several articles and monographs offer a comparative analysis of the earliest changes in the Middle East from late antiquity to the early Islamic era. Ira M. Lapidus, *A History of Islamic Societies* (Cambridge: Cambridge University Press, 2002), pp. 67–80; Hugh Kennedy, "From Polis to Medina: Urban Change in Late Antique and Early Islamic Syria," *Past and Present* 106 (1985): 3–27; Nancy Khalek, *Damascus after the Muslim Conquest: Text and Image in Early Islam* (Oxford: Oxford University Press, 2011); Tayeb El-Hibri, *Reinterpreting Islamic Historiography: Harūn al-Rashīd and the Narrative of the ʿAbbāsid Caliphate* (Cambridge: Cambridge University Press, 1999).

2 A number of studies have investigated the fragmentation of power between the military center of Samarra, the caliphal and administrative capital of Baghdad, and regional centers such as Fusṭāṭ, where appointments of Samarra-based sultans produced enduring military dynasties. Matthew Gordon, "The Commanders of the Samarran Turkish Military: The Shaping of a Third/Ninth-Century Imperial Elite," in *A Medieval Islamic City Reconsidered: An Interdisciplinary Approach to Samarra*, ed. Chase Robinson (Oxford: Oxford University Press, 2001), pp. 119–40; idem, *The Breaking of a Thousand Swords: A History of the Turkish Military of Samarra (AH 200–275/815–889 CE)* (Albany: State University of New York Press, 2001).

3 The respective monographs of Maribel Fierro and Janina Safran on the Andalusī Umayyads offer key starting points for considering the various facets of the dynasty's power, authority, and legitimacy. Maribel Fierro, *La heterodoxia en Al-Andalus durante el periodo Omeya* (Madrid: Instituto Hispano-Arabe de Cultura, 1987); Janina Safran, *The Second Umayyad Caliphate: The Articulation of Caliphal Legitimacy in Al-Andalus* (Cambridge, MA: Harvard Center for Middle Eastern Studies, 2001).

4 A multifaceted analysis of this evolution of religious authority, including the negotiation of authority between rulers and scholars, can be found in the following: Muhammad Qasim Zaman, *Religion and Politics under the Early ʿAbbāsids: The Emergence of the Proto-Sunni Elite* (Leiden: Brill, 1997); Christopher Melchert, "Religious Policies of the Caliphs from al-Mutawakkil to al-Muqtadir, AH 232–295/AD 847–908," *Islamic Law and Society* 3 (1996): 316–42.

5 The intersection between these structures of political and religious authority became particularly complex and unpredictable in the decades of the Imāmī (Twelver) Shiite Buyid dynasty's military control over the Sunnī Abbasid caliphate in the tenth century. Buyid ascendancy was followed by the arrival of the Sunnī Seljuks during the lifetime of the powerful vizier Niẓām al-Mulk, who sought to professionalize the Sunnī scholarly establishment in full-time paid positions. Key aspects of this changing framework of authority have been examined in the following: Jonathan Berkey, *The Formation of Islam: Religion and Society in the Near East, 600–1800* (New York: Cambridge University

Press, 2003), pp. 111–76; Roy Mottahedeh, *Loyalty and Leadership in Early Islamic Society* (Princeton, NJ: Princeton University Press, 2001), pp. 3–39.

6 Kevin Thomas van Bladel, *The Arabic Hermes: From Pagan Sage to Prophet of Science* (New York: Oxford University Press, 2009), pp. 121–63.

7 The respective of works of Dimitri Gutas and Peter Adamson have provided analytical overviews of the institutions and figures involved in this transmission of thought in Abbasid Iraq. Dimitri Gutas, *Greek Thought, Arabic Culture: The Graeco-Arabic Translation Movement in Baghdad and Early ʿAbbāsid Society (2nd–4th/8th–10th centuries)* (New York: Routledge, 1998); Peter Adamson, *al-Kindī* (New York: Oxford University Press, 2006), pp. 21–45.

8 Peter Heath has contextualized ʿAbd al-Raḥmān III's reputation as a patron of the letters against the backdrop of Cordoba's emergence as a kind of Baghdad of the western Islamic world. Peter Heath, "Knowledge," in *The Literature of al-Andalus*, eds. Maria Rosa Menocal, Raymond P. Scheindlin, and Michael Sells (Cambridge: Cambridge University Press, 2000), pp. 96–125. His overview draws on Ṣāʿid al-Andalusī (d. 462/1070), *Tabaqāt al-Umam. Science in the Medieval World: "Book of the Categories of Nations."* ed. Ḥayā al-ʿĪd Bū Alwān (Beirut: Dār al-Ṭāliʿa lī-l-Ṭabāʿa wa-l-Nashr, 1985), trans. Sema'an I. Salem and Alok Kumar (Austin: University of Texas Press, 1991), pp. 158–62.

9 Among rulers and scholars in the early centuries of Islam, the perception of a crisis of authority that emerged with the rise of the Fatimids is clear in the extant sources. Heinz Halm, *The Fatimids and Their Traditions of Learning* (London: I. B. Tauris, 1997), pp. 41–78; Paul Walker, *Exploring an Islamic Empire: Fatimid History and Its Sources* (London: I. B. Tauris, 2002), pp. 17–39.

10 Marshall Hodgson's early overview of esoteric hermeneutics as a method of discovering hidden textual meanings and worldly realities remains a foundational starting point for understanding how, in Sunnī contexts, scholarly assessment of esoteric exegesis became entangled with the controversy over Fatimid Ismāʿīlī politics. Maribel Fierro's more recent study on esoteric hermeneutics in Islamic intellectual history, specifically in al-Andalus, highlights two points that are key to the current chapter's discussion: the use of esoteric scriptural hermeneutics was part of the intellectual history of both Sunnism and Shiism, and the scholarly debate about it became particularly contentious with the rise of the Fatimids, the so-called Esotericists. *Encyclopaedia of Islam*, 2nd ed., s.v. "Bāṭiniyya," (by Marshall Hodgson); Maribel Fierro, "Bāṭinism in al-Andalus: Maslama b. Qāsim al-Qurṭubī (d. 353/964), author of the *Rutbat al-ḥakīm* and the *Ghāyat al-ḥakīm (Picatrix)*," *Studia Islamica* 84 (1996): 87–112.

11 As Paul Walker and Farhad Daftary have both shown, Ismāʿīlī theologians increasingly integrated Neoplatonic doctrines into Ismāʿīlī cosmology in the early centuries of Ismāʿīlism's history, with early Fatimid-era figures having taken steps in this direction from the dynasty's first century in the 900s. Paul Walker, *Early Philosophical Shiism: the Ismāʿīlī Falsafa of Abū Yaʿqūb al-Sijistānī* (Cambridge: Cambridge University Press, 1993), pp. 3–67; Farhad Daftary, *The Ismāʿīlīs: Their History and Doctrines* (Cambridge: Cambridge University Press, 1992), pp. 144–255.

12 Leon Gauthier, *Ḥayy ibn Yaqẓān: Roman philosophique d'Ibn Thofail, texte arabe avec les variantes des manuscrits et de plusieurs editions et traduction francaise*, 2e edition, revue, augmentee et completement remaniee (Beirut: Imprimerie Catholique, 1936), pp. 11–12.
13 al-Maqqarī, *Nafḥ al-Ṭīb min Ghuṣn al-Andalus al-Raṭīb*, ed. Iḥsān ʿAbbās (Beirut: Dār Ṣādir, 1968), 1:221.
14 Ibid., 1:221.
15 Reinhart Dozy summarized the history of philosophy in al-Andalus by offering an image of a contrast between a more intellectually closed al-Andalus and a cosmopolitan Abbasid Baghdad. Reinhart Dozy, *Histoire des Musulmans d'Espagne: jusqu'à la conquete de l'Andalousie par les Almoravides (711–1110)* (Leiden: Brill, 1861), 3:409. For a similar presentation in contemporary scholarship, see Lawrence I. Conrad (ed.), *The World of Ibn Ṭufayl* (Leiden: Brill, 1997), p. 9ff.
16 This representation of al-Andalus continued to permeate the scholarship in the late twentieth century and was laden not only in discussions of broad Andalusī resistance to *falsafa*, but also references to Mālikī resistance to Ashʿarism before the arrival of al-Ghazālī's works. Montgomery Watt, for example, wrote that, "Though in the east there was some connection between Mālikite law and Ashʿarite theology, there is hardly any trace of Ashʿarism in the west before the Almoḥad movement." W. Montgomery Watt, *Islamic Philosophy and Theology* (Edinburgh: Edinburgh University Press, 1962), p. 134.
17 This assumption is especially obvious in discussions of Sufism in al-Andalus, which is often perceived to have been barely visible or nonexistent before the impact of al-Ghazālī in al-Andalus. This view can be found most concisely in the articles on key Almoravid-era Sufis in *Encyclopaedia of Islam*, 2nd ed. s.v. "Ibn al-ʿArīf," "Ibn Barrajān," "Ibn Qasī." (by A. Faure).
18 Maribel Fierro discusses why this quotation and others like it in sources on the medieval Islamic West belie the true theological diversity of early al-Andalus. Maribel Fierro, "Heresy in al-Andalus," in *The Legacy of Muslim Spain*, eds. Salma Jayyusi and Manuela Marín (Leiden: Brill, 1992), pp. 895–908. Fierro demonstrates in particular that a critical reading of early theological treatises and chronicles indicates that political resistance to various intellectual currents is indicative of the existence and even the flourishing of those various currents.
19 Roger Idris, "Reflections on Mālikīsm under the Umayyads of Spain," in *The Formation of al-Andalus: Part 2 Language, Religion, and Culture in the Sciences*, eds. Maribel Fierro and Julio Samso (Hampshire: Aldershot, 1998), pp. 85–101.
20 On the more systematic absorption of *ḥadīth* science beyond the *ḥadīth* texts in Mālik's *al-Muwaṭṭāʾ* as well as the embrace of legal theory (*uṣūl al-fiqh*), see Manuela Marín, "Baqī b. Majlad y la introduccion del studio del Hadīt en al-Andalus," *al-Qantara* 1 (1981): 165–208; Maribel Fierro, "The Introduction of *Ḥadīth* in al-Andalus (2nd/8th–3rd/9th centuries)," *Der Islam* 66 (1989): 68–93; idem, "Los Mālikīes de al-Andalus y los dos arbitros (*al-ḥakamān*)," *al-Qantara* 6 (1985): 79–102; idem, "Heresy in al-Andalus," pp. 896–8.

21 José Maria Forneas, "De la transmisión de alguna obras de tendencia aš'arī en al-Andalus," *Awraq* 1 (1978): 4–11; Abdel Magid Turki, *Polémiques entre Ibn Ḥazm et Bāǧi sur les principes de la loi musulmane. Essai sur le littéralisme ẓāhirīte et la finalité mālikīte* (Algiers: Argel, 1973).

22 Manuela Marín, "*Zuhhād* de al-Andalus 300/912–420/1029," *al-Qantara* 12 (1991): 439–69.

23 Biographical evidence of the existence among the *'ulamā'* of Andalusī students of the scholar and mystic Abū Ṣa'īd al-A'rābī is particularly notable. Marín, "*Zuhhād* de al-Andalus," 439–69. For a historical contextualization of early mystics among the Mālikī *'ulamā'* as early as the Taifa period, see Maribel Fierro, "Opposition to Sufism in al-Andalus," in *Islamic Mysticism Contested: Thirteen Centuries of Controversies and Polemics*, eds. Frederick de Jong and Bernd Radtke (Leiden: Brill, 1999), pp. 174–206.

24 These bio-bibliographical dictionaries are the following: al-Khushanī, *Ṭabaqāt 'Ulamā' Ifrīqiya, Classes des Savantes de l'Ifriqiya*, ed. trans. M. Ben Cheneb (Algiers: Publications de la Faculté des Lettres d'Alger, 1915–20); Ibn al-Faraḍī, *al-Mawṣūl fī Tārīkh al-'Ulamā' wa-Ruwāt al-'Ilm bi-l-Andalus (Tārīkh 'Ulamā' al-Andalus)*, ed. Francisco Codera Zaidín, 2 vols. (Madrid: Bibliotheca Arabico-Hispana, 1890–2); Ibn Bashkuwāl, *al-Ṣila fī Akhbār A'immat al-Andalus*, ed. Francisco Codera Zaidín (Madrid: Bibliotheca Arabico-Hispana, 1892); Ibn al-'Abbār, *al-Takmila li-Kitāb al-Ṣila*, ed. Francisco Codera Zaidín (Madrid: Bibliotheca Arabico-Hispana, 1887–9).

25 Ibn Ḥazm, *al-Taqrīb li-Ḥadd al-Manṭiq*, ed. Iḥsān 'Abbās (Beirut: Dār Maktabat al-Ḥayā, 1959), p. 6ff.

26 This picture is also clear from the evidence shown in Maribel Fierro's work. Fierro, "Bāṭinism in al-Andalus," 87–112; idem, "The Polemic about the *Karamāt al-Awliyā'* and the Development of Sufism in al-Andalus Fourth/Tenth–Fifth/Eleventh Centuries," *Bulletin of the School of Oriental and African Studies* 55 (1992): 236–49.

27 Ibn al-Faraḍī, *Tārīkh 'Ulamā' al-Andalus*, no. 1202.

28 Emilio Tornero's examination of Ibn Masarra's work remains a useful starting point for understanding Ibn Masarra's legacy. Emilio Tornero, "Noticia sobre la publicación de obras inéditas de Ibn Masarra," *al-Qantara* 14 (1993): 47–64.

29 A succinct picture of mystics among the early Sunnī scholars, who drew on both *ḥadīth* traditions and speculative theology (*kalām*) in the articulation of their mysticism, can be found in the respective works of Ahmet Karamustafa and Christopher Melchert. Karamustafa compares Abū Bakr al-Kalābādhī (d. ca 380/990), a Ḥanafī in jurisprudence, and Abū 'Abd al-Raḥmān al-Sulamī (d. 412/1021), a Shāfi'ī in jurisprudence. In their respective articulations of mysticism, al-Kalābādhī drew on speculative theology (*kalām*), while al-Sulamī drew more exclusively on *ḥadīth*. Abū l-Qāsim al-Qushayrī (d. 465/1072) emerged in the next generation as a central figure among the scholars of the Shāfi'ī school of jurisprudence and Ash'arī school of theology. Ahmed Karamustafa, *Sufism: The Formative Period* (Edinburgh: Edinburgh University Press, 2007), pp. 83–113. Christopher Melchert, *The Formation of the Sunni Schools of Law* (Brill: Leiden, 1997), pp. 68–86. The analysis of Orfali and Böwering offer further context on al-Sulāmī's intellectual background, which can be compared with Nguyen's analysis of al-Qushayrī's

work. Gerhard Böwering and Bilal Orfali, *Sufi Treatises of Abū 'Abd Al-Raḥmān al-Sulamī* (Beirut: Dār al-Mashriq, 2009). Martin Nguyen, *Sufi Master and Qur'ān Scholar: Abū'l-Qasim al-Qushayrī and the Laṭā'if al-Ishārāt* (Oxford: Oxford University Press, 2011). Despite Ibn Masarra's multiple references to Sahl al-Tustarī, the respective works of Sarah Stroumsa, Sara Sviri, and Michael Ebstein have placed less emphasis on Ibn Masarra's connection with the Sunnī scholars of Iraq interested in mysticism, investigating instead the possible impact of Ismāʿīlī thought in al-Andalus. This approach departs from the conclusions of Tornero and Cruz Hernandez (n. 31) on the lack of evidence of Ismāʿīlī connections in Ibn Masarra's work, and instead relies in part on an early dating of the *Epistles of the Pure Brethren*. Sarah Stroumsa, "Ibn Masarra and the Beginnings of Mystical Thought in al-Andalus," in *Mystical Approaches to God: Judaism, Christianity, and Islam*, ed. Peter Schäfer (Munich: Oldenbourg Verlag, 2006), pp. 97–112; Sarah Stroumsa and Sara Sviri, "The Beginnings of Mystical Philosophy in al-Andalus: Ibn Masarra and His Epistle on Contemplation," *Jerusalem Studies in Arabic and Islam* 36 (2009): 201–53; Michael Ebstein, *Mysticism and Philosophy in al-Andalus: Ibn Masarra, Ibn al-'Arabī and the Ismā'īlī Tradition* (Leiden: Brill, 2013).

30 Maribel Fierro's foundational article on esotericism in al-Andalus remains a key starting point for understanding how the scholarly debate about the widespread use of esoteric scriptural hermeneutics became a contentious controversy with the rise of the Fatimids. Fierro, "Bāṭinism in al-Andalus," pp. 87–112.

31 Emilio Tornero's and Miguel Cruz Hernandez's respective overviews of philosophy in early al-Andalus provides important context for understanding where Ibn Masarra's work fit in early Andalusī intellectual history. Emilio Tornero, "Filosofía," in *Historia de España Menéndez Pidal – El retroceso territorial de al-Andalus. Almorávides y almohades, siglos IX–XIII*, eds. José María Jover Zamora and María Jesús Viguera Molíns (Madrid: Espasa-Calpe, 1997), 8-2:587–602; Miguel Cruz Hernandez, *Historia del pensamiento en el mundo islámico, vol. 2, El pensamiento de al-Andalus (Siglos IX–XIV)* (Madrid: Alianza Editorial, 1996), pp. 344–57.

32 Ibn al-Faraḍī states that the judge Ibn al-Ḥabbāb (d. 323/934) wrote a *ṣahīfa*, a written treatise, responding to Ibn Masarra's work. Ibn al-Faraḍī, *Tārīkh 'Ulamā al-Andalus*, no. 1202. As with Ibn al-Ḥabbāb, as Fierro has noted, the refutation here is cited specifically as a written refutation (*ṣahīfa*) in Ibn al-Faraḍī, *Tārīkh 'Ulamā' al-Andalus*, no. 1361.

33 These refutations are also mentioned in Ibn al-Faraḍī, *Tārīkh 'Ulamā' al-Andalus*, no. 1202.

34 See n. 27.

35 An example of a later scholar describing Ibn Masarra as a philosopher is al-Qifṭī, who refers to him as a follower of "Anbaduqlis" (Empedocles) in al-Qifṭī, *Ikhbār al-'Ulamā' bi-Akhbār al-Ḥukamā'* eds. Julius Lippert and August Mueller (Leipzig: Dieterich'sche Verlagbuchhandlung, 1903) pp. 16–17.

36 Ibn Masarra's identification as a Sufi is found in the writings of al-Ḥumaydī (d. 488/1095), who was a student of Ibn Ḥazm and lived only a century after Ibn Masarra. He indicates that Ibn Masarra "*kāna 'alā tarīqa min al-zuhd wa-l-'ibāda … lahū tarīqa fī l-balāgha wa tadqīq fī ghawāmiḍ ishārāt al-ṣūfiyya.*" al-Ḥumaydī, *Jadhwat al-Muqtabis fī Dhikr Wulāt al-Andalus*, ed. Muḥammad

al-Ṭanjī (Cairo: Maktab Nashr al-Thaqāfa al-Islāmiyya, 1952), no. 83. The Andalusī Sufis Ibn ʿArabī, Ibn Sabʿīn, and Ibn Marʾa (Ibn Sabʿīn's teacher), all writing in al-Andalus more than three centuries after Ibn Masarra's death, write of Ibn Masarra as though he were a foundational figure in Andalusī mysticism. Ibn ʿArabī writes that Ibn Masarra was "the first in the states and stations." Ibn ʿArabī, *al-Futūḥāt al-Makkiyya* (Cairo: Dār al-Kutub al-ʿArabiyya al-Kubrā, 1329/1911), 1:147–8. As Massignon has shown, Ibn Marʾa indicates that Ibn Masarra argued in the latter's non-extant *Tawḥīd al-Mūqinīn* that God's attributes are limitless, and that the unity of the attributes is part of his doctrine on God's Oneness. Louis Massignon, *Recueuil des texts inedits concernant l'histoire de la mystique en pays d'Islam* (Paris: Geuthner, 1929), p. 70. As discussed in Chapter 4, this last doctrine is central to the representation of the Almoravid-era Sufis by their Nasrid-era critics, including Ibn al-Khaṭīb and Ibn Khaldūn.

37 The Andalusī biographical tradition, particularly the works of al-Faraḍī and Ibn ʿAbbār, locates him among the students and teachers of the Mālikī scholars, while his own texts indicate that he thought of himself as among both the scholars and the philosophical and mystical *ḥukamāʾ*.

38 Ṣāʿid al-Andalusī, *Kitāb Tabaqāt al-Umam. Livre des categories des nations*, ed. L. Cheiko (Beirut: al-Maktaba l-Kāthulikiyya, 1912), trans. Regis Blachère (Paris: Larose, 1935), pp. 20–1.

39 Everett K. Rowson, *A Muslim Philosopher on the Soul and Its Fate: Al-ʿĀmirī's Kitāb al-Amad ʿAlā l-Abad* (New Haven, CT: American Oriental Series, 1988), pp. 70, 207–8.

40 For Ibn ʿArabī in *al-Futūḥāt al-Makkiyya*, see note 35.

41 Ibn al-Faraḍī states, referring to Muḥammad b. Fatḥ from the people of Guadalajara, "*balagha-nī anna-hū allafa li-bn al-Aʿrābī kitāb al-ikhlāṣ wa ʿilm al-bāṭin.*" See Ibn al-Faraḍī, no. 1300.

42 Ibn al-Faraḍī states, referring to Muḥammad b. Aṣbagh b. Labīb from the people of Astija, that he "*raḥala ilā l-mashriq fa-samiʿa bi-Makka min Abī Jaʿfar al-ʿUqaylī wa-Abī Saʿīd b. al-Aʿrābī wa-ghayrihimā wa-nsafara ilā l-Andalus wa lazima l-zuhd wa-l-ʿibāda ... wa kāna yatakallamu fī madhāhib al-ʿilm al-bāṭinī.*" Ibn al-Faraḍī, no. 1227.

43 Some mystics suggested a kind of dichotomy that represented interior knowledge as otherworldly knowledge, while exterior knowledge was central to legal and ritual principles governing believers' lives in this world. Some mystics even argued that knowledge of jurisprudence (*fiqh*) was part of *ʿilm al-ẓāhir*. Other mystics like al-Kharrāz were critical of this kind of dichotomous understanding given the possibility of problematically emphasizing the importance of one over the other. Ahmet Karamustafa discusses Ibn al-Jawzī's criticism of this distinction in the context of scholarly concerns for preservation of the law, ritual, and ultimately prophecy. Karamustafa, *Sufism*, p. 158ff. Jamil Abun-Nasr, *Muslim Communities of Faith: The Sufi Brotherhoods in Islamic Religious Life* (New York: Columbia University Press, 2007), pp. 40–5.

44 al-Qifṭī, *Ikhbār al-ʿUlamāʾ bi-Akhbār al-Ḥukamāʾ*, pp. 16–17.

45 al-Dhahabī, *Siyar Aʿlām al-Nubalāʾ* (Beirut: Muʾassasat al-Risāla, 1985) 15:558. That *bāṭiniyya* here is specifically the epithet "esotericists" used in criticism of the Fatimid Ismāʿīlīs is clear given that Ibn Masarra's refutation

came at a time of Umayyad–Fatimid competition, when the use of the word *bāṭinī* for the Fatimids had become widespread. Decades before al-Ṭalamankī's career, the controversy over Ibn Masarra's works had already erupted politically. Specifically, ʿAbd al-Raḥmān III condemned the Masarrīs at the pulpit of the grand mosque of Cordoba and palace city outside Seville in a period coinciding with his condemnation of the Fatimids. On the condemnations, see Fierro *La heterodoxia*, Section 9:2–4 and Safran, *The Second Umayyad Caliphate*, p. 36ff.

46 The use of the term *tashayyuʿ* in scholarly works in al-Andalus is important in this context as evidence of contemporary political concern over any local claims to knowledge and authority that resembled the model of the proselytizing Ismāʿīlī teachers. Makkī contextualizes this concept in M. A. Makkī, "al-Tashayyuʿ fī l-Andalus," in *Revista del Instituto Egipcio de Estudios Islámicos en Madrid* 2 (1954): 93–149. As discussed in Chapter 3, al-Ghazālī's detailed description of how to identify an Ismāʿīlī teacher in his eleventh-century *Faḍāʾih al-Bāṭiniyya*, written in the context of Abbasid-Fatimid political and ideological competition, closely echoes in Baghdad the earlier environment in Cordoba of Umayyad–Fatimid political and ideological competition. Limitations of source documentation of this earlier period of Fatimid controversy mean that the full extent to which the lost refutations of Ibn Masarra may have emphasized suspicion of *tashayyuʿ* remains elusive. However, the other evidence examined in this chapter points strongly to this conclusion. al-Ghazālī, *Faḍāʾiḥ al-Bāṭiniyya wa-Faḍāʾil al-Mustaẓhiriyya*, ed. ʿAbd al-Raḥmān al-Badawī (Cairo: Dār al-Qawmiyya, 1964), p. 19.

47 *Risālat al-Iʿtibār* is available in two Arabic editions: Muḥammad Kamāl Jaʿfar, *Min Qaḍāya l-Fikr al-Islāmī: Dirāsa wa Nuṣūs* (Cairo: Maktabat Dār al-ʿUlūm, 1976), pp. 310–69; Pilar Garrido, "Edición crítica de la *Risālat al-Iʿtibār* de Ibn Masarra de Córdoba," *Miscelánea de estudios árabes y hebraicos* 56 (2007): 81–104.

48 *Kitāb Khawāṣṣ al-Ḥurūf* is available in two Arabic editions: Muḥammad Kamāl Jaʿfar, *Min Qaḍāya l-Fikr al-Islāmī: Dirāsa wa Nuṣūs* (Cairo: Maktabat Dār al-ʿUlūm, 1976), pp. 310–69; Pilar Garrido, "Edicion critica de *K. jawāṣṣ al-hurūf* de Ibn Masarra," *Al-Andalus Magreb: Estudios árabes e islámicos* 14 (2007): 51–89.

49 As mentioned, Emilio Tornero's concise overview of both works continues to be a useful starting point for analyzing Ibn Masarra's thought. Tornero, "Noticia sobre la publicación de obras inéditas de Ibn Masarra," 47–64.

50 Echoing al-Qifṭī's description of Ibn Masarra as a philosopher (see n. 35), Ṣāʿid al-Andalusī indicates that the *ḥikma* of Luqman passed to Empedocles and had intellectual adherents in Islam, including Ibn Masarra. Ṣāʿid al-Andalusī, *Kitāb Tabaqāt al-Umam. Livre des categories des nations*, ed. L. Cheiko (Beirut: al-Maktaba l-Kāthulikiyya, 1912), trans. Regis Blachère (Paris: Larose, 1935), pp. 20–1.

51 Qur'an 16:44.

52 *Kitāb Khawāṣṣ al-Ḥurūf*, pp. 58–9.

53 In what points to continuity between Ibn Masarra's thought and those of the later Andalusī Sufis who drew on his work, *iʿtibār* reappears as a key doctrine in the Sufism of Ibn ʿArabī immediate predecessors in the twelfth century.

Denis Gril, "'La lecture supérieure' du Coran selon ibn Barrağān," *Arabica* 47 (2000): 510–22.

54 *Kitāb Khawāṣṣ al-Ḥurūf*, pp. 60–1.

55 In this text, as in the *Risālat al-Iʿtibār*, Ibn Masarra does not aim for a systematic or exhaustive theory of the soul and intellect as might be found in the works of al-Fārābī or Avicenna. For these latter philosophers, Neoplatonic doctrines such as the logical emanation of the world's causality, or the mediation of higher levels of agency through the hypostases of Intellect and Soul, are elaborated systematically in a way that draws explicitly and methodologically on the ideas and goals of texts such as the pseudo-Aristotelian Plotinian *Theology of Aristotle*. In Ibn Masarra's own work examined here, he acknowledges the explanatory power of such philosophical concepts in elaborating the workings of divine agency in the world while criticizing the terms themselves. D'Ancona provides a closer look at this Neoplatonic cosmology of One, Intellect, and Soul that Ibn Masarra engages. Cristina D'Ancona, "La doctrine de la creation 'mediante intelligentia' dans le *Liber de Causis* et dans ses sources," *Revue des sciences philosophiques et theologiques* 76 (1992): 209–33; idem "Porphyry, Universal Soul, and the Arabic Plotinus," *Arabic Sciences and Philosophy* 9 (1999): 47–88.

56 *Kitāb Khawāṣṣ al-Ḥurūf*, p. 61.

57 Many of the later twelfth-century Andalusī Sufis' uses of the Names in cosmological discussions that drew on Graeco-Arabic philosophy have a clear source to draw on in al-Andalus in Ibn Masarra's tenth-century legacy. As mentioned, even before this treatise was discovered, Massignon pointed out this connection between Ibn Masarra's and the later Andalusī Sufis' discussion of the Names by highlighting Ibn Marʾa's reference to Ibn Masarra's lost *Tawḥīd al-Mūqinīn*. A contemporary of Ibn ʿArabī, Ibn Marʾa explained that Ibn Masarra believed God's attributes to be limitless, and that the unity of the attributes is part of the doctrine of the oneness of God. Massignon, *Recueuil des texts inedits concernant l'histoire de la mystique en pays d'Islam*, p. 70. It is notable that while the Muʿtazilites do not make this exact type of Names–cosmology connection, they do connect the Names as attributes with God's agency, which seems to be what Ibn Masarra asserts here by interpreting the Names as referents to God's agency in the act of creating the world. In this way, one can interpret Ibn Masarra's use of the Names in cosmology and the Andalusī Sufis' later use of the Names in cosmology as likely drawing on common philosophical and theological sources. These sources include the early Muʿtazilite work of figures such as Ibn Kullāb, who identified the divine Names with God's qualities, or likewise Abū l-Hudhayl al-ʿAllāf, who identified the divine Names with God "in His Oneness." It is worth recalling, as mentioned in Chapter 1, that Ibn Masarra's father is associated with Muʿtazilism in Ibn al-Faraḍī's biographical work, and that Ibn Ḥazm likewise represented Ibn Masarra as drawing on the Muʿtazilites. On the Muʿtazilites' own connections to Graeco-Arabic philosophers such as al-Kindī, see note 72. Frank and Peters have each provided early overviews of these previously mentioned Muʿtazilī arguments. Frank, "The Divine Attributes According to the Teaching of Abū l-Hudhayl al-ʿAllāf," pp. 451–506; J. R. T. M. Peters, *God's Created Speech: A Study in the Speculative Theology of the Mutʿazilī Qāḍī l-Quḍāt Abū l-Ḥasan ʿAbd al-Jabbār b. Aḥmad al-Hamadhānī* (Leiden: Brill, 1976),

pp. 231–75. Suleiman Mourad's analysis of the legacy of Muʿtazilī hermeneutics in *tafsīr* more broadly provides further context for understanding Ibn Masarra's approach. Suleiman A. Mourad, "The Survival of the Muʿtazila Tradition of Qurʾanic Exegesis in Shīʿī and Sunnī *tafāsīr*," *Journal of Qurʾanic Studies* 12 (2010): 83–108.

58 Fierro's picture of the mix of philosophy and scriptural esotericism in tenth-century Andalusī intellectual history includes treatment of the question of when the philosophical and esoteric *Epistles of the Pure Brethren* was transmitted to al-Andalus. Fierro, "Bāṭinism in al-Andalus," 87–112.

59 The considerable legacy of the philosopher and theologian al-Kindī and his students is the obvious candidate here when considering how Graeco-Arabic philosophical doctrines and Muʿtazilī doctrines could have arrived in al-Andalus in a mixed form. Peter Adamson has traced this early mix. Peter Adamson, "al-Kindī and the Muʿtazila: Divine Attributes, Creation and Freedom," *Arabic Sciences and Philosophy* 13 (2003): 45–77.

60 The prominent twelfth-century scholar and philosophical Sufi Ibn Barrajān, discussed in Chapter 4, wrote similarly in his characterization of the philosophers. In his larger Qur'an commentary, he indicates that he is in agreement with much of the philosophers' claims, even as the philosophers erred in their language and neglected the language of scripture's clearer presentation of God's omnipresent agency. al-Ghazālī made the same point as Ibn Barrajān, and ultimately both of these scholarly Sufis represent the common paradigm of philosophically oriented scholar Sufis having criticized the philosophers' neglect of prophecy while simultaneously drawing on philosophical cosmologies and philosophical conceptions of prophecy. Frank Griffel and Alexander Treiger have each offered analyses of al-Ghazālī's work that illustrate this simultaneous criticism and absorption of philosophy. Frank Griffel, "al-Ġazālī's Concept of Prophecy: The Introduction of Avicennan Psychology into Ashʿarite Theology," *Arabic Sciences and Philosophy* 14 (2004): 101–44. Treiger, A. "Monism and Monotheism in al-Ghazālī's *Mishkāt al-Anwār*." *Journal of Qur'anic Studies* 9 (2007) pp. 1–27.

61 Qur'an 2:1, 3:1, 29:1, 30:1, 31:1, 32:1.

62 Qur'an 13:1.

63 Qur'an 7:1.

64 Qur'an 19:1.

65 Qur'an: 26:1, 28:1.

66 *Kitāb Khawāṣṣ al-Ḥurūf*, p. 316.

67 This project of representing esoteric hermeneutics as an Islamic science accepted by the scholars departs, to some extent, from the previously mentioned contentious representation of esoteric knowledge found in the writings of some near-contemporary Sufis. In this context, Ibn Masarra appears as a scholar interested in both mysticism and the project of introducing the mystics' esoteric scriptural hermeneutic into the scholarly sciences. Karamustafa, *Sufism: The Formative Period*, p. 158ff; Abun-Nasr, *Muslim Communities of Faith*, pp. 40–5.

68 Ibn Ḥazm, discussed in Chapter 2, emphasized that it is in the *ẓāhir* where there is certainty and a proper consensus among the scholars. For Ibn Ḥazm, this *ẓāhir* contrasts with the unsystematic attempts at non-literal scriptural meanings found in the symbolism and numerology of alchemists, the

speculative theology of the dialectical theologians, and the esoteric hermeneutics of the mystics and Shiites. Interestingly, as scholars like Albert Hourani and Christopher Melchert have shown, and as the next chapter shows, even Ibn Ḥazm's *ẓāhir* is laden with heavy amounts of speculative thought and possibilities for interpretive debate. In what reflects the common philosophical and speculative nature of Ibn Masarra's esoteric approach and Ibn Ḥazm's anti-esoteric approach, Ẓāhirism appealed unsurprisingly to court sophisticated elites. Albert Hourani, *Reason and Tradition in Islamic Ethics* (Cambridge: Cambridge University Press, 1985), pp. 172–200; Christopher Melchert, *The Formation of the Sunni Schools of Law*, pp. 178–97.

69 As discussed, there were several scholars who studied *ʿilm al-bāṭin* and who studied with Abū Saʿīd Ibn al-Aʿrābī in Iraq. Moreover, Marín's discussion of the early ascetics and mystics in al-Andalus, coupled with Melchert and Chabbi's discussion of the fluid boundary between early ascetics and mystics in Iraq, suggests the following: in ninth- and tenth-century al-Andalus, there likely were many figures among these Andalusī ascetics who studied in Baghdad who were also interested in mystical doctrines, and who may not have been remembered as "Sufis" by name. Manuela Marín, "*Inqibāḍ ʿan al-sulṭān: ʿulamāʾ* and Political Power in Al-Andalus," in *Saber, religioso, y poder político en el Islam: acts del Simposio Internacional (Granada, 15–18 Octubre 1991)* (Madrid: Agencia Espanola de Cooperacion Internacional, 1994), pp. 127–39; Marín, "*Zuhhād* de al-Andalus" *al-Qantara* 12 (1991): 439–69.

70 *Kitāb Khawāṣṣ al-Ḥurūf*, pp. 62–3.

71 There are parallels here with al-Ghazālī's Sufism. The continuity points to the importance of Sufis as key interlocutors in the absorption of Graeco-Arabic philosophy into Islamic theology in the centuries leading up to al-Ghazālī's synthesis of philosophy with speculative theology and Sufism. Alexander Treiger, *Inspired Knowledge in Islamic Thought* (New York: Routledge, 2011).

72 *Risālat al-Iʿtibār*, p. 90.

73 The fact that there are shared Sufi and philosophical understandings of the world and scripture, which they see as two "texts" to be read for their exterior and interior meanings, is reflected in the Brethren of Purity's widely transmitted legacy. In Treatise 31 on "The Causes of the Diversity of Languages," the Brethren of Purity present their understanding of the connections between the meanings of scripture and the world, relying in large part on the numerical value they assign to the letters of the Arabic alphabet and the correspondences they identify between these letters and both the signs of the Zodiac and qualities of the body and soul. Ikhwān al-Ṣafāʾ, *Rasāʾil Ikhwān al-Ṣafāʾ*, ed. Khayr al-Dīn Ziriklī (Cairo: al-Maktaba al-Tijāriyya al-Kubrā, 1928), 3: 151–8 / Ikhwān al-Ṣafāʾ, *Rasāʾil Ikhwān al-Ṣafāʾ*, ed. Butrus al-Bustānī (Beirut: Dar Ṣādir, 1957), 3:143–51. Ibn Ḥazm contests this way of understanding the world, which he identifies as a kind of pre-Islamic Iranian dualism, calling for a more sound recognition of the world's ontology as a corporeal set of created visible bodies and invisible subtle bodies. The true "interior" or "hidden" for Ibn Ḥazm is the unseen superworldly realm, unseen both in terms of vision and in terms of understanding. See Chapter 2 for discussion of Ibn Ḥazm, *al-Fiṣal wa-l-Milal fī l-Milal wa-l-Ahwāʾ wa-l-Niḥal*, ed. Muḥammad Ibrāhīm Naṣr and ʿAbd al-Raḥmān Umayra (Beirut: Dār al-Jayl, 1995), 1:40–2.

74 *Kitāb Khawāṣṣ al-Ḥurūf*, pp. 63–4.
75 *Kitāb Khawāṣṣ al-Ḥurūf*, p. 64.
76 *Kitāb Khawāṣṣ al-Ḥurūf*, pp. 79–80.
77 In the rest of the passage, Ibn Masarra explains that "The *Qāf* from the letters of the Pen – and likewise with the *Mīm* and the *Ḥa* from the letters of the Well-Preserved Tablet, [together] with the *Kāf* from the letters of the Command and the *Nūn*, and with the *Ṣād* that is the other name of the truthful, [together] with the *Ḥa* that is from the primordial dust and the air, and with the *Ra* from the wind, and so on – from these things occurred the Throne, the Pedestal, the Heaven and Fire, the seven firmaments, the earth, the seas, the angels, *jinn*, mankind, the animals, and the plants." *Kitāb Khawāṣṣ al-Ḥurūf*, p. 80.
78 The Brethren of Purity make an explicit connection between philosophical language and scriptural language by explaining scriptural notions of divine agency in terms of Neoplatonic philosophical concepts like Universal Soul and Universal Intellect. According to this philosophical conception of the world as being alive, complete with universal principles of body, soul, and intellect, Nature is a faculty of the Universal Soul that has causal force in the sublunary world. Among the various places where they tie together scriptural and philosophical explanations of cosmological doctrines in this way, and in what offers an important parallel with what some Sufis and eclectic scholars like Ibn Masarra were writing, the Brethren's discussion in Epistle 18 (Meteorological Phenomena) and Epistle 20 (The Essence of Nature) is most notable. Ikhwān al-Ṣafā', *Rasā'il Ikhwān al-Ṣafā'*, ed. Khayr al-Dīn Ziriklī (Cairo: al-Maktaba al-Tijāriyya al-Kubrā, 1928), 2:54–75, 112–22; Ikhwān al-Ṣafā', *Rasā'il Ikhwān al-Ṣafā'*, ed. Butrus al-Bustāni (Beirut: Dar Ṣādir, 1957), 2:62–8, 2:132–49.
79 *Kitāb Khawāṣṣ al-Ḥurūf*, p. 328.
80 *Kitāb Khawāṣṣ al-Ḥurūf*, pp. 74–5.
81 The Brethren of Purity's analogous intersection of esoteric scriptural hermeneutics with Neoplatonic philosophical language was identified by its critics in later centuries of Andalusī history as being not specifically or exclusively or even originally an Ismāʿīlī approach, but rather a more generally philosophical and sometimes philosophical Sufi approach. However, the parallels with Fatimid Ismāʿīlī doctrine remained recognizable to contemporaries as late as the fourteenth century just as the parallels were recognizable back in the tenth century. As Knysh has discussed, the fourteenth-century Nasrid-era contemporaries and one-time colleagues Ibn al-Khaṭīb and Ibn Khaldūn each described the twelfth-century Andalusī Sufis as philosophically oriented Sufis who interpreted the elusive scriptural references to the Pen, the Tablet, the divine Names, the Throne, and the Pedestal as glosses for concepts in the Graeco-Arabic philosophers' cosmologies. According to Ibn al-Khaṭīb in his *Garden of Knowledge*, the Sufis systematized a cosmological mixture of *falsafa* and scriptural ideas that he believed crossed some boundaries of sound theological writing. Alexander Knysh, *Ibn ʿArabī in the Later Islamic Tradition* (Albany: State University of New York Press, 2007), pp. 180–5.
82 Ibn al-Khaṭīb's thirteenth-century analysis of later Almoravid-era and Almohad-era Andalusī Sufis is specific enough to criticize this very set of

doctrines, namely the intersection of the scriptural discussion of the Names with philosophical discussion of cosmological phenomena. Ibn Masarra was a source for some of these Sufis of this later era, as is clear from references such as those of Ibn Marʾa to Ibn Masarra's influential works. Massignon, *Recueuil des texts inedits concernant l'histoire de la mystique en pays d'Islam*, p. 70ff.

83 The widespread existence of this approach of integrating philosophical cosmologies into both Sufi metaphysics and formal Islamic theology (*kalām*) points broadly to the way Sufis and theologians adopted specific philosophical doctrines without adopting an entire Aristotelian-Neoplatonic cosmological system. That is, Sufis and theologians sought to draw on select philosophical doctrines and methods without compromising key intellectual commitments in scriptural understandings of divine agency. For Sufis, including the philosophical Sufis like Ibn ʿArabī, their eclectic approach reflected their belief that a superior epistemic approach draws on scripture-informed mysticism and includes inductive reasoning without an overreliance on the philosophers' logical methods. Among writers of philosophical theology, Ibn Ḥazm, discussed in the next chapter, appears as an almost Kindīan figure by claiming to use logic more critically than even the logicians themselves. Against this backdrop, al-Ghazālī made the eclectic move of pursuing both a logic-oriented theology and a more loosely Platonizing Sufi metaphysics, which Treiger has shown to have intersected. Considering all of these figures together reflects not only how contested the place of Graeco-Arabic philosophy was in Islamic thought, but also more interestingly the large number of ways various Islamic intellectual movements beyond the classical *falāsifa* (Avicenna, al-Fārābī) drew on Graeco-Arabic philosophical doctrines while criticizing *falsafa*. A comparative picture of the legacies of some of these approaches to drawing selectively on Graeco-Arabic philosophy can be found in the following: Melchert, *The Formation of the Sunni Schools of Law*, 178–97; Hourani, *Reason and Tradition in Islamic Ethics*, pp. 172–200; Kenneth Garden, *The First Islamic Reviver: Abu Ḥamīd al-Ghazālī and His Revival of the Religious Sciences* (New York: Oxford 2014), pp. 63–103.

84 See Chapter 2.

85 *Kitāb Khawāṣṣ al-Ḥurūf*, pp. 86–7.

86 As mentioned, several studies have pointed out the importance of Andalusī–Fatimid political and ideological competition in understanding the controversy over Ibn Masarra. Fierro, *La heterodoxia*, especially Section 9; Cruz Hernandez, "La persecución anti-Massarí durante el reinado de ʿAbd al-Raḥmān al-Nāṣir lī-Dīn Allāh según Ibn Ḥayyān," pp. 51–67; Safran, *The Second Umayyad Caliphate*, pp. 32–7. Fierro's study of esotericism in al-Andalus is especially important to recall in this context for highlighting how specific philosophical sciences and approaches to esoteric scriptural hermeneutics, particularly in the sphere of astrology and alchemy, were criticized by the scholars for having epistemologically unsound bases as pseudo-sciences and for having morally problematic applications. Fierro, "Bāṭinism in al-Andalus," pp. 87–112.

87 *Kitāb Khawāṣṣ al-Ḥurūf*, pp. 72–3.

2 A Third Caliphate in Cordoba

Following the scholarly controversy in Cordoba over Ibn Masarra's philosophical and Sufi legacy, the bibliophile Andalusī Umayyad emir and later caliph ʿAbd al-Raḥmān III (r. 912–961) took the surprising step of publicly condemning Ibn Masarra's works despite his own caliphal patronage of Graeco-Arabic philosophy. This condemnation offers a lens into how ruling circles, through the patronage or public criticism of specific books, navigated scholarly theological debates in a dialogue of leadership that involved ruling administrators, political rivals, and successive generations of scholars (*ʿulamāʾ*). Following the collapse of the short-lived Andalusī Umayyad caliphate (r. 929–1031) and the rise of the first Taifa kingdoms, a supporter of the fallen Cordovan caliphate and a self-styled reformer of the scholars named Ibn Ḥazm emerged. A critic of both Ibn Masarra's scholarly movement (*masarriyya*) and the neighboring Fatimid political movement, Ibn Ḥazm adopted a school of jurisprudence, namely Ẓāhirism of Iraq, which he revised in al-Andalus to include its own dedicated school of philosophical theology. In contrast with the Platonizing doctrines of Ibn Masarra and the Fatimid theologians, Ibn Ḥazm drew on Aristotelian logic to the exclusion of basic tenets in Neoplatonic psychology and cosmology. Ibn Ḥazm's and Ibn Masarra's respective legacies as philosophically minded theological writers lived on side by side among the scholars in the eleventh century, setting the stage for the Mālikī scholars' twelfth-century absorption of al-Ghazālī's dual legacy as an Aristotelian-Avicennan Ashʿarī theologian and Platonizing Sufi metaphysician.

A Rivalry of Caliphs in Cordoba, Cairo, and Baghdad

While the tenth-century predominantly Mālikī scholars (*ʿulamāʾ*) of al-Andalus were having an internal debate about whether their knowledge and conception of communal guidance should embrace Graeco-Arabic philosophy and the Sufis' esoteric scriptural hermeneutics according to Ibn Masarra's example, the tenth-century ruler and emir ʿAbd al-Raḥmān

Figure 2.1. The prayer niche (*miḥrāb*) facing Mecca, the direction of prayer, in the Great Mosque of Cordoba, established in 784 during the reign of the Andalusī Umayyad emirate.

III (r. 912–961) was in the process of reshaping his own model of leadership as a political ruler. In the decades following the Fatimids' declaration of a caliphate in 909 that rivaled the Abbasids, ʿAbd al-Raḥmān III was preparing to change his title from emir of the Andalusī Umayyad emirate to caliph of the Andalusī Umayyad caliphate.[1] That step came in 929 in Cordoba, just twenty years after the Fatimids declared their caliphate in North Africa and Cairo, and some 229 years after the Abbasids declared their caliphate in Baghdad in defiance of the original Umayyad caliphate of Damascus (r. 650–750).[2]

Sharing a border in the Maghrib and competing for allies among the Berber tribes, the Andalusī Umayyads and Fatimid Ismāʿīlīs were neighbors with a tense relationship from the earliest years of the Fatimid movement. In 917, just eight years after the Fatimids' establishment of a caliphate and twelve years before the establishment of the caliphate of Cordoba, the Andalusī Umayyad emir and future caliph ʿAbd al-Raḥmān III could be seen sending military forces to North Africa in an effort to win tribal allies against the Fatimids.[3] By 931, just two years after claiming the caliphate, he captured Ceuta and brought over to the Umayyad side the Miknasa chief and former Fatimid governor in Fez,

Mūsa b. Abī l-ʿĀfiya. The history of these Berber tribes and leaders like the Miknasa chief demonstrate that during the tenth-century Andalusī Umayyad–Fatimid rivalry for political authority in North Africa, local allies could and did switch sides, transferring allegiance between Iberia and North Africa or, alternatively, establishing an independent power base.[4] This transfer of allegiance constituted not only a geopolitical challenge, but also one entangled with rival conceptions of religious authority.

That a North African Ismāʿīlī figure who claimed esoteric or "interior" (*bāṭinī*) knowledge of scripture and jurisprudence stood at the head of a newly declared semi-messianic (*mahdī*) Fatimid caliphate meant that the Fatimids' military challenge against Andalusī Umayyad interests in North Africa was heightened by specific hermeneutical and theological underpinnings. This situation was compounded by the fact that in the mid-tenth century, the Fatimids formally assimilated philosophically oriented Ismāʿīlī theories of ideal political leadership that conceived of the Fatimid caliph as a Platonizing guide. The Fatimids absorbed this theory into their model of leadership in Cairo during the reign of the caliph al-Muʿizz (r. 953–975).[5] This two-tiered military and ideological challenge explains why the political and religious landscape back in al-Andalus during ʿAbd al-Raḥmān III's reign was so contentious. The challenge of the Fatimid movement, which the predominantly Sunnī scholars had been writing about from the early tenth century, engendered substantial political concerns over local Andalusī alignment with the Fatimid Ismāʿīlīs' political and intellectual cause.[6] The fact that local Andalusīs, such as the rebel ʿUmar b. Ḥafsūn, claimed allegiance to the competing caliphate made the movement's hermeneutical and theological dimensions an imminent and present challenge to Andalusī Umayyad political authority.[7] What deepened these concerns were reports that the Fatimids had sent out proselytizing teachers throughout the Abbasid lands to win followers to their cause.

It is in this climate of the Andalusī ruling circles' perception of an imminent geopolitical challenge posed by the rising Fatimid Ismāʿīlī "esotericists" (*bāṭiniyya*), a challenge entangled with a growing stereotype of Fatimid Ismāʿīlī political theories as being Platonizing in their cosmological orientation, that the Sunnī scholarly debate over Ibn Masarra and his students erupted into political controversy several decades after his death. The previous chapter showed that the theological parallelism between Ibn Masarra's writings and Fatimid philosophical theology likely explains the sudden appearance of a number of now lost scholarly refutations directed posthumously at Ibn Masarra in the tenth century. In a continued investigation of a dialectic of authority between ruling political and scholarly circles, what follows in the next sections of this chapter is a closer look at two questions: First, how exactly did the Cordovan caliph become so attuned to these earlier tenth-century scholarly debates that a scholarly critique of Ibn Masarra could spill over into public caliphal condemnation? Second, how did the climate of political rivalry between the Andalusī Umayyad and Fatimid caliphates, which saw these public caliphal condemnations of both Ibn Masarra's and the Fatimids' philosophical theologies, impact the philosophical activities of a later generation of eleventh-century scholars, specifically the logic-oriented Andalusī Ẓāhirīs?

Philosophical Caliphs Navigating the World of the Scholars

ʿAbd al-Raḥmān III's claim in 929 to being a "caliph" in Cordoba indicated that he was "commander of the faithful" (*amīr al-muʾminīn*) across the entire Islamic world, putting him in direct competition with the identical claims of the Fatimid and Abbasid caliphs. This move from emirate to caliphate also theoretically changed the relationship between ʿAbd al-Raḥmān III's ruling political authority and the local predominantly Mālikī scholars' religious authority. In an attempt to centralize political and religious authority more closely than seen in the example of contemporary Abbasid Baghdad, the Andalusī Umayyad emirate had already sought in the ninth century to work more closely with the scholars long before the declaration of a Cordovan caliphate.[8] The claim to a caliphate in 929 foreshadowed the way ʿAbd al-Raḥmān III would take an unusually direct position in the scholarly debate under way about Ibn Masarra, going as far as condemning his posthumous legacy at the pulpit of the Great Mosque of Cordoba and the palace city of Madīnat al-Zahrāʾ. ʿAbd al-Raḥmān III publicly condemned the intellectual movement of Ibn Masarra posthumously in 952 and 957, and an unusual book-burning spectacle took place in 961 that appears to have been sanctioned by some figures in both ruling and scholarly circles.[9] These events occurred in the same era as the Andalusī caliph's public condemnations of the neighboring Fatimid caliphate. Shortly thereafter, a similar interplay of scholarly and ruling attempts at redefining theological boundaries took place in 979. In that year, Andalusī Umayyad chamberlain al-Manṣūr b. Abī ʿĀmir (d. 392/1002), the de facto ruler in the early years of the reign of caliph al-Hishām II (r. 976–1009), brought several scholars to the library amassed by caliph al-Ḥakam II (r. 961–976) to remove specific books on philosophy deemed problematic.[10] This event took place despite the fact that the Andalusī Umayyad caliphs, like the Abbasid caliphs, were historically patrons of Graeco-Arabic philosophy. Significantly, it took place against the backdrop of a rivaling Ismāʿīlī political culture that projected an image of the Fatimid caliph as a Platonizing semi-messianic guide. Notably, the Andalusī Umayyads' tenth-century reassessment of the place of philosophy in caliphal political culture foreshadowed a similar caliphal reassessment of philosophy in eleventh-century Abbasid Baghdad, a process evidenced in al-Ghazālī's court-sponsored critique of the Ismāʿīlīs' political use of Graeco-Arabic psychology and cosmology.[11]

A key question that emerges from these public condemnations in Cordoba of both Ibn Masarra's work and the Fatimids' political claims, together with the subsequent reshaping of the place of Graeco-Arabic philosophy in Cordovan political culture, is the following: While the climate that shaped the eruption of a scholarly debate about Ibn Masarra into the political sphere is clear, how exactly did ruling circles come to identify the parallelism between Ibn Masarra's scholarly movement and the neighboring Fatimids' political theology to the point of publicly condemning Masarrism? Based on the discussion thus far, one possible and somewhat limited explanation points to the intellectual profile of an Andalusī Umayyad sovereign as that of a well-educated bibliophile emir and later caliph, who ruled within a courtly culture resembling that of the earlier philosophical Abbasid caliphs of Baghdad.[12] This explanation would highlight the fact that contemporary scholarly debates about Ibn Masarra were not outside the realm of the discussion of ruling political circles. A more precise explanation is the following: ʿAbd al-Raḥmān III may have been more acutely aware of the parallelism between, on the one hand, the growing stereotype of Fatimid Ismāʿīlīs as Platonizing political theologians and "esotericists" (*bāṭiniyya*), and, on the other hand, Ibn Masarra's reconception of the Sunnī scholars as Platonizing sage-like figures (*ḥukamāʾ*) interested in the mystics' esoteric hermeneutics, through the activities of particular Mālikī scholars connected with ruling circles. One key candidate for such an intermediary is the powerful scholar Qāsim b. Aṣbagh.

Qāsim b. Aṣbagh (d. 340/951) was a highly influential Mālikī scholar and contemporary of Ibn Masarra, even sharing three previously mentioned teachers who included Ibn Masarra's father. What is notable about these scholars is the distinction between their legacies. While Qāsim b. Aṣbagh was remembered as a foundational figure in early Andalusī Mālikism, Ibn Masarra was remembered as a Sufi and philosopher. That is, despite their originally close connections in recorded teachers and students, only Qāsim b. Aṣbagh between the two was accorded an enduring memory as a scholar.[13] As mentioned, their shared teachers included the renowned Mālikī *ḥadīth* transmitter Ibn Waḍḍāḥ and Ibn Masarra's own Muʿtazilī-leaning father.[14] According to Ibn al-Faraḍī, there were several other scholars who were also students of Ibn Masarra's and Qāsim b. Aṣbagh's shared teachers. One example is Muḥammad b. Qāsim, who was a legal consultant during the reign of ʿAbd al-Raḥmān III.[15] Qāsim b. Aṣbagh and Ibn Masarra also shared several students, which points to how closely they were connected in tenth-century Cordovan scholarly circles. Where their scholarly activities significantly differ is in their connections with ruling circles. Biographical evidence indicates that Qāsim b. Aṣbagh was one of the teachers of ʿAbd al-Raḥmān III and his son al-Ḥakam II (r. 961–976) prior to the latter's political ascendancy.[16] Qāsim b. Aṣbagh even dedicated a compilation of *ḥadīth* to the future caliph in 936, less than ten years before the book-burning spectacle that took place during his father's reign. The picture of Qāsim b. Aṣbagh's connections with ruling circles in the era of Ibn Masarra, coupled with the image of the previously mentioned scholar Muḥammad b. Qāsim as a legal consultant for the caliph, sheds light on the various channels for the emirs and caliphs to learn about the scholarly debate over Ibn Masarra's synthesis of theological writing with Graeco-Arabic psychology and the mystics' esoteric hermeneutics. In what points to the possibility that Qāsim b. Aṣbagh and his students were remembered by later scholars as a group opposed to Ibn Masarra's scholarly movement, Ibn al-Faraḍī presents a very consistent type of ambiguity in the reliability of students of Qāsim b. Aṣbagh who were also associated with Ibn Masarra's teachings.

Specifically, Ibn al-Faraḍī offers bibliographical representations that reflect the posthumous virtue of being associated with Qāsim b. Aṣbagh and the questionability of being associated with Ibn Masarra.[17] By the time the Taifa-era biographer al-Ḥumaydī (d. 488/1095) wrote, the earlier biographical report that Qāsim b. Aṣbagh studied with Ibn Masarra's father even disappeared.[18] The image evoked by this evidence of Qāsim b. Aṣbagh and Ibn Masarra's originally close connections and highly divergent legacies is that of one group of scholars, who were skeptical of Ibn Masarra's approach and connected to Qāsim b. Aṣbagh, refuting another group of scholars, namely the mysticism-influenced, philosophically minded followers of Ibn Masarra, in a debate that bore on questions of communal guidance and scholarly religious authority. After declaring a caliphate in the former Andalusī Umayyad emirate, it appears that ʿAbd al-Raḥmān III sought to participate as a politician in this debate about communal guidance through his public condemnations of Masarrism long after Ibn Masarra had already died. As mentioned, this heightened political scrutiny over specific aspects of Graeco-Arabic philosophy, which took place against the backdrop of a rivalry with the Platonizing Fatimid caliphs, foreshadowed the way the Abbasid caliph al-Mustaẓhir (r. 1094–1118) commissioned al-Ghazālī's *Scandals of the Esotericists* in Baghdad. As discussed in the next chapter, the text offered a philosophical critique of the Fatimid caliphate's "esotericist" claim to communal guidance and its underpinnings in Graeco-Arabic and specifically Plotinian psychology and cosmology.[19]

These three examples of the intersection of political controversies and scholarly theological debates – namely the political rise of the Fatimids impacting a scholarly theological debate over Ibn Masarra, the rise of a scholarly theological debate over Ibn Masarra erupting into political condemnation of his followers, and the further evolution of caliphal political culture impacting the articulation of scholarly opinions on philosophy and theology through the patronage of books – are illustrative of this dialectic of authority between ruling circles and scholarly circles examined in the current study. By the early eleventh century, a new iteration of this pattern developed in al-Andalus with the rise in appeal of the Ẓāhirī school of jurisprudence and theology at the peak of the rivaling Fatimids' power.

That ʿAbd al-Raḥmān III in the tenth century went as far as hiring a previously mentioned chief jurist who followed the Ẓāhirī school of jurisprudence foreshadowed the rise in popularity in the eleventh century of a local Andalusī form of Ẓāhirism in both jurisprudence and theology.[20] That is, the political environment of the late tenth century appears to have fostered the successful scholarly reception in al-Andalus of the scholar Ibn Ḥazm's reform of the Andalusī scholars' theological methods through the articulation of a new Ẓāhirī theology. The remainder of this chapter shows that his project included an absorption of Aristotelian logic to the exclusion of popular Platonizing conclusions in psychology and cosmology in anticipation of the same arguments al-Ghazālī made in the politically supported *Scandals of the Esotericists*. Like al-Ghazālī's reform of the scholars' understanding of theology and his appeal to Aristotelian logic, Ibn Ḥazm's very similar and slightly earlier project in his revision of Ẓāhirism occurred against the backdrop of an enduring political and theological challenge posed by the Platonizing Fatimid Ismāʿīlī caliphate. Ẓāhirism rose to prominence on the ruins of the Andalusī Umayyad caliphate just as Masarrism was pushed into the margins of the Andalusī scholarly world and biographical dictionaries.[21] As discussed in the remainder of this chapter, in contrast with Ibn Masarra's reconceptualization of scholars as Platonizing sage-like figures (*ḥukamāʾ*), Ibn Ḥazm offered the notion of scholars as Aristotelian logicians who nonetheless rejected contemporary logic's Neoplatonic conclusions in psychology and cosmology.

The Rise of Aristotelian Logic-Oriented Scholars in Cordoba

After the fall of the short-lived Andalusī Umayyad caliphate in 1031, with the rise of the eleventh-century Taifa period of competing city-states, Ibn Masarra's movement appears to have diminished or at least to have become less widely transmitted among the scholars (*ʿulamāʾ*).[22] In his *Book of Religions and Sects* (*Kitāb al-Fiṣal fī l-Milal*), the Cordovan scholar Ibn Ḥazm attests to the continued existence of groups of Masarrīs (*masarriyya*) in his own lifetime, including some followers who broke with a particular Masarrī leader in early eleventh-century Almería named Ismāʿīl b. al-Ruʿaynī.[23] As discussed later in this chapter, Ibn Ḥazm's analysis of Ismāʿīl b. al-Ruʿaynī and Masarrīs was substantial, but not extensive. What loomed larger in the eleventh-century world of scholars was the spread of Ẓāhirism as a new reform movement in jurisprudence, theology, and scriptural hermeneutics. Ibn Ḥazm was the principal transmitter and systematizer of Ẓāhirism in al-Andalus, and it offered scholars a new approach to earlier forms of Ẓāhirī jurisprudence that also included a dedicated school of Ẓāhirī theology. Ibn Ḥazm and his theological positions offered what should be read as an alternative approach to contemporary models of philosophically oriented theological writing. Ibn Ḥazm presented ultimately a corrective to both Ibn Masarra's and the Fatimid Ismāʿīlīs' legacies, which epitomized in the previous century the rise of Platonizing theologies and esoteric scriptural hermeneutics among both Sunnī scholars and Ismāʿīlī Shiite theologians, respectively.

Ibn Ḥazm's explicit criticisms of the Masarrīs and the Fatimid Ismāʿīlīs in his *Book of Religions and Sects*, examined more closely later, offer evidence of how he articulated his univocal scriptural hermeneutic and Aristotelian logic-oriented epistemology partly as a direct counterpoint to the contemporary synthesis in both Sunnism and Shiism of scriptural esotericism and more loosely Platonizing Islamic cosmologies. At a hermeneutical level, in contrast with Ibn Masarra and the Fatimids' similar integration of the philosophers' (*falāsifa*) cosmological doctrines into some interior (*bāṭin*) level of the scriptural text's meaning, Ibn Ḥazm's approach called for the use of Aristotelian logic as an essential tool for bringing out the true univocal "literal" (*ẓāhir*) meaning of the text.[24] He argued that this univocal meaning and its logical support excluded philosophical discussions of emanationist cosmologies and hypostases beyond time and space. Emanationism and hypostases, he argued, were logically impossible and ontologically dualist positions that he identified not with true logic-based philosophy, but rather errors of the ancients and ancient Iranian emanationist premises proliferated by contemporary "esotericist"

Ismāʿīlī theologians.[25] In his revision of *falsafa*, he offered a nominalist critique by reframing the immaterial Plotinian abstractions of Universal Soul and Universal Intellect as logical categories that properly exist only in their diverse particular corporeal substantiations, that is, as distinct individual human souls and human intellects. Specifically, he claimed that "the soul of every individual is distinct from the soul of another ... the Universal Soul of man is [simply] a genus, below the species of the Universal Soul [of all creatures], under which falls all of the living things as different individuals carrying different characteristics."[26] This argument was part of his larger nominalist critique of the Peripatetics' ontological theory of universals, according to which the philosophers saw the universals as somehow distinct from or able to be abstracted from their particular substantiations. In his own words:

> Matter (*hayūla*) is [simply] the body itself carrying all of its accidents. But only the ancients [among the Hellenistic philosophers] singled it out by this name as they spoke of it in isolation of all of its accidents and in isolation from form, isolating it from its accidents even as there is no way for [matter] to exist devoid and stripped from its accidents.[27]

As part of his alternative understanding of the created world as being corporeal and spatially finite, and in what rounds out his historically early nominalist critique, he claims in the same passage that "to speak of Universal Man as more than the species only means that we are speaking of the individuals of man and nothing else. Likewise to speak of Universal Red means the individuals of red where red is found and nothing else." In a synthesis of logic with scriptural hermeneutics, he even applied this ontology of particular corporeal souls and intellects to the ontology of the *jinn* mentioned in scripture, claiming that the *jinn* are invisible but corporeal in a manner similar to air and other "subtle bodies." That is, in his revisionist logic-oriented ontology, souls, intellects, and the *jinn* are three types of subtle bodies or invisible corporeal bodies that take up space and exist in time in contrast with what he believed to be the mind-body "dualism" of the ancient philosophers, the Zoroastrians, and contemporary Ismāʿīlīs.[28] Ibn Ḥazm popularized this new logic-oriented reformist philosophical theology in al-Andalus decades before al-Ghazālī presented his Aristotelian-Avicennan logic-oriented nominalist critique of Neoplatonism in Iraq, where Ashʿarī theology became increasingly oriented around Aristotelian-Avicennan logical methods (neo-Ashʿarism).[29]

Like Ibn Masarra's Platonizing philosophical theology, Ibn Ḥazm's Aristotelian logic-oriented philosophical theology was contested in his own homeland of al-Andalus in a larger eleventh-century controversy over the absorption of Ẓāhirī jurisprudence among the predominantly

Mālikī scholars. However, in what points to the slow emergence of enduring and shared western (*maghrib*) and eastern (*mashriq*) trends in agreement with both Ibn Masarra's and Ibn Ḥazm's respective absorptions of Graeco-Arabic philosophy into theological writing, Mālikī scholars in al-Andalus by the twelfth century unsurprisingly absorbed al-Ghazālī's dual legacy as a philosophical theologian and Sufi metaphysician. The transmission in al-Andalus of al-Ghazālī's work in effect gave Ibn Ḥazm and Ibn Masarra's original philosophical projects a certain permanence.[30]

In terms of the historical appeal of Ẓāhirism, one of the key findings of Camilla Adang's and Samir Kaddouri's respective analyses is that Ibn Ḥazm's work was widely transmitted and read by scholars in al-Andalus to an extent that contextualizes the large number of scholarly refutations against Ẓāhirism.[31] These refutations echo what was seen in the last chapter of refutations against Ibn Masarra's earlier work. As in the case of the followers of Ibn Masarra, some of the followers of Ibn Ḥazm appear to have found his work's philosophical dimensions and methods of argumentation appealing. Christopher Melchert is among a group of recent historians whose findings confirm the earlier conclusions of Albert Hourani and Ignaz Goldziher regarding this philosophical orientation of Ẓāhirism in al-Andalus. Specifically, all three historians have shown that Ẓāhirism was far from anti-rationalist despite the way the movement's name implies a kind of literal (*ẓāhir*) orientation.[32] As mentioned, Ẓāhirism and its conceptualization of the *ẓāhir* might be better translated as a type of hermeneutical anti-esotericism and univocalism, one that was a counterpoint to the use of an esoteric scriptural hermeneutic among Ismāʿīlīs and mystics and the use of metaphorical interpretation among speculative theologians. From an anti-esotericism perspective, Ibn Ḥazm was specifically critical of the notion of an elect (*khāṣṣa*) with access to special *bāṭin* meanings. From the perspective of revising metaphorical interpretation, Ibn Ḥazm's appeal to Aristotelian logic as a tool of scriptural hermeneutics and his simultaneous call for unpegging words from primary "literal" meanings and secondary "metaphorical" meanings can be interpreted as having offered an alternative rationalist position to that of the earlier theologians. In this regard, Ibn Ḥazm appears as a precursor to his younger near-contemporary al-Ghazālī, or rather a parallel western (*maghrib*) formulator of logic-oriented theological conclusions that arose at the same time in eastern (*mashriq*) centers. Against a shared backdrop of a Platonizing Fatimid Ismāʿīlī "esotericist" challenge and the development of seemingly unsystematic trends in speculative theology that many Sunnī scholars thought needed to be reined in, Ibn Ḥazm and al-Ghazālī emerged almost simultaneously as intellectual reformers who called for a more systematic absorption of Aristotelian logic in Sunnī

Islamic theology to the exclusion of specific Neoplatonic psychological and cosmological conclusions.[33]

The simultaneous emergence of Ibn Ḥazm and al-Ghazālī in the late eleventh century, and their respective impacts, reflects how Sunnī theology in the eleventh century was in the process of becoming an increasingly Aristotelian-influenced, logic-oriented philosophical theology, and how the Sunnī scholars were increasingly becoming scholarly logicians adept in Aristotelian (Aristotelian-Avicennan) logic. Ibn Taymiyya was notably skeptical that this process could occur without Islamic theology inadvertently absorbing Aristotelian logic's conclusions in psychology and cosmology, conclusions that we know to have been Plotinian conclusions of late antique Neoplatonism.[34] The remainder of this chapter shows how Ibn Ḥazm constructed his thought partly in response to the scholarly and political controversies of the previous century over Ibn Masarra and the Fatimids' Platonizing "esotericist" theologies. This evidence underscores the overlooked significance of politics, and more specifically the previously discussed dialectic between ruling political authority and scholarly religious authority, in helping shape how successive generations of scholars conceived and reconceived of their own theological knowledge and communal theological guidance in a political context.

Ibn Ḥazm's Critique of Platonizing Cosmologies

The foundation of Ibn Ḥazm's criticism of the cosmological doctrines of the philosophers, Ibn Masarra, and the Ismāʿīlīs in his *Book of Religions and Sects* (*Kitāb al-Fiṣal fī l-Milal*) is his simultaneous acceptance of logic as part of a non-esoteric "literalist" or univocal hermeneutic and his rejection of many of the philosophers' cosmological conclusions. His support for Aristotelian logic appears in his *Treatise on the Categories of the Sciences* (*Risālat Marātib al-ʿUlūm*), in which he recommends a course of study that amounts to a scholarly curriculum of specific philosophical sciences. This curriculum, he explains, should begin with the study of language, grammar, and numbers. One should then study the books of Euclid and Ptolemy in order to understand the arrangement of the celestial spheres, their orbits, and the orbits of the celestial bodies.[35] He argues that a sound approach to this philosophical program will carry the individual through a series of questions, beginning with whether the world is originated or is pre-eternal, and moving to conclusions that include a surprising rejection of many positions in psychology and cosmology widely held by the philosophers themselves. His didactic narrative of questions in these parts of the *Marātib al-ʿUlūm* shows how his appeal to scriptural conclusions about the nature of the world, such as the creation of the world *ex nihilo*, is equally an appeal to philosophical tools of analysis that he argues underpin these conclusions. In these examples, much of what emerges as a kind of philosophical theology turns around the philosophical distinction between logical impossibility, logical possibility, and necessity. His approach builds a metaphysical system based on what he describes as being both "manifest" (*ẓāhir*) to the senses and manifestly true according to logical necessity. That information is brought together with the large sphere of information that he determines to be logically possible. As far as what is necessarily true among these possibilities, such as the existence of angels, scripture provides key additional information given the necessary validity of prophecy.[36]

Curiously, in the process of simultaneously drawing on the tools of philosophy while reining in the philosophers' erroneous conclusions, he does not identify the contemporary Graeco-Arabic philosophers (*falāsifa*) or the Baghdad Peripatetics (*mashshā'iyyūn*) specifically as the face of these errors. Rather, he turns to pre-Islamic Zoroastrianism, Ismāʿīlism, and Masarrism. The case of his representation of Zoroastrianism and Ismāʿīlism is most illustrative of the political dimensions of his reform of Graeco-Arabic philosophy's discussion of emanationism and hypostases beyond time and space.

> One can distinguish those who claim that the agent of the world is more than one into several groups. These groups go back to two groups: one of the two groups says that the world and its agents are different, and these are the ones who speak of the governance of the seven celestial bodies and their eternal permanence. These are the Magians ... their manifest (*ẓāhir*) claim is that God, [whom they call] *Ormon*, and *Ahriman* [which is Darkness], as well as *Kam* which is Time, and *Jam* which is Space and also the Void, and *Nom* which is Substance and also Prime Matter (*hayūla*) ... are five pre-eternal things, and that *Ahriman* is the agent of evil, and that *Ormon* is the agent of good.... Among [the Magians] are the Mazdakians ... and the Khurramians [who] are the people of Babak and [who] are among the people of the Mazdakians, and they are also the secret of the method of the Ismāʿīlīs and whoever numbers among the [Ismāʿīlī] Qarmatians.[37]

The title of this section, "Discourse on those who believe that the cause and orderer of the world is more than one," suggests a typical theological attack on the Graeco-Arabic philosophers. However, the discussion opens with a discussion of Zoroastrian cosmology, which at first appears out of place for an eleventh-century text on the Islamic world written so far west of Iraq. However, the ascription of Zoroastrian cosmology to the Ismāʿīlīs at the end of the passage clarifies that his discussion is entangled with a familiar and contemporary criticism of the neighboring

Fatimids' philosophical cosmology, which he seeks to distinguish from his own logic-oriented philosophical approach. He describes the Ismāʿīlīs as inheritors of pre-Islamic Zoroastrian doctrines, and he characterizes the Zoroastrians as believers in an emanationist cosmology built on the causation of divine self-reflection and five hypostases. Specifically, quoting earlier theologians who wrote about what the Zoroastrians believed, Ibn Ḥazm explains that the Zoroastrians claimed that the Creator's act of thought, caused by "the duration of His Oneness" as He "felt solitude," brought about a series of principles like the perfect void, prime matter, and time in an emanation that included the pre-eternal celestial bodies that govern agency in the sublunary world.[38] His identification of Zoroastrianism and Ismāʿīlīsm with doctrines that contemporary readers would identify as part of the Graeco-Arabic philosophers' emanationist cosmology is significant because it illustrates a kind of medieval intellectual stereotype or typology with which some Fatimid-era Sunnī scholars reexamined Graeco-Arabic philosophy's soundness. Specifically, what links Zoroastrianism and Ismāʿīlīsm in medieval doxographies is a representation, often polemical, of a common genealogy of ontological dualism in cosmology and esoteric textual hermeneutics.[39] This doxographical representation of Zoroastrianism and Ismāʿīlīsm as "dualist" explains why common Graeco-Arabic philosophical doctrines were sometimes represented as having origins in pre-Islamic Iranian religions, which contrasts with the modern European historiography of these doctrines being representative of late antique Platonism with an emphasis on Plotinus, Porphyry, and other late antique Hellenistic figures.

Ibn Ḥazm's reticence to point out this connection between the Ismāʿīlīs' and Zoroastrians' philosophical cosmology, on the one hand, and the Graeco-Arabic philosophers, on the other hand, illustrates the following: During the peak of Abbasid–Fatimid competition, the classical Avicennan philosophers (*falāsifa*, *mashshāʾiyyūn*) were not always central to a Sunnī doxographer's representation of widely circulating philosophical doctrines in Platonizing psychology and cosmology. Rather, groups of more significant political import, especially the Platonizing Ismāʿīlīs, loomed just as large in the Sunnī image of philosophical doctrines in cosmology and psychology. This point is significant because it shows how politically controversial movements in philosophical theology that integrated philosophical doctrines into an esoteric scriptural hermeneutic, including both Ismāʿīlīsm in Shiism and Sufi-influenced Masarrism in Sunnism, offered a more immediate motivation than al-Fārābī's (d. 235/950) or Ibn Sīna's (Avicenna d. 428/1037) activities in inspiring the Sunnī scholars' critical reexamination of Graeco-Arabic philosophy as a source of sound theological knowledge and scholarly communal guidance. A closer look at Ibn Ḥazm's identification of controversial Graeco-Arabic philosophical doctrines in a later group of Masarrīs' internal debates will shed further light on how the tenth-century political controversy over the Platonizing Fatimid Ismāʿīlī and Masarrī movements, influential in respectively Shiite and Sunnī writings of esoteric scriptural hermeneutics, was a key counterpoint to his eleventh-century Aristotelian logic-oriented theology.

Philosophy in Ẓāhirism and Masarrism

Like his criticism of Zoroastrianism and Ismāʿīlīsm, Ibn Ḥazm's critique of his Cordovan predecessor Ibn Masarra and his later Masarrī followers in eleventh-century Almería offers the reader an additional window into the following point: Ibn Ḥazm rejected specific doctrines in Graeco-Arabic psychology and cosmology by criticizing not al-Fārābī or the Baghdad Peripatetics, but rather philosophically oriented theological writers who drew on the philosophers' Platonizing conclusions. Ibn Ḥazm's critique emerges in his fascinating encounter with the later followers of Ibn Masarra who were living in Almería a century after the Andalusī Umayyads' book-burning campaign. Ibn Ḥazm describes a contemporary figure named Ismāʿīl b. ʿAbdullāh al-Ruʿaynī as an influential Masarrī thinker who deviated so far from mainstream Masarrī theological positions about God's pre-eternal existence and God's omniscience that even his own followers parted ways with him.

> I myself saw him, but I did not meet him … he said seven things that made all of the Masarrīs (*masarriyya*) wash their hands of him and ascribe disbelief to him, except those who followed him. He said that bodies are never resurrected, and that only the spirits are resurrected.… It is also said that he used to claim that upon the death of man and the separation of his spirit from his body, his spirit encounters the final reckoning and goes either to heaven or to hell, and that [Ismāʿīl b. al-Ruʿaynī] did not recognize resurrection except in this way. It is also said that he used to claim that the world does not end (*yufnā*), but rather that it will be as it is [in eternal existence] with no end.[40]

Ibn Ḥazm presents the case of Ismāʿīl b. al-Ruʿaynī, who was an important figure among at least one group of later followers of Ibn Masarra, but who appears to have been a source of controversy among the Masarrīs themselves for his theological claims.[41] Ismāʿīl b. al-Ruʿaynī's reading of Ibn Masarra's texts undergirded certain philosophical claims that clashed with the scriptural notion of God's omnipotence and omniscience. Specifically, Ibn Ḥazm's account attributes to Ismāʿīl b. al-Ruʿaynī the claim that only souls and not bodies are resurrected, and that the world has no finite end in time. Ibn Ḥazm explains that he also heard from the jurist Abū Aḥmad al-Maʿāfirī al-Ṭulayṭulī that a certain Yaḥyā b. Aḥmad al-Ṭabīb, the maternal grandson of Ismāʿīl b. al-Ruʿaynī, remembered that "My grandfather [Ismāʿīl b. al-Ruʿaynī] used to say that the Throne is what orders and governs (*mudabbir*) the world, and that God Most High is more exalted than to be described with agency at all. He used to attribute this saying to Muḥammad b. ʿAbdullāh b. Masarra [Ibn Masarra]."[42] That is, Ismāʿīl b. al-Ruʿaynī was associated with yet another controversial claim in theology, namely that it is not God but the divine Throne that is the ultimate ordering and governing agent of the world. Ibn Ḥazm also attributes to Ismāʿīl b. al-Ruʿaynī the opinion that God does not have foreknowledge of the world's particular events before they occur. Specifically, he characterizes the followers of Ismāʿīl b. al-Ruʿaynī as a group who ascribed disbelief to anyone who said that God "knows everything that will be before it is."[43] The entire discussion of Ismāʿīl b. al-Ruʿaynī is in fact framed in this section of Ibn Ḥazm's work as one example of a theological group that considers divine agency a separate attribute. Rounding out the controversial claims attributed to Ismāʿīl b. al-Ruʿaynī, Ibn Ḥazm points to the most controversial doctrine that he was accused of, which is the claim that prophecy could be acquired. Specifically, Ibn Ḥazm says that, "those disagreeing with [Ismāʿīl b. al-Ruʿaynī] as well as those following him ascribed to him discussion of the acquisition of prophecy, meaning that whoever reached the limit of goodness and purity of the soul can achieve prophecy, [which implies] that it is not a specialized trait. We have seen among them some who ascribe this saying to Ibn Masarra."[44] Interestingly, this claim is the same one that the Andalusī scholar al-Ṭalamankī, a contemporary of Ibn Ḥazm, ascribed to Ibn Masarra in a lost refutation quoted by several later sources.[45] Given that Ibn Masarra's works do not show evidence of this doctrine, its association with both Ibn Masarra and Ismāʿīl b. al-Ruʿaynī may have emerged as part of polemical refutations.

This list of controversial doctrines that Ibn Ḥazm associated with the head of the eleventh-century Masarrīs is significant because it highlights how Ibn Ḥazm ascribed common Graeco-Arabic philosophical doctrines to movements beyond the philosophers themselves. In total, Ibn Ḥazm's discussion has identified five sources of theological contention among the followers of Ismāʿīl b. al-Ruʿaynī: (1) denial of bodily resurrection, (2) denial of the creation of the world from nothing in time (*ex nihilo*), (3) denial of God's agency as the ultimate governing agent, (4) denial of God's foreknowledge of the world's particular events, and finally (5) denial of the inimitability of prophecy. The parallel between this representation of the Masarrīs and al-Ghazālī's later representation of the Graeco-Arabic philosophers is critical. The five philosophical doctrines associated with Ismāʿīl b. al-Ruʿaynī here, which overlap with Ibn Ḥazm's representation of aspects of Zoroastrianism and Ismāʿīlīsm, are the exact same philosophical doctrines that al-Ghazālī takes up a few decades later against both the Graeco-Arabic philosophers and Fatimid Ismāʿīlīs in the *Incoherence of the Philosophers* and the *Scandals of the Esotericists*, respectively. It was in the *Incoherence of the Philosophers* where al-Ghazālī issued his famous opinion condemning the philosophers' doctrines on the same issues, three of which al-Ghazālī deemed as most problematic: the world's pre-eternity, limitations on God's particular knowledge, and the resurrection of the soul without the body.[46] This parallel between Ibn Ḥazm and al-Ghazālī's identification of philosophical doctrines in the writings of philosophically oriented theological movements can be summarized in the following way. Just as the political and ideological challenge of Fatimid Ismāʿīlism framed al-Ghazālī's combined defense of Aristotelian logic and critique of select doctrines in Neoplatonic cosmology as an Ashʿarī philosophical theologian, so the political controversy in Cordoba over Fatimid Ismāʿīlism and Masarrism shaped Ibn Ḥazm's own support of logic and criticism of popular Platonizing cosmologies as a Ẓāhirī philosophical theologian. That is, Sunnī scholarly articulations of Aristotelian-Avicennan logic-oriented philosophical theologies were significantly entangled with the rise of politically controversial Platonizing theologies, whether Masarrism in Sunnism or the more politically influential Fatimid Ismāʿīlism in Shiism.

From a hermeneutical perspective, Ibn Ḥazm's counterarguments in Ẓāhirism were also similar to those of al-Ghazālī in his Ashʿarism in that they were both framed from a position of philosophical skepticism.[47] In the rest of his criticism of Ibn Masarra's legacy in the *Book of Religions and Sects*, Ibn Ḥazm articulates this skepticism through his interpretation of the scriptural reference to the term *ghayb*. Ibn Masarra understood the term *ghayb* as the phenomenological "unseen," while Ibn Ḥazm offered an interpretation closer to the totality of epistemic and ontological unknowns. Ibn Ḥazm explains that this difference of opinion is at the center of the problem of Ismāʿīl b. al-Ruʿaynī's Masarrī thought.

Muḥammad b. ʿAbdullāh b. Masarra b. Najīḥ al-Andalusī [Ibn Masarra] agreed with the Muʿtazila on the issue of *qadar* [that is, the question of God's foreknowledge and agency]. He used to say that God's knowledge and agency (*qudra*) are two originated created attributes, and that God Most High has two knowledges. One of them is composite, the knowledge of the Book, which is knowledge of the unseen (*ghayb*). This, for example, is His [general] knowledge that there will be those with faith and those who disbelieve, or knowledge of redemption (*qiyāma*), recompense (*jazāʾ*) and so on. The other is knowledge of the particulars (*juzʾiyyāt*), which is knowledge of the visible (*shahāda*). [This knowledge includes] for example, the [particular knowledge of] the disbelief of [a specific individual, say] Zayd, or the faith of [a specific individual, say] ʿUmar and so on. [Ibn Masarra claims] therefore that God does not know of something until it is. He mentioned [in support of this doctrine] the saying of God Most High, "Knower of the unseen and visible (*al-ghayb wa-l-shahāda*)" ... which is not the meaning He intended. On the contrary, on its manifest (*ẓāhir*) level, [the verse means] that He knows what you do [in reference to the *shahāda*] even if you hide it, and that he knows what your knowledge has not seen of what was, what will be, and what is [of the *ghayb*].[48]

In an important example of his counterarguments against Ibn Masarra's philosophical theology, Ibn Ḥazm identifies the problem in Ismāʿīl b. al-Ruʿaynī's understanding of God's knowledge as Ibn Masarra's original misinterpretation of the scriptural paradigm of "the visible and the unseen" (*al-shahāda wa-l-ghayb*). He explains that Ibn Masarra understood these terms to indicate something akin to the philosophers' particulars and universals, with the former interpreted by Ibn Masarra as man's immediate particular knowledge and occurrences of the world, and the latter being God's knowledge of universal truths or realities that man can aspire to know. Ibn Ḥazm prefers translating scripture's "visible and unseen" not in a way that suggests the Graeco-Arabic philosophers' "particulars and universals," but rather the more skeptical "known and unknown." Specifically, Ibn Ḥazm argues that while the scriptural notion of the *ghayb* is indeed part of God's knowledge as Ibn Masarra originally argued, this *ghayb* is not the ontological totality of the philosophical universals or universal realities, such as a universal concept existing in some superlunary Intellect that faith exists. Rather the "unseen" is the epistemic totality of "unknowns" outside of man's comprehension and within God's knowledge, knowledge that he believes only prophets have some limited access to. Likewise, Ibn Ḥazm believes that the "visible" (*shahāda*) is not the totality of philosophical particulars or particular realities in the world like the particular faith of some specific person, or some particular knowledge within man's knowledge. Rather, Ibn Ḥazm asserts that the "visible" (*shahāda*) is actually the "known" of what God knows and what man can aspire to grasp through scripture and logic.[49]

Ibn Ḥazm's interpretation of the "seen and unseen" as the "known and unknown" essentially scales back what man can claim to know, and attributes to God knowledge of both the universals and the particulars. Ibn Ḥazm further builds on his counter position to Ibn Masarra's ontology by additionally connecting this epistemic "unknown" (*ghayb*) with a revised ontology of a spatially finite world, which more clearly demarcates the limits of the known created world. Specifically, while Ibn Ḥazm presents Ibn Masarra's interpretation of the Throne as some cosmic ordering or governing principle of agency distinct from God, Ibn Ḥazm's own interpretation of the "Throne" is as the outer limits of the created world.

The truth is that beyond the Throne, there is no creation, and that [the Throne] is the end of the corporeality (*jaram*) of the created things, beyond which there is no [so-called] void nor expanse [as the philosophers claim]. Whoever denies that the world has an ending (*nihāya*) in area, time, and space has followed the saying of the materialists (*dahriyya*).[50]

In contrast with conception of the Throne as an ontologically distinct principle of agency or knowledge, as a kind of pre-eternal divine attribute in theology or pre-eternal hypostasis in philosophy, Ibn Ḥazm presents the Throne as the outer limits of the cosmos and the world's corporeal existence. Drawing on the Qur'an, he offers something of an early modern European picture, contrasting with late antique Neoplatonism and medieval Graeco-Arabic philosophy, of a spatial break or ontological endpoint that constitutes the end of the corporeal world and the epistemic limits of what exactly man can discover about creation with the help of the senses and logic and without the additional help of scripture. He seems to imply that this break marks the distinction between the cosmos's created corporeal existence and the unknown ontology of an incorporeal supercosmic spiritual realm of the divine, but he does not articulate this point in this particular section of the text. What his conception of the Throne does articulate is a rejection of the ostensibly "dualist" and emanationist cosmology of the Graeco-Arabic philosophers, Ismāʿīlīs, and Masarrīs, as well as a rejection of the far-reaching epistemic claims of the mystics, the latter in particular having claimed to be able to attain special saintly knowledge of the divine realm beyond the Throne.[51] Particularly in contrast with the Graeco-Arabic philosophers' claims, Ibn Ḥazm explains that the Throne, as in the scriptural reference that God "established upon the Throne," should be read neither as God having "established Himself" on the Throne nor as God having established some kind of universal principle of agency akin to Soul. Rather, he asserts, "He established His [creative] act in the Throne, which is the [outer limits or] end of His creation."[52] That is, he argues that the verb "established" (*istawā*) in this case is a transitive verb indicating a type of ending or finality, and that therefore "established on the Throne" indicates that God established with finality the totality of creation as the world reached the outermost limits of created existence following God's act of creating and ordering (*mudabbir*).

Ibn Ḥazm, thus, gives an impression of a world created *ex nihilo* from the inside moving outward. This picture contrasts with the common Graeco-Arabic philosophical presentation of a pre-eternal world of emanating causality, in which logical agency pre-eternally proceeds from the outside moving inward, that is, from the Aristotelian First Cause or the Neoplatonic One to the microcosm of man. For Ibn Ḥazm, the phrase "established on the Throne" is additional scriptural evidence of a logically acceptable understanding of the created cosmos being self-contained with a finite beginning in time, and that beyond this finite world, no conclusions about ontology can be made. The Throne represents the end of man's comprehension to an extent that demarcates the kinds of conclusions mankind can make about the nature of the Creator. That is, in contrast with both the philosophical and speculative theologians, Ibn Ḥazm leans toward a scrupulous suspension of judgment about the nature of the Creator who brought this finite realm into existence, arguing in sum that God simultaneously transcends the world ontologically and is immanent in the world in terms of omnipotent agency and omniscient knowledge. Interestingly, this last outcome of Ibn Ḥazm's arguments reemerges as a central part of the later Andalusī scholar Ibn Barrajān's pursuit of a mystical witnessing of the divine through, more specifically, a mystical witnessing of God's immanent agency.[53]

Taken together, Ibn Ḥazm's positions should be thought of as an attempt to rein in philosophical and speculative theology, tying speculative thought about the nature of God and the world down to the limits of what one can know through logical and textual evidence. He thus limits not only what can be claimed speculatively or logically about the world, but he also limits the scope of scriptural theological interpretation to what can be known with certainty, this method being part of his larger program of reining in sound knowledge acquisition to what can be learned from sense-based knowledge and scripture. Everything else is "unknown" (*ghayb*). From the perspective of his jurisprudence, this doctrine contextualizes how he notably assigns the judgment of "permissible" to a much larger category of activities than other jurisprudential schools based on the same position of skepticism seen here in his theology. From the perspective of theology and the examples seen in this chapter, this doctrine lies at the heart of not only his criticism of questions of causality and cosmology among the philosophers, Ibn Masarra, Fatimid Ismāʿīlīs, and theologians, but also his very specific criticisms of esoteric hermeneutics found in the writings of some of these philosophical groups.

In sum, Ibn Ḥazm's logic-oriented counterarguments to Ibn Masarra's and the Ismāʿīlīs' simultaneously Platonizing and scripturally esoteric legacies marked the high point of a politically charged debate in predominantly Mālikī-trained Andalusī circles of scholars. This debate was principally about Graeco-Arabic conceptions of psychology and cosmology that had become part of politically controversial conceptions of leadership and communal guidance, epitomized especially in the tenth-century Fatimid notion of the Cairene caliph as a Platonizing Ismāʿīlī semi-messianic guide. As authors of distinct forms of philosophically oriented theological writing, Ibn Masarra and Ibn Ḥazm offered arguments that point to how Sunnī scholars continued to debate in a political context a question that the scholars asked from the earliest days of Islamic history's intersection with late antique history: What makes a Sunnī scholarly guide of the community's faith, and should Graeco-Arabic philosophy number among scholarly modes of theological knowledge? By the eleventh century in al-Andalus, a region popularly perceived in medieval and modern scholarship as a peripheral region of conservative Mālikism, the idea that a scholar of scriptural sciences and jurisprudence might also be a scholar of the Graeco-Arabic philosophical sciences became widespread. For Ibn Masarra, such philosophical scholars were sage-like figures adept in a Platonizing theology, who located Neoplatonic doctrines in psychology and cosmology in what the mystics called the interior knowledge (*ʿilm al-bāṭin*) of the scriptural text's meaning and the world's phenomena. For Ibn Ḥazm, true philosophical theologians were Aristotelian logic-oriented scholars who combined sensory knowledge, logical methods, and scriptural evidence emerging from a univocal hermeneutic to discover that there was no Universal Intellect or Soul, which Platonizing groups such as the Fatimids had popularized in politically contentious cosmologies.

Notes

1 Several studies offer analytical overviews of the full implications for religious authority of the Andalusī Umayyad emirate's proclamation of a caliphate in 929. Two articles offer particularly useful starting points: Janina Safran, "The Command of the Faithful in Al-Andalus: A Study in the Articulation of Caliphal Legitimacy," *International Journal of Middle Eastern Studies* 30 (1998): 19–50; Maribel Fierro, "La política religiosa de ʿAbd al-Raḥmān III (r. 300/912-350/961)," *al-Qantara* 25 (2004): 120–56.

2 On the impact of Fatimid Ismāʿīlī doctrine on ʿAbd al-Raḥmān III's overall construction of caliphal authority, including the latter's appointment of a judge from the anti-esoteric Ẓāhirī legal school of thought, see Maribel Fierro, "The Movable Minbar of Cordoba: How the Umayyads of al-Andalus Claimed the Inheritance of the Prophet," *Jerusalem Studies in Arabic and Islam* 33 (2007): 149–68.

3 The respective works of Michael Brett and Hanna E. Kassis offer critical analyses of Umayyad–Fatimid rivalries in North Africa, highlighting the contingencies of North African tribal allegiances as these tribes moved between rivaling alliances. Michael Brett, *The Rise of the Fatimids: The World of the Mediterranean and the Middle East in the 10th Century CE* (Leiden: Brill,

2013), pp. 135–75; Hanna E. Kassis, "Coinage of an Enigmatic Caliph: The Midrārid Muḥammad b. al-Fatḥ of Sijilmāsah," *al-Qantara* 9 (1988): 489–504.

4 Ibn al-Qiṭṭ of the Umayyad family led a rebellion in 901 during which he gained the support of some Berber tribes and eventually made semi-messianic (*mahdī*) claims to authority. Maribel Fierro, *La heterodoxia en al-Andalus durante el Periodo Omeya* (Madrid: Instituto Hispano-Arabe de Cultura, 1987), Section 7:3.

5 Paul Walker, *Ḥamīd al-Dīn al-Kirmānī: Ismāʿīlī Thought in the Age of al-Ḥakīm* (New York: I. B. Tauris, 1999), pp. 25–30; Paul Walker, *Early Philosophical Shiism: The Ismāʿīlī Falsafa of Abū Yaʿqūb al-Sijistānī* (Cambridge: Cambridge University Press, 1993), pp. 10–24; Farhad Daftary, *Ismāʿīlī Literature: A Bibliography of Sources and Studies* (New York: I. B. Tauris, 2004), pp. 20–36; Wilfred Madelung, "Das Imamat in der fruhen ismailitischen Lehre," *Der Islam* 37 (1961): 43–135.

6 On *tashayyuʿ* in al-Andalus, see M. A. Makkī, "al-Tashayyuʿ fī l-Andalus," *Revista del Instituto Egipcio de Estudios Islámicos en Madrid* 2 (1954): 93–149.

7 Safran has offered a useful contextualization of the quelling of ʿUmar b. Ḥafsūn's rebellion in the articulation of Andalusī caliphal legitimacy. Safran, "The Command of the Faithful in al-Andalus," pp. 183–98.

8 Hussain Mones, "Le rôle des hommes de religion dans l'histoire de l'Espagne musulmane jusqu'à la fin du califat," *Studia Islamica* 20 (1964): 47–88. Maribel Fierro, "Los Mālikīes de al-Andalus y los dos arbitros (*al-ḥakamān*)," *al-Qantara* 6 (1985): 79–102; idem, "El derecho Mālikī en al-Andalus, ss. II/VIII-V/sXI," *al-Qantara* 12 (1991): 119–31.

9 These details are based on the account of Mālikī jurist al-Nubāhī (= al-Bunnāhī) (d. after 1392). By the time of ʿAbd al-Raḥmān's condemnations between 952 and 957, Mālikī scholars were already condemning their fellow scholar Ibn Masarra. The bio-bibliographical evidence examined in the previous chapter indicates that this scholarly controversy over Ibn Masarra began well before public condemnations between 952 and 957. Some of the scholars who wrote refutations died close to this time and had already written refutations. On this account of the condemnation of the Masarrīs and the book burning, see Abū Ḥasan ʿAlī b. ʿAbdullāh b. al-Ḥasan al-Malaqī al-Andalusī al-Nubāhī (= al-Bunnāhī), *Taʾrīkh Quḍāt al-Andalus*, ed. E. Levi Provencal (Cairo: Dar al-Kātib al-Miṣrī, 1948), p. 201. Muhammad Bencherifa has argued that the *nisba* of al-Nubāhī was more likely al-Bunnāhī. Muhammad Bencherifa, "al-Bunnāhī la al-Nubāhī," *Académia Revue de l'Académie du Royaume du Maroc* 8 (1998): 17–89.

10 Fierro, *La heterodoxia*, pp. 161–2.

11 See Chapter 3.

12 Peter Heath has offered an analytical picture of ʿAbd al-Raḥmān III's patronage of the letters in an era when Cordoba had emerged as a kind of second Baghdad for the western Islamic world. Peter Heath, "Knowledge," in *The Literature of al-Andalus*, eds. Maria Rosa Menocal, Raymond P. Scheindlin, and Michael Sells (Cambridge: Cambridge University Press, 2000), pp. 96–125. For more context on the notion of bibliophile political leaders in al-Andalus, see Tornero's and Cruz Hernandez's discussions of the various

dimensions of philosophy in Andalusī history. Emilio Tornero, "Filosofía," in *Historia de España Menéndez Pidal – El retroceso territorial de al-Andalus. Almorávides y Almohades, siglos IX–XIII*, eds. José María Jover Zamora and María Jesús Viguera Molíns (Madrid: Espasa-Calpe, 1997): 8-2:587–602; Miguel Cruz Hernandez, *Historia del pensamiento en el mundo islámico, vol. 2, El pensamiento de al-Andalus (Siglos IX–XIV)* (Madrid: Alianza Editorial, 1996), pp. 344–57.

13 Bosch Vilá provides a concise overview of Qāsim b. Aṣbagh's legacy in *Encyclopaedia of Islam*, 2nd edition, s. v. "Qāsim b. Aṣbagh" (Jacinto Bosch Vilá).

14 On Ibn Waḍḍāḥ and his critical role in systematizing the place of *ḥadīth* science in Mālikī jurisprudence, see the introduction to Ibn Waḍḍāḥ, *Kitāb al-Bidʿa: Tratado Contra Las Inovaciones*, ed. Maribel Fierro (Madrid: CSIC, 1988); Manuela Marín, "Baqī b. Majlad y la introduccion del studio del Hadit en Al-Andalus," *al-Qantara* 1 (1981): 165–208.

15 These scholars include Thābit b. Ḥazm from Saragossa (Ibn al-Faraḍī, no. 306); Muḥammad b. Qāsim (Ibn al-Faraḍī, no. 1216), who was a legal consultant during the reign of ʿAbd al-Raḥmān III; and finally ʿUthmān b. ʿAbd al-Raḥmān (Ibn al-Faraḍī, no. 895).

16 *Encyclopaedia of Islam*, 2nd edition, s. v. "Qāsim b. Aṣbagh" (Jacinto Bosch Vilá).

17 In Ibn al-Faraḍī's bio-bibliographical reports, the contested credibility of those students of Qāsim b. Aṣbagh who were associated with Ibn Masarra's doctrines appears to reflect the posthumous virtue of being associated with Qāsim b. Aṣbagh and the questionability in being associated with Ibn Masarra. One example is Cordovan *ḥadīth* transmitter Muḥammad b. Mufarrij al-Maʿāfirī (Ibn al-Faraḍī, no. 1329), a pioneer in semantic and syntactic Qur'anic analysis who also studied under mystic Ibn al-Aʿrābī in Mecca during his travels to the Islamic East. Ibn al-Faraḍī tells us that he was abandoned as an authority on *ḥadīth*. The Cordovan scholar Muḥammad b. ʿAbdullāh al-Qaysī or Ibn al-Khayr of Jaen (Ibn al-Faraḍī, no. 1364) is described in very similar terms. Muḥammad b. Aḥmad al-Khawlānī likewise lost his credibility specifically because of his association with the "school of Ibn Masarra" (*madhhab Ibn Masarra*).

18 Qāsim b. Aṣbagh studied with Ibn Masarra's father, a point that Ibn al-Faraḍī mentions but that does not appear in some later biographies, such as the one found in al-Ḥumaydī's (d. 488/1095) work. The latter mentions the other two teachers of al-Qāsim b. Aṣbagh whom we know were also Ibn Masarra's teachers, namely al-Khushanī and Ibn Waḍḍāḥ, but does not mention Ibn Masarra's father. al-Ḥumaydī was notably also the first to refer to Ibn Masarra as a Sufi. He indicates that Ibn Masarra "*kāna ʿalā tarīqa min al-zuhd wa-l-ʿibāda … lahū tarīqa fi-l-balāgha wa tadqīq fī ghawāmiḍ ishārāt al-ṣūfiyya.*" al-Ḥumaydī, *Jadhwat al-Muqtabis fī Dhikr Wulāt al-Andalus*, ed. Muḥammad al-Ṭanjī (Cairo: Maktab Nashr al-Thaqāfa al-Islāmiyya, 1952), no. 83.

19 See Chapter 3.

20 The respective works of Fierro and Safran have traced the impact of the neighboring Fatimid "esotericist" challenge on Andalusī affairs in a way that contextualizes the appointment of a judge of the Ẓāhirī school of thought.

Fierro, "The Movable Minbar of Cordoba," pp. 149–68; Janina M. Safran, *Defining Boundaries in al-Andalus: Muslims, Christians, and Jews in Islamic Iberia* (Ithaca, NY: Cornell University Press, 2013), pp. 35–80, esp. 71ff.

21 While twelfth-century writers of chronicles and bio-bibliographical works such as Ibn Bashkuwāl (d. 578/1183) did not spill much ink discussing Ibn Masarra's legacy in the context of late tenth-century and eleventh-century developments, the legacy of Ibn Masarra did ultimately reemerge in the late twelfth and thirteenth centuries in the bio-bibliographical work of Ibn al-ʿAbbār (d. 658/1260) and the mystical writing of his Sufi contemporaries, namely Ibn ʿArabī, Ibn Sabʿīn, and Ibn Marʾa. Referring to a lost book on Ibn Masarra and his followers, a book not mentioned by Ibn Bashkuwāl, Ibn al-ʿAbbār describes two figures as *faqīh*s of Cordoba, namely, Aḥmad b. Ghānim and Aḥmad Hāmid, as followers of Ibn Masarra (Ibn al-ʿAbbār no. 8, no. 7). Ibn al-ʿAbbār reports that two sons of Abū l-Ḥakam Mundhir b. al-Saʿīd, the chief *qāḍī* of Cordoba during the lifetime of Ibn Masarra, were followers of Ibn Masarra. The two sons are Ḥakam b. Mundhir and Saʿīd b. Mundhir. Ibn al-ʿAbbār mentions both together in his discussion of yet another follower of Ibn Masarra, namely their cousin and the *qāḍī*'s nephew, the Cordovan Muḥammad b. Faḍlallāh b. Saʿīd (Ibn al-ʿAbbār, no. 389). Ibn al-ʿAbbār, *al-Takmila li-Kitāb al- Ṣila*, ed. Francisco Codera Zaidín (Madrid: Bibliotheca Arabico-Hispana, 1887–9). As mentioned, the jurist Ibn Ḥazm names the first, Ḥakam b. Mundhir, as someone he was personally acquainted with and who served as a source for his discussion of Ibn Masarra's doctrine. Ibn Ḥazm, *Al-Fiṣal wa-l-Milal fī-l-Milal wa-l-Ahwāʾ wa-l-Niḥal*, eds. Muḥammad Ibrāhīm Naṣr and ʿAbd al-Raḥmān Umayra (Beirut: Dār al-Jayl, 1995), 4:80. On the mystics' connection with Ibn Masarra, see Chapter 1, note 34.

22 Maribel Fierro has provided an analytical overview of key political and religious debates during the Taifa period, highlighting the diminishing relevance of Masarrism and the rise of Ẓāhirīsm in the eleventh century. Maribel Fierro, "La religión," *Historia de España Menéndez Pidal – Los reinos de taifas: Al-Andalus en el siglo XI*, eds. José María Jover Zamora and María Jesús Viguera Molíns (Madrid: Espasa-Calpe, 1994), 8-1:399–496.

23 Miguel Asín Palacios originally located this contemporary of Ibn Ḥazm in the context of an early Andalusī Sufi tradition initiated by Ibn Masarra and systematized by Ibn ʿArabī. The recent scholarship of Maribel Fierro has more cautiously characterized him as a peripheral figure with controversial interpretations of Ibn Masarra's ideas. Fierro contrasts this figure with al-Ṭalamankī, a scholar with a significant following who believed in the notion of saintly miracles. Maribel Fierro, "The Polemic about the *karāmāt al-awliyāʾ* and the Development of Sufism in al-Andalus Fourth/Tenth–Fifth/Eleventh Centuries," *Bulletin of the School of African and Oriental Studies*, 55 (1992) p. 246ff; Miguel Asín Palacios, *Abenmasarra y su escuela. Origenes de la filosofía hispano-musulmana* (Madrid: Imprenta Ibérica – E. Maestre, 1914); Fierro, *La heterodoxia*, pp. 166–8.

24 This interpretation of scriptural words and phrases avoids pegging individual Arabic words to primary and secondary meanings, such that a reader might read the same word in one passage literally and in another passage metaphorically according to contextual clues. The latter approach, commonly

found in speculative theology, uses *ta'wīl* as a way to "deflect" the apparent meaning in order to discover the metaphorical (*majāz*) meaning of the term. This literal-metaphorical hermeneutic is familiar to modern readers of English-language prose. While Ibn Ḥazm departed from this approach in his exclusion of metaphors, he did not argue for a literal interpretation of all Arabic terms in the Qur'an such that a reference to the divine "hand" should be understood anthropomorphically. Rather, in a manner perhaps comparable to Derrida's analysis of language, he argued that every term needs to be understood in its context in order to discover the intended or literal meaning of the term in each case. That is, he simply unpegged words from primary meanings. This hermeneutic, thus, was opposed to the dichotomous literal-esoteric scriptural hermeneutic adopted by many Sufis and also to the literal-metaphorical hermeneutic of speculative theology. Sands offers an analysis of Sufi *ẓāhir-bāṭin* esoteric scriptural hermeneutics, which can be compared to Weiss's analysis of Ashʿarī discussions of primary meanings and metaphorical meanings (*majāz*). Elias has called attention to the extent that commonly Sufi hermeneutical techniques are part of more widespread historical trends in scriptural exegesis. Kristen Sands, *Sufi Commentaries on the Qur'an in Classical Islam* (Routledge: New York, 2006), pp. 35–64. Bernard Weiss, *The Spirit of Islamic Law* (Athens: University of Georgia Press, 1998), pp. 96–103; Jamal Elias, "Sufi *tafsīr* Reconsidered: Exploring the Development of a Genre," *Journal of Qur'anic Studies* 12 (2010): 41–55.

25 *al-Fiṣal wa-l-Milal*, 5:86. See n. 39.

26 *al-Fiṣal wa-l-Milal*, 5:217.

27 Ibn Ḥazm uses the example of philosophical discussions of prime matter as a starting point for his larger critique of the way the philosophers conceived of the ontology of universals in abstraction of their particular substantiations. "[Matter's] existence cannot even be conceived as such … it is nonsense that is impossible, just as the Universal Man and all of the species and the genera [like Universal Intellect and Universal Soul] are nothing but their [particular] individuals, which are the bodies as they are [and that they adhere in]. The genus [of body] is in fact the genus of [these] bodies, which comprise [the totality of] the individuals of the accidents, and the species is [simply] the species of the accidents and nothing more.… This breaks down the assessment of anyone among the ignorant who thinks [in agreement with the philosophers] that the genus and species and the category are all substances and not bodies." *al-Fiṣal wa-l-Milal*, 5:200.

28 Ibn Ḥazm's explanation of the ontology of the invisible *jinn* is particularly illustrative of his commitment to reading the scriptural text using an eclectic hermeneutic that draws on both logical arguments and sensory evidence. "We do not recognize [*jinn*] by the senses nor do we know either the necessity of their existence nor the necessity of the impossibility of their existence in the world by the intellect. However, we do know by the necessity of intellect the possibility of their existence.… It is when the prophets … reported that *jinn* exist in the world that knowledge of God's creation of them and their existence became necessary [and no longer just possible]. Moreover, [scriptural] text was revealed both on this point and on the point that they are a community (*umma*), in cognition, discerning,

worshipping, moving about until they pass away ... the Muslims have come to a consensus upon this point, as have the Christians, Magians, Sabians and Jews.... They are subtle airy bodies with no color in them, and their base element is fire, just like our base element is dust. On that point, God (Mighty and Exalted) said in the Qur'an [15:27], 'And as for the *jinn*, We created them aforetime from the fire of scorching winds.' Fire and air are two base elements that have no color, as color only comes upon enflamed fire in our [visual] perspective because of its mix with the humidity of things that are enflamed in it, from wood and flint stones to other things. If they [the *jinn*] had color we would see them by the naked eye, and if they were anything other than pure subtle airy bodies, we would recognize them by the sense of touch." *al-Fiṣal wa-l-Milal*, 5:112.

29 Historians have argued that al-Ghazālī's nominalist critique stood at the start of the historical nominalist critique of Neoplatonism in Arabic, Hebrew, and Latin philosophy. However, Ibn Ḥazm's arguments discussed in the current chapter preceded those of al-Ghazālī, pointing thus to how similar solutions were being developed across the medieval Islamic world in this era of Sunnī scholarly scrutiny of Graeco-Arabic philosophy's theological value. On al-Ghazālī's critique, see Frank Griffel, *al-Ghazālī's Philosophical Theology* (New York: Oxford University Press, 2009), pp. 97–110.

30 See Chapter 3.

31 Camilla Adang, "The Spread of Ẓāhirism in al-Andalus in the Post-Caliphal Period: The Evidence from the Biographical Dictionaries," in *Ideas, Images, Methods of Portrayal: Insights into Classical Arabic Literature and Islam*, ed. Sebastian Gunther (Leiden: Brill, 2005), pp. 297–345; Samir Kaddouri, "Refutations of Ibn Ḥazm by Mālikī Authors from al-Andalus and North Africa," in *Ibn Ḥazm of Cordoba: The Life and Works of a Controversial Thinker*, eds. Camilla Adang, Maribel Fierro, and Sabine Schmidtke (Leiden: Brill, 2013), pp. 539–600.

32 The medieval and modern view that Ẓāhirism rejected rationalism or was "anti-rationalist" appears to draw on later Arabic sources writing about Ẓāhirism. Ignaz Goldziher and Roger Arnaldez were among the first modern historians to recognize these philosophical contours of Ibn Ḥazm's understanding of the "literal" meaning of the text. Ignaz Goldziher, *The Ẓāhirīs: Their Doctrine and Their History*, trans. Wolfgang Behn (Leiden: Brill, 1971), especially pp. 160–70; Roger Arnaldez, *Grammaire et théologie chez Ibn Ḥazm de Cordoue: essai sur la structure et les conditions de la pensée musulmane* (Paris: Vrin, 1956). In agreement with the notion that Ẓāhirism should not be understood as simplistic literalism, Christopher Melchert has written on Ẓāhirism's appeal among sophisticated courtly elites. Melchert has also identified the reasons for the decline of Ẓāhirism as a school of jurisprudence, pointing not to its supposed anti-rationalism, but rather to its associations with theological heterodoxy, the history of its patronage, and methods of teaching. Christopher Melchert, *The Formation of the Sunni Schools of Law* (Brill: Leiden, 1997), 178–97. See also George F. Hourani, *Reason and Tradition in Islamic Ethics* (Cambridge: Cambridge University Press, 1985), pp. 172–200. Albert Hourani, *Reason and Tradition in Islamic Ethics* (Cambridge: Cambridge University Press, 1985), pp. 172–200; Roger

Arnaldez, *Grammaire et théologie chez Ibn Ḥazm de Cordoue: essai sur la structure et les conditions de la pensée musulmane* (Paris: J. Vrin, 1956).

33 What remains to be seen in this chapter is how much this criticism of philosophy was tied up with a response to the Fatimids, a point that would demonstrate how philosophical knowledge increasingly took on political dimensions following the rise of the three competing caliphates (the Andalusī Umayyads, the Fatimids, the Abbasids) that negotiated the place of philosophy in political culture. The Andalusī Umayyads and Abbasids appear to have narrowed the originally wide variety of genres under patronage. Examples can be seen in the removal of certain books on philosophy from the Andalusī courtly library in 979 (see n. 10) as well as the Abbasid patronage of al-Ghazālī's reform of philosophy (see Chapter 3). In their respective works on al-Andalus, Maribel Fierro, Janina Safran, and several other historians have analyzed broad changes in Abbasid and Andalusī political culture that contextualize the increasingly contested political place of philosophy in the tenth and eleventh centuries. Fierro, *La heterodoxia*, especially Section 9; Miguel Cruz Hernandez, "La persecución anti-Massarí durante el reinado de ʿAbd al-Raḥmān al-Nāṣir lī-Dīn Allāh según Ibn Ḥayyān," *al-Qantara* 2 (1981): 51–67; Janina Safran, *The Second Umayyad Caliphate: The Articulation of Caliphal Legitimacy in al-Andalus* (Cambridge, MA: Harvard Center for Middle Eastern Studies, 2001), pp. 32–7.

34 See n. 47.

35 *Marātib al-ʿUlūm*, 4:67.

36 The passage in note 27 offers an illustrative example of Ibn Ḥazm's methods of analysis. al-Ghazālī's criticism of the philosophers in the *Incoherence of the Philosophers* (*Tahāfut al-Falāsifa*) similarly argues that many positions claimed by the philosophers as logically necessary or rejected as logically impossible are, in fact, logically possible. For both al-Ghazālī and Ibn Ḥazm, scriptural information, read according to the exigencies of a logic-oriented hermeneutic, fills in missing information about what is necessarily true within the logically possible. Despite this overlap in approach, al-Ghazālī and Ibn Ḥazm did not arrive at identical conclusions. al-Ghazālī conceded in the *Incoherence* that the soul's immateriality is a possibility, while Ibn Ḥazm concluded that the soul is necessarily corporeal. Dutton has examined al-Ghazālī's discussion of possibility in the context of causality. B. D. Dutton, "al-Ghazālī on Possibility and the Critique of Causality," *Medieval Philosophy and Theology* 10 (2001): pp. 23–46. In agreement with Ibn Ḥazm's work, al-Ghazālī's discussion of causality in the *Incoherence* is oriented around the claim that "the connection between what is typically believed to be a cause and what is typically believed to be the effect is not necessary." al-Ghazālī, *Tahāfut al-Falāsifa. The Incoherence of the Philosophers*, trans. Michael E. Marmura (Provo, UT: Brigham Young University Press, 2000), pp. 166–70.

37 *al-Fiṣal wa-l-Milal*, 5:86.

38 The reference to God's self-reflection as the starting point of a procession of existence in an emanationist cosmology appears in the full passage of this section of the text. *al-Fiṣal wa-l-Milal*, 5:86.

39 In these passages, Ibn Ḥazm represents doctrines in psychology and cosmology that he does not agree with as Zoroastrian and Ismāʿīlī, which pushes

the reader to think of these doctrines as dualist, evocative of Manicheanism, and therefore heterodox. De Blois offers an overview of the connections of these latter three terms with Ismāʿīlism in Islamic doxographies in *Encyclopaedia of Islam*, 2nd Edition, s.v. "Manichaeism," (by F. C. De Blois). Specifically, al-Masʿūdī and al-Bīrūnī offered an account of the etymology of the term *zindīq* as originally meaning dualist and esotericist Manicheans. al-Masʿūdī points out that upon the Arab adoption of the Persian term *zandī*, which originally referred to Zoroastrians who turned toward allegorical interpretations of the Avesta that clashed with the Avesta's apparent meaning, the Persian term *zandī* became the Arabic *zindīq* and meant dualists (*thanawiyya*) and anyone who believed in the doctrine of the world's pre-eternity (*qidam*). De Blois points out that this etymology, in fact, constitutes a medieval projection backward onto pre-Islamic Manichaeism of popular medieval conceptions of the Ismāʿīlīs, who were entangled with the Manicheans with common epithets such as dualists (*thanawiyya*) and esotericists (*bāṭiniyya*). Ibn Ḥazm's comments, taken together with those of al-Masʿūdī and al-Bīrūnī, indicate the extent to which philosophical doctrines perceived today as quintessentially Aristotelian-Neoplatonic were, in medieval Islamic history, equally associated with a wide variety of groups such as the Zoroastrians, the Ismāʿīlīs, Ibn Masarra's scholarly followers, and the Sufis. al-Masʿūdī's comments are found in al-Masʿūdī, *Murūj al-Dhahab wa Maʿādin al-Jawhar*, ed. Charles Pellat (Beirut: Manshūrāt al-Jāmiʿa al-Lubnāniyya, 1965), 2:167–8.

40 *al-Fiṣal wa-l-Milal*, 5:66.

41 Fierro and Asín Palacios have each discussed Ismāʿīl b. al-Ruʿaynī in the context of the elusive eleventh-century history of Sufism in al-Andalus. While Asín Palacios saw him as a key figure in a continuous Ibn Masarra-based Sufi tradition that began with Ibn Masarra and continued through Ibn ʿArabī, Fierro sees him more cautiously as one of several figures inspired by Ibn Masarra who was not necessarily part of a coherent group. Ismāʿīl b. al-Ruʿaynī was accused by Ibn Ḥazm of having claimed that prophecy could be acquired. A similar accusation against Ibn Masarra was attributed to al-Ṭalamankī, as discussed in Chapter 1. See Fierro, *La heterodoxia*, Section 10.3; Asín Palacios, *Abenmasarra y su escuela*, pp. 80–6.

42 *al-Fiṣal wa-l-Milal*, 5:66.

43 *al-Fiṣal wa-l-Milal*, 5:66.

44 *al-Fiṣal wa-l-Milal*, 5:66.

45 al-Ṭalamankī studied with Ibn Ḥazm and was himself the object of criticism for arguing in favor of the legitimacy of saintly miracles (*karamāt al-awliyāʾ*). The fact that he was an eleventh-century critic of the late Ibn Masarra is ironic because the two shared an interest in doctrines popular among the mystics. The accusation that Ibn Masarra did not adhere to the doctrine of the inimitability of prophecy comes from later authors' references to the text. Interestingly, Morris and Fierro have both discussed the lost manuscript of al-Ṭalamankī's refutation against Ibn Masarra using two different references indicative of the changing legacy of Ibn Masarra, which was discussed in Chapter 1. Morris refers to this refutation as *al-Radd ʿalā Ibn Masarra* in James Morris, "Ibn Masarra: A Reconsideration of the Primary Sources"

(unpublished article), appendix. Fierro refers to it as *al-Radd ʿalā l-Bāṭiniyya*. Fierro, *La heterodoxia*, p. 163, n. 7. Morris's reference is based on Asín's and Cheneb's reference to a refutation of Ibn Masarra attributed to al-Ṭalamankī in a Tunisian manuscript, discussed by Codera in Francis Codera Zaidín, "Un manuscrito árabe-español en Túnez," *Boletín de la Real Academia de la Historia* 58 (1911): 285–96. That manuscript describes the contents of the text as *kitāb yashtamilu ʿala ashyāʾ fī-hī kashf madhhab Muḥammad Ibn Masarra ajzāʾ kathīra*. Fierro's reference, in contrast, is based on al-Dhahabī's later reference to al-Ṭalamankī's accusation that Ibn Masarra claimed prophecy: *qāla l-Ṭalamankī fī raddihī ʿalā l-Bāṭiniyya: Ibn Masarra iddaʿā l-nubuwwa*. The reference to al-Ṭalamankī's refutation of Ibn Masarra as *al-Radd ʿala l-Bāṭiniyya*, which is a late reference, is potentially further indicative of the way in which Ibn Masarra's legacy became entangled with anti-Fatimid polemics. Fierro, "The Polemic over the *karamāt al-awliyāʾ*," p. 245; idem *La heterodoxia*, p. 163, n. 7; al-Dhahabī, *Siyar Aʿlām al-Nubalāʾ* (Beirut: Muʾassasat al-Risāla, 1985), 15:558.

46 See Chapter 3's discussion of the criticism of these doctrines in the later writings of al-Ghazālī.

47 As scholars such as Lagerlund have pointed out in this context, Ibn Ḥazm should be thought of as part of the medieval history of skepticism prior to al-Ghazālī. Henrik Lagerlund, *Rethinking the History of Skepticism: The Missing Medieval Background* (Leiden: Brill, 2010), pp. 11–14, 44–7. See also Wael Hallaq, *Ibn Taymiyya against the Logicians* (Oxford: Clarendon Press, 1993) pp. xlv–xlviiii.

48 *al-Fiṣal wa-l-Milal*, 5:65.

49 Ibn Ḥazm's understanding of *al-shahāda wa-l-ghayb*, "known and unknown," as opposed to the Masarrīs' "particulars and universals," offers some parallels with al-Ghazālī's use of a cosmology. al-Ghazālī's approach is oriented around *al-shahāda*, which denotes the present world for al-Ghazālī, and *al-malakūt*, which refers to the divine realm. However, as Whittingham shows, al-Ghazālī's *al-shahāda* and *al-malakūt* also parallel his bipartite cosmology of *al-jismānī* and *al-rūḥānī* and his discussion of "the visible world" as a ladder to the "world of dominion," which echoes the writings of the Graeco-Arabic philosophers and mystics or Iraq. Indeed, in stating that the "cosmos" is "two worlds: spiritual and corporeal," al-Ghazālī described a world that was very different from Ibn Ḥazm's emphasis on a created corporeal cosmos, and that was in significant agreement with the world imagined by the Graeco-Arabic philosophers, many Sufi metaphysicians, and Ibn Masarra. Whittingham provides an overview of these terms in Martin Whittingham, *al-Ghazālī and the Qur'an: One Book, Many Meanings* (New York: Routledge, 2007), pp. 49–54. As Rustom has shown, Mullā Ṣadra, like many Sufis, also distinguished between the *ʿālam al-shahāda* and *ʿālam al-ghayb*, with man characterized as having both unseen and visible dimensions (*al-ghayb wa-l-shahāda*). God, in this discussion, is the unseen of unseens (*ghayb al-ghuyūb*). There is, in sum, a spectrum of uses of these terms, with Ibn Ḥazm having stood firmly on the side of avoiding using *ghayb* as some phenomenological unseen that was ostensibly embedded within the created realm. Ibn Ḥazm preferred interpreting the

ghayb as the collective phenomenological and epistemic unknown. Ibn Masarra, like many Sufis and philosophers, stood on the other side of this spectrum by including the *ghayb* as what lies beyond the visible. This doctrine in ontology was one that Ibn Ḥazm would certainly have criticized as the kind of ontic dualism that he believed was found in Graeco-Arabic philosophy, Iranian philosophy, and Ismāʿīlism. For Mullā Ṣadra's use of the terms, see Mohammed Rustom, *Triumph of Mercy: Philosophy and Scripture in Mullā Ṣadra* (Albany: State University of New York Press, 2012), pp. 75, 128. al-Ghazālī's mixed use of these terms can be seen in al-Ghazālī, *Mishkāt al-Anwār*, trans. D. Buchman, *The Niche of the Lights* (Provo, UT: Brigham Young University Press, 1998), pp. 11–14.

50 *al-Fiṣal wa-l-Milal*, 2:290.

51 The Throne here as the outer limits of created existence parallels to some extent the earlier sage al-Ḥakīm al-Tirmidhī's understanding of the Throne in the *Sīrat al-Awliyā'* as the outer limits of the created world beyond which lie divine realms of light. In contrast with the mystics, however, Ibn Ḥazm specifically eschewed not only the mystics' notion that the saintly can attain special knowledge of the divine realm beyond the Throne, which he associated with prophetic knowledge, but he also eschewed the philosophical notion that the Throne constitutes a universal principle of agency akin to the philosophers' Plotinian Soul. Griffel's analysis of al-Ghazālī argues that al-Ghazālī subscribes to this philosophical idea that the Throne denotes the entire system of secondary causes as found in philosophical literature. An overview and analysis of al-Ḥakīm al-Tirmidhī's writings, including the *Sīrat al-Awliyā'*, is available in Muḥammad b. ʿAlī al-Ḥakīm al-Tirmidhī, *Thalāthat Muṣannafāt li-l-Ḥakīm al-Tirmidhī: Kitāb Sīrat al-Awliyā', Jawāb Masā'il Allatī Sa'alahū Ahl Sarakhs ʿanhā, Jawāb Kitāb min al-Rayy*, ed. Bernd Radtke (Stuttgart: F. Steiner, 1992), 1–134. Griffel, *al-Ghazālī's Philosophical Theology*, pp. 235–74. See also Bernd Radtke and John O'Kane, *The Concept of Sainthood in Early Islamic Mysticism: Two Works by al-Ḥakīm al-Tirmidhī* (New York: Routledge, 2013), 38–212. Bernd Radtke, "The Concept of Wilāya in Early Sufism," in *The Heritage of Sufism. Vol. 1, Classical Persian Sufism from Its Origins to Rumi (700–1300)* (Oxford: Oneworld, 1999), pp. 483–96; idem "al-Ḥakīm al-Tirmidhī on Miracles," in *Miracle et karāma*, ed. Denise Aigle (Brepols: Turnhout, 2000), 287–99.

52 *al-Fiṣal wa-l-Milal*, 2:290.

53 See Chapter 4.

3 Political Reform among the Later Abbasids

The political rise of the Fatimid caliphate in the tenth century constituted a challenge not only to the authority of the Andalusī Umayyad caliphate and the scholars of al-Andalus and North Africa (*maghrib*), but also to the authority of the Abbasid caliphate and scholars further east (*mashriq*). The chief judge in Baghdad, al-Ghazālī (d. 505/1111), wrote a court-sponsored work called *Scandals of the Esotericists and Virtues of the Followers of the Caliph al-Mustaẓhir* in this political context. Significantly, the treatise had strong parallels with his more famous *Incoherence of the Philosophers*, which was widely transmitted in Europe. Both texts show that like his Andalusī predecessors, al-Ghazālī sought to incorporate Aristotelian-Avicennan logic into a more philosophical form of Islamic theology while simultaneously offering a nominalist critique of various Neoplatonic conclusions in psychology and cosmology. al-Ghazālī's embrace of a philosophical form of Sufi metaphysics, however, opened the door for a deeper engagement through mystical epistemologies with Platonizing theories in psychology and cosmology. Contemporary critics noted the extent to which his logic-oriented theology appeared to extend more deeply into the philosophers' doctrines. One of his students, the Andalusī jurist Abū Bakr b. al-ʿArabī (d. 543/1148), offered a nuanced opinion on his teacher's writings and on philosophy and mysticism more broadly. His critique foreshadowed the way the Ghazālian Sufi metaphysicians of the Almoravid and Almohad eras of al-Andalus, discussed in Part II, would rise to the center of a new political and scholarly controversy as the Fatimid "esotericist" challenge came to a close in 1171.

al-Ghazālī's Legacy between Philosophy and Sufism

Debates over Graeco-Arabic philosophy, esoteric hermeneutics, and the contours of political and religious authority in al-Andalus ran parallel with those in Baghdad, where they came to a political and intellectual climax in the time of the Abbasid caliph al-Mustaẓhir (r. 1094–1118)

Figure 3.1. Distinctive concentric three-ring design of the Fatimid gold denarius in Cairo, inscribed with the name of the caliph and the testimony of faith, and minted during the reign of the Fatimid caliph al-Muʿizz (r. 953–975).

just decades after Ibn Ḥazm wrote the *Book of Religions* in Cordoba. The caliph's title, al-Mustaẓhir, like the Andalusī caliph's appointment of a Ẓāhirī judge, was evocative of the ideological dimensions of competition with the Fatimid "Esotericists" (*bāṭiniyya*). The Fatimid movement's claims to knowledge of the esoteric dimensions of the scriptural text undergirded the Ismāʿīlī theologians' conceptions of the caliph as a Platonizing semi-messianic (*mahdī*) guide. The Fatimids' projection of this philosophical image of Ismāʿīlī theology, as seen in Ibn Ḥazm's work in the previous chapter, and as depicted in al-Ghazālī's refutations of the Ismāʿīlīs in this chapter, constituted a challenge to the majority Sunnī Islamic world on multiple fronts. Not only did it challenge conceptions of sound knowledge and leadership among the networks of predominantly Sunnī and growing Imāmī (Twelver) Shiite scholars, but it also challenged the authority of the Abbasid caliphs themselves. The Abbasid caliphs projected a specific model of leadership not as semi-messianic

Figure 3.2. Ptolemaic model of a celestial map or macrocosm, as represented in a sixteenth-century Ottoman manuscript.

guides, as in the Fatimid case, but rather as sources of imperial unity and bibliophile guarantors of the scholars' wide-reaching religious authority.

The Fatimid Ismāʿīlī challenge became a more immediate political threat with the rise of the non-Fatimid breakaway Nizārī Ismāʿīlī movement, whom the Fatimids called polemically the *Ḥashīshiyya* (figuratively "the rabble"), and who became the famous "Assassins" of European literary imagination.[1] The Nizārī Ismāʿīlīs politically threatened the Abbasid caliphate and its Seljuk military governors from centers very close to Baghdad and were accused of planning assassinations, making them a much more imminent threat than Fatimid proselytizing missions. The political significance of al-Ghazālī's *Scandals of the Esotericists (Faḍā'iḥ al-Bāṭiniyya)* is in how it illustrates a continuing Fatimid political backdrop of Sunnī scholarly debates about the theological soundness of Aristotelian logic and Platonizing theories in psychology and cosmology.[2] This Fatimid political context of al-Ghazālī's writings has been the subject of much research.

Albert Hourani placed the writing of the *Scandals of the Esotericists* (*Faḍā'iḥ al-Bāṭiniyya*) as chronologically later than the *Incoherence of the Philosophers* (*Tahāfut al-Falāsifa*) and earlier than the *Moderation in Belief* (*al-Iqtiṣād fī l-Iʿtiqād*).[3] This possible chronology suggests that the Abbasid–Fatimid rivalry was secondary to the motivations of many of the text's arguments, which include philosophical criticisms of Fatimid cosmology and esoteric scriptural hermeneutics. Frank Griffel, however, has pointed out recently that although the text was court-commissioned, it was likely based on an earlier lost Persian text titled *Proof of Truth in Response to [and Refutation of] the Esotericists* (*Ḥujjat al-Ḥaqq fī l-Radd ʿalā l-Bāṭiniyya*).[4] For the purposes of the current study, this chronology is important because it recalls an important question that was asked about the work of Ibn Ḥazm and the refuters of Ibn Masarra in the last chapter: Were some of al-Ghazālī's fundamental positions on Graeco-Arabic philosophy and esoteric knowledge shaped by the political threat of the Fatimids, whose theologians integrated these forms of knowledge into a major challenge to the Abbasid caliphs' political authority and the predominantly Sunnī scholars' religious authority? One could ask more cautiously if the Fatimid presence more simply colored the way al-Ghazālī articulated the gravity of certain positions, particularly given that he condemned in a non-binding legal opinion (*fatwā*) certain philosophical positions in the *Incoherence of the Philosophers* (*Tahāfut al-Falāsifa*). Recent studies by Omid Safi and Farouk Mitha are important in this regard in helping illustrate the following point: Although al-Ghazālī's nuanced discussions of philosophy and Sufism show significant continuity throughout his early and later work, suggesting that his basic intellectual positions were formulated independent of the contingencies of Abbasid–Fatimid politics, the challenge of the Fatimids nonetheless loomed large in the articulation of his positions.[5] Paul Walker, in this context, has highlighted how the development of a Abbasid-Ismāʿīlī political and theological polemic colored juridical discourse.[6] The relevance of the Fatimid context in the current chapter is especially significant as it helps contextualize a particular aspect of al-Ghazālī's work, namely what Alexander Treiger has argued to be the philosophical orientation of al-Ghazālī's Sufi metaphysics.[7]

The Fatimid context of al-Ghazālī's work is important for understanding the development of two interrelated sides of his legacy, namely his methodologically Aristotelian-Avicennan logic-oriented philosophical theology (neo-Ashʿarism) and his more loosely Platonizing Sufi metaphysics. In the latter case, his Platonizing Sufism became entangled with new eleventh- and twelfth-century scholarly debates in al-Andalus about Graeco-Arabic philosophy and Sufi esoteric hermeneutics with the rise of the Ghazālian Sufis, when the Fatimid political context continued to inform scholarly debates about philosophy and scriptural esotericism.

Kenneth Garden and Delfina Serrano have both shown how al-Ghazālī's conceptions of the Sufis' saintliness were at the center of the political and religious controversy over his work in Almoravid-era al-Andalus, when philosophical forms of Sufism were flourishing in the decades leading up to the scholar and Sufi Ibn ʿArabī's (d. 638/1240) career.[8] Whether this later twelfth- and thirteenth-century flourishing of a Ghazālian or Ghazālī-influenced Sufism in al-Andalus was directly connected with the early tenth-century Platonizing metaphysics of Ibn Masarra remains to be investigated, but the continuity in early and later Andalusī scholarly interest in Graeco-Arabic philosophy and the mystics' esoteric hermeneutics is clear.

Treiger's examination of al-Ghazālī's conceptualization of inspiration points to key philosophical dimensions of al-Ghazālī's Sufism that might explain why later philosophically oriented Sufi metaphysicians in al-Andalus like Ibn Qasī had a strong interest in al-Ghazālī's corpus.[9] At the same time, in an effort to highlight how these more philosophical forms of Sufi metaphysics existed alongside forms of Sufism that were less philosophical, Vincent Cornell has identified how even this Ghazālian tradition in al-Andalus had a much more practical and ethical bent in the writings of many Andalusī Sufis who did not theorize elaborate systems of metaphysics. This point has called into question Miguel Asín Palacios' original theory that Ibn Masarra initiated a tenth-century philosophical form of Sufism that dominated Andalusī Sufism until the thirteenth-century rise of Ibn ʿArabī. Maribel Fierro, however, has brought new attention to early trends in al-Andalus that likely primed the scholars for the reception of al-Ghazālī's writings.

Fierro's research examines evidence in the era immediately preceding the transmission of al-Ghazālī's work, when scholars of the eleventh-century Taifa era debated whether saintly miracles (*karāmāt al-awliyā'*) were a genuine phenomenon.[10] Ibn Ḥazm in this era argued that the only miracles to speak of soundly are those of prophets. Other scholars, including some of his students, argued that miracle performance of a lesser degree is possible and scripturally verified. They pointed to the case of the Qur'anic representation of a miraculous event in the life of Mary, the mother of Jesus. Ibn Ḥazm argued that scripture does indeed ascribe a miracle to Mary, namely her communication with angels, but explains it by arguing that Mary was a female prophet, and that therefore the miracle associated with her is a prophetic miracle (*muʿjiza*) and not what the Sufis in al-Andalus came to identify as saintly miracles (*karāmāt al-awliyā'*). Fierro's work suggests that the connection of these twelfth-century Ghazālian Sufis to the tenth-century controversy over Ibn Masarra was mediated by the rise of Taifa-era scholars such as al-Ṭalamankī, who absorbed aspects of the mystics' ritual piety. This Taifa-era debate in al-Andalus about mysticism during the rise of an early Sufi metaphysics is significant because it points to a new post-Masarrī chapter of scholarly debate about Graeco-Arabic philosophy and esoteric scriptural hermeneutics. This new debate was still shaped by the continuing ascendancy of the Fatimids in the early twelfth century, and it erupted with the rise of politically powerful Almoravid-era Sufis, such as the political revolutionary Ibn Qasī (d. 546/1151). The writings of al-Ghazālī's most important Andalusī student and critic, Abū Bakr b. al-ʿArabī (d. 543/1148), show that already in the period of al-Ghazālī's Almoravid-era transmitters, this new controversy over Andalusī Sufi metaphysics emerged against the backdrop of a continuing set of Sunnī scholarly concerns over the Fatimids' Platonizing doctrines in psychology and cosmology and their esoteric hermeneutical underpinnings. That is, in an echo of the political and religious debate about Ibn Masarra's mysticism-influenced Platonizing theological writing in the Andalusī Umayyad period, and also echoing the rise of Ibn Ḥazm's logic-oriented Ẓāhirī response to Neoplatonism and scriptural esotericism in the Taifa period, the Almoravid period (r. 1040–1187) saw the Fatimid political challenge continuing to inform how the Sunnī-majority scholarly world articulated positions about the place of Graeco-Arabic philosophy in Sunnī conceptions of theological knowledge and communal guidance in belief.

In the case of al-Ghazālī, who lived in Abbasid-Seljuk Baghdad when the Almoravids ruled al-Andalus, his simultaneous critique and defense of philosophy in his court-commissioned condemnation of the Fatimids, together with his influential and Platonizing Sufi metaphysics, illustrate the following point: three centuries of caliphal rivalry between the Fatimids and their neighbors in al-Andalus and Abbasid Iraq informed debates in the majority-Sunnī world about the validity of Graeco-Arabic philosophy in conceptions of ruling political culture and scholarly guidance of the community. Before turning to the controversy over the Ghazālian Sufis in al-Andalus and the political rise of Ibn Qasī in Chapters 4 and 5, the remainder of this chapter offers a critical analysis of how the Fatimids' Platonizing political leadership and theology became part of al-Ghazālī's counterpoint to his call for an Aristotelian-Avicennan logic-oriented theology.

A Political Response to Platonizing Cosmologies

As a political critique of Fatimid and Nizārī Ismāʿīlīsm, al-Ghazālī's *Scandals of the Esotericists* is especially illustrative of a point seen in Part I. Specifically, intellectual debates about modes of knowledge such as Graeco-Arabic philosophy and esoteric scriptural hermeneutics became particularly contentious among scholars and politicians because of their contemporary implications for political authority. The *Scandals of the Esotericists*, often overlooked by scholars in favor of al-Ghazālī's *Incoherence of the Philosophers*, sheds light on how the political framework of contemporary criticisms of the Ismāʿīlīs' philosophical theology shaped Sunnī-majority articulations of where Graeco-Arabic philosophy fit in scholarly conceptions of valid theological knowledge and guidance of the community. The text is especially notable for what was already seen in al-Andalus in Chapter 2, namely the Ibn Ḥazm-like acceptance of Aristotelian logic as a counterpoint to the Ismāʿīlīs' Platonizing psychology and cosmology. At the start of the text, in a section indicating that the Ismāʿīlīs' methods "draw on ideas of the dualists and the philosophers (*falāsifa*)," al-Ghazālī sums up their overall approach:

> They [Ismāʿīlīs] mixed the ways of the ancients, as they are between the schools of the [Iranian] dualists and the philosophers (*falāsifa*), going back and forth between the two, [but] they only move around the [outer] limits of [Aristotelian] logic in their arguments.[11]

al-Ghazālī's representation of Ismāʿīlīsm closely echoes Ibn Ḥazm's representation of Ismāʿīlīsm. Both authors identified problematic aspects of Graeco-Arabic philosophy in their larger critique of Ismāʿīlī theology. In the case of Ibn Ḥazm's representation, while he discussed Ismāʿīlīsm as philosophical in its cosmology, he typically avoided explicitly naming Graeco-Arabic philosophy (*falsafa*) as part of the basis of Ismāʿīlī metaphysics and preferred to represent Ismāʿīlīsm as being entangled with "dualist" and emanationist doctrines of Zoroastrianism. In Ibn Ḥazm's case, there appeared to be a rhetorical strategy in this representation, which was to claim that Graeco-Arabic philosophy was indeed a legitimate science that was useful for the Islamic sciences because of its logical underpinnings despite the apparent unsoundness of its Platonizing emanationist cosmologies. al-Ghazālī, in contrast, explicitly identifies Graeco-Arabic philosophy alongside pre-Islamic "dualism" as part of the basis of Ismāʿīlī doctrines, but like Ibn Ḥazm, he indicates that true logic leads to conclusions different than what Ismāʿīlī metaphysics claims. As in the writings of Ibn Ḥazm, al-Ghazālī does entangle Ismāʿīlism in a specific way with one side of philosophy, namely what he identifies as dualist doctrines evocative of Zoroastrianism, which he believes contrasts with an ostensibly more sound side of philosophy, namely logic. This dichotomy of a good and bad side of philosophy is more explicit in al-Ghazālī's work than in Ibn Ḥazm's work, but in both cases, Ismāʿīlism and Iranian religious traditions are represented as part of the unsound side of that dichotomy. From a modern perspective, one can say that both scholars took issue with Aristotelian logic's Neoplatonic conclusions in cosmology and psychology, even as al-Ghazālī appeared to have been more receptive of those doctrines in some of his later texts.

> But ultimately, they [the Ismāʿīlīs] took counsel with a group among the Zoroastrians (*majūs*) and Mazdians (*mazdakiyya*) and a smattering of the transgressing dualists and a large group among the transgressing ancient philosophers (*al-falāsifa al-mutaqaddimūn*).[12]

Taken together, al-Ghazālī's coupling of ancient Hellenistic philosophy and pre-Islamic Iranian religions with contemporary Ismāʿīlism is important in how it frames a fundamentally important point that runs through both this text and the earlier texts of Ibn Ḥazm: Graeco-Arabic philosophical doctrines, when misinterpreted, undergird problematic models of political and religious authority that challenge the sound communal leadership of the scholars and the Abbasid caliph.[13]

As one might expect based on Ibn Ḥazm's similar presentation, and in what further contextualizes the earlier controversy over Ibn Masarra, al-Ghazālī's representation of Ismāʿīlism as an Islamic intellectual tradition that inherited a philosophically oriented Iranian dualist set of doctrines is part of a familiar argument. Specifically, he faults the doctrinal liberties taken by Ismāʿīlī theologians and proselytizers in their esoteric scriptural hermeneutics and in their application of this hermeneutic to the world's ontology.[14] He makes this point in his explanation of the names he associates with Ismāʿīlism, including the "Esotericists" (*bāṭiniyya*) and "Seveners" (*sabaʿiyya*). He suggests that the latter term has two explanations: (1) the seven imams of Ismāʿīlism, to whom we know the Fatimid Ismāʿīlīs added in their own claim to a continuing Ismāʿīlī imamate, and (2) the seven planets that they claim order the world, a doctrine that Ibn Ḥazm indicated was central to the Ismāʿīlīs' esoteric hermeneutic.

The first section [of this text] is on the names that they have been called through different periods and times ... As for the Esotericists (*bāṭiniyya*), they are called this because of their claim that for all the manifests (*ẓawāhir*) of the Qur'an and the [Prophetic] reports are hiddens (*bawāṭin*) that go into the manifests like the course of a seed in its shell. [They claim that the manifests'] form in the imagination is [as a set of] clear images for the ignorant, while they are for the intellectual ones and the clever ones [only] symbols and allusions to [hidden] realities.... As for the [name] Seveners (*sabaʿiyya*), they are called this for two reasons ... the second is their saying that the ordering of the lower [sublunary] world, meaning what is encompassed by the sphere of the moon, is explained by the seven celestial bodies, the highest of which is Saturn, followed by Mercury, Mars, the Sun, Venus, Saturn, and the Moon. This method is taken from the transgressions of the astrologers and goes back to the ways of the dualists who claim that through these seven planets, light controls those parts mixed with darkness.[15]

al-Ghazālī shares familiar concerns seen earlier in Ibn Ḥazm's work about Ismāʿīlīsm's esoteric scriptural hermeneutics, highlighting the problematic association of an elect with a special layer of meaning hidden from the masses. He takes issue in particular with their use of a macrocosm-microcosm paradigm of causality. This presentation of these names' meanings is illustrative of how Ismāʿīlīsm's mix of philosophical doctrines and esoteric hermeneutics continued to be a challenge to the Sunnī-majority scholars. Specifically, this philosophically oriented scriptural esotericism suggested the notion of a philosophical and esotericist Ismāʿīlī elect who could potentially undermine the theological basis of the role of the scholars as communal guides. For al-Ghazālī, this notion was epitomized in another name for the Ismāʿīlīs, the *taʿlīmiyya*, which he discusses in the same section as the passage cited earlier.

In combination with the philosophical and hermeneutically esoteric nature of Fatimid Ismāʿīlī theology, and in the context of Abbasid awareness of proselytizing followers throughout Abbasid lands, the Ismāʿīlī notion of *taʿlīm* appears to have indicated to scholars like al-Ghazālī that the Fatimid leadership was using a didactic method of popularizing its theological methods in order to attract followers to its philosophical cosmology and its belief in the caliphal leadership of a semi-messianic Platonizing Ismāʿīlī guide.[16] This teaching to potential initiates, he explains, includes these various esoteric readings of scripture and philosophical readings of the world. In the passage that follows, he offers a picture or stereotype of this didactic process in Ismāʿīlīsm, describing proselytizing followers inspiring popular interest in these hermeneutical methods and readings of worldly phenomena in order to instill doubt in the minds of the masses about the current state of their Islamic knowledge.

Doubt-instillation (*tashkīk*) refers to when an [Ismāʿīlī] proselytizer befriends individuals and intellectually endeavors to change their belief by shaking their belief in what they already sincerely believe. The way [the proselytizer] does this is that he begins questioning them about the wisdom in the decisions of the rules of Islam, the more obscure elements of [doctrinal] issues, unclear meanings among the verses, and anything that does not have a clear meaning. So he says of the unclear meanings in scripture, "What is the meaning of [the set of letters] *Alif Lām Ra* and *Kāf Ha Ya ʿAin Ṣād* and *Ḥa Mīm* and *ʿAin Sīn Qāf* and so on, which are found at the beginnings of the [scriptural] chapters?". He asks, "Do you see that the designation of these letters were made to coincide with the utterance of tongues, meaning that they designate secrets underneath them that have not occurred in other cases [of these letters' use]? It does not appear to me that this is just for amusement or done pointlessly without some purpose."[17]

It is important to keep in mind the extent to which the specific process of looking for interior or esoteric meanings in scripture and applying a *ẓāhir-bāṭin* hermeneutic to a reading of the world as a text is not specific to Ismāʿīlīsm and applies to various other hermeneutically esoteric traditions, especially Sufi esotericism and particular Graeco-Arabic sciences such as alchemy and astrology. al-Ghazālī is specifically critical of Ismāʿīlī esoteric hermeneutics in the passage just cited because he finds it particularly subversive of sound conceptions of communal guidance and valid notions of political and religious leadership.[18] From the extraction of ostensibly hidden meanings of the isolated letters of scripture to the symbolic interpretation of worldly phenomena, the methods of Ismāʿīlī hermeneutical esotericism are for al-Ghazālī part of a larger problematic method used by Ismāʿīlī proselytizers of the Fatimid and Nizārī political movements to induce in the scripture-reading masses certain skepticism of the scholars' (*ʿulamāʾ*) ability to identify the deepest cosmological truths of the Qur'an. In inspiring this doubt, he explains, they inspire interest in an alternative layer of theological belief and ultimate guidance provided by the Ismāʿīlīs' leadership. The fact that al-Ghazālī finds Ismāʿīlī forms of hermeneutical esotericism subversive of the scholars' religious authority in particular emerges in the rest of his discussion:

[The Ismāʿīlī proselytizer] instills doubt in [these individuals] in the [meanings of] the reports of the Qur'an, so he says, "What is the reason the gates of heaven are eight and the gates of hell are seven? And what is the meaning of His saying, 'and carrying the throne of your Lord above them that day are eight,' and His saying (Most High), 'Upon them are nineteen?' … It appears to me that all of this is not devoid of a secret." Then [the proselytizer] instills doubt in [these individuals] in [their understanding of] the creation of the world and the body of man and says, "Why are the skies seven without being six or eight? And why were the celestial bodies that move about seven, and the constellations twelve? Why in the head of man are there seven orifices: two eyes, two ears, two nostrils, and mouth, but in his body two orifices only? And why was the human head made according to the structure of the letter *Mīm* – and his hands if he extends them posteriorly according to the structure of the *Mīm*, and the two feet according to the structure of the *Dāl* such that if all were brought together – it becomes the image of [the written name] Muḥammad? Do you see that there is a figural meaning and symbol here? How great are these wonders! And how great is creation's neglect of it!" He continues bringing out this type of discussion until he instills doubt in his interlocutor and makes him believe that below these manifests (*ẓawāhir*) are [hidden] secrets that were blocked from him and his companions, and he brings out in [them] a longing to seek it further.[19]

What emerges in his longer discussion is the extent to which the Ismāʿīlīs' use of esoteric hermeneutics and Graeco-Arabic philosophical doctrines in psychology and cosmology is ultimately entangled with the Ismāʿīlīs' challenge in religious authority. The epistemic methodology he references – including the notion of man as a microcosm of a world, and the appeal to scripture to validate a philosophical understanding of complex cosmological phenomena – is not unique to the Ismāʿīlīs given this methodology's parallelism in the early writings of the philosophers and some Sufis. It is specifically in the way these doctrines proceed forth from the Fatimid leadership and proselytizing circles as an argument in favor of defining a new Ismāʿīlī elect that informs al-Ghazālī's special criticism of Ismāʿīlīsm's philosophical and hermeneutically esoteric doctrinal mix.[20] Given how closely connected each of his criticisms are – from his discussion of their esoteric hermeneutics and their philosophical cosmology to their notions of religious authority – one can begin to identify how his criticism of Ismāʿīlī authority shapes his Ibn Ḥazm-like critique of Graeco-Arabic philosophy in this particular text. In this critique, discussed in the next section of this chapter, he problematizes common Platonizing cosmological doctrines and defends a scaled-down approach to logic.

A Philosophical Critique of Fatimid Political Authority

Foremost among the problems al-Ghazālī identifies in Fatimid Ismāʿīlī theology is a philosophical misunderstanding of divine agency. al-Ghazālī characterizes Ismāʿīlī cosmology as inclusive of the notion of hypostases that mediate God's agency in the world, and he sees in Ismāʿīlī discussions of the Pen and Tablet a problematic glossing of scriptural notions using unsound philosophical meanings. He begins by asking the reader how many groups one can find with erroneous beliefs "imitating [blindly] Plato and Aristotle and some group of sages claiming virtue?"[21] Among these types of groups, he asserts, are some among the "philosophers and dualists and those confused in religion. They believed that the legal injunctions are just constructed traditions, and that the miracles are embellished stories."[22] Though he appears to dismiss Plato and Aristotle, he actually points the reader to the conclusion that Plato and Aristotle should be distinguished from the problematic philosophical doctrines of those who claim to follow these two ancient philosophers. Among these claimants, he points to the Ismāʿīlīs, whose theology he characterizes in classic Neoplatonic terms of logical emanationism. Specifically, in the passage that follows, he criticizes the Ismāʿīlīs as one of the various philosophically oriented groups that articulate non-temporal emanationist cosmologies, and he makes the explicit argument that such groups are, in essence, pseudo-philosophers. That is, while Ibn Ḥazm identified this emanationist cosmology as Iranian metaphysics inherited by the Ismāʿīlīs, al-Ghazālī describes this emanationist cosmology as an Ismāʿīlī attempt to follow Plato and Aristotle, distinguishing both philosophers from the Platonizing doctrines in cosmology and psychology found in the Ismāʿīlīs' writings.

Some of the doctrines transmitted in [the Ismāʿīlīs'] treatises indicate that they speak of two pre-eternal deities, with none being first in terms of time, yet one of them is the [logical] cause of the existence of the second. The name of the first one that causes is the "prior" one. This first one is Intellect. The second one is Soul. They claim that the first is complete in actuality and the second is deficient because it is caused [by the first]. Perhaps they [likely] presented this to the masses, deriving this [concept] from verses of the Qur'an, as in His saying, "We sent down"[23] or "We portioned out."[24] They allege that these are indications of plurality not produced by one [creative cause], and that for this reason He says, "Glorify the Name of Your Lord the Most High," as an allusion to the prior of the two deities as though referring to the higher one.... They might also say: Revelation called the two the Pen and the Tablet, and the first is the Pen, as the Pen issues forth (*mufīd*) and the Tablet gains (*mustafīd*), and the one that issues forth is above the one that gains. They might also say that the name of the latter is *qadar* (measure, proportion) in the language of revelation, and this is that with which God created the world when he said, "We created everything by measure."[25]

Ismāʿīlīsm is at the center of al-Ghazālī's criticism of contemporary theological movements that claim to follow the ancient philosophers. In his criticism of their cosmology, which is nearly identical to contemporary

Neoplatonic cosmology and psychology, he in effect argues that the Plotinian cosmology of Intellect and Soul is simply pseudo-philosophy. He represents this cosmology as philosophical dualism that contemporary claimants to philosophy teach to the masses using esoteric readings of scriptural notions like the Pen and the Tablet in an unsuccessful attempt to, as he previously mentioned, follow Plato and Aristotle. Whether claimants to philosophy choose to talk about the scriptural Pen or the philosophical Intellect, which they identify as the same cosmological concept, their understanding of the Pen's or Intellect's priority to the scriptural Tablet or philosophical Soul is problematically a priority in causality and not in time. The specific problem al-Ghazālī has with this framework parallels Ibn Ḥazm's criticism of Masarrī conceptions of the Throne. Both al-Ghazālī and Ibn Ḥazm argue that these concepts compromise God's oneness and God's voluntary agency as the singular *mudabbir* (governing orderer) of the world. As discussed in Chapter 2, this notion of *mudabbir* is a notion of agency that does not quite fit in the philosophical categories of primary and secondary causality, but rather deals with the question of the existence of a principle of voluntary agency that creates, encompasses, and governs all other agents as an independent cause and independent voluntary agent. For both al-Ghazālī in this text and for Ibn Ḥazm in his *Book of Religions*, that specific principle of voluntary agency is God, Who has a Divine Will. Therefore, in their respective views, the Ismāʿīlīs' philosophical and scripturally esoteric interpretations of the Pen and Tablet as Graeco-Arabic philosophical principles misinterpret this divine agency in the problematic suggestions of a necessary procession of causality and the existence of pre-eternal causes that exist alongside God.[26] The problems created by the notion of the Pen and Tablet (or Intellect and Soul) as pre-eternal principles of agency are exacerbated by the fact that the atemporal priority of the Pen or Intellect implies their existence outside of time, such that their preexistence in a pre-eternal world contradicts the notion of God's creation of the world out of nothing (*ex nihilo*).

They [the Ismāʿīlīs] say that the world is pre-eternal, that is, its existence is not preceded by a lack of time but rather that the latter originated from the prior, which in turn was the first originated thing, and that from the first originated thing occurred the Universal Soul instilling its particulars in these bodies. [They say that] from the movement of the Soul, heat is produced, and that coldness is produced from stationariness, and that from these two come humidity and dryness, and that from these are produced the qualities of the four elements: fire, air, water, and earth.[27]

al-Ghazālī explains that the Ismāʿīlī theologians argue that the Pen and Tablet, or the Intellect and Soul, issue forth from the Universal Intellect as a generation of the Soul, and that the Soul's movement and stationariness is responsible for the existence of heat, coldness, and ultimately the earthly elements. al-Ghazālī, in sum, represents Ismāʿīlī esoteric hermeneutics as encompassing a familiar Neoplatonic cosmology that the Ismāʿīlīs interpret through scriptural terminology. Ibn Ḥazm was somewhat coy about identifying this Ismāʿīlī cosmology as a form of Graeco-Arabic philosophical cosmology, preferring to peg this emanationist cosmology to Iranian dualism. In this text, al-Ghazālī is eager to identify this cosmology as a problematic interpretation of Plato and Aristotle, identifying both by name. Like Ibn Ḥazm, however, al-Ghazālī also ascribes some of these cosmological errors to Zoroastrianism. He claims that these beliefs are:

... inherited from the dualists and the Magians [that is, Zoroastrians] in speaking of two deities, changing the phrase [used by the Magians] from "light and darkness" to "prior and subsequent" in an error taken from the language of the philosophers (*falāsifa*) in their claim that the first principle is the cause of the existence of the Intellect by way of necessity, not by way of intention and will, and that [Intellect] came from His essence without intermediary. They affirm pre-eternal existences with necessary causal relations, and they call them intellects, and they connect the existence of every sphere to an intellect from among these intellects.[28]

Arguing that Ismāʿīlīsm shares erroneous cosmological assumptions with Zoroastrianism, and that Ismāʿīlīsm drew on the philosophers, al-Ghazālī presents very familiar objections to the implications of emanationist doctrines. Not only do these emanationist cosmologies imply the problem of the pre-eternity of the world, but they also associate each sphere with ensouled cognizant celestial beings in a cosmology that implies a world of multiple pre-eternal intellects mediating God's agency, this agency being furthermore a non-contingent necessary agency by virtue of God's existence and not by virtue of God's Divine Will.[29] For al-Ghazālī, the fact that the Ismāʿīlīs apply a philosophical framework to what he sees as a mix of Zoroastrian cosmology and Islamic scriptural language does not alleviate the problem of this Zoroastrian-like dualism. al-Ghazālī seems to indicate that the use of philosophical language compounds the problem, a point that harmonizes with his claim that the philosophers themselves erred in major areas of cosmology and psychology on the basis of their flawed philosophical interpretation of prophecy:

As for their [the Ismāʿīlīs] belief in the prophets, what they transmit is close to the method of the philosophers, that the prophet is a person upon whom a pure holy faculty emanated from the prior [causal principle] by way of the subsequent [caused principle], that is, [a holy faculty] that is ordered because it receives what is in the Universal Intellect of particulars upon [the holy faculty's] contact with the

Universal Intellect, just as this happens to some of the more clever souls in their sleep. [They believe that while such clever souls] see the occurrences of the conditions of the future [in their dreams], either explicitly as it is, or in degrees through images that need interpretation, the prophet is the one who is able to do this while awake. [They claim that] the prophet realizes the intellectual universals upon the appearance of that light and through the purity of the prophetic faculty, just as the images of sensible objects appear in the visual faculty of the eye in accordance with the appearance of the light of the sun upon the surfaces of bodies. [The Ismāʿīlīs] claim that the archangel Gabriel is this Intellect that emanates upon [the prophetic faculty] and is a symbol of this [Intellect], meaning they reject the idea that [the archangel Gabriel] is a corporeal individual composed of a subtle body that is dense and occupies space, moving [and descending] from above to below.[30]

The nature of the Ismāʿīlīs' philosophical interpretation of prophecy represents the climax of al-Ghazālī's criticism of the Ismāʿīlīs' philosophical theology and their use of Platonizing doctrines in psychology and cosmology.[31] He is particularly critical of their use of Graeco-Arabic philosophy's understanding of prophecy as the pinnacle of philosophical truth acquisition in a Plotinian emanationist cosmology oriented around the spiritual ascent of the human intellect to the Universal Intellect. One of the problematic results of a philosophical interpretation of prophecy, according to his argument, is this explanation of theological doctrines according to the metaphysical principles of Neoplatonic emanationist cosmology. Despite his later theories about the workings of inspired knowledge and prophecy, al-Ghazālī in this text contests how the philosophers and some of the Ismāʿīlīs represent Gabriel as one of the intellects in a Plotinian, or more accurately, a Fārābian cosmology. The entire edifice of a Fārābian philosophical interpretation of scripture is based on the contested notion that scripture agrees with the cosmological conclusions of the philosophers. As discussed in Chapter 1, Ibn Masarra and the Ismāʿīlīs locate this harmony between philosophy and scripture in the esoteric meaning of scriptural references to concepts like the Pen and Tablet. In Chapter 2, Ibn Ḥazm turned this philosophically oriented scriptural esotericism upside down by scaling back what falls under philosophical certainty and expanding what falls under philosophical possibility, leaving a logic-oriented, univocal, scriptural hermeneutic to fill in that knowledge. Here, al-Ghazālī's critique of the Ismāʿīlīs' philosophical theology likewise criticizes how they, like the philosophers, deduced philosophical conclusions based on intellectual leaps that were not logically deduced but were rather inherited blindly from philosophical predecessors without giving enough weight to either logic or evidence in the scriptural text.[32]

In the passages that follow, al-Ghazālī brings together all of the elements of his criticism of the Ismāʿīlīs' Platonizing cosmology and their esoteric scriptural hermeneutic by criticizing Ismāʿīlī conceptions of religious authority, which are built on these philosophically oriented forms of knowledge. al-Ghazālī argues that the Ismāʿīlī conception of a philosophical *imām* encourages creedal imitation, or *taqlīd*, of the Ismāʿīlī *imām*'s philosophical doctrines, which are informed by the claim to having a special esoteric hermeneutical ability inherited from the previous Ismāʿīlī *imāms*. He describes the philosophical Ismāʿīlī *imām* as a figure who claims infallibility, who dictates certain claims as truths, and who expects creedal imitation (*taqlīd*) by a general populace that looks to the *imām* for salvation. In this framework, he critiques in particular the Ismāʿīlīs' philosophically oriented doctrines on the soul and its eschatology, highlighting like Ibn Ḥazm before him what he sees as a misinterpretation of the scriptural notion of the *ghayb*.

> [They claim that] every time the soul increases in distance from the world of the sensory things, it increases in its [non-sensory] spiritual knowledge. [They claim that] likewise when [the soul] is removed from the senses in sleep, it rises to the world of the unseen (*ghayb*), and it senses what will appear in the future either as it is, such that it does not need to be interpreted, or through images, such that interpretation is necessary.... [They claim that] in the case of the degenerate soul sunken in the world of nature that turns away from guidance of the infallible *imāms*, it stays forever in fire, [which they interpret as] meaning that it is forever in the corporeal world, transmigrating through different bodies, so it is constantly in pain and does not separate from the body except when it goes to meet another body.... This is their school of thought in the matter of resurrection, and it is at its core the school of thought of the philosophers (*falāsifa*).[33]

al-Ghazālī criticizes the Ismāʿīlī conception of the *imām*'s religious authority by criticizing the Ismāʿīlī leadership's claims to special access as an elect to philosophical truths in psychology, cosmology, and soteriology. He is particularly critical of the philosophical doctrine of the body's eschatology as being independent of the soul, a doctrine that follows from the philosophical claim that the soul's intellectual progress dissociates it from the corporeal world of the body as the soul achieves a cognitive spiritual ascent toward higher intellects in ultimate philosophical salvation.[34] Painting Ismāʿīlism and Graeco-Arabic philosophy with a very broad brush, al-Ghazālī even claims that the Ismāʿīlīs and philosophers coalesce around the doctrine of the transmigration of souls. Certainly he was aware that there was significant diversity in doctrines on the soul among the many schools of thought in Ismāʿīlism and Graeco-Arabic philosophy. His use of a broad brush in what amounts to an intellectual stereotype indicates that certain dimensions of his discussion serve the text's larger goal of conflating together Ismāʿīlism with the following: the philosophers' cosmologies, the ontological dualism popularly associated with Zoroastrianism, esoteric scriptural hermeneutics, and the philosophers' soteriology. In effect, he has contrasted all of these with what he believes to be the sound knowledge of a scaled-down use of Aristotelian logic and the scriptural text read less esoterically. In his presentation, he builds what amounts to a dichotomy between two sets of knowledge: one a scripturally esoteric Platonizing theology in Ismāʿīlīsm and the other an Aristotelian logic-oriented theology. This dichotomy is simultaneously one between the communal leadership of a Platonizing "esotericist" Ismāʿīlī guide or *imām*-caliph and the communal leadership of the methodologically logic-oriented majority-Sunnī scholars and the caliph, the latter who guarantees the communally guiding role of the scholars (*ʿulamāʾ*). This argument appears more explicitly at the end of the text, where he claims that the true leader of the community is not the Ismāʿīlī *imām* who claims infallibility, but rather the Abbasid caliph, who makes a more limited religious claim to being the uniting figure of the community by guaranteeing the religious authority of the scholars. The strong political dimension of this argument, and the fact that he wrote this text as the chief judge of the Abbasid caliphate under caliphal patronage, sheds light on the extent that the continuing Fatimid–Abbasid and rising Nizārī–Abbasid rivalry informed the way al-Ghazālī articulated his critique of Platonizing theologies and scriptural esotericism as a counterpoint to his defense of Aristotelian-Avicennan logic, which he believed was a useful tool for Sunnī theology and jurisprudence.

When stepping away from the text and reconsidering the way he places a very broad set of philosophical and esoteric hermeneutical methods under the umbrella of Ismāʿīlīsm, one can recognize that the critique of Ismāʿīlīsm in the text's title is only one part of the treatise. His critique also applies to methodological trends among contemporary Sunnī scholars who were already synthesizing Graeco-Arabic philosophy with esoteric scriptural hermeneutics in their theological writing. Eleventh- and twelfth-centuries Sufis like Ibn Barrajān, discussed in the next chapter, are of particular interest in this case. Paradoxically, al-Ghazālī himself took a step in the direction of this philosophical Sufi tradition upon leaving Baghdad in what modern historians should read as a kind of backtracking of some of his earlier public criticisms of the Ismāʿīlīs' embrace of Platonizing doctrines seen here. The gateway to this turn to Sufism more generally was the corpus of early Sufi manuals in Iraq that included al-Makkī's tenth-century *Nourishment of Hearts* (*Qūt al-Qulūb*), a text transmitted by the same generation of Sahl al-Tustarī's followers that included Ibn Masarra.

In a development that paralleled Ibn Masarra's work, al-Ghazālī drew on Platonizing doctrines in psychology and cosmology in his mysticism-inspired writings, particularly the *Niche of the Lights*. Treiger's analysis of the Neoplatonic-Avicennan orientation of his mystical writings and conceptions of mystical inspiration may help explain how his Aristotelian-Avicennan logic-oriented Ashʿarism came to take on what historians such as Richard Frank argued to be a surprisingly Neoplatonic strand of thought that runs through some of his theological corpus.[35] While other historians continue to caution against overemphasizing the Neoplatonic strands of al-Ghazālī's Ashʿarism, the enduring medieval representation of al-Ghazālī as a figure who delved more deeply into philosophy than he originally intended is illustrative of how specific approaches to the mix of Islamic theology and Graeco-Arabic philosophy had achieved widespread acceptance in Sunnī theological writing by the twelfth century.

More specifically, as Part II shows, the philosophical dimensions of al-Ghazālī's parallel Ashʿarī and Sufi legacies developed a scholarly following in Almoravid-era and Almohad-era al-Andalus, where Ibn Ḥazm's logic-oriented philosophical theology and Ibn Masarra's Platonizing theological writing had already achieved widespread renown. Notably, the scholar and Sufi Ibn ʿArabī (d. 638/1240), who referred to al-Ghazālī's work throughout his writings, considered himself a follower of Ẓāhirism in jurisprudence and represented Ibn Masarra as a founding figure in Andalusī mysticism.[36] Equally notable is the Andalusī judge Abū Bakr b. al-ʿArabī (d. 543/1148), who was one of the figures responsible for transmitting al-Ghazālī's legacy westward and who was also a critic of both philosophy and Sufism. His political and theological opinions, discussed in the next and last section of this chapter, shed light on how the political controversy over the Fatimid Ismāʿīlīs continued to influence the way Sunnī-majority scholars articulated the contours of sound theology and acceptable forms of communal guidance.

Abū Bakr b. al-ʿArabī on the Philosophers and Sufis

In the previous chapter, Ibn Ḥazm's alternative to the Andalusī scholars' (*ʿulamāʾ*) diverse overtures to trends in esoteric hermeneutics, speculative theology, and Neoplatonic cosmology was his newly systematized version of Ẓāhirism. His new approach systematized the school of jurisprudence to include a dedicated Aristotelian logic-oriented theology that foreshadowed al-Ghazālī's own work further east.[37] When considering the intersection of Graeco-Arabic philosophy and esoteric scriptural hermeneutics as a single intertwined story from al-Andalus to Iraq, one can point to the career of one of Ibn Ḥazm's major critics – namely, the *qāḍī* of Seville Abū Bakr b. al-ʿArabī – as a period that bookmarks the end of one era and the beginning of another. In the first era, the focus of Part I of this book, the politics of the Fatimid caliphate loomed large in the scholarly and political discourse of the majority Sunnī world. In the second era, the focus of Part II of this book, the rise of Sufi political activists began to eclipse the earlier political controversy over the Fatimids. What linked the two eras were enduring Sunnī scholarly debates about modes of knowledge undergirding controversial models of political leadership, especially Graeco-Arabic philosophical doctrines in psychology and cosmology and esoteric scriptural hermeneutics.

The *qāḍī* Abū Bakr b. al-ʿArabī (d. 543/1148) lived at the end of the Taifa period of al-Andalus and the beginning of the Almoravid period, precisely when he could criticize Ibn Masarra, the Fatimids, Ibn Ḥazm, al-Ghazālī, and the Sufis together. While his father was a close student of Ibn Ḥazm, he himself was a student of al-Ghazālī following a trip together with his father to Baghdad.[38] In a fascinating mix of legacies very illustrative of the career of a reformist scholar of his era, Abū Bakr b. al-ʿArabī's historical and heresiographical *Protections from Catastrophes* (*al-ʿAwāṣim min al-Qawāṣim*) shows him to be a critic of the most important intellectual phenomena found in Andalusī intellectual history. In a single volume of writing, he demonstrated that he was equally a critic of esoteric scriptural hermeneutics, a critic of Ẓāhirī scriptural hermeneutics, a critic of the historical intersection of philosophical doctrines with the doctrines of the Ismāʿīlīs and Sufis, a major transmitter and follower of al-Ghazālī's works, and a critic of some of the philosophical and Sufi epistemological doctrines that he identified in al-Ghazālī's work.

As for his critique of esoteric scriptural hermeneutics, in a statement in his *ʿal-Awāṣim min al-Qawāṣim* that captures a major cross section of Part I of the current study, the *qāḍī* objects to the method of those who claim to read scripture for its ostensibly "interior" (*bāṭin*) and "exterior" (*ẓāhir*) meanings. Specifically, he begins his criticism by stating that "those who hear God's speech can be divided into some who make it entirely [hidden or] interior (*bāṭin*) [in meaning] and others who make it entirely [manifest or] exterior (*ẓāhir*) [in meaning]."[39] In this discussion, in a widely quoted statement about his travels between the *maghrib* and Baghdad, he asserts that "The first innovation (*bidʿa*) I encountered on my journey was the doctrine of the *bāṭin*, but when I returned I found the whole of the Maghrib had been filled with the doctrine of the *ẓāhir* by a foolish man from the outskirts of Seville named Ibn Ḥazm."[40] Kaddouri and Adang contextualize this famous passage in what they show to be the biographical dictionaries' representation of a Mālikī scholarly environment in the late Taifa and early Almoravid era of al-Andalus that was challenged by a robust and controversial Ẓāhirism movement, led by Ibn Ḥazm.[41] What remains elusive is what exactly this earlier interest in *bāṭin* was that had since been eclipsed by Ẓāhirism. From the perspective of Part I's examination of controversies over philosophical cosmologies and esoteric scriptural hermeneutics, one would expect that the Fatimid Ismāʿīlī movement should loom large in his discussion of esotericism.

As expected, in what echoes Ibn Ḥazm's and al-Ghazālī's discussion, the *qāḍī* takes on the Ismāʿīlī "esotericists" (*bāṭiniyya*) in a dedicated critique that represents the esoteric hermeneutics of the Fatimids and Ismāʿīlīs more broadly as a method entangled with Graeco-Arabic philosophical doctrines and pre-Islamic Iranian religious traditions. In a genealogy that he elaborates of the origins of the Ismāʿīlī "esotericists" in early Abbasid history, he claims that the powerful early Abbasid-era Barmakid ministers were among the original Ismāʿīlī "esotericists" who controlled the caliphate. He describes these early Ismāʿīlī "esotericists" as having "followed the creed of the philosophers (*yaʿtaqidūna ārāʾ al-falāsifa*)" and having "revived Zoroastrianism (*majūsiyya*)."[42] The *qāḍī* argues, furthermore, that it was under the Barmakids that a set of theologians, whom he names individually in the text, flourished and promoted problematic doctrines under the guise of further developing formal speculative theology (*ʿilm al-kalām*). In his elaboration of these doctrines, he presents and refutes a set of problematic cosmological theories that deal with, among other subjects, the nature of the superlunary world and questionable principles of causality.[43]

In other words, as seen in his predecessor Ibn Ḥazm's work, the *qāḍī*'s writings shed further light on how Sunnī doxographical writing represented Graeco-Arabic philosophy and esoteric hermeneutics as having become problematically entangled with Ismāʿīlī theology. What is critical to note is the other group that the *qāḍī* identifies in his analysis of problematic applications of Graeco-Arabic philosophy and esoteric hermeneutics. In what echoes conclusions in Part I about the importance of esoteric hermeneutics and Graeco-Arabic philosophy in understanding the controversy over Ibn Masarra's mysticism-influenced work in the Andalusī Umayyad era, the *qāḍī* discusses the Sufis of Iraq.

The criticism of the Sufis' esoteric hermeneutics appears specifically in the context of what the current study identified in Chapters 1 and 2 as that particular aspect of the early mystics' interior knowledge (*ʿilm al-bāṭin*) that uncovered certain ontological interior realities (*ghayb/bāṭin, ghuyūb/bawāṭin*) veiled behind various apparent or exterior phenomena (*shahāda/ẓāhir*) in the sensory world. As mentioned in Chapter 2, Ibn Ḥazm argued that these scriptural terms were hermeneutically misinterpreted by the Masarrīs. In Abū Bakr b. al-ʿArabī's own discussion of the problem of epistemology among the Sufis and early mystics, and specifically in his analysis of the scholar-mystics al-Muḥāsibī and al-Qushayrī, the *qāḍī* criticizes the Sufi claim that the purification of the soul (*ṭahārat al-nafs*) and chastening of the heart (*tazkiyat al-qalb*) as well as ascetic practices are somehow connected to the unveiling of certain hiddens or unseen ideas or realities (*yankashifu l-ghuyūb*).[44] Similarly, in the section of this text where he criticizes "the philosophers' discussion of God's essence," he mentions the Sufis again in a point that anticipates Nasrid-era criticisms leveled against Almoravid-era and Almohad-era Sufis of al-Andalus who were among the Sufi Ibn ʿArabī's contemporaries and immediate predecessors. Specifically, using the same terms of analysis articulated two centuries later by the Nasrid-era colleagues Ibn al-Khaṭīb and Ibn Khaldūn, the *qāḍī* states in this text that some Sufis believe problematically that it is God's essence that brings about all things, and that all things come about from God's essence according to an arrangement (*tartīb*) of causes and effects in which the singularity of God causes (*mubdiʾ*) the plurality of the world.[45] For al-Ghazālī, this doctrine was more a philosophical doctrine than one of the Sufis' doctrines. al-Ghazālī's famous critique of the philosophers in the *Incoherence of the Philosophers* included a criticism of this very doctrine on the necessity of causality in the Neoplatonic emanationist cosmology from the One, a doctrine that ran counter to the theological notion of God's Will and its divine contingencies.[46] The *qāḍī*, in contrast, has identified the Sufis as part of his criticism of the philosophers' discussion of God's essence. The commonality between his twelfth-century Almoravid-era representation of the Sufis' philosophically oriented metaphysics and the later fourteenth-century Nasrid-era representation of the Sufi metaphysicians offered by Ibn Khaldūn and Ibn al-Khaṭīb points to the following: from an early period dating back to the Taifa and Almoravid eras, and in a manner that echoed Ibn Ḥazm's criticism of Ibn Masarra, a scholarly criticism was in formation of the way the Sufis' doctrines were becoming controversially entangled with doctrines in Graeco-Arabic philosophy.[47] In this context, Ibn Masarra was likely one among many followers of the early mystic Sahl al-Tustarī who simultaneously engaged the philosophers, just as the writers of formal speculative theology, the Ismāʿīlīs, writers of legal theory, litterateurs, alchemists, astrologers, mathematicians, astronomers, physicians, and caliphs all engaged the philosophers from the earliest centuries of Islamic history. From the *qāḍī*'s perspective, this intersection of Graeco-Arabic philosophy and Sufism was a problematic one, as it potentially introduced into Islamic theological writing the same scripturally and inherently quesionable Platonizing doctrines in psychology and cosmology that made their way into Ismāʿīlī writing.

In sum, in what illustrates the enduring impact of the Platonizing and semi-messianic (*mahdī*) Fatimid Ismāʿīlī movement on the contours of Sunnī scholarly conceptions of sound theology between Cordoba and Baghdad, Ibn Ḥazm, his younger contemporary al-Ghazālī, and al-Ghazālī's one-time Andalusī student Abū Bakr b. al-ʿArabī all expressed concern over the mix of Graeco-Arabic philosophy and esoteric scriptural hermeneutics in Islamic theological writing in a dedicated critique of how this mix undergirded problematic Fatimid conceptions of communal leadership. It is the *qāḍī*'s additional criticism of the Sufis and early mystics of Iraq in his larger critique of the philosophers, the Fatimid Ismāʿīlīs, and the reformist Ẓāhirīs that makes his career bookmark the end of Part I and introduce Part II. In this book's examination of the dialectic of authority between ruling circles and scholars, analyzed through the lens of politically salient debates about Graeco-Arabic philosophy and esoteric scriptural hermeneutics, Part I traced the impact of the Abbasid–Fatimid and Andalusī Umayyad–Fatimid political rivalries on ongoing Sunnī scholarly debates about sound conceptions of scholarly leadership and communal guidance in belief. Part II of this book traces the diminishing of this Fatimid political backdrop amidst the rise of a second Platonizing and semi-messianic (*mahdī*) political movement that arose not within Ismāʿīlī circles, but among the Sufi metaphysicians – namely, Ibn Qasī's political revolt. Against the backdrop of Ibn Qasī's rebellion in Almoravid Portugal, Sufi metaphysicians among Ibn ʿArabī's immediate predecessors represented the new political challenge of the synthesis of Neoplatonic psychology and esoteric hermeneutics in a post-Fatimid age. In a significant pattern of continuity between the controversy over the Fatimids in the tenth and eleventh centuries and the critique of the Sufi metaphysicians in the twelfth and thirteenth centuries, scholarly positions on Graeco-Arabic philosophy's place in theological writing and conceptions of communal guidance continued to be articulated with an eye toward contemporary political phenomena.

Notes

1 Farhad Daftary discusses this point in the following: "Origins and Early Formation of the Legends," in Farhad Daftary, *The Assassin Legends: Myths of the Ismāʿīlīs* (London: I. B. Tauris, 2001), pp. 88–128.

2 As previously discussed, the role of the Ismāʿīlī theologians Muḥammad b. Aḥmad al-Nasafī (d. 332/943) and Ḥamīd al-Dīn al-Kirmānī (d. 411/1020) in incorporating Neoplatonic doctrines into Ismāʿīlī theological writing at an early period helps explain doxographical representations of the Ismāʿīlīs as a philosophically oriented group. Paul Walker, *Abū Yaʿqūb al-Sijistānī: Intellectual Missionary* (New York: I. B. Tauris 1998), pp. 14–25; idem, *Early Philosophical Shiism: The Ismāʿīlī Falsafa of Abū Yaʿqūb al-Sijistānī* (Cambridge: Cambridge University Press, 1993), pp. 3–66; idem *Ḥamīd al-Dīn al-Kirmānī: Ismāʿīlī Thought in the Age of al-Ḥakīm* (New York: I. B. Tauris, 1999), pp. 25–61.

3 George F. Hourani, "The Chronology of al-Ghazālī's Writings," *Journal of the American Oriental Society* 79 (1959): 225–33; idem, "A Revised Chronology

of al-Ghazālī's Writings," *Journal of the American Oriental Society* 104 (1984): 284–302.

4 Referencing passages from both *al-Munqidh min al-Ḍalāl* and *Faḍā'iḥ al-Bāṭiniyya*, Frank Griffel has pointed out that while the text was commissioned by the caliph's court, it may have drawn on this earlier Persian text. Frank Griffel, *al-Ghazālī's Philosophical Theology* (New York: Oxford University Press, 2009), p. 36ff.

5 Omid Safi, *The Politics of Knowledge in Premodern Islam: Negotiating Ideology and Religious Inquiry* (Chapel Hill: University of North Carolina Press, 2006), pp. 105–24; Farouk Mitha, *Ghazālī and the Ismā'īlīs: A Debate on Reason and Authority in Medieval Islam* (New York: I. B. Tauris, 2001).

6 Walker, *Early Philosophical Shiism*, pp. 3–23; Farhad Daftary, *Ismā'īlī Literature: A Bibliography of Sources and Studies* (New York: I. B. Tauris 2004), pp. 84–103.

7 Alexander Treiger, "Monism and Monotheism in al-Ghazālī's *Mishkāt al-Anwār*," *Journal of Qur'anic Studies* 9 (2007): 1–27; idem., *Inspired Knowledge in Islamic Thought* (New York: Routledge, 2011).

8 Kenneth Garden, "Al-Ghazālī's Contested Revival: *Iḥyā' 'Ulūm al-Dīn* and Its Critics in Khorasan and the Maghrib" (University of Chicago dissertation, 2005), pp. 144–223; idem, *The First Islamic Reviver* (New York: Oxford University Press, 2013), pp. 143–68; Delfina Serrano, "Why Did the Scholars of al-Andalus Distrust al-Ghazālī: Ibn Rushd al-Jadd's *Fatwā* on *Awliyā' Allāh*," *Der Islam* 83 (2006): 137–56.

9 Treiger, "Monism and Monotheism in al-Ghazālī's *Mishkāt al-Anwār*," pp. 1–27. For an early analysis of Ibn Qasī's use of passages from al-Ghazālī's work, see David R. Goodrich, "A Ṣūfī Revolt in Portugal: Ibn Qasī and His *Kitāb Khal' al-Na'layn*" (Columbia University dissertation, 1978).

10 Maribel Fierro, "The Polemic about the *Karamāt al-Awliyā'* and the Development of Sufism in al-Andalus Fourth/Tenth–Fifth/Eleventh Centuries," *Bulletin of the School of Oriental and African Studies* 55 (1992): 236–49.

11 *Faḍā'iḥ al-Bāṭiniyya*, p. 4

12 *Faḍā'iḥ al-Bāṭiniyya*, p. 18.

13 As Alexander Knysh has shown, Ibn Khaldūn makes this same argument in the interesting case of his criticism of Almoravid-era and Almohad-era Sufism more than one century after the Sufi rebellion of Ibn Qasī. Ibn Khaldūn even issued a *fatwā* in condemnation of Ibn Qasī's writings upon leaving Granada for Mamluk Cairo. Alexander Knysh, *Ibn 'Arabī in the Later in the later Islamic Tradition: The Making of a Polemical Image* (Albany: State University of New York Press, 2007), pp. 167–96.

14 Historians have pointed out that figures like al-Ghazālī may have had an imperfect understanding of the doctrinal distinctions between various Ismā'īlī groups based on limited access to their respective writings. Given that this treatise was a politically commissioned response to the Fatimids and Nizaris, however, it is worth considering the extent to which any inaccuracies can be explained by the treatise's entanglement with a political climate of polemics. In this context, references to the Magians and Mazdaism, which are together

a reference to the Zoroastrians, are illustrative of some of the rhetorical goals of the text. Like his student Abū Bakr b. al-ʿArabī and his predecessor Ibn Ḥazm, al-Ghazālī sought to argue more broadly that the Ismāʿīlīs owed something to the various syncretic traditions of early Islamic history that were connected to Iranian spiritual traditions and that were broadly deemed dualist in Islamic doxographies. An analysis of the development of an early critique of Iranian religious traditions, including how that critique overlapped with representations of the Ismāʿīlīs, can be found in *Encyclopedia of Islam*, 2nd edition, s.v. "Thanawiyya" (by Guy Monnot) and "Madjūs" (by Michael Morony); Guy Monnot, *Penseurs musulmans et religions iraniennes: ʿAbd al-Jabbār et ses devanciers* (Paris: Vrin, 1974), pp. 77–81, 88–91; Christoph J. Burgel, "Zoroastrianism as Viewed in Medieval Islamic Sources," in *Muslim Perceptions of Other Religions: A Historical Survey*, ed. Jacques Waardenburg (Oxford: Oxford University Press, 1999), pp. 202–12.

15 *Faḍāʾiḥ al-Bāṭiniyya*, p. 11.

16 In the context of this connection of philosophical knowledge and esoteric hermeneutics with a dynamic model of religious authority, one can identify noteworthy parallels between al-Ghazālī's representation of the Fatimid caliph's religious authority in the eleventh century and the saintly or semi-messianic authority of the Almohad caliph of the Islamic West (*maghrib*) in the twelfth century. Maribel Fierro has examined this connection, and it further illustrates how scholars and rulers in the Fatimid and post-Fatimid eras were engaged in an enduring process of debate over the implications for religious authority of philosophically oriented theological writing, whether the writing of Sufi metaphysicians or the Fatimid Ismāʿīlīs. Maribel Fierro, "The Almohads and the Fatimids," in *Ismāʿīlī and Fatimid Studies in Honor of Paul E. Walker*, ed. Bruce D. Craig (Chicago: Middle East Documentation Center, 2010), pp. 161–75; Dominique Urvoy, "La pensée d'Ibn Tumart," *Bulletin d'études orientales* 27 (1974): 19–44.

17 *Faḍāʾiḥ al-Bāṭiniyya*, p. 19.

18 To be sure, esoteric scriptural hermeneutics was seen as subversive of religious authority outside of and prior to the specifically Fatimid context, as discussed in Chapter 1. Early Graeco-Arabic philosophy, mysticism, and Shiism were all entangled with conceptions of an elect with special knowledge of interior scriptural meanings. Influential studies that have highlighted the place of esoteric hermeneutics in early scholarly debates include the following: James W. Morris, "Ibn ʿArabī's 'Esotericism': The Problem of Spiritual Authority," *Studia Islamica* 71 (1990): 37–55; Maribel Fierro, "Bāṭinism in al-Andalus: Maslama b. Qāsim al-Qurṭubī (d. 353/964), author of the *Rutbat al-ḥakīm* and the *Ghāyat al-ḥakīm* (Picatrix)," *Studia Islamica* 84 (1996): 87–112; Shlomo Pines, "The Limitations of Human Knowledge According to al-Fārābī, Ibn Bājja, and Maimonides," in *Studies in Medieval Jewish History and Literature*, ed. Isadore Twersky (Cambridge, MA: Harvard University Press, 1979), pp. 82–109; Mohammad Ali Amir-Moezzi, *The Divine Guide in Early Shi'ism: The Sources of Esotericism in Islam*, trans. D. Streight (Albany: State University of New York Press, 1994).

19 *Faḍāʾiḥ al-Bāṭiniyya*, p. 19.

20 Fatimid proselytizing was often represented by its opponents as being a somewhat secretive process oriented around esoteric scriptural hermeneutics. These representations echo what surviving evidence from early Ismāʿīlism indicates about the political manifestations of early Ismāʿīlism. What makes this representation potentially simplistic is the recorded diversity of groups that were connected to Ismāʿīlīsm but that had distinct political goals and that developed divergent epistemologies and models of religious authority. What is questionable in al-Ghazālī's picture of Ismāʿīlīsm, among other points, is the notion that the Ismāʿīlīs exclude the *ẓāhir* in their analysis of the *bāṭin*, when in fact esoteric exegesis was not identical across Ismāʿīlī traditions. In fact, writers using esoteric scriptural hermeneutics among Sufis and Ismāʿīlīs often emphasized the intertwining importance of the *ẓāhir* and *bāṭin* meanings in their *ẓāhir-bāṭin* hermeneutic. Some of this diversity of *ẓāhir-bāṭin* scriptural hermeneutics in Ismāʿīlī contexts is discussed in the following studies: Heinz Halm, *The Empire of the Mahdi: The Rise of the Fatimids* (Leiden: Brill, 1996); idem, *Kosmologie und Heilslehre der fruher Ismāʿīlīyya* (Wiesbaden: Franz Steiner, 1978); idem, "Methoden und Formen der frühesten ismailitischen Daʿwa," in *Studien zur Geschichte und Kultur des Vorderen Orients. Festschrift für Bertold Spuler zum siebzigsten Geburtstag* (Leiden: Brill, 1981), pp. 123–36; Samuel Miklós Stern, "The Early Ismāʿīlī Missionaries in North-West Persia and in Khurasan and Transoxania," *Bulletin of the School of Oriental and African Studies* 23 (1960): 56–90.

21 *Faḍāʾiḥ al-Bāṭiniyya*, p. 35. al-Ghazālī's question here is important because it reflects an aspect al-Ghazālī's eclectic epistemology that we know in previous chapters to have been found in the works of Ibn Masarra and Ibn Ḥazm. Specifically, in the writing of all three scholars, broad criticisms of Greek and Graeco-Arabic philosophy were entangled with a readiness to accept the veracity of key tenets of philosophy as part of larger reorientation of scriptural hermeneutics and Islamic theological writing. Walker has noted that even the Ismāʿīlīs, despite the strong association of their cosmologies with Neoplatonic doctrines, also criticized Graeco-Arabic philosophy in their larger assimilation of the philosophers' conclusions. Walker, *Early Philosophical Shiism*, pp. 3–67.

22 *Faḍāʾiḥ al-Bāṭiniyya*, p. 36.

23 Qur'an 15:9, 76:23.

24 Qur'an: 43:32.

25 Qur'an 54:49; *Faḍāʾiḥ al-Bāṭiniyya*, p. 38.

26 Historians have recognized al-Ghazālī's use of philosophical language in his Sufism, including his *Niche for the Lights*, which introduces the question of who the text's intended audience was. Lazuar-Yafeh has argued that the *Niche* was intended for a smaller audience receptive to Sufism, even as the text was nonetheless widely transmitted and circulated. The broad scholarly reception of the text in the medieval Islamic world might be explained by Michael Marmura's reading of al-Ghazālī's corpus, which suggests that philosophical notions in al-Ghazālī's work were tied down to or harmonized with Ashʿarī notions of causality. Hawa Lazuar-Yafeh, *Studies in al-Ghazzali* (Jerusalem: Magnes Press, 1975); Michael Marmura, "al-Ghazālī's Chapter on Divine Power in the *Iqtiṣād*," *Arabic Sciences and Philosophy* 4 (1994): 279–315.

27 *Faḍā'iḥ al-Bāṭiniyya*, p. 39.
28 *Faḍā'iḥ al-Bāṭiniyya*, p. 39.
29 In addition to the previously mentioned research on al-Ghazālī's interpretation of causality and the studies in note 48, Marmura's research remains a useful starting point for considering how al-Ghazālī sought to reconcile philosophical approaches to causality with principles in Ash'arism. Michael Marmura, "Ghazālian Causes and Intermediaries," *Journal of the American Oriental Society* 115 (1995): 89–100; idem, "Did al-Ghazālī Deny Secondary Causality?" *Studia Islamica* 47 (1978): 83–120.
30 *Faḍā'iḥ al-Bāṭiniyya*, p. 42.
31 Farouk Mitha soundly identifies that there is something complex or elusive about al-Ghazālī's specific criticisms of Ismā'īlī epistemology and his later adoption of Sufism, but he problematically locates the contradiction as a change of position on Ismā'īlī *ta'līm* doctrine. What is more likely is a change of position on Sufi religious authority as an acceptable locus for elaborating an esoteric scriptural hermeneutic that engaged select aspects of Aristotelian-Neoplatonic cosmology and psychology. Mitha, *al-Ghazāli and the Ismā'īlīs*, pp. 1–48; Treiger, *Inspired Knowledge in Islamic Thought*, pp. 48–80; idem, "Monism and Monotheism in al-Ghazālī's *Mishkāt al-Anwār*," pp. 1–27.
32 While figures like the philosophers, including the Brethren of Purity, offered philosophical interpretations of knowledge transmission that influenced their understanding of prophecy, their arguments did not necessarily challenge the inimitability of prophecy as much as they challenged the scholars. Yves Marquet, *La philosophie des Ikhwān al-Ṣafā'* (Algiers: Societe Nationale d'Edition et de Diffusion, 1975), pp. 477–508; idem, "Révélation et vision véridique chez les Ikhwān al-Ṣafā'," *Revues des Etudes Islamiques* 32 (1964): 27–44.
33 *Faḍā'iḥ al-Bāṭiniyya*, p. 46.
34 Interestingly, particularly in al-Andalus, philosophers and Sufis often faced this same accusation of adherence to theories of *ḥulūl* and *ittiḥād*. Ibn Sab'īn and his student al-Shushtarī, both Sufis who integrated Graeco-Arabic philosophy with Sufism, were accused of *ḥulūl*. Ibn Taymiyya faulted Ibn 'Arabī's doctrine of *waḥdat al-wujūd* for promoting a kind of *ḥulūl*. Philosophers were accused of *ḥulūl*, but more so in the form of the similar doctrines of intellectual *ittiṣāl* and *ittiḥād*. Lourdes M. Alvarez, *Abū al-Ḥasan al-Shushtarī: Songs of Love and Devotion* (Mahwah: Paulist Press, 2009), 15–20; *Encyclopedia of Islam*, 2nd edition, s.v. "*Waḥdat al-Shuhūd*" (by William Chittick); *Encyclopedia of Islam*, 2nd edition, s.v. "Ghulāt" (by Marshall G. S. Hodgson). See also Calero Sacall's discussion of this accusation in María Isabel Calero Secall, "El proceso de Ibn al-Jaṭīb," *al-Qantara* 22 (2001): 421–61.
35 While Richard Frank highlighted ways that al-Ghazālī should be read as an Avicennan philosopher within the Ash'arī theological tradition, Michael Marmura examined al-Ghazālī's commitment to doctrines in Ash'arī occasionalist causality in a way that highlights the limits of interpreting al-Ghazālī's works too philosophically. Griffel has sought to harmonize the analysis of Frank and Marmura by examining ways that al-Ghazālī's causality, while framed in terms of Ash'arī causality and cosmology, were laden with Avicennan commitments in a manner that was not always obvious from

al-Ghazālī's language. Treiger's analysis is critical in this context for highlighting how some of those Avicennan commitments may have been connected to his Avicennan approach to Sufi epistemology and conceptions of inspired knowledge. These findings further contextualize the results of Sands and Whittingham regarding the cosmological concepts in Ghazālī's Sufi interpretations. Richard Frank, *Creation and the Cosmic System: Al-Ghazālī and Avicenna* (Heidelberg: Carl Winter-Universitätsverlag, 1992). Michael Marmura, "Avicenna's Theory of Prophecy in the Light of Ash'arite Theology," in *The Seed of Wisdom: Essays in Honour of T. J. Meek*, ed. W. S. McCullough (Toronto: Toronto University Press, 1964), pp. 159–78; Griffel, *al-Ghazālī's Philosophical Theology*, pp. 3–18; Martin Whittingham, *al-Ghazālī and the Qur'an: One Book, Many Meanings* (New York: Routledge, 2007); Kristen Sands, *Sufi Commentaries on the Qur'an in Classical Islam* (London: Routledge, 2006).

36 Ignaz Goldziher's appreciation of the point that later Sufis were "easily accommodated" within Ẓāhirism appears to be based on his sound recognition that the *ẓāhir* for Ibn Ḥazm is not the first meaning that comes to one's mind upon hearing a word. This approach to the *ẓāhir* meaning allowed Sufis such as Ibn 'Arabī as well as predecessors like Ibn Barrajān (see Chapter 4) to identify in some cases the *ẓāhir* meaning with the *bāṭin* meaning. Ignaz Goldziher, *The Ẓāhirīs: Their Doctrine and Their History*, trans. Wolfgang Behn (Leiden: Brill 2008), pp. 160–70.

37 In addition to both early and more recent analyses of the development of Ẓāhirīsm in al-Andalus, the studies of Kaddouri have shed light specifically on how Ibn Ḥazm became a controversial figure in al-Andalus both during his lifetime and posthumously. Samir Kaddouri, "Refutations of Ibn Ḥazm by Mālikī Authors from al-Andalus and North Africa," in *Ibn Ḥazm of Cordoba: The Life and Works of a Controversial Thinker*, eds. Camilla Adang, Maribel Fierro, and Sabine Schmidtke (Leiden: Brill, 2013), pp. 539–600; idem "Ibn Ḥazm al-Qurtubī (d. 456/1064)," in *Islamic Legal Thought: A Compendium of Muslim Jurists*, eds. Oussama Arabi, David S. Powers, and Susan A. Spectorsky (Leiden: Brill, 2013), pp. 211–38. Key earlier works include Goldziher, *The Ẓāhirīs*, pp. 160–70; Roger Arnaldez, *Grammaire et théologie chez Ibn Ḥazm de Cordoue: essai sur la structure et les conditions de la pensée musulmane* (Paris: J. Vrin, 1956); Camilla Adang, "The Spread of Ẓāhirism in al-Andalus in the Post-Caliphal Period: The Evidence from the Biographical Dictionaries," in *Ideas, Images, Methods of Portrayal: Insights into Classical Arabic Literature and Islam*, ed. Sebastian Gunther (Leiden: Brill, 2005), pp. 297–345. Christopher Melchert, *The Formation of the Sunni Schools of Law, 9th–10th Centuries C.E.* (Leiden: E. J. Brill, 1997).

38 Drawing especially on Abū Bakr b. al-'Arabī's *al-'Awāṣim min al-Qawāṣim*, Griffel has offered a critical analysis of the *qāḍī*'s pedagogical connections with al-Ghazālī. Griffel, *al-Ghazālī's Philosophical Theology*, pp. 62–70. An overview of his life can be found in Ibn Khallikān, *Wafayāt al-A'yān wa-Anbā' Abnā' al-Zamān* (Bullaq, 1858), 1:697; *Encyclopedia of Islam*, 2nd Edition, s.v. Abū Bakr b. al-'Arabī (by J. Robson).

39 Abū Bakr b. al-'Arabī, *al-'Awāṣim min al-Qawāṣim*, ed. 'Ammār Ṭālibī (Cairo: Maktabat Dār al-Turāth, 1997), p. 248.

40 Abū Bakr b. al-ʿArabī, *al-ʿAwāṣim min al-Qawāṣim*, p. 248. This passage also attracted the interest of al-Dhahabī. al-Dhahabī, *Tadhkirat al-Ḥuffāẓ* (Hyderabad: Dāʾirat al-Maʿārif al-ʿUthmāniyya, 1968–70), 3:1149.

41 Kaddouri, "Refutations of Ibn Ḥazm by Mālikī Authors from al-Andalus and North Africa," pp. 539–600. Adang, "The Spread of Ẓāhirism in Al-Andalus," pp. 297–345.

42 *al-ʿAwāṣim min al-Qawāṣim*, pp. 61–2.

43 *al-ʿAwāṣim min al-Qawāṣim*, pp. 63–70.

44 *al-ʿAwāṣim min al-Qawāṣim*, p. 23. Griffel has analyzed the *qāḍī*'s criticisms of al-Ghazālī's philosophical and Sufi doctrines, summing up this particular section of the text by highlighting that the *qāḍī* was critical of the idea that there was a "connection between certain practices in one's worship and the unveiling of some kind of hidden knowledge. The subject of whether Sufi practice or the asceticism of the 'friends of God' (*awliyāʾ*) leads to superior religious insight seems to be the focal point of the dispute about al-Ghazālī's work in the Muslim West." Griffel, *al-Ghazālī's Philosophical Theology*, pp. 62–70. While Griffel's analysis is not framed in terms of the issue of Sufi esoteric hermeneutics, one can argue that esoteric hermeneutics is at the heart of this issue, given the larger context of how both the *qāḍī* and earlier figures in al-Andalus debated the way the Fatimids, Sufis, and others sought to articulate knowledge of *bāṭin* and *ghayb* in scripture and in the world as "text." In this way, the current study further contextualizes the controversy over al-Ghazālī's conceptualization of Sufi saints (*awliyāʾ*), analyzed in depth by Garden and Serrano, as part of a longer debate in al-Andalus about the Sufis' interior knowledge (*ʿilm al-bāṭin*). Kenneth Garden and Delfina Serrano have both analyzed the controversy over Sufi sainthood in al-Andalus, which we know to have been related in many cases to Sufi esoteric hermeneutics. Serrano, "Why Did the Scholars of al-Andalus Distrust al-Ghazālī;" Garden, *Al-Ghazālī's Contested Revival*, pp. 144–89.

45 Abū Bakr b. al-ʿArabī, *al-ʿAwāṣim min al-Qawāṣim*, pp. 122–30.

46 B. D. Dutton, "Al-Ghazālī on Possibility and the Critique of Causality," *Medieval Philosophy and Theology* 10 (2001): 23–46; T. Kukkonen, "Possible Worlds in the *Tahāfut al-Falāsifa*: al-Ghazālī on Creation and Contingency," *Journal of the History of Philosophy* 38 (2000): 470–502.

47 Knysh, *Ibn ʿArabī in the Later Islamic Tradition*, pp. 184–96.

Part II

Philosophical Sufis among Scholars (*ʿulamāʾ*) and Their Impact on Political Culture

4 Sufi Metaphysics in the Twelfth Century

The twelfth century saw the rise of the Almoravid and Almohad dynasties, which took over al-Andalus's Taifa-period city-states and incorporated them into larger polities based in modern-day Morocco. The rise of Sufism in scholarly circles of this era was a product of the way itinerant Mālikī scholars (*'ulamā'*) in North Africa transmitted al-Ghazālī's works westward to al-Andalus, where the Cordovan scholar Ibn Masarra's earlier mysticism-influenced legacy remained influential. The most prominent Sufis among the scholars in the Almoravid era included Ibn Barrajān (d. 536/1141) of Seville and Ibn al-'Arīf (d. 536/1141) of Almería. Both were summoned to the Almoravid capital of Marrakesh in 1141, their lives cut short in mysterious circumstances shortly thereafter. Their reputations as scholarly Sufis appear to have become entangled in their own lifetimes with the political and scholarly controversies over more politically activist Sufi movements such as the rebellion of Ibn Qasī (d. 536/1151), who revolted in 1144 and founded a separate state. Ibn Qasī emerged from outside of or on the margins of scholarly circles. His revolt against the Almoravids was part of a contentious period at the end of the Almoravid era that saw several political movements turn against the Almoravids, including the rising Almohads. This chapter examines the controversy over Ibn Barrajān's legacy in a political context. It asks in particular whether his mystical conception of scholarly knowledge and communal guidance, which drew on philosophical doctrines and esoteric hermeneutics, helps explain why he fell afoul of Almoravid ruling circles. Notably, these circles sought to participate politically in ongoing scholarly debates about sound models of communal leadership.

Sufism and Its Integration of Philosophical Doctrines

Ibn Barrajān (d. 536/1141) was a *ḥadīth* scholar and Sufi who was remembered both as the "al-Ghazālī of al-Andalus" and as a kind of

Figure 4.1. The Almohad mosque of Tinmel, built in 1156 in the High Atlas Mountains south of Marrakesh.

spiritual *imām* of 137 villages throughout North Africa and al-Andalus.[1] Like his one-time student Ibn al-ʿArīf (d. 536/1141), his career was abruptly cut short the year that both scholars were summoned in separate incidents to the Almoravid capital for questioning. They died

Figure 4.2. Entry portal of the Mosque of the Booksellers (Jāmiʿ al-Kutubiyya), built in Almohad-era Marrakesh in the late twelfth century and once adjacent to a marketplace (*sūq*) for books.

shortly thereafter in mysterious circumstances, just three years before Ibn Qasī (d. 546/1151), whom Ibn al-ʿArīf wrote about, led a rebellion against the Almoravids (r. 1040–1147) and captured the city of Mértola.[2] There, Ibn Qasī eventually aligned himself with the advancing Almohads

(r. 1121–1269), who replaced the Almoravids and whose ascendancy saw the rise of two of al-Andalus's most famous Peripatetic philosophers and four of its most famous Sufi metaphysicians: the philosopher and Sufi Ibn Ṭufayl (d. 580/1185), the philosopher and *qāḍī* Ibn Rushd (Averroes d. 595/1198) who was Ibn Ṭufayl's protégé, the Ashʿarī theologian and Sufi al-Shūdhī (d. ca. 600/1203), the later Ashʿarī theologian and Sufi Ibn Marʾa (d. 611/1214), the influential Sufi Ibn Sabʿīn (d. 669/1270), and perhaps the most famous of the Andalusī Sufi metaphysicians, Ibn ʿArabī (d. 638/1240).[3] As previously mentioned, the latter three Sufis all identified Ibn Masarra (d. 319/931) as a foundational figure in Andalusī Sufi metaphysics, even as al-Ghazālī's dual legacy as a philosophical Ashʿarī theologian and Platonizing Sufi metaphysician loomed just as large in al-Andalus. Ibn ʿArabī in particular also made reference to his immediate predecessors in the Almoravid period, praising Ibn Barrajān and Ibn al-ʿArīf and calling into question the mystical credibility of the political revolutionary Ibn Qasī. The intersection of Ibn Masarra and al-Ghazālī's legacies in twelfth-century Andalusī Sufism has been the subject of recent studies that have grappled with the philosophical underpinnings of many Andalusī examples of Sufi metaphysics, which later medieval scholars such as Ibn Khaldūn criticized in the late fourteenth century.

Modern historians have contextualized Ibn Barrajān's legacy as part of a larger twelfth-century flourishing of Sufism in al-Andalus following an earlier tenth-century transmission of Iraq's mysticism in the era of Ibn Masarra. In agreement with the early research of Miguel Asín Palacios, both Maribel Fierro and Claude Addas have identified tenth- and eleventh-century Andalusī figures like Ibn Masarra and his critics, including al-Ṭalamankī, as influential figures in the rise of Sufism in al-Andalus long before the transmission of al-Ghazālī's popular writings of philosophical theology and Sufism.[4] According to Fierro, the influence of al-Ṭalamankī, who was a scholarly critic of Ibn Masarra and supporter of the doctrine that saint miracles (*karāmāt al-awliyāʾ*) exist, may have helped prime al-Andalus for the reception of al-Ghazālī's works.[5] The fact that he was simultaneously a critic of Ibn Masarra, a student of Ibn Ḥazm, and a supporter of the doctrine on saint miracles points to multiple episodes in al-Andalus of interest in mysticism and specifically Sufi ritual piety prior to the transmission of al-Ghazālī's writings. What underlines the lasting legacy of Ibn Masarra's early tenth-century articulation of a mysticism-influenced philosophical theology is how Sufi metaphysicians of the twelfth and thirteenth centuries represented Ibn Masarra. As mentioned, al-Andalus's most famous Sufis, including Ibn Sabʿīn's student al-Shushtarī (d. 668/1269) and their contemporary Ibn ʿArabī, explicitly represented Ibn Masarra as one of the founders of their Sufi tradition.[6] At the same time, they recognized the importance of al-Ghazālī in their writings.

Though he wrote in the Islamic East, al-Ghazālī was an extremely important figure in the eleventh and twelfth centuries among circles in the Maghrib interested in the trajectory of the scholarly sciences in Baghdad. Vincent Cornell and Kenneth Garden have shown how al-Ghazālī's *Revival of the Religious Sciences* (*Iḥyā' 'Ulūm al-Dīn*), which brought together elements of ethics, philosophical theology, legal theory, and Sufi ritual piety, was a source of great interest among Andalusī scholarly Sufi circles.[7] By the twelfth century, Mālikī scholars who were receptive to al-Ghazālī's *Revival of the Religious Sciences* and to Sufi notions of theological belief and communal guidance found themselves at the center of both scholarly and political controversy when the *Revival* became part of a book-burning campaign, which was sanctioned by the Almoravids in collaboration with particular Mālikī scholars critical of al-Ghazālī's writings.[8] That the Almoravids countenanced this polemic against al-Ghazālī's legacy reflects how at least some figures within the political administration were interested in curbing the rise of Sufism, including the notion of the living Sufi saint as a model of communal leadership found increasingly within and outside of scholarly circles.[9] In the case of Sufis such as Ibn Barrajān, this chapter shows how his dynamic model of communal leadership was built on a mystical articulation of philosophical doctrines and esoteric hermeneutics, one that critics appear to have found problematically reminiscent of Fatimid Ismā'īlī doctrine. As Part I shows, esoteric hermeneutics and philosophical doctrines in cosmology and psychology were pulled into contentious political and scholarly debates. These debates focused on the intellectual underpinnings of controversial models of communal leadership, especially that of the Platonizing semi-messianic (*mahdī*) "esotericist" Fatimid caliphs of tenth-century Cairo. The Fatimids and their theologians were rivals of the bibliophile Andalusī Umayyad and Abbasid caliphs, whose simultaneously Islamic, Persianate, and Hellenistic forms of political culture saw an enduring patronage of Graeco-Arabic philosophy together with a distinct conception of the Sunnī caliph: the caliph as a uniting figure of empire and a supporter of the Sunnī scholarly networks' religious authority.

The current chapter argues that Ibn Barrajān fell afoul of ruling circles in part because of the way his Sufi metaphysics resembled aspects of philosophically oriented theological writing that undergirded two contemporary political circles: the philosophical theology of the once powerful Ismā'īlī "esotericist" theologians, who were still influential in the contemporary late Fatimid era (r. 909–1171), and the newly controversial Sufi metaphysics of the political revolutionary Ibn Qasī (d. 546/1151) and his political contemporaries, examined in the next chapter. In both cases, claims to communal leadership and guidance in belief were built on a synthesis of esoteric hermeneutics and Platonizing philosophical doctrines in psychology and cosmology. Since the early centuries of the Islamic-era Middle East, and in continuity with patterns of the late antique period, these modes of knowledge had significant salience for questions of leadership among a scripture-valuing, semi-Hellenizing, Middle Eastern urban population. Muslims in the early Islamic-era Middle East were familiar with the widely circulating notion that ancient sages, such as Hermes-Idrīs and Plato, achieved some kind of spiritual ascent to cognitive and spiritual enlightenment that resembled Islam's prescribed path toward communal virtue in the present life and the afterlife.[10]

In what points to how medieval politicians identified and took issue with Ibn Barrajān's mystical model of communal guidance and its underpinnings in philosophy and esoteric hermeneutics, the one-time Nasrid courtier and Mamlūk *qāḍī* Ibn Khaldūn represented the Almoravid-era Sufis, including Ibn Barrajān himself, as "people of theophany" (*aṣḥāb al-tajallī*) in criticism of their mystical use of philosophical doctrines, which he found evocative of philosophical monism and the Fatimid Ismāʿīlīs' semi-messianic religious authority.[11] Alexander Knysh has contextualized Ibn Khaldūn's criticism of the philosophical and mystical predecessors of Ibn ʿArabī, including Ibn Barrajān, in an analysis that shows how medieval political administrators were well attuned from the tenth century through the fourteenth century and beyond to the politically controversial parallels between the Fatimid Ismāʿīlīs and the Andalusī Sufi metaphysicians in terms of their related conceptions of theological knowledge and communal guidance. In the eyes of critics, the notion of a saintly Sufi mystic was in some cases too similar to the historical model of a Platonizing "esotericist" Ismāʿīlī theologian and semi-messianic Ismāʿīlī caliph. In both his historical *Muqaddima* and in a *fatwā* that he issued as one of four head judges in Mamluk Egypt after he left Nasrid al-Andalus, Ibn Khaldūn made three specific points on the issue of Ibn Barrajān's and the Andalusī Sufis' respective claims to knowledge and authority.[12]

First, Ibn Khaldūn represented the "people of theophany" (*aṣḥāb al-tajallī*) as those Andalusī Sufis, including Ibn Barrajān, whom he accused of believing that God's oneness has two opposite tendencies, transcendence and immanence, with the latter tendency causing the unfolding of divine existence into the multiplicity of the world. This point attributes philosophical monism to Andalusī Sufis in a way that echoes al-Ghazālī's similar criticism of the Fatimid Ismāʿīlīs' use of philosophical psychology in their understanding of God and the world.[13] Second, Ibn Khaldūn represented Andalusī Sufis, including Ibn Barrajān, as imprudently claiming knowledge of the "unseen" (*ghayb*) in what directly echoes al-Ghazālī's court-sponsored criticism of the Fatimid Ismāʿīlī conception of the Ismāʿīlī *imām*-caliphs and proselytizing theologians as questionable claimants of hidden or interior (*bāṭin*) knowledge of scripture and the world.[14] In agreement with Ibn Ḥazm's criticisms of Ibn Masarra and the Fatimids, Ibn Khaldūn argued that the "unseen" (*ghayb*) is knowledge that should be left to the prophets. He explained that the masses' ability to fulfill their religious obligations and achieve salvation should not be shattered by complex theories of metaphysics articulated in an unsound manner.[15] Third, and most importantly, Ibn Khaldūn argued that Ibn Barrajān and the other Andalusī Sufis offered conceptions of saintly Sufi guidance that problematically resembled Fatimid Ismāʿīlī conceptions of semi-messianic leadership.[16] In this regard, his sharpest criticism was reserved for the writings of the political revolutionary and Sufi Ibn Qasī (d. 536/1151), who emerged from outside scholarly circles and whose extant treatise Ibn Khaldūn argued should be burned. In what illustrates how esoteric hermeneutics and certain philosophical doctrines in psychology and cosmology continued to be politically salient long after the fall of the Fatimids and during the rise of Akbarian (Ibn ʿArabīan) Sufi metaphysicians, Ibn Khaldūn's one-time colleague Ibn al-Khaṭīb, the chief Nasrid minister, was even prosecuted unsuccessfully by the Nasrid-era chief *qāḍī* al-Nubāhī (al-Bunnāhī) for his attempt to integrate these doctrines into the political culture of the Nasrids. Ironically, the Nasrids were themselves patrons of philosophy and Sufi metaphysics.[17]

In sum, the writings of fourteenth-century Nasrid- and Mamluk-era politicians like Ibn al-Khaṭīb and Ibn Khaldūn, together with the case against Ibn al-Khaṭīb by the chief *qāḍī* al-Nubāhī (al-Bunnāhī), point to specific aspects of the way medieval philosophically oriented Sufi doctrines on theological knowledge and communal guidance attracted enduring political and scholarly suspicion in a premodern political context in which philosophical doctrines were closely tied to controversial political movements, from the Fatimid caliphate in Cairo to Ibn Qasī's rebel state in Almoravid Portugal. Ibn Khaldūn's points suggest that politically influential Almoravid-period ruling circles and scholarly critics likely viewed Ibn Barrajān using the same lens through which more politically activist Sufi movements, such as Ibn Qasī's revolution, were analyzed and criticized.[18]

The political controversy over Ibn Barrajān's Sufi metaphysics and communal leadership in the twelfth century demonstrates strong continuity with the earlier controversy over Ibn Masarra's scholarly movement

Figure 4.3. The Konya manuscript of the scholar (*ʿālim*) and Sufi Ibn Barrajān's (d. 1141) major Qur'an commentary (*tafsīr*), which includes examples of Graeco-Arabic analysis of the celestial bodies and mystical exegesis.

in the tenth and eleventh centuries, which emerged against the enduring backdrop of the Fatimids' claim to a distinct caliphate. This continuity in political contexts indicates the following point: with the rise of Sufi metaphysicians within and outside scholarly circles, the intellectual solutions that Andalusī scholars were articulating in defining their own knowledge and scholarly religious authority had become, in the twelfth century, as much a challenge to the Andalusī ruling circles' political leadership as the Fatimid movement had been in the tenth and eleventh centuries. That this new challenge in authority came from within Sunnism and specifically within scholarly circles, in contrast with the Fatimids' ideological challenge as a Shiite political theology, foretold the way the dialectic of authority in Sunnism between ruling circles and scholars was about to shift. The Almoravid rulers could either have used their political power to suppress the religious authority of these new scholarly Sufis, or alternatively to adapt their own political culture by assimilating and appropriating these new conceptions of knowledge and leadership.[19] As discussed in Chapter 6 of this book, the Almohads attempted the latter approach, celebrating al-Ghazālī as a kind of patron saint of the dynasty, sponsoring the works of Ibn Ṭufayl and Averroes at the court, and representing the Almohad dynasty's founder, Ibn Ṭūmart, as a type of saintly and semi-messianic figure evocative of both the Sufis and the Fatimids. The earlier Almoravids, however, attempted the former approach, publicly clashing with the Sufi followers of al-Ghazālī's legacy, including Ibn Barrajān, in a manner reminiscent of the Andalusī Umayyads' condemnation of the scholar Ibn Masarra.[20]

The Konya Manuscript of Ibn Barrajān's Major *Tafsīr*

Ibn Barrajān's major Qur'an commentary (*tafsīr*), *Tafsīr Ibn Barrajān* (MS Yusuf Ağa 4744–6), offers a critical window into the elusive tradition of Andalusī Sufi metaphysics in the generation before Ibn ʿArabī. Examined here in its manuscript form, the text provides a window into the reality that Ibn Khaldūn's representation of Ibn Barrajān, as one of various Andalusī Sufis who brought together philosophical and mystical doctrines in a dynamic conception of communal guidance, echoes some of what the text itself actually argues.[21]

Recent examinations of the major *tafsīr* by Gril, Idrīsī, and Mazyādī have indicated that for Ibn Barrajān, reasoned contemplation (*iʿtibār*) is one key element in Ibn Barrajān's goal of realizing the intellect's (*ʿaql*) full potential to discover the interior dimensions of the Qur'an and the world, and that the Names of God are an essential aspect of Ibn Barrajān's overall method.[22] Bringing the study of Ibn Barrajān's Sufism more squarely into its political context, Bellver has argued recently that the tensions were more religious than political given how the judiciary saw the rise of Sufis as a challenge in authority.[23] However, in agreement with Fierro and Cornell, Serrano's and Garden's research on the controversy over Sufism in the Almoravid era shows that such religious tensions had deep political implications in their contemporary context because of the way scholarly religious authority, including in its more Sufi-oriented forms, was contested and negotiated at the highest ruling levels.[24] That is, religious and political controversies were hardly distinguishable in cases when ruling circles participated directly in scholarly debates, which occurred both in the context of ruling participation in the judiciary and in the case of ruling participation in scholarly writerly culture through the patronage of books and authors.[25] In this regard, the doctrinal system of Ibn Barrajān's major *tafsīr* remains a key unexamined piece of evidence of how Fatimid- and post-Fatimid-era political controversies over the theological use of philosophical doctrines in psychology and cosmology ultimately pushed Sufi metaphysics into the center of a new political controversy, one informed both by the earlier alarm over the Fatimid political movement and the rising alarm over Sufi political movements.

A closer examination of the text that follows, with an eye on the familiar intersection of esoteric hermeneutics and philosophical doctrines, demonstrates that Ibn Barrajān framed his *tafsīr* in a way that conceived of the ideal Sufi among the scholars as a philosophically minded Sufi metaphysician, one able to witness mystically the divine omnipotence Ibn Barrajān characterized as immanent in the celestial macrocosm. As discussed in the next sections, Ibn Barrajān's Sufi method was based on a theory of knowledge oriented around esoteric hermeneutics integrated into a system of mystical metaphysics, one that engaged common Graeco-Arabic philosophical ideas such as the agency of the celestial bodies in the world and the nature of man as a microcosm. The mystical elect for Ibn Barrajān were the gnostics (*ʿārifūn*) and saints (*awliyāʾ*), whose mystical knowledge included knowledge of the meanings of God's Names (*maʿānī al-asmāʾ*). As in the case of Ibn Masarra's writings, Ibn Barrajān understood the Names to be indicative of God's omnipresent agency that is veiled by the secondary causality of the created world. In this text, Ibn Barrajān acknowledges that key aspects of his representation of a cognitive and spiritual ascent toward mystical witnessing of the divine realm make his approach look like the methods of the Peripatetic philosophers. In a manner reminiscent Ibn Masarra's writings and his near contemporary al-Suhrawardī's Platonizing critique of logic, Ibn Barrajān in fact distinguishes himself from the Peripatetic philosophers, whom he alludes to as previous claimants to "wisdom" (*ḥikma*) in a series of passages. In a nuanced critique and embrace of philosophy, he argues that while the philosophers were correct in much of what they claimed about the nature of the world, they used imprecise terminology in their neglect of prophecy. For Ibn Barrajān, the true claimants of "wisdom" (*ḥikma*) are not the philosophers but the contemplative mystical saints, whom he represents as a group that overlaps with the scholars in their role as guides of the community.

The Epistemology of Sufi Metaphysics

Ibn Barrajān introduces his major *tafsīr* (MS Yusuf Ağa 4744–6) with an overall framework for understanding his theory of knowledge. All knowledge for Ibn Barrajān, whether sensory knowledge derived from the phenomenological world or knowledge derived from scripture, is important as a gateway to knowledge of the divine realm. The way Ibn Barrajān introduces his method for acquiring knowledge of God in his major Qur'an commentary is illustrative of how his method, while ultimately mystical, is at its foundation a speculative one that leads to mystical experience. Like Ibn Masarra's method, its starting point is contemplation (*iʿtibār*) of scripture and the created world.

Verily God has laid out the path of guidance directing man to Him and has established signs of what is right and what leads to Him. He brought into existence all that exists for those who contemplate (*muʿtabirūn*), and sent down the scriptures for those of remembrance, and He sent guides, the leaders of the pious. The rope was stretched to them and the Straight Path was made clear to them.[26]

Those who contemplate (*muʿtabirūn*) are the focus of Ibn Barrajān's proposed path to knowledge of God. Ibn Barrajān takes interest in the Qur'anic notion that revelation and the created things of the world have meaning and purpose as signs for the contemplating intellect (*ʿaql*). Contemplation (*iʿtibār*), pondering (*tadabbur*), reflection (*naẓar*), remembrance (*tadhakkur*), and thought (*tafakkur*) are among the most frequently occurring concepts in Ibn Barrajān's major Qur'an commentary and constitute the essential vehicles for the ideal mystical aspirant's acquisition of saintly insight.[27] A key assumption of his approach to knowledge is the existence of a spiritual or intellectual elect that is able to contemplate with greater success than the masses, these masses themselves being diverse in their intellectual abilities. He presents people's differing abilities to contemplate as seemingly deterministic, tempering this determinism throughout his *tafsīr* by highlighting the way individuals with strong desire and ability to contemplate can eventually progress to the point where they themselves can perceive what the elect perceive of the world's "unseen" (*ghayb*) and hidden (*bawāṭin*) realities.

God (Exalted and Glorious) clarified to us, with what we recite of His Book and from what is understood of His supreme discourse, that He created us out of earth and a mixture of what is based in it and what emerges from it of seed in plants and animals. Among the various types of people is … he in whom dominates the attribute of intellect. He inclines toward the attributes of quick-wit, insight, and discernment in unseen (*ghayb*) matters, being one who knows to the fullest extent. He discerns the manifest [realities] of things (*ẓawāhir al-ashyāʾ*) and raises his view to what is unseen (*ghayb*) in them. There is [also] he in whom dominates the attribute of angels. He is faithful, in submission to God, obedient, full of modesty, little in the way of conflict, strong in support, aspires for the [true] realities, desires fairness and good qualities, leaves aside bad qualities, keeps away from vice, acts with justice, and inclines towards grace.[28]

Ibn Barrajān describes human nature (*jibilla*) as a non-uniform and complex mix of elements that vary according to certain elements that are inherent in human nature and that correspond with certain categories of created existence, including earth, plants, animals, and angels. The highest levels, the level quoted in the excerpt just cited, include individuals whose natures are dominated by an intellectual attribute that explains their insight and knowledge of unseen (*ghayb*) matters. An individual in this group is a kind of knower (*ʿārif*) who identifies the apparent realities of things (*ẓawāhir al-ashyāʾ*) as distinct from the hidden realities (*ghawāmiḍ/bawāṭin al-ashyāʾ*), both of which he grasps. At a higher level of human nature, an angel-like attribute is predominant that explains these individuals' moral character and inclination toward understanding all levels of reality and truth. In contrast with both of these higher levels of nature are lower levels of nature dominated by more earth-like and plant-like elements, such that individuals in these groups are inclined toward lower levels of perception lacking in insight.[29]

This preliminary definition of an elect constitutes a central part of the framework of his spiritual-intellectual method for acquiring knowledge of the divine realm. The taxonomy he develops in describing this spiritual-intellectual capacity is a central part of the framework for the way his doctrines in ontology, epistemology, and religious authority are built into his metaphysics. It is particularly the second highest contemplative and intellectual level among the elect whom Ibn Barrajān is interested in highlighting, the level below the angelic level. He characterizes them by their advanced abilities of contemplation (*iʿtibār*), highly developed intellect (*ʿaql*), and perception of the hidden realities of things (*ghawāmiḍ al-ashyāʾ*).[30] In a passage discussed later in this chapter, he will identify this group as the mystical saints, the *awliyāʾ*, whom he will characterize has having highly developed knowledge of the meanings of the Names of God. He will characterize these meanings as being semantically indicative of God's omnipresent agency, witnessed by the saintly *awliyāʾ* at the level of the unseen hidden realities of the world. For Ibn Barrajān, this mystical witnessing follows from their deep contemplation of the interior dimensions of both the Qur'an as God's discourse and the created phenomenological world.

In later parts of the text, he identifies the highest angelic level among the elect as the "veracious" or "truthful ones," the *ṣiddīqūn*, whom he describes as being above the contemplative saints according to the *ṣiddīqūn*'s more direct access to the knowledge that the contemplative saints aspire to acquire. The "truthful ones" gain this knowledge through direct intuition without necessary prior contemplation. Unsurprisingly, he describes the prophets as numbering among the *ṣiddīqūn*. That is, he distinguishes between, on the one hand, the prophets as being among the highest *ṣiddīqūn*, and on the other hand, the saints as the *awliyāʾ*. Between them lies a distinction in modalities of knowledge acquisition and distinct limits of knowledge acquisition. According to this dichotomy, and in a manner reminiscent of al-Ghazālī's use of Avicennan psychology in Ashʿarism and Sufi metaphysics, Ibn Barrajān represents the mystical saints as having a limited grasp of the hidden realities of the world based on a level of contemplation that contrasts with the prophets' fuller grasp through prophetic intuition.[31]

While the *ṣiddīqūn* are named far more regularly than the *awliyāʾ* in the text, saintly contemplation of the Qur'an and the created world as a mode of knowledge acquisition is the central focus of the method he describes, which means that it is these contemplative "saints" (*awliyāʾ*) who are the center of the text's metaphysical theories. Critically, the final section of this chapter shows how he intertwines the religious authority of the contemplative saints with the authority of the scholars, the latter whom he characterizes in familiar terms as inheritors of the religious authority of the prophets.

Against the backdrop of this framework of knowledge acquisition and the elect, the starting point of the intellectual and spiritual ascent that he describes is his esoteric scriptural hermeneutic. As in the case of Ibn Masarra's Platonizing scripturally esoteric method, his esoteric hermeneutic includes contemplation of the interior dimension of both the Qur'an and the created world as part of a joint gateway to a cognitive witnessing of the "hidden realities of things," a level of cognition and perception in which God's veiled omnipotence appears manifest to the mystical aspirant. This vision leads in the section after that to the philosophical recognition of the world, including the celestial bodies that are part of the collective macrocosmic macroanthropon (*insān kabīr*) and Universal Servant of God's omnipotent agency in a unique mystical cosmology that he describes as *ḥikma* (wisdom, philosophy).

Philosophical Knowledge and Esoteric Hermeneutics

In what echoes the approach of both Ibn Masarra and the early Sufis of Iraq, Ibn Barrajān represents the Qur'an as the single most important door to mystical knowledge of the divine realm, focusing especially on scripture's individual letters and presentation of the Names of God. His presentation focuses on the notion that scripture, integrated into ritual piety, brings about deeper faith, which serves as a transitional element in the development of a human intellect that ultimately develops a kind of sixth sense of perception. Specifically, with faith, the "lower intellect" (*al-ʿaql al-adnā*) that grasps only the manifest realities of things (*ẓawāhir al-ashyāʾ*) develops into the "higher intellect" (*al-ʿaql al-aʿlā*), which grasps the world's hidden realities (*bawāṭin al-ashyā'*). In this way, the Qur'an, particularly through ritual invocation of the Names of God found in the sacred text and through recitation of the sacred text, can facilitate a mystical perception of the created world's hidden realities.

The starting point of this scripture-oriented mystical elaboration of knowledge can be found in his treatment of the opening chapter of the Qur'an, as Ibn Barrajān discovers that the interior meanings of the opening verses' letters correspond to the interior or hidden realities of the world.[32] Specifically, he indicates that as much as the Qur'an is a source of guidance for man to help distinguish between virtue and vice and realize the requirements of divine law and ritual, scripture also provides a kind of manifest and hidden knowledge that can be identified among other places in scripture's presentation of the Names of God. For the contemplative, one of the first goals in contemplation of the Qur'an is to discover the Names of God in the manifest and hidden levels of the text's discourse. Ibn Barrajān demonstrates the discovery process:

> The mother of the Qur'an is made up of seven sections and seven well-known verses, if one counts them. It is also seven names, five of which are apparent: His Name God (Exalted be His Invocation), His Name the Lord, the Compassionate, the Merciful, the Sovereign, His Name understood from the attribute Praise, that is, The Praiseworthy, and His name hidden between the attribute and the Name in His saying, "Praise be to God," and, "the Compassionate, the Merciful," which is [the Name] He declares when you say [in prayer, the scriptural phrase], "To You do we worship and to You do we turn for help."[33]

Ibn Barrajān explains that the first chapter of the Qur'an can be analyzed not only as seven verses, but also as seven names, two of which are hidden and five of which are manifest in the text: God, the Lord (*Rabb*), the Compassionate (*Raḥmān*), the Merciful (*Raḥīm*), the Sovereign (*Mālik*). He infers two others as part of the interior level of scriptural discourse. The first is the Praiseworthy, derived from the phrase "Praise be to God." He does not identify the second hidden name in this passage, but he indicates that it can be derived from the phrase "To You do we worship and to You do we turn for help." His allusion to a hidden name is evocative of the historical practice of referring to God's unfathomable name using the pronoun "He" in some forms of Sufi ritual invocation, a practice for which Ibn Taymiyya two centuries later criticized the Andalusī Sufis.[34] The key conclusion to draw from Ibn Barrajān's method is that he believes that the number of divine Names emerging from both the interior and exterior dimensions of scriptural discourse is higher than the number of Names derived only from the manifest level. The key question this discussion suggests is the following: How do the Names discovered at the exterior and interior levels of scriptural discourse serve as a vehicle to a higher state of knowledge of the "unseen" (*ghayb*) that he referred to earlier? His answer, integrated into several points he makes later, is that the Names in scripture are indicative of God's agency in the world, which can be grasped and witnessed by the contemplative mystical aspirant at the level of the world's hidden realities. He frames this connection between esoteric scriptural hermeneutics and knowledge of the world's hidden realities with a basic question that was asked by many early Islamic theologians and linguists: "The scholars among the forebears differed on [the debate about] the name: [Do names] refer to the name or the named, or other than the named?"[35]

In a manner reminiscent of Ibn Ḥazm's linguistic theories, Ibn Barrajān's answer to the question of the connection between the signifier and the signified avoids strict connections between words and their meanings. In the case of Ibn Ḥazm, his linguistic theories about words and their highly contextual and contingent meanings helped him read the scriptural text univocally according to a *ẓāhirī* hermeneutic, such that the same word could be read "literally" with two different meanings in two different verses without the use of metaphorical or esoteric interpretation. In an interesting twist, Ibn Barrajān's similar loosening of the strict connection between words and meanings helps him employ not a *ẓāhirī* hermeneutic, but an esoteric hermeneutic. In an Ibn Masarra-like way, he applies this hermeneutic to a reading of worldly phenomena in order to claim that commonplace semantic articulations of perceived realities are actually just apparent (*ẓāhir*) realities, which veil more real hidden (*bāṭin*) realities.

> Most of the names of created things among distinguishing traits and signs perhaps [refer to] what mark them and distinguish them from other things, while [the names of things] are only [truly] the named if what is understood from the name is the [hidden] reality of the named. However, we are hidden from [that true reality of the named, when pondering created things] in the prison into which He (Glorious be His Majesty) has confined us, separated from [that true reality]. [Grasp of] this [hidden] abode is built upon faith in the unseen realities (*ghuyūb*) in accordance with what was decreed [by God] of trials and tribulation. [It is according to this that] He (Glorious be His Majesty) established reports about Himself in the absence of His presence, and signs of Himself in place of witnessing, and invocation in place of the invoked, and the [Divine] Name in place of the [hidden] Named, as in His saying, "So glorify in the Name of your Lord the Supreme,"[36] and [even] closer than this, His saying, "Glorify in the Name of your Lord the Most High."[37] He established cognizance and knowledge of Him in place of vision, and the report in place of the reported. He then raised hearts to the secret of what is intended in His saying, "Call upon Me, and I will answer you."[38]

Ibn Barrajān illustrates the importance of the Names as gateways to the world's hidden realities in his assertion that God, rather than allowing man the actual vision of Himself, revealed to man out of His mercy His Most Beautiful Names "in place of the Named." God in this way is the ultimate Hidden (*al-bāṭin*), even as he is the ultimate Manifest (*al-ẓāhir*). Likewise, the names of the created things are simply words used to distinguish one thing from another based on certain distinguishing characteristics. Such names of created things are only truly meaningful if they refer to the reality or true nature of a named entity or concept.[39] In the rest of his discussion, it becomes clear that this reality or true nature is the particular aspect of these entities and concepts that reveal God's agency in their existence, such that entities and concepts are in reality created entities and created concepts.

> The establishment of the divine law and the existence of divine inspiration stipulates that He is closer to His servants than themselves and their very essences, and the same for His Power over affairs and His command in all of existence. His Names are [to be understood] from this perspective. Do you not see that He is Majestic in His Glory in the Oneness of His Pre-eternity, such that when He brought into existence the existent things altogether, He was also in them and with them in terms of His (Exalted be His Glory) [act of] creation and command. [He is] also a Guardian to whom He wills, meaning that a spirit from Him supports [the servant]. He, Exalted be His Glory, made Himself known to us with what is His in the created world of [the act of] creation and command, and [the Names] are named by that.[40]

Ibn Barrajān explains that the true nature of the created things is, in simplest terms, their createdness. That is, knowledge of the true nature of created things is knowledge of God's agency in these things. What follows from this discussion is his understanding that God is immanent, but not in a pantheistic or monistic sense. Rather, he speaks of God's immanence in His agency, or more specifically, in terms of His "command" to create and His realization of this command by "bringing creation into existence" (*amr*, *khalq*). God's command presented in this way alludes to the Qur'anic notion of God as the Creator Who causes and sustains the world's existence through the formula "Be, and it is" (*kun fa-yakūn*), which was similarly the basis of Ibn Masarra's discussion in Chapter 1 of the Names as indicative of God's agency.[41] In other words, as Ibn Barrajān explains, God is omnipresent and immanent specifically in His agency, and more specifically in terms of His role as both of the following: the Living (*Ḥayy*) who brings creation into existence (*ījād*), and the Sustaining (*Qayyūm*) who upholds creation's existing or enduring state (*imsāk*). He defines this knowledge as interior knowledge of the "hidden realities of things."

One example he gives in this part of the text is that of a bird in flight. Semantically speaking, the bird is a "flying" bird at the apparent level of phenomenological reality, but at the level of the hidden realities, the "flying" bird is more accurately a bird that is divinely "made to fly." Ibn Barrajān's discussion appears in reference to Qur'anic language that describes the flight of birds in terms of divine agency. The verse in question states, "Have they not seen the birds held (flying) in the midst of the sky? None holds them up but God. Most surely in this are signs for those who believe."[42] According to Ibn Barrajān's method, the mystical aspirant is ideally able to witness this divine agency in the flight of birds as part of this mystically oriented cognitive ascent built on contemplation of the Qur'an and the world.

In his discussion, Ibn Barrajān was careful to clarify that God is "in and with" the created existent things specifically in terms of "creation and command," that is, in terms of agency. Still, despite this distinction, his discussion of the Names provides some clues about controversial aspects of his doctrine that contextualize how Ibn Khaldūn managed to lump him together with Ibn Sabʿīn and Ibn ʿArabī as "people of theophany" (*asḥāb al-tajallī*), who ostensibly integrated philosophical and theological doctrines into virtually monistic discussions of the Names and Attributes. In the following passage, Ibn Barrajān argues that the Names of God "traverse their courses of the world" in a way comparable to both "the way souls act in bodies" and the "adherence of accidents to bodies," ultimately making God's Names encompass all creation in terms of "knowledge and meaning."

> The [Divine] Names traverse their courses of the world in the way that souls act in bodies, and they constitute the locus of the command (*amr*) in creation. They adhere to it [like] the adherence of accidents in bodies, such that every created thing trifling or large is encompassed in knowledge and meaning by the Names of God (Majestic is His Invocation). What is required [in understanding] of the Name of divinity encompasses [an understanding of] the meanings of all of the Names. God divided the entire world according to [the act of] the command and the creation, and then among the Names, according to the Living and the Sustaining in bringing about existence and holding it up [respectively], and then [dividing the world] according to His Name the Lord and the Merciful in His mercy and establishment of a link.[43]

What is interesting about Ibn Barrajān's language of the Names and creation is that it seems to indicate at first glance something akin to a manifestation ontologically of God's Names in the world, which is similar to the Akbarian (Ibn ʿArabīan) theory that Ibn Khaldūn criticized as monistic. A closer look at this reference in the passages cited previously suggests that Ibn Barrajān's understanding of the Names of God "traversing their courses of the world" is actually presented in the context of God's creative agency in bringing things into existence. Specifically, his discussion ties together various pairs of terminology that point to a discussion of God's omnipresent agency, specifically pairs of divine Names like "Living and Sustaining" Who simultaneously "gives life" and "sustains life" as part of the "the [act of] command" and "[act of] creation." This last pair, command and creation as an act, parallels Ibn Barrajān's discussion of God's omnipresence in agency when He creates things in such a way that God is ultimately "in them and with them … in the [act of] creation and command." That is, his discussion of God's omnipresence is in fact a discussion of God's omnipresent agency in a theory that echoes Ibn Ḥazm's discussion of omnipresent angels carrying out God's command, and he ultimately ties all of these pairs of agency-oriented terms to the most significant pair of agency-oriented words: the Qur'anic creation formula, "Be, and it is" (*kun fa-yakūn*). In other words, what Ibn Khaldūn saw as monistic "theophany" among Andalusī Sufis appears to be, at least in the specific case of Ibn Barrajān, more accurately a doctrine about God's omnipresent agency as illustrated in the meanings of God's Names that "traverse their courses in the world."[44]

The way Ibn Barrajān understands the divine Names and meanings as pathways for the contemplative mystic's perception of the world's hidden realities can be summarized in the following way. According to Ibn Barrajān, God reveals Himself to the world through knowledge or awareness of His agency, and in man's attempt to grasp the true meaning of God's Names and the true meanings of the created things, he discovers that God is the ultimate agent. In this way, the Names guide man's understanding of God and even his encounter with God as the Living and the Sustainer Who gives life and sustains it. In place of the actual vision of God, man is given signs and tools of His presence. Invocation of the Names is one of the signs and tools God gives man in place of vision of God. Most critically, in Ibn Barrajān's attempt to grasp the single unfathomable Named indicated by all of God's Most Beautiful Names, he turns to the mystics' favored form of supererogatory ritual – namely ritual invocation (*dhikr*) of the Names – in order to call on the unfathomable divine Creator and witness the world's hidden realities.[45]

For Ibn Barrajān, ritual invocation is one of the keys to this contemplative methodology toward mystical witnessing of God's immanent agency. In Ibn Barrajān's representation of the mystical aspirant's spiritual-intellectual ascent, invocation of the Names as part of Sufi piety brings the aspirant closer to a kind of mystical communion in which God's agency is finally witnessed in an encounter similar to the one described by Sahl al-Tustarī's notion of the "eye of certainty" that sees the *ghayb*.

[God] the Most High, the Supreme, says, "When my servant invokes me to himself, I invoke him to Myself, and when he invokes me in a gathering, I invoke him in a gathering better and more upright," and in another narration, "better and more upright than his gathering," expanding in explanation. God (Glorious and Majestic) says, "If there were a Qur'an with which the mountains were moved or the earth were cloven asunder or the dead were made to speak,"[46] then it would be as mentioned, [that is, scripture's] account would be shown as truth, as everything lifeless as well as the plants and the animals, that is, existence in its entirety, exalts and recognizes Him.… [Indeed, it is] with the Will of God in His Names (Majestic is His Invocation) that He implements His dispensation and decrees His command, and through [the Will of God] all of existence is brought into being. This invocation is what is indicated by His True saying, "And the invocation of God is greater,"[47] that is, the invocation of God in His Names and Attributes is greater, and God's invocation of His servant in [the servant's] prayer is superior to the [servant's] prayer [toward God]. This [greater] invocation [of God to man] is what, if God facilitates it on the one who prays and makes it present in his heart, keeps him away from anything disgraceful and reprehensible. God says (Glorious is He Who speaks), "Indeed I am God, there is no deity except Me, so worship Me and perform prayer for My remembrance,"[48] that is, [remember and] invoke Me in it [prayer] and I will [remember and] invoke you.[49]

Ibn Barrajān presents the Names of God as found in the Qur'an not simply as vocabulary to be identified and discovered by Qur'an readers, but as critical components in a specific ritual that is a vehicle of mysticism: remembrance and invocation of God *(dhikr)* in His Names. The value he assigns to invocation of God in His Names is so high that he identifies it as a central part of a state one should aspire to reach during the actual prayer (*ṣalā*), namely, mutual invocation. In this communication, man's remembrance and invocation of God is answered by God's invocation of His servant, in line with Qur'anic language describing this mutual invocation or remembrance: "Therefore remember [or invoke] Me, and I will remember [or invoke] you."[50] Ibn Barrajān's intellectual-spiritual approach to the Qur'an, in which he discovers the Names of God in the Qur'an's exterior and interior levels of discourse in an esoteric hermeneutic, is thus integrated into common ritual practices that are reconceptualized with greater mystical emphasis: ritual invocation *(dhikr)* of the Names identified as part of scriptural recitation and utterances of prayer itself, whether compulsory prayers or supererogatory prayers.[51] In his explanation of invocation's virtues, he locates its value in the inspired knowledge of the prophets, which the Sufi teachers and scholars pass on. In his own words:

The virtues of invocation are such that the Prophet has spoken explaining it, disclosing this in his knowledge of divine inspiration and in what is known of prophecy. The virtue of invocation *(dhikr)* is well known to the point that its virtues have surpassed [the limits of] intellects. The elect among the learned teachers (*shuyūkh*), may God be pleased with us and them, have said that only in submission [to God] is known the measure of what has come [to man] of the virtues of invocation's reward, and [only in submission] is faith reached.[52]

The role of the learned teachers (*shuyūkh*) as specialists of this ritual knowledge is worth noting as part of his larger endeavor to highlight the religious authority of Sufis alongside, or within, the authority of the scholars. Together with *dhikr*, there is a second process in which these teachers' intellectual-spiritual approach to the Qur'an is accompanied by a key ritual component, one that he also describes mystically and more specifically in terms of a cognitive and spiritual ascent. In the passages that follow, he integrates contemplation of the individual Qur'anic letters (the isolated letters at the start of the Qur'anic chapters) with the dedicated practice of ritually reciting the Qur'an (*tilāwa*). In recitation, thee letters point not only other parts of the text, but also the Well-Preserved Tablet mentioned in the Qur'an. He represents the Well-Preserved Tablet as a kind of mystical locus of otherworldly knowledge and divine inspiration, much like Sahl al-Tustarī's association of otherworldly knowledge with the Throne, and he ultimately describes access to this knowledge in terms of the same notion of "certainty" used by Sahl al-Tustarī.[53] In this way, the letters constitute a kind of "intermediary between the letters of the Clear Book and the Noble Qur'an."[54] That is, in agreement with Ibn Masarra and Sahl al-Tustarī before him, Ibn Barrajān believes that the letters serve as a gateway into the realm of the unseen (*ghayb*) and the hidden realities of the world.

> The scholar is not in [a state of] true certainty (*yaqīn*) until he brings together his pondering into the Well-Preserved Tablet with recitation of the Glorious Qur'an, [then] through this acquires some qualities of the truthful ones (*ṣiddīqūn*) if [the scholar] attaches himself to this act [of pondering and recitation]. His statement (Glorious and Exalted) "This book,"[55] may refer to what is unseen (*ghayb*), as this [book] is the Well-Preserved Tablet. That is, these letters *Alif Lām Mīm* are signs of it.[56]

Ibn Barrajān identifies the individual Qur'anic letters as intermediaries between the manifest Qur'an and the hidden Well-Preserved Tablet. In an interesting framing of this mystically conceptualized ritual piety and knowledge, which he identifies as part of the broader knowledge of the scholars, he argues that the simultaneous recitation and contemplation of Qur'anic discourse together constitute the ultimate intellectual-experiential vehicle for passing cognitively to the realm of the Well-Preserved Tablet and the "unseen" (*ghayb*). In this way, the letters epitomize the role of the Qur'anic text as a platform for man's mystical encounter with the divine world. In sum, recitation and contemplation of the text are part of a mystically oriented set of rituals that includes remembrance or invocation (*dhikr*), which leads to the grasp of the Well-Preserved Tablet and allows the mystical aspirant and scholar to perceive and grasp the hidden realities of the world. At this interior level of the world's ontology, the mystic witnesses God's omnipresent agency in the phenomenal world and is bestowed with gifts of insight. In explaining this process, Ibn Barrajān qualifies that even the most advanced of the saints can never reach the fully inspired level of the prophets, who are the highest among the more advanced truthful ones (*ṣiddīqūn*).[57] Thus far, while the key steps of his methodology for attaining mystical insight are clear, the contents of that mystical insight remain vague beyond his explanation of the saint's witnessing of God's omnipresent agency. A closer look at his discussion of the hidden realities of things reveals that the mystical knowledge of the world that Ibn Barrajān ascribes to the contemplative saints includes markedly philosophical truths that he intertwines with doctrines found in contemporary philosophical cosmologies.

Celestial Agency and the Mystical Ascent

Ibn Barrajān's incorporation of doctrines from the philosophers' cosmologies into his discussion of the "hidden realities of things" is a nuanced one typical of many philosophically oriented systems of Sufi metaphysics. On one level, Ibn Barrajān acknowledges the soundness of key aspects of these cosmologies. On another level, his discussion of the "hidden realities of things" flips the causal orientation of these cosmologies upside down by criticizing the philosophers' claims about divine agency and secondary causality. His method is reminiscent of the writings of al-Ghazālī in the *Incoherence of the Philosophers* and *Niche of the Lights*, and he calls his own results in Sufi metaphysics "wisdom" (*ḥikma*), using the same term that the philosophers identified with "philosophy" (*falsafa*, *ḥikma*).[58] He accomplishes this intellectual task using the concept mentioned earlier: the ascent from the "lower intellect" to the "higher intellect." At the lower intellect, one recognizes cosmological doctrines in agreement with the philosophers, particularly the notion of the philosophical macrocosm and the agency of the celestial bodies as they act on the sublunary world. At the level of the higher intellect, which recognizes the incorporeal hidden realities of things, one recognizes that common philosophical notions of agency in the macrocosm are in fact veils of the true agency of God as the real governor of causality (*mudabbir*) in the world. The world in this framework is actually the obedient macrocosmic Universal Servant. His detailed explanations of the faculties of the individual planets, from Mars to Venus, represent a very unique and even surprising integration of diverse philosophical doctrines into his own mystical metaphysics. The first passage here discusses the faculties of the celestial bodies, while the second turns to the parallel agency that occurs in the microcosm at the level of the man's bodily organs.

Raised between every two firmaments of these seven raised firmaments are [more] firmaments, celestial spheres, and what takes the place of the celestial spheres in the descent of the [creative] command, as explained in His saying (Majestic is His Invocation), "And He inspired in each firmament His command,"[59] among which are the planets, which are indications and signs of [the command]. [The planets] resemble man's principal organs [of the body], in which [the celestial faculties] are present and around which [the celestial faculties] turn.

In what demonstrates the extent to which Andalusī Sufis had diverse philosophical sources to draw on, Ibn Barrajān describes the role of human organs in the body as being directly related to the role of the planets in the world according to a macrocosm-microcosm parallelism of causality, which he elsewhere describes as a Universal Servant–Particular Servant relationship (*al-ʿabd al-kullī, al-ʿabd al-juzʾī*).[60] The planets act on the world in a manner similar to the sun, each with its own faculty. In the case of the sun, it generates primordial heat essential to the formation and sustenance of plant and animal life. The sun "provides heat to the areas it comes upon, and from it radiates primordial heat necessary for creation. From it comes the animal soul by the permission of God (Exalted and Majestic, Supreme in His Sublimity and Affairs)."[61] The other planets act on the world likewise:

Similarly [in the case of] the moon, God (Exalted and Glorious, Supreme is His Affair) ascribed to it an intermediary role [of agency] and a role of subjection. It regulates what the sun has heated, preparing it for growth and facilitating its ripening by the permission of God, its creator and its subjector. Likewise [in the case of] Venus, God (Majestic is His glory and Supreme is His Exaltedness) made an attraction faculty for it, which is what extracts the appetitive faculty [in the world] that is receptive of things. [Venus] supports the sun in extracting [the appetitive faculty] from the earth, bringing out moisture where the sun does not reach [directly] but only [indirectly] through heat from the womb of the earth. [As for] Mercury, God (Exalted is His Majesty and Supreme is His Sublimity) made for it a mixed faculty, regulating [the Earth] and inclining toward the dominant element in nature such that it inclines toward every nature. [As for] Saturn, God assigned it a power that regulates heat in whatever it comes upon and moves away from, such as earth, fruit, animals and the like. Similarly [in the case of] Mercury, God (Exalted and Glorious) made for it a nutritive power for all things among the animals and plants. It regulates things through sustenance, balance, and equitable measure. As for Mars, God (Exalted, Glorious, and Supreme in His Sublimity) made for it a power that stirs all appetites, anger, temerity, and impetuousness. Likewise in all things attributed to nature, God (Exalted in His Invocation) made for them a good condition in this world through the moderation of these celestial bodies as well as decay ...[62]

Just as the moon regulates the sun's heat by stimulating the development of moisture, Jupiter with its nutritive faculty brings balance to all of creation. Saturn regulates heat throughout the world, while Venus with its faculty of attraction governs desire with particular respect to creation's need for the sun to sustain life. Mars excites various elements in the nature of creation from anger and impulsiveness to desire and appetite. He explains that the body works similarly through the faculty of "seven hidden parts," the effects of which make them apparent on the "manifest aspect of the body of man."

The heart in man directs [in the body] what is [akin to] the role of the sun in this world. It is the place of primordial heat. From [the heart], [heat] radiates to the entire body. Then there is the kidney, which is in the position of the moon in the world with respect to to the sun. [That is, the kidney] takes away heat from the heart, breaking it down and making it less dense in the body, processing it into steam. Then the kidney modifies food and processes it, clarifying it for the heart in balanced weight and equitable measure ... The spleen is associated with a holding power, as it holds the heaviness of the food, dries it, and nourishes [the body] by the grace of God (Most High). [The spleen] in man is in the position of Saturn in the world. As for the stomach, it possesses an appetitive faculty that accepts food and desires it with a growing appetite. [The stomach] in man is in the position of Venus in the world. The gallbladder possesses a fiery faculty heating the stomach, stirring it up to the point of boiling, increasing appetites, and from it is the appetite emitted in the body. [The gallbladder] governs the body's fiery desires, and it is in man in the position of Mars in the world. The brain possesses a faculty of thought, bringing together things that connect with it. It is the locus of the connection of forms and formation of patterns, and it is in man in the position of Saturn in this world.[63]

This discussion of the parallel faculties of the planets and organs offers strong evidence of how Almoravid-era Sufis in the twelfth century likely drew on philosophical texts like the *Epistles of the Pure Brethren* (*Rasā'il Ikhwān al-Ṣafā'*). The *Rasā'il*'s discussion of astronomy and astrology similarly identifies man as a microcosm (*'ālam ṣaghir*) and the world as the macroanthropon (*insān kabīr*).[64] While the writings of ancient philosophers like Ptolemy and Proclus likewise associated the bodily organs with the planets, the writings of the Pure Brethren (*Ikhwān al-Ṣafā'*) offer more immediate examples of textual links in Arabic writerly culture connecting the Sufis with the Graeco-Arabic philosophical tradition. At first glance, this philosophical material seems to present a major gap in Ibn Barrajān's method. Why does Ibn Barrajān think a macrocosm-microcosm paradigm for understanding planetary agency in the world will help the reader of his Sufi Qur'an commentary recognize God's universal agency as the orderer and planner (*mudabbir*) of the world? Ibn Barrajān's answer is that one must recognize that the philosophers' discussion of the planets' causality is only true agency from one perspective, which is the perspective of the lower intellect. The truly contemplative mystical aspirant ascends cognitively from the lower intellect to the higher intellect, witnessing and discovering the most hidden and unseen levels of reality that illustrate God's manifest agency. This latter agency, he indicates, is ultimately unveiled to the mystical aspirant in a manifest perception of God's omnipotence.[65]

In the passages that follow, and in a manner reminiscent of al-Ghazālī's philosophical theology and Platonizing Sufi metaphysics, Ibn Barrajān makes this very point by tying these two levels of intellectual perception to distinct understandings of agency. What the lower intellect perceives is specifically the "lower agent" (*al-fāʿil al-adnā*), which is any perceived agent in the world that a regular observer recognizes in terms of secondary causality. The higher intellect sought by the mystical aspirant perceives the "higher agent" (*al fāʿil al-aʿlā*). This higher agent is the singular agency of God as the planner (*mudabbir*), Whose singular pervasive agency is carried out by the pervasive presence of piously obedient angels implementing God's command at all levels of the world "at every handspan of existence."[66] He explains this doctrine in what amounts to a simultaneous defense and critique of philosophical discussions of causality, echoing not only the analysis of al-Ghazālī, but also that of Ibn Hazm's discussion of angels and angency.

Perhaps the reader of our book is struck by what he hears of our discussion of faculties and natures, and ascribing acts to what cannot correctly be said to have an act or choice. He should know that this [is said] on our part in concession to what is dominant in the current custom of [philosophical] discourse, that is, the curtailing of the mention of the Higher Agent [God] (Blessed and Most High). Indeed, the act [or agency] only [truly] belongs to the One [Who] possesses it, encompasses it, and from Whom come its sources and origins, [the One] to Whom belongs its first and last and its manifest and hidden, and to Whom everything goes back and is the source: He is the First and Last, the One who plans and implements (*mudabbir*) everything, the One who advances and the One who delays, the Sustainer of everything, its Trustee and the Encompasser of everything from behind every encompassment and the Trustee over every Trustee. So even with flexibility in the course of discourse, this [curtailing of the mention of the Higher Agent in discussion of perceived acts] is allowed and understood, though this is usually the cause of obscuring the path [to knowledge of God], and it encourages the neglect of speculation into the reality behind the verification of truth. In this way, confusion can result in people to the point where it brings them to think incorrectly because of persistence in this [method] of forgetting the Higher Agent, the True One, Exalted be His Glory and Supreme is his Sublimity and Affair.[67]

Ibn Barrajān's distinction of the Higher Agent and lower agent resolves the problems of causality introduced by his philosophically oriented discussion of celestial agency. His resolution is notably in keeping with Ibn Ḥazm and al-Ghazālī's recognition of verifiable patterns of secondary causality in the world coupled with their simultaneous identification of

God as the only omnipotent orderer and planner (*mudabbir*) and ultimate agent.[68] His specific point, which constitutes a defense of his use of doctrines found in philosophical cosmologies, is the following: When Ibn Barrajān presents discussion of planetary "faculties" that "act upon" the world or uses concepts like "nature," he is conceding to what he thinks is an acceptable custom of discussing philosophically what is witnessed of the causally connected patterns of the world using terms that are common in philosophical discourse. His point is that a philosophical framework for understanding causality is not inherently problematic. The philosophers and ordinary people simply neglect the interior reality behind the apparent phenomena they describe, which is the veiled omnipresent agency of God as the "Higher Agent" and only real agent.[69] The philosophical discussion of "nature" and "faculties," while acceptable enough for him to assimilate into his Sufi metaphysics in agreement with Ibn Masarra and al-Ghazālī, is only truly sound when the reality that God is behind those faculties is simultaneously recognized. Most importantly, he seeks to bring about this recognition in the mystical aspirant's perception not simply through logical conclusions or the arguments of speculative theology, which have their place in other sciences, but rather through a more experiential process characterized by a loosely Platonizing cognitive and spiritual ascent of the mystic's intellect to an elusively described "higher intellect" (*al-ʿaql al-aʿlā*). At this level, the mystic can finally witness and draw insight from the realm of the "unseen" (*ghayb*) and Well-Preserved Tablet. His Sufi metaphysics, which constitutes a kind of mystical theology with Neoplatonic overtones, indicates that inspiration, contemplation, scripture, apparent phenomena, and their hidden realities all point to a shared truth witnessed at the level of the hidden realities of the world: God is indeed transcendent and the Hidden, but His immanence in agency means that He is the Manifest Who is closer to you "than your jugular vein." The manifestation of the Names' meanings that refer to God's agency (*tajallī maʿānī al-asmāʾ*) allow people to understand how the world is encompassed by His omnipresent agency and knowledge in a way that makes it possible for an individual to witness mystically God's omnipresence by witnessing His agency in the "hidden realities of things," thus gaining insight into truth, virtue, and in the afterlife, salvation.

This method for achieving a philosophically oriented mystical ascent brings the reader to a key question: How does Ibn Barrajān conceive of the social role of these saintly mystics who achieve this level of contemplative philosophically oriented mystical knowledge? Particularly given the fact that he was himself one of the scholars (*ʿulamāʾ*), and given that the scholars were understood by Muslims to inherit post-prophetic guiding authority through their theological, ethical, and jurisprudential knowledge, how does he conceive of the relationship between the Sufis and the scholars if he sees both as communal guides? His integration of the Sufis' mystical piety into the knowledge of the scholars, seen in this section, offers the biggest clue to the fact that Ibn Barrajān saw the scholars and the Sufis as one group. In his characterization of the Sufis' saintly knowledge as a philosophical and mystical "wisdom" (*ḥikma*), seen in the next section, the legacies of the Cordovan scholar Ibn Masarra, his teacher Sahl al-Tustarī, and Ibn Masarra's own fusion of the scholars and sages (*ḥukamāʾ*) is brought back to life.

Ibn Barrajān's Reform of Philosophy

Ibn Barrajān offers a very nuanced answer to the question of the authority of the saintly individuals who achieve these highest levels of philosophical and mystical knowledge. His comments are oriented around a specific criticism of Graeco-Arabic philosophy and an alternative definition of philosophy as, unsurprisingly, philosophically oriented mysticism.

> *Ḥikma* (wisdom), then, is the knowledge of the realities of things: how and why they were generated, what the intention in them is, what they lead to, and the knowledge of their Creator and its Maker in them. Following that, [wisdom includes the following questions:] What is required of *ḥikma* and [what are] the truths desired and the accepted methods – that is, [what is literally] the wisdom (*ḥikma*) in acquiring knowledge of existent things? The knowledge of the realities of the existent things goes back to four foundations: (1) knowledge of their beginnings (2) their manifest elements (3) knowledge of their hidden elements, given that what is sought is based on questions of how and knowledge of why its creator brought it into existence, and (4) are they from the right side [of virtue] such that one should bring them close in friendship or [are they] from individuals of the left side such that one should distance them ... The hidden [dimension] of the servant that submits to *ḥikma* (wisdom) is radiant and luminous, and is the sun of the hidden [dimension of the world]. With its light, the forms of the hidden realities of the worldly existences – their good and their bad, as well as their benefits and harms – are elucidated, and this is a light emitted from the reality of the heart in which the light of faith is established.[70]

Ḥikma (wisdom) is a term that Graeco-Arabic philosophers used to describe their Peripatetic (Aristotelian-Neoplatonic) philosophical tradition as a synonym for *falsafa*, and it is the same term used in many examples of Sufi exegesis to describe the path and intellectual results of mystical knowledge (*maʿrifa*). Sahl al-Tustarī used the term in the tenth century to describe the goals of his mystical method in his *tafsīr*. One author of a work of Platonizing Sufi metaphysics, Shihāb al-Dīn al-Suhrawardī, identified Plato and Hermes-Idrīs as specialists of "wisdom" (*ḥikma*), or simply, "sages" (*ḥukamāʾ*), in effect making a Sufi claim against the Baghdad Peripatetics on ancient Hellenistic philosophy.[71] As a philosophical and mystical form of knowledge, *ḥikma* (wisdom) in Ibn Barrajān's framework in this passage is a somewhat elusive reference to understanding how created things function, including knowledge of their veiled true causal dimensions as well as why and how they came to be. He describes the foundation of this knowledge as the pursuit of the "beginnings" of things, a description that points to an investigation of existence not in terms of itself (the Peripatetic philosopher's "being *qua* being"), but rather understanding existence in terms of its Creator (being *qua* Creator). If this Sufi *ḥikma* sounds like a variation of the Graeco-Arabic philosophers' intellectual inquiry, Ibn Barrajān was fully aware of the resemblance. As the next passage shows, Ibn Barrajān attempts to reclaim Graeco-Arabic philosophy in an approach to Sufi metaphysics that emphasizes the contemplative mystical ascent to a higher intellect without an emphasis on logical methods. Ibn Barrajān's simultaneous engagement with and criticism of the Graeco-Arabic philosophers very closely echoes Ibn Masarra's earlier attempt to criticize the philosophers as the *falāsifa* (Graeco-Arabic philosophers) while championing the philosophical and scholarly "sages" (*ḥukamāʾ*).

> Most [of those who claimed knowledge of *ḥikma*] were overcome by ignorance when they looked to *ḥikma* ... They said [*ḥikma*] is knowledge of first pre-eternal essential things. They sought it from the existent things and they approached them through comparison of what exists in nature, and they categorized them according to genus, which are the final forms of being and their perfection. Then they brought them to [the level of] species above [the existence things], then to the species of the species until they ended at what they claimed to be the first being created without intermediary from the agency of the Creator (Glory be to Him) – namely the soul breathed into Adam (peace be upon him). They found it yet they were ignorant of it in knowledge, and so they said this [Soul] gives to people their names and their definitions.[72]

In a clear reference to the philosophers, Ibn Barrajān makes a direct critique of an unnamed group of flawed claimants to knowledge of *ḥikma* (wisdom). He indicates that their incomplete approach to *ḥikma* led them astray from its true goals. True *ḥikma*, Ibn Barrajān explains, is not simply the project of classifying the order of things "as they are," but rather classifying things in terms of God's agency.[73] He indicates that the philosophers' failure to take note of God's agency left them in the unenviable position of forgetting the original goal of the entire enterprise, which was to witness God's agency as the ordering voluntary agent (*mudabbir*). This witnessing is central to his claim on philosophy as a method oriented towards the Sufi goals of mystically witnessing divine agency and the divine realm. While his analysis parallels the Platonizing critique of the Baghdad Peripatetics written by his contemporary Shihāb al-Dīn al-Suhrawardī, it more closely anticipates Ibn al-Khaṭīb's Nasrid-era representation of Socrates and the ancient philosophers as proto-Sufis whose legacy was inherited by the contemporaries of Junayd in Iraq.[74] Ibn Barrajān indicates that the philosophers explain the existence of the world in terms of concepts like Soul, as they claim that Soul is God's first creation and the giver of formal names and definitions in the created world. Their flawed conclusions, he explains, are based on their pursuit of the so-called pre-eternal first essences that they categorize into genus and species. In his more detailed analysis that follows, he criticizes how the philosophers define Nature as an element present in all creation that explains movement as well as generation and decay. He rejects, furthermore, how the philosophers identify Nature in terms of the faculties of the celestial spheres.[75]

> They said that Nature characterizes the four elements: fire, air, water, and earth, and that this is really an allusion from God in language to the origins [of things] in the two [universal] souls from which creation is brought into being.... [They speak of Nature] in terms of the celestial sphere and the celestial power that the Creator (Exalted and Glorious) adorned the celestial sphere with. [They say] that He has empowered [the celestial sphere] with influence over being, generation, decay, degradation, excess, dissolution, movement, motionlessness, and [they claim] to know this from truths that come from [celestial sphere], and that [these truths] come to this world on account of the precise cycles of the orbits.[76]

Ibn Barrajān explains that the philosophers characterize Soul and Nature as principles characterized by agency, volition, life, knowledge, and wisdom. According to this framework, he argues, the discussion of God and His angels is overlooked and marginalized. Ibn Barrajān contends that if the philosophers pursued *ḥikma* (wisdom, philosophy) by also pursing the Names and Attributes of God, which are indicative of His agency, they would have discovered that it is not Soul and Nature but the agency of God and His angels that ultimately gives meaning to every aspect of the world's existence, from generation and decay to their names and definitions. According to this critique, the philosophers fell short of sound discovery of God by overlooking divinely revealed prophecy.[77] At the same time, despite the philosophers' problematic use of terminology, he indicates later that he actually accepts many of the philosophers' conclusions in cosmology in the same way that Ibn Masarra accepted their framework. The main caveat of his acceptance of philosophy is that, as he explains in a manner reminiscent of Ibn Masarra, "The language of prophecy is more precise and the discourse of divine inspiration is more complete, revealing, higher, and closer in its approach."[78] This simultaneous acceptance and criticism of the philosophers' cosmological doctrines is best captured in the following passage.

They said also that Nature is a subtle substance governing the creation of things. Now, if they mean by "substance governing the creation of things" that it is God, then it is true, and their mistake is simply in their using the names "Nature" and "Substance." Otherwise, [if they mean other than God] they are far from correct, as Nature is not what they claim to prove and define it to be, that is, something characterized with life, knowledge, agency, and desire, characterized therefore with wisdom and the ability to create and fashion.[79]

Like Ibn Masarra before him, Ibn Barrajān partially accepts Graeco-Arabic philosophy at the level of a general cosmological picture of the world, but not necessarily its methodology or full ontological implications, which are at odds with his contemplative mystical methodology and his emphasis on God's Will and omnipotence. His representation of the philosophers having understood "Nature" correctly, as a governing principle that explains agency in the world, while simultaneously faulting their ignorance of God's agency as the hidden reality of "Nature," closely echoes Ibn Masarra's adoption of Graeco-Arabic philosophy's doctrines on Soul and Intellect and simultaneous critique of the philosophers. For Ibn Masarra, the scholarly articulators of his own revised form of Platonizing philosophy were the *ḥukamāʾ* (sages), while for Ibn Barrajān they are the *ḥikma*-elaborating Sufi saints (*awliyāʾ*). Like Ibn Masarra and al-Ghazālī, Ibn Barrajān blends the role of these philosophically oriented saintly sages with that of the scholars. His blending of roles appears in the following two passages that round out this chapter's analysis of Ibn Barrajān's Sufi metaphysics and his reconceptualization of the social role of the polymathic scholars as philosophically oriented mystical guides.

When the prophets and messengers (peace upon them) were in a position that connected mankind and the angels, it was out of God's wisdom that He also put the saints (*awliyāʾ*) in a position that connected the masses among the faithful and Muslims with the prophets and messengers. Faith in the necessity of existence of the saints and in the necessity of following them is in a position that follows only after the requirement of faith in the prophets and messengers, as they are the leaders.[80]

In his discussion of the religious authority of the saint in the first passage just quoted, Ibn Barrajān represents the Sufi saints as intermediaries between the prophets and the masses, which was a historically controversial claim in the eyes of earlier scholars from al-Andalus to Iraq.[81] In that same discussion, he asserts that "As for those of authority who are God's saints (*awliyāʾ*) and His deputies in his earth, listening and obedience to them is [in scriptural meaning] an exterior and interior [truth]."[82] In this same passage, in part of his explanation of a scriptural verse on acceptance of prophetic guidance, he resolves this potential theoretical tension between the religious authority of the Sufi saints and that of the scholars by blurring the categories in the same way that Ibn Masarra blurred the lines between the sages and the scholars.

"But nay, by your Lord, they do not believe until they make you [O Prophet] judge of what is in dispute between them and then find within themselves no discomfort from what you have decided and accept with full conviction," and as the scholars (*ʿulamāʾ*) are the inheritors of the prophets (peace be upon them), obedience to them privately and publicly is required.[83]

Ibn Barrajān accomplishes this fusion of saintly and scholarly religious authority by explicitly describing the scholars as inheritors of prophetic authority while simultaneously speaking of the saints in essentially the same terms. On the one hand, he does not identify the categories with each other, as specific modes of knowledge and authority are associated with each category. The *awliyāʾ* are distinguished by their role as guides for mystical aspirants to achieve the intellectual and spiritual ascent that deepens philosophical insight about the true nature of the world and God's omnipotence. The *ʿulamāʾ* are distinguished by their polymathic expertise in jurisprudence, speculative theology and belief, ethics, and other scriptural sciences. On the other hand, he quite clearly indicates that these models of authority can be found in a single person, that is, a scholarly Sufi who is ideally accomplished in all of these sciences. That *ḥikma* became a simultaneously philosophical and Sufism-oriented scholarly science in the Ottoman era, when Akbarian (Ibn ʿArabīan) Sufi metaphysics rose to prominence among the scholars, is perhaps a testament to Ibn Barrajān's vision of the ideal scholar also being a scholarly Sufi metaphysician. What is especially interesting about this harmony of roles is the reality that he himself appears to have been seen by contemporaries and later writers as the type of multifaceted scholarly Sufi that his work describes, earning him the posthumous reputation as the "Ghazālī of al-Andalus."

This continuity with both Ibn Masarra and al-Ghazālī highlights the likelihood that Ibn Barrajān's self-presentation as a philosophically oriented Sufi metaphysician and mystical guide among the scholars placed him in tension with other non-Sufi scholars and Almoravid ruling circles. As mentioned, the friction that developed between him and the Almoravid ruling circles took place against the backdrop of two political contexts: the continued prominence of the Platonizing semi-messianic Fatimid caliphs in neighboring North Africa and the rise of new political movements such as Ibn Qasī's Sufi-oriented political revolution, which was in formation at the end of Ibn Barrajān's life.[84] Ultimately, as much as Almoravid ruling circles grew wary of the rise of Sufis like Ibn Barrajān within scholarly circles, it was the rise of political reformist Sufi movements like that of Ibn Qasī that became the biggest political challenge to the dynasty. Just three years after the untimely death of Ibn Barrajān, Ibn Qasī channeled his religious authority as a Sufi into an explicitly political model of leadership resulting in a political revolution and separate state in Almoravid Portugal. The rebellion against the dynasty, discussed in the next chapter, sent shockwaves throughout the ruling and scholarly circles of the western Islamic world. Ibn Qasī's writings were even censured in a posthumous *fatwā* issued by Ibn Khaldūn (d. 808/1406) more than 200 years later in Cairo. That this political movement emerged from within growing local Sufi circles as opposed to Fatimid Ismāʿīlī circles appears to have played a role in how the Almohads, discussed in Chapter 6, turned against the Almoravids' earlier politics and absorbed both philosophy and Sufi metaphysics into their own political culture and court patronage.

Notes

1 An analytical study of the bibliographical sources on Ibn Qasī's life is available in several studies. José Bellver, "al-Ghazālī of al-Andalus: Ibn Barrajān, Mahdism, and the Emergence of Learned Sufism on the Iberian Peninsula," *Journal of the American Oriental Society* 133 (2013): 659–81; Denis Gril, "'La lecture supérieure' du Coran selon ibn Barrağān," *Arabica* 47 (2000): 510–22.

2 For a contextualization of the Almoravids' friction with these Sufis in the larger history of religious authority in al-Andalus, see Maribel Fierro, "Opposition to Ṣūfism in Al-Andalus," in *Islamic Mysticism Contested: Thirteen Centuries of Controversy and Polemics* (Brill: Leiden, 1999) pp. 174–206; J. Katura, "al-Taṣawwuf wa-l-Ṣulta: Namādhij min al-Qarn al-Sādis al-Hijrī fī l-Maghrib wa-l-Andalus," *al-Ijtihad* 12 (1991): 181–212.

3 Alexander Knysh's analysis of the political and scholarly debates throughout the Islamic world of the Almoravid-era and Almohad-era Sufis of al-Andalus offers a useful starting point for understanding the historical background and legacy of these figures. Alexander D. Knysh, *Ibn ʿArabī in the Later Islamic Tradition* (Albany: State University of New York Press, 1999).

4 Maribel Fierro and Claude Addas have traced the rise of saintly Sufis as an increasingly important and controversial locus of religious authority in their respective studies on the development of Sufism in al-Andalus. Maribel Fierro, "The Polemic about the *karamāt al-awliyāʾ* and the Development of Ṣūfism in al-Andalus Fourth/Tenth–Fifth/Eleventh Centuries," *Bulletin of the School of Oriental and African Studies* 2 (1992): 236–49; Claude Addas, "Andalusī Mysticism and the Rise of Ibn ʿArabī," in *The Legacy of Muslim Spain*, ed. Salma Khadra Jayyusi (Leiden: Brill, 1994), pp. 909–36.

5 Fierro, "The Polemic about the *karamāt al-awliyāʾ*," pp. 236–49.

6 Ibn ʿArabī, Ibn Sabʿīn, and Ibn Marʾa (Ibn Sabʿīn's teacher), all writing more than three centuries after Ibn Masarra's death, wrote of Ibn Masarra as a foundational figure in Andalusī mysticism. Andalusī mysticism, however, did not appear to flourish until almost two centuries after Ibn Masarra's death in the Almoravid period, though the validity of saint miracles was being debated in the Taifa period. Ibn ʿArabī wrote that Ibn Masarra was "the first in the states and stations" in Ibn ʿArabī, *al-Futūḥāt al-Makkiyya* (Cairo: Dār al-Kutub al-ʿArabiyya al-Kubrā 1329/1911), 1:147–8. As Massignon has shown, the writings of Ibn Marʾa indicate that Ibn Masarra argued in the latter's non-extant *Tawḥīd al-Mūqinīn* that God's attributes are limitless, and that the unity of the attributes is part of the doctrine of the oneness of God. This doctrine is central to the image of Andalusī mysticism presented by Andalusī mysticism's critics, including Ibn al-Khaṭīb, Ibn Khaldūn, and Ibn Taymiyya. Massignon's discussion is found in Louis Massignon, *Recueuil des texts inedits concernant l'histoire de la mystique en pays d'Islam* (Paris: Geuthner, 1929), p. 70. al-Ḥumaydī, who was a student of Ibn Ḥazm and lived only a century after Ibn Masarra, indicated that Ibn Masarra "*kāna ʿalā tarīqa min al-zuhd wa-l-ʿibāda … lahū tarīqa fi l-balāgha wa tadqīq fī ghawāmiḍ ishārāt al-ṣūfiyya*," in al-Ḥumaydī, *Jadhwat al-Muqtabis fī Dhikr Wulāt al-Andalus*, ed. Muḥammad al-Ṭanjī (Cairo: Maktab Nashr al-Thaqāfa al-Islāmiyya, 1952), no. 83, p. 58.

7 Vincent Cornell highlights how Ashʿarī theology first began to enter and merge with the Andalusī tradition of legal theory under the influence of the North African legist Abū ʿImrān al-Fāsī (d. 430/1039), whose Andalusī students mixed the studies of theology and jurisprudence with asceticism. He argues that the development in the later eleventh and early twelfth centuries of a theological and juridical consensus among legal theory-oriented scholars and Ashʿarī theologians led these scholars to strike a doctrinal compromise that Sufis supported. The result, he argues, conditioned the twelfth-century flourishing of a kind of Sufism that was heavily oriented around the reception of Ghazālī's Ashʿarī and Sufi *Iḥyāʾ ʿUlūm al-Dīn*. These developments saw the further transmission to al-Andalus of mysticism from Iraq, which included the writings of al-Sulamī, Abū Nuʿaym al-Iṣfahānī, and al-Qushayrī. Vincent Cornell, *Realm of the Saint* (Austin: University of Texas Press, 1998), pp. 3–31.

8 Kenneth Garden, "Al-Ghazālī's Contested Revival: *Iḥyāʾ ʿUlūm al-Dīn* and Its Critics in Khorasan and the Maghrib" (University of Chicago dissertation, 2005), pp. 144–223, idem, *The First Islamic Reviver* (New York: Oxford University Press, 2013), pp. 143–68; Delfina Serrano, "Why Did the Scholars of al-Andalus Distrust al-Ghazālī: Ibn Rushd al-Jadd's *Fatwa* on *Awliyāʾ Allāh*," *Der Islam* 83 (2006): 137–56.

9 Vincent Cornell, "Faqīh versus Faqīr in Marinid Morocco: Epistemological Dimensions of a Polemic," in *Islamic Mysticism Contested: Thirteen Centuries of Controversies and Polemics*, eds. Frederick de Jong and Bernd Radtke (Leiden: Brill, 1999), pp. 207–24. Manuela Marín has argued that while most of the eleventh-century *zuhhād* (ascetics) were *munqabiḍūn* or had believed in withdrawing from politically connected religious posts, some among the *zuhhād* did not refrain from holding administrative and legal offices. This

distinction may explain the slow development of a circle of Mālikīs interested in mysticism who were closer to ruling circles. Manuela Marín, "*Inqibāḍ ʿan al-sulṭān: ʿUlamāʾ* and Political Power in al-Andalus," in *Saber, Religioso, y Poder Politico en el Islam: Acts del simposio* internacional (Granada, 15–18 Octubre 1991) (Madrid: Agencia Espanola de Cooperacion Internacional, 1994), pp. 127–39; idem, "*Zuhhād* de al-Andalus 300/912–420/1029," *al-Qantara* 12 (1991): 439–69; Garden, "Al-Ghazālī's Contested Revival," pp. 144–223; Serrano, "Why Did the Scholars of al-Andalus Distrust al-Ghazālī," pp. 137–56.

10 One Nasrid-era example of the blending of Socrates' legacy with that of the Sufis, which makes the ancient philosophers appear as proto-Sufi mystics, can be found in the writings of Ibn al-Khaṭīb. Ali Humayun Akhtar, "The Political Controversy over Graeco-Arabic Philosophy and Sufism in Nasrid Government: The Case of Ibn al-Khaṭīb in al-Andalus," *International Journal of Middle Eastern Studies* 47 (2015): 323–42.

11 Knysh discusses this term as used by Ibn Khaldūn, as well as Ibn Khaldūn's various criticisms of the Andalusī Sufis. Knysh, *Ibn ʿArabī in the Later Islamic Tradition*, pp. 190–7.

12 Knysh's analysis focuses on the particular accusations found in Ibn Khaldūn's *Muqaddima* and Ibn Khaldūn's *fatwā*, transmitted by al-Fāsī. Ibn Khaldūn, *The Muqaddimah*, 3 vols., trans. Franz Rosenthal (Princeton, NJ: Princeton University Press, 1958); al-Fāsī, *al-ʿIqd al-Thamīn fī Taʾrīkh al-Balad al-Amīn*, 8 vols., eds. Muḥammad Ḥāmid al-Fiqī, Fuʾād Sayyid, and Maḥmūd Muḥammad Tanāhī (Cairo: Maṭbaʿat al-Sunna al-Muḥammadiyya, 1958).

13 Ibn Khaldūn, *The Muqaddima*, 3:89; al-Fāsī, *ʿIqd*, 2:180–1; al-Ghazālī, *Faḍāʾiḥ al-Bāṭiniyya wa-Faḍāʾil al-Mustaẓhiriyya*, ed. ʿAbd al-Raḥmān al-Badawī (Cairo: Dār al-Qawmiyya, 1964), p. 38.

14 al-Ghazālī, *Faḍāʾiḥ al-Bāṭiniyya*, p. 46.

15 al-Fāsī, *ʿIqd*, 2:180–1.

16 Ibn Khaldūn, *The Muqaddima*, 3:92.

17 See discussion of this accusation in María Calero Secall, "El proceso de Ibn al-Jaṭīb," *al-Qantara* 22 (2001): 421–61; Akhtar, "The Political Controversy over Graeco-Arabic Philosophy and Sufism in Nasrid Government," pp. 323–42.

18 Notably, Ibn Khaldūn groups Ibn Sabʿīn and Ibn ʿArabī with these earlier Almoravid-era Sufis in the same *fatwā*, as quoted in al-Fāsī, *ʿIqd*, 2:180–1.

19 In hindsight, historians know that the latter scenario occurred throughout the Islamic world, especially in Almohad, Nasrid, Mamluk, and Ottoman administrative circles that attempted to represent the court as a center of Sufi patronage. However, the fact that some scholars like Ibn Taymiyya began to fold Sufis into the polemical umbrella term "esotericists" long after the fall of the Fatimids is relevant in this context, because his position represents an alternative trajectory that religious discourse and politics could have followed. However, scholars and ruling circles sidelined Ibn Taymiyya's unpopular positions as they were perceived as extreme at the time. To be sure, as Michot has shown, even Ibn Taymiyya's interests and engagement with philosophy and Sufism were deeper than his modern revived legacy suggests. Yahya Michot, "Ibn Taymiyya's Commentary on the Creed of al-Ḥallāj," in *Sufism and Theology*, ed. Ayman Shihadeh (Edinburgh: Edinburgh University

Press, 2007), pp. 123–36. Ibn Taymiyya, *al-Radd ʿAlā l-Manṭiqiyyīn*, ed. ʿAbd al-Ṣamad Sharaf al-Dīn al-Kutubī (Bombay: al-Maṭbaʿat al-Qayyima, 1949), pp. 509–10.

20 The hagiographical text of Ṭāhir al-Ṣadafī is of particular interest as a source on how the scholars, by the Almohad period, were widely associated with forms of piety characteristic of Sufis, including saintly miracle performance. This source helps contextualize changes in Almohad-era political policies that appear to have responded favorably to these Sufi-oriented scholarly developments. Halima Ferhat, "As-Sirr al-Maṣūn de Ṭāhir as-Ṣadafī: un itinéraire mystique au Xiie siècle," *al-Qantara* 16 (1995): 237–88; Cristina de la Puente, "Vivre et mourir pour Dieu, oeuvre et héritage d'Abū ʿAlī al-Ṣadafī (m. 514/1120)," *Studia Islamica* 88 (1998): 77–102; Maribel Fierro, "La religión," in *Historia de España Menéndez Pidal – El retroceso territorial de al-Andalus. Almorávides y Almohades, siglos IX–XIII*, eds. José María Jover Zamora and María Jesús Viguera Molíns (Madrid: Espasa-Calpe, 1997), 8-2:435–546.

21 This reading agrees with key aspects of the early analysis of Asín Palacios, who surmised that Ibn Barrajān might be connected with Ibn Masarra's legacy. Miguel Asín Palacios, *Abenmasarra y su escuela. Origenes de la filosofía hispano-musulmana* (Madrid: Imprenta Ibérica – E. Maestre, 1914).

22 The manuscript tradition of this text is discussed in Gril, "'La lecture supérieure' du Coran selon ibn Barrağān." What is less accurate in Gril's discussion is his explanation that the Names of God, for Ibn Barrajān, have agency in the creation of the world. Gril's analysis of Ibn Barrajān's introduction makes the Names of God appear as though they serve a kind of intermediary causal function between God and man. In this analysis, Ibn Barrajān's doctrines on the Names of God resemble Ibn ʿArabī's later interpretation of the Names of God, an overview of which is found in William Chittick, *The Sufi Path of Knowledge: Ibn ʿArabī's Metaphysics of Imagination* (Albany: State University of New York Press, 1989), pp. 31–76. The current chapter points to how Ibn Barrajān discusses the Names not as independent agents, but rather as sources of meanings for the mystical aspirant's understanding of God's agency. The analysis in this chapter is based on an examination of the Konya manuscript, which is the oldest manuscript available. Following the completion of this study, an edition of the *tafsīr* based on this manuscript was published by Mazyādī in Beirut. Ibn Barrajān, *Tafsīr Ibn Barrajān: Tanbīh al-Ifhām ilā Tadabbur al-Kitāb al-Ḥakīm wa-Taʿarruf al-Āyāt wa-l-Nabaʾ al-ʿAẓīm*, ed. Aḥmad Farīd Mazyādī (Beirut: Dār al-Kutub al-ʿIlmiyya, 2013). A partial edition using a later manuscript in Munich, which does not include the first half of the text that is examined in this chapter, was recently published in Casablanca by Idrīsī. Ibn Barrajān, *al-Tafsīr al-Ṣūfī lil-Qurʾān aw Tanbīh al-Ifhām ilā Tadabbur al-Kitāb al-Ḥakīm wa-Taʿarruf al-Āyāt wa-l-Nabaʾ al-ʾAẓīm*, ed. Muḥammad al-ʿAdlūnī Idrīsī (Casablanca: Dār al-Thaqāfa, al-Muʿassasa lil-Nashr wa-l-Tawzīʿ, 2011). An edition of Ibn Barrajān's minor *tafsīr*, which echoes many of the key doctrines found in the major *tafsīr* examined in this chapter, has recently been published by Böwering and Casewit. Ibn Barrajān, *A Qurʾan Commentary by Ibn Barrajān of Seville (D. 536/1141): Īḍāḥ Al-Ḥikma bi-Aḥkām al-ʿIbra (Wisdom Deciphered: The Unseen Discovered)*, eds. Gerhard Böwering and Yousef Casewit (Leiden: Brill, 2015). Purificación de la Torre

was one of the pioneers of the study of Ibn Barrajān's work, and published an edition of his dedicated writing on the Names. Ibn Barrajān, *Sharḥ Asmā' al-Ḥusnā*, ed. Purificacion de la Torre (Madrid: CSIC, 2000).

23 Bellver, "al-Ghazālī of al-Andalus."

24 Serrano, "Why Did the Scholars of al-Andalus Distrust al-Ghazālī"; Garden, "Al-Ghazālī's Contested Revival," pp. 166–79; Fierro, "La religión," pp. 3–31.

25 See this book's introduction.

26 Konya, Yusuf Ağa Library (hereafter cited as KYA), MS Yusuf Ağa 4744 fol. 2r.

27 These concepts have a range of meanings in speculative theology. Ibn Barrajān seeks to extend their meanings into a mystical context in much the same way that al-Ghazālī and the Sufis of Iraq had done so. Ibn al-ʿArīf's extant Sufi writings offer a good reference in this regard for understanding how other Sufis at the time likewise interpreted some of these concepts mystically. His writings also illustrate some of the channels and networks of students through which Ibn Barrajān's works were transmitted. Using Ibn al-ʿArīf's letters, edited under the title *Miftāḥ al-Saʿāda*, Paul Nwyia showed that Ibn al-ʿArīf was not the teacher of Ibn Barrajān and Ibn Qasī, as Asín Palacios thought, but was rather a student. Evidence from Ibn al-ʿArīf's letters indicates that he addressed Ibn Barrajān as an authoritative master and teacher. Paul Nwyia, "Notes sur quelques fragments inédits de la correspondence d'Ibn al-ʿArīf avec Ibn Barrajān," *Hespéris: Archives Berberes et Bulletin de l'Institute des Hautes Études Marocaines* 48 (1955): 217–21.

28 KYA, MS Yusuf Ağa 4744 fol. 2v.

29 This typology resembles the Andalusī philosopher Ibn Bājja's taxonomies of human souls and their predispositions. Ibn Bājja categorized people according to the predominance of various faculties, including the rational, imaginative, and nutritive, with some Sufis included among those whose souls have a predominance of spiritual forms over corporeal forms. Ibn Bājja, *al-Qawl fī l-Ṣuwar al-Rūḥāniyya*, in *Rasā'il ibn Bājja al-Ilāhiyya*, ed. Mājid Fakhrī (Beirut: Dar al-Nahār, 1968), pp. 50–5; Ibn Bājja, *Tadbīr al-Mutawaḥḥid*, in *Rasā'il ibn Bājja al-Ilāhiyya*, ed. Mājid Fakhrī (Beirut: Dār al-Nahār, 1968), p. 80.

30 In the context of Sufi hermeneutics and the importance of bringing together *ẓāhir* and *bāṭin* meanings, al-Ghazālī also spoke of *iʿtibār* as a kind of crossing over from the manifest (*ẓāhir*) to the secret (*sirr*). al-Ghazālī, *Mishkāt al-Anwār*, trans. David Buchman, *The Niche of the Lights* (Provo, UT: Brigham Young University Press, 1998), p. 32ff. With reference to Ibn Taymiyya, *al-Tafsīr al-Kabīr*, Sands notes how Ibn Taymiyya wrote approvingly of Sufi shaykhs who spoke, in a manner akin to legal judgments, of allusions (*ishārāt*) in connection with those teachings taken from the Qur'an that fall under the category of consideration (*iʿtibār*) and analogy (*qiyās*). He stated that "if the allusion is considerative (*iʿtibāriyya*) by virtue of a sound type of analogy (*qiyās*), it is good and acceptable." Kristen Sands, *Sufi Commentaries on the Qur'an in Classical Islam* (Routledge: New York, 2006), p. 121. Ibn Taymiyya, *al-Tafsīr al-Kabīr* (Beirut: Dār al-Kutub al-ʿIlmiyya, 1988), 5:423.

31 In Sufi writing, this representation of the *ṣiddīqūn* near to the prophets in virtue has some early precedent in Sahl al-Tustarī's Qur'an commentary.

In reference to the prophets, he asserts that the "truthful ones" (*ṣiddīqūn*) are "heirs to the secrets of their sciences" in *Tafsīr al-Tustarī*, 58:22. Sahl al-Tustarī describes purity in character (*akhlāq*) and propriety (*adab*) attained by prophets and "some among the truthful ones" in *Tafsīr al-Tustarī*, 79:40. On Avicennan conceptions of intuition, see Frank Griffel, "Al-Ghazāli's Concept of Prophecy: The Introduction of Avicennan Psychology into Ashʿarite Theology," *Arabic Sciences and Philosophy* 14 (2004): 101–44; Alexander Treiger, "Monism and Monotheism in al-Ghazālī's *Mishkāt al-Anwār*," *Journal of Qur'anic Studies* 9 (2007): 1–27.

32 This correspondence between scriptural and worldly hidden realities is central to the esoteric hermeneutics described in Chapter 1 as a phenomenon that was widespread in early Islamic theological systems. For Ibn Masarra in early Sunni scholarly circles, as for Ismāʿīlīs in early Shiite theological circles, the notion of the world as text with manifest and hidden layers of meaning was entangled with philosophical and mystical methods of expanding the Qur'an's call to ponder the signs of the world. *Encyclopaedia of Islam*, 2nd ed., s.v. "Bāṭiniyya"; Maribel Fierro, "Bāṭinism in al-Andalus: Maslama b. Qāsim al-Qurṭubī (d. 353/964), author of the *Rutbat al-ḥakīm* and the *Ghāyat al-ḥakīm (Picatrix)*," *Studia Islamica* 84 (1996): 87–112.

33 KYA, MS Yusuf Ağa 4744 ff. 6v-7r.

34 There are parallels in this context with the use of apophatic discourse in the writings of Ibn ʿArabī. Michael A. Sells, *Mystical Languages of Unsaying* (Chicago: University of Chicago Press, 1994). It is notable that in a *fatwā* on *dhikr*, Ibn Taymiyya criticized particular ways that Sufis used the name of God in isolation in *dhikr*, specifically in the form of the proper noun *Allāh* and the pronoun *huwa* (*al-ism al-mufrad al-muẓhar wa-l-muḍmar*). He objected specifically to what he thought was the imprecise use of terms. In the first case, in the use of the proper noun *Allāh* in *dhikr*, he objected to its use in grammatical isolation of a meaningful phrase or sentence, such as the semantically fuller profession of faith: "There is no God but God (*Allāh*)." In the second case, in the use of the pronoun *huwa* in *dhikr*, he likewise objected to its use in isolation given that the phrase does not indicate grammatically a referent and can refer to anything. In his own words, "Some of those who persisted in this kind of *dhikr* ended up in various kinds of deviations and ideas of *waḥdat al-wujūd* (oneness of being)." Interestingly, he connects this practice to the Andalusī Sufis in the era of Ibn ʿArabī by referring to the "people of oneness of being." al-Maqrīzī, *Kitāb al-Sulūk li-Maʿrifat Duwal al-Mulūk*, ed. Muḥammad Muṣtafa Ziyāda (Cairo: Kulliyyat al-ādāb bi-Jāmiʿat al-Qāhira, 1934–72), 2:40–94.

35 KYA, MS Yusuf Ağa 4744 fol. 16.4r.

36 Qur'an, 56:96, 56:74, 69:52.

37 Qur'an, 87:1.

38 Qur'an, 40:60. KYA, MS Yusuf Ağa 4744 fol. 16.4r.

39 It is significant that Ibn Barrajān offers esoteric hermeneutics and mysticism as tools for resolving the question of the name and the named. Ibn Ḥazm distinguished the name and the named in agreement with some of Ibn Barrajān's conclusions, but Ibn Ḥazm's conclusions were based on a different approach. Here, Ibn Barrajān suggests that the true meaning of a name is not

what immediately comes to mind from the referent but is rather the interior or *bāṭin* reality of what is signified, which he elaborates later in this chapter. Ibn Ḥazm made a similar claim, but identified the real meaning as the *ẓāhir* meaning, which is likewise not necessarily the first meaning that comes to mind but rather the true meaning upon investigation of context and logical evidence. Drawing on Ibn Ḥazm's method, later Andalusī Sufis including Ibn ʿArabī could call themselves Ẓāhirīs by identifying *bāṭin* realities with the *ẓāhir* meaning of the text as a single meaning. This approach appears to be what is sometimes found in Ibn ʿArabī's hermeneutics, and he perhaps justified it based on this mutual Ẓāhirī–Sufi agreement on the notion that any given name (signifier) and its conventionally associated named (signified) do not have a universal binary relationship. Goldziher's appreciation of the point that later Sufis were "easily accommodated" within Ẓāhirism appears to be based on his recognition that the *ẓāhir* for Ibn Ḥazm and the Sufis was not necessarily the first meaning that came to mind upon hearing a word. Ignaz Goldziher, *The Ẓāhirīs: Their Doctrine and Their History*, trans. Wolfgang Behn (Leiden: Brill, 2008) pp. 160–70.

40 KYA, MS Yusuf Ağa 4744 fol. 16.4r.

41 Ibn Masarra likewise discussed the Names of God as manifest and hidden pathways to specific subtle pieces of knowledge about God's role as creator of the world, knowledge that he believed could be witnessed at the level of the phenomenal world's interior realities and that he articulated in Neoplatonic terms. One example of the way he attempted to derive information about agency, including names indicative of agency, from other names was in his analysis of the *basmala*. From the *basmala*, he discovered three names: the name of divinity (God), the Beneficent, and the Merciful. His analysis of the name Merciful included the following point: "From [the Name] the Merciful is derived [the information] that God is the One Who fashions (*muṣawwir*), the One Who witnesses (*shāhid*), the One Who gives life (*muḥyī*)." Ibn Masarra, *Kitāb Khawāṣṣ al-Ḥurūf* in Pilar Garrido, "Edición critica de *K. jawāṣṣ al-ḥurūf* de Ibn Masarra," *Al-Andalus Magreb: Estudios árabes e islámicos* 14 (2007): 61ff.

42 Qur'an 16:79.

43 KYA, MS Yusuf Ağa 4744 fol. 16.4v.

44 As mentioned, in his analysis of the text, Gril understands Ibn Barrajān's discussion of the Names of God in a slightly different way. From Gril's perspective, the Names for Ibn Barrajān have agency in the creation of the world. Gril's analysis of Ibn Barrajān's introduction makes the Names of God appear as though they serve a kind of intermediary function between man and God in a way that resembles Ibn ʿArabī's later interpretation of the Names of God. As the current chapter argues, Ibn Barrajān's approach more likely echoes Ibn Masarra's writing, in which the Names are indicative of the different facets of God's agency. Denis Gril, "'La Lecture Supérieure' du Coran selon Ibn Barrağān," *Arabica* 47 (2000): 510–22.

45 There are important parallels in this doctrine with Sahl al-Tustarī and Ibn Masarra's discussion of the Names, which highlights the important connection in mysticism between Sahl al-Tustarī and Ibn Barrajān. Both Sahl al-Tustarī and Ibn Barrajān integrate their discussion of the Names into specific rituals for the mystical aspirant oriented around *dhikr*. This element is not a

key aspect of Ibn Masarra's surviving texts, which emphasize contemplation more exclusively. Still, Andalusī historiography ascribes ascetic rituals to Ibn Masarra and his students, who organized ascetic retreats in the mountains outside Cordoba. Given Ibn Masarra's asceticism and inclination toward the writings of Sahl al-Tustarī, together with Ibn Masarra's textual reference to the importance of invocation (*dhikr*) of the Names of God, there may indeed have been some ritual oriented around *dhikr* and mysticism in his mountain retreats that may have been preserved in his other non-extant writings. Marín has investigated Ibn Masarra's connections with both ascetics and early Sufis in al-Andalus. Marín, "*Zuhhād* de al-Andalus," 439–69.

46 Qur'an 13:31.

47 Qur'an 29:45.

48 Qur'an 20:14.

49 KYA, MS Yusuf Ağa 4744 fol. 7r.

50 Qur'an 2:152.

51 Marion Katz provides an overview of ways that various types of *dhikr*, which include the two-way *dhikr* discussed here, relate to other forms of ritual piety, including mystical piety. Marion Katz, *Prayer in Islamic Thought and Practice* (Cambridge: Cambridge University Press, 2013), pp. 10–43, 75–120. The use of the phrase "mystical piety" in this chapter refers to piety that incorporates remembrance of God (*dhikr*) within and outside of prayer in addition to any other ritual (such as scriptural recitation) in the mystical aspiration for intellectual or spiritual witnessing of the divine realm. This use of the term mysticism draws on the respective works of Melchert and Chabbi. Christopher Melchert, "The Transition from Asceticism to Mysticism at the Middle of the Ninth Century CE," *Studia Islamica* 83 (1996): 51–70; Jacqueline Chabbi, "Remarques sur les développement historique des mouvements ascétiques et mystiques au Khurâsân," 46 (1977): 5–72.

52 KYA, MS Yusuf Ağa 4744 fol. 7r.

53 Sahl al-Tustarī discusses the pinnacle of mystical experience as gnosis (*ma'rifa*) that connects the light of certainty, the eye of certainty, and the knowledge of certainty. Sahl al-Tustarī, *Tafsīr al-Tustarī*, 2:40.

54 KYA, MS Yusuf Ağa 4744 fol. 15r.

55 Qur'an 2:1.

56 KYA, MS Yusuf Ağa 4744 fol. 15r.

57 It is notable that Ibn Barrajān emphasizes clearly the inimitability of prophecy and distinguishes sharply between prophets and other pious figures, whether the truthful ones or the saints. Despite this distinction, Ibn Khaldūn still lumps Ibn Barrajān with those Sufis whom he collectively blames for doctrines on religious authority that appear Fatimid-like and specifically semi-messianic (*mahdī*). At the same time, in his *fatwā* issued in Cairo, preserved by al-Fāsī, he isolates the writings of Ibn Qasī, not those of Ibn Barrajān, as texts worthy of being burned, a distinction that points either to his understanding of Ibn Barrajān's work as being more theologically scrupulous or simply his criticism of the unique political manifestations of Ibn Qasī's Sufism. al-Fāsī. *al-'Iqd al-Thamīn fī Ta'rīkh al-Balad al-Amīn*, 2:180–1.

58 This method of integrating doctrines found in the philosophers' cosmologies into an esoteric scriptural hermeneutic is common among early

philosophers themselves, such as the classical *falāsifa* and the Brethren of Purity. Concomitant with this method is the notion of an elect, whether philosophers, philosophically oriented Sufis, or Platonizing Ismāʿīlī theologians, who can grasp the esoteric meanings of scripture. Ibn Masarra, the Brethren of Purity, and al-Ghazālī in his Sufism are among the most notable predecessors for Ibn Barrajān in this context. Sands has provided a useful overview of some of the points of contention among defenders and critics of an esoteric scriptural hermeneutic. Sands, *Sufi Commentaries on the Qur'an in Classical Islam*, pp. 47–64.

59 Qur'an 41:12.

60 Ibn Barrajān's use of this Universal–Particular Servant relationship offers a window into the philosophical background of Sufis in this era, who had a wide variety of philosophical models to draw on. The Ikhwān al-Ṣafāʾ and al-Ghazālī are two of the most obvious sources. Fierro has argued that the *Rasāʾil Ikhwān al-Ṣafāʾ* were transmitted in al-Andalus as early as the tenth century, which is earlier than the widely accepted medieval report that the *Epistles* were transmitted by Abū Ḥakam al-Kirmānī in the first half of the eleventh century. Both the *Rasāʾil* and al-Ghazālī's discussions of macrocosm–microcosm connections overlap with discussions of divine agency. al-Ghazālī, *Mishkāt al-Anwār*, ed. ʿAbd al-Azīz Izz al-Dīn al-Sayrawān (Beirut: ʿĀlam al-Kutub, 1986), p. 158ff.

61 KYA, MS Yusuf Ağa 4744 fol. 77r–77v.

62 KYA, MS Yusuf Ağa 4744 fol. 77r–77v.

63 KYA, MS Yusuf Ağa 4744 fol. 77r–77v.

64 See epistles 26 (vol. 7) and 34 (vol. 8) in *Rasāʾil Ikhwān al-Ṣafāʾ wa Khullān al-Wafāʾ*, ed. Butrus al-Bustānī (Beirut: Dar Ṣādir, 1957).

65 In what suggests the influence of al-Ghazālī's work on Sufism in this era, Ibn Barrajān's distinction here between the lower intellect's perception of secondary causality and the higher intellect's transcendence of secondary causality to recognize divine omnipotence echoes al-Ghazālī's discussion of how human judgment of causality follows not from the necessity of their connection, but from a hidden syllogism. al-Ghazālī, *Tahāfut al-Falāsifa*, ed. Maurice Bouyges (Frankfurt: Institute for the History of Arabic-Islamic Science, 1999), p. 278.

66 This discussion of angels as being fundamental to understanding divine omnipotence is central to Ibn Ḥazm's theological approach, in which the angels are identified as carrying out God's command in the scriptural reference to the ones who "carry the Throne" (Qur'an 40:7). Ibn Ḥazm, *al-Fiṣal*, 2:291. See Chapter 2.

67 KYA, MS Yusuf Ağa 4744 fol. 78r.

68 In an analysis that is worth comparing to Ibn Barrajān's assessment of philosophy, Marmura's work has offered a classic overview of al-Ghazālī's own balance of these perspectives. Michael Marmura, "Did al-Ghazālī Deny Secondary Causality?" *Studia Islamica* 47 (1978): 83–120.

69 What distinguishes Ibn Barrajān and Ibn Ḥazm from the *falāsifa* is that both emphasize an understanding of God as a voluntary agent Who, as the only planner (*mudabbir*), acts out of His Will and not out of necessity. Still, like Ibn Masarra, Ibn Barrajān is willing to acknowledge critical aspects of the

philosophers' doctrines in psychology and cosmology, particularly in the case of specific faculties of the celestial bodies. Ibn Ḥazm rejected philosophical descriptions of the faculties of the celestial bodies beyond the obvious heating effect of the sun on the world. His position followed from his skepticism that these faculties could be studied empirically. He argued that there simply is not enough evidence to test in a repeated manner and based on sensory evidence how exactly the planets have an effect on the earth. Still, he admitted that there might be some celestial effect on the earth akin to the sun's heat. Ibn Ḥazm, *al-Fiṣal*, 5:148–9.

70 KYA, MS Yusuf Ağa 4744 ff. 189v–190r.

71 See this book's introduction.

72 KYA, MS Yusuf Ağa 4744 ff. 190v–191r.

73 As noted in Chapter 2, al-Kindī and Ibn Masarra are important predecessors and possible sources in paving the way for this integration of philosophical doctrines into Islamic theology. They share an understanding that the philosophers identified correctly key elements of cosmology despite misunderstanding fundamental principles of causality. For this reason, Ibn Masarra criticized the philosophers while still using their language of Universal Soul and Universal Intellect, in effect reinterpreting these terms.

74 See this book's introduction.

75 KYA, MS Yusuf Ağa 4744 ff. 193r–193v. Ibn Barrajān's language echoes Ibn Masarra's writings, especially where Ibn Masarra indicates that the *falāsifa* identified God's attributes but "explained them in other terms" out of ignorance of scripture. The idea of criticizing the philosophers and simultaneously adopting their doctrines and language is so common that it appears almost like a literary trope in the writings of many early and later Sufi metaphysicians (Ibn Barrajān, Ibn Ṭufayl, Ibn ʿArabī), as well as in the writings of the Platonizing Ismāʿīlī theologians. The use of this argument in Sufi texts tends to betray the author's interest in actually absorbing select doctrines in *falsafa*, or repurposing *falsafa* for mysticism. Ibn Khaṭīb, as mentioned, criticizes this particular aspect of Sufism in al-Andalus, even as he unsurprisingly represents Socrates and the ancient philosophers as a proto-Sufis. Ibn al-Khaṭīb, *Rawḍat al-Taʿrīf bi-l-Ḥubb al-Sharīf*, p. 555ff.

76 KYA, MS Yusuf Ağa 4744 ff. 193r–193v.

77 Ibn Barrajān's point suggests that some philosophers discarded religious ritual. This point echoes Ibn al-Jawzī's criticism mentioned previously of the Sufi distinction between *ʿilm al-bāṭin* and *ʿilm al-ẓāhir* in his scrupulous defense of the preservation of law, ritual, and ultimately prophecy. For Ibn Barrajān, like al-Ghazālī before him, one can strike a balance in the use of a *bāṭin-ẓāhir* scriptural hermeneutic while avoiding compromising ritual. Ibn al-ʿArīf's discussion of the *bāṭin* meanings of rituals is notable. He claims that these meanings strengthen one's understanding of their value rather than compromising their importance. Ibn al-ʿArīf, *Maḥāsin al-Majālis*, ed. Miguel Asín Palacios (Paris: Paul Geuthner, 1933).

78 KYA, MS Yusuf Ağa 4744 ff. 193r–193v.

79 KYA, MS Yusuf Ağa 4744 ff. 193r–193v.

80 KYA, MS Yusuf Ağa 4745 fol. 184v.

81 Fierro provides an analysis of how the doctrine that the scholars inherit the authority of the prophet operated in tension with the idea that Sufis provide continuing communal guidance or are a source of emulation for the community. Maribel Fierro, "Spiritual Alienation and Political Activism: The *ġurabā'* in Al-Andalus during the Sixth/Twelfth Century," *Arabica* 47 (2000): 230–60.

82 KYA, MS Yusuf Ağa 4745 fol. 185v.

83 KYA, MS Yusuf Ağa 4745 fol. 185v.

84 Evidence for a clash between Ghazālīan Sufi scholars and other scholars can be seen in the example of the former *qāḍī* of Almería, Abū l-Ḥasan al-Barjī (d. ca. 1115). The *qāḍī* issued a juridical opinion criticizing the pro-Almoravid chief *qāḍī* of Cordoba for calling for the destruction of al-Ghazālī's *Iḥyā' 'Ulūm al-Dīn*. Accusations against al-Barjī and his students resulted in the decades that followed. These later accusations were directed against Ibn al-'Arīf, Ibn Barrajān's contemporary. Ibn Barrajān may have been caught up in an anti-Ghazālīan movement among the Andalusī scholars that erupted originally with the book-burning campaign and lasted throughout the final years of the twelfth-century Almoravid period. Cornell has contextualized this controversy in the context of a debate over *uṣūl al-fiqh* more than Sufism. However, Garden's and Serrano's previously mentioned works indicate that the debate over Sufi religious authority was at the center of this tension. Cornell, *Realm of the Saint*, pp. 20–2. The details of this condemnation against the Cordovan chief *qāḍī* who called for the destruction of al-Ghazālī's works are found in 'Abbās b. Ibrāhīm, *al-I'lām bi-man Ḥalla Marrākush wa-Aghmāt min al-A'lām*, ed. 'Abd al-Wahhāb b. Manṣūr (Rabat: al-Maṭba'a al-Malakiyya, 1974), 2:6ff.

5 A New Political Model and Its Sufi Dimensions

The political reformer and Sufi Ibn Qasī (d. 546/1151) was both the head of a short-lived city-state in present-day Portugal and a writer of Sufi metaphysics. His mysticism, like that of his predecessors, synthesized philosophical doctrines in psychology and cosmology, esoteric hermeneutics, and controversial claims about the religious authority of Sufis. In the later Mamluk era in the fourteenth century, Ibn Khaldūn strongly condemned Ibn Qasī's Sufi treatise, *Doffing of the Sandals* (*Kitāb Khalʿ al-Naʿlayn*), in a *fatwā* issued as one of four head judges in post-Fatimid Cairo. The late date of this *fatwā*, written more than 200 years after Ibn Qasī's death and in a city far from al-Andalus, is indicative of how Ibn Qasī's striking political activity as an anti-Almoravid separatist earned him enduring notoriety among ruling and scholarly circles. Ibn Khaldūn's one-time colleague Ibn al-Khaṭīb, the chief minister in Nasrid Granada, was likewise a critic. In contrast with Ibn Barrajān's (d. 536/1141) and Ibn al-ʿArīf's (d. 536/1141) theories of communal leadership, which blended the roles of Sufi metaphysicians and scholars, Ibn Qasī's conception of communal leadership blended the roles of Sufi metaphysicians and political reformers. His political movement and that of the advancing Almohads of Marrakesh, who represented their founder as a saintly semi-messianic (*mahdī*) figure, marked the diminishing of the earlier political challenge of the Platonizing Ismāʿīlī *imām*-caliphs and the rise of a variety of new political models from within Sunnī political circles that drew on Sufism.

A Sufi Debate about Communal Leadership

In many ways, Ibn Barrajān and Ibn Qasī were very different figures, and their lives were cut short under very different circumstances. Ibn Barrajān, like Ibn al-ʿArīf, was a Sufi among the twelfth-century scholars (*ʿulamāʾ*) of al-Andalus, while Ibn Qasī does not appear to have had a strong scholarly background. He is represented in the sources as having turned to a more austere and ascetic life following an early career as a

Figure 5.1. The castle and surrounding town of Mértola, site of Ibn Qasī's (d. 1151) short-lived state in Almoravid Portugal.

tax collector under the Almoravids.[1] Upon becoming an itinerant mystic, he absorbed diverse intellectual influences, possibly including the philosophical *Epistles of the Brethren of Purity* of Iraq, and he led a separatist movement in the Algarve city of Mértola against the Almoravids.[2] Ibn Qasī's contemporaries Ibn Barrajān and Ibn al-ʿArīf, in contrast, were not political revolutionaries and did not make any known claims to political power or articulate aspirations to rule. While they died mysteriously after being summoned to the Almoravid court in Marrakesh for questioning, Ibn Qasī was killed ten years later by his followers. His demise took place while trying to maintain the autonomy of his short-lived revolutionary state in Mértola, threatened on two fronts by the advancing North African Almohads and by Christian kingdoms descending as far south as Coimbra and Lisbon.[3] Ibn Qasī made treaties on both fronts in an attempt to maintain the autonomy of his state, and it was apparently his treaty with the Portuguese conqueror Afonso de Henriques (d. 1185) that formed part of the immediate sequence of events leading to his demise at the hands of his own supporters.

Ibn Qasī's most famous work, *Doffing of the Sandals* (*Kitāb Khalʿ al-Naʿlayn*), is available in three editions, edited respectively by David Goodrich, Josef Dreher, and Muḥammad al-Amrānī. The studies included in these editions highlight that Ibn Qasī was unique among Sufis during his lifetime for actually claiming ruling political power and founding a short-lived separatist state.[4] While Goodrich and Dreher have pointed out that Ibn Qasī's political claims appear to be based in a specific conception of Sufi religious authority found in the text, Amrānī focused more on the question of Ibn Qasī's cosmological interpretation of the Names in an analysis that contextualizes Ibn ʿArabī's work decades later. All three historians have contributed to an understanding of how Ibn Qasī defined the mystical elect in a manner indicative of a new theory of Sufi political authority, which earned Ibn Khaldūn's famous criticism. Building on these studies, the current chapter explores the unanswered question of how philosophical knowledge and esoteric hermeneutics in particular became integrated into his politically reformist model of religious authority. In this context, it is important that the *ḥadīth*-based notion of the *ghurabāʾ*, virtuous people who become "strangers" in a decadent environment at the end of time, is referenced in Ibn Qasī's work.

The respective works of Maribel Fierro and Mercedes García-Arenal have pointed out how the political use of doctrines such as the "strangers" (*ghurabāʾ*) and the semi-messianic "guided one" (*mahdī*) links Ibn Qasī's movement with several other twelfth-century political movements, including the late Fatimids and early Almohads.[5] Scholarly critics of some of these political reformist movements, including critics of Sufi and non-Sufi political movements, objected to the way these political theories echoed the Fatimid Ismāʿīlīs' conception of a semi-messianic Shiite *imām*-caliph. As Knysh has shown, Ibn Khaldūn, the one-time colleague of the chief Nasrid vizier Ibn al-Khaṭīb, ascribed to Ibn Qasī and other Andalusī Sufis a theory of religious authority that he believed problematically resembled the notion of the semi-messianic Fatimid Ismāʿīlī caliph.[6] That Ibn Khaldūn's condemnation of Ibn Qasī's writings came in the form of a *fatwā* that he issued as one of four chief judges in post-Fatimid Mamluk Cairo speaks to the extent to which the controversy over the Fatimid Ismāʿīlīs' Platonizing theories of leadership continued to loom large in the background of Sunnī political and theological debates about leadership long after the Fatimids' collapse in 1179.[7] In this regard, Ibn Qasī's work offers a key counterpoint to Ibn Barrajān's writings because it shows how Sufi metaphysics was becoming entangled in the twelfth century not only with changes in scholarly conceptions of communal guidance, but also new models of political leadership that drew on the scholars' Sufi religious authority. By the Almohad, Nasrid, Mamluk, and Ottoman eras, Sunnī political circles were beginning to converge upon a common and enduring pattern of ruling patronage of scholarly Sufi metaphysicians and their writings, a pattern reminiscent of the earlier and continued patronage of philosophical theologians and philosopher-physicians in the Abbasid and Andalusī Umayyad periods.[8]

The previous chapter explored how Ibn Barrajān's understanding of the mystical elect was based on a theory of mystical knowledge drawing on Graeco-Arabic philosophy (*falsafa*) and esoteric scriptural hermeneutics. The mystical elect for Ibn Barrajān were the saints (*awliyāʾ*), whose mysticism was articulated in terms of witnessing God's agency throughout the world in the "hidden realities of things." The contemplative mystics grasp this level of ontology through an understanding of the meanings of God's Names (*maʿānī al-asmāʾ*), which Ibn Barrajān believed were indicative of God's immanent and omnipresent agency, and which Ibn Barrajān found to be illustrative of various philosophical truths identified as *ḥikma* (wisdom).

This chapter examines how Ibn Qasī's representation of the elect was likewise based on a theory of contemplative mystical knowledge drawing on a system of philosophical cosmology, one that strongly echoed Ibn Masarra's Platonizing doctrines in psychology. In a departure from Ibn Masarra's work, however, Ibn Qasī emphasizes the gnostics' witnessing of God's omnipresent agency in greater continuity with Ibn Barrajān and Sahl al-Tustarī's mysticism.[9] Specifically, in his *Doffing of the Sandals*, Ibn Qasī describes the mystical elect as the gnostics (*ʿārifūn*) and saints (*awliyāʾ*), who employ an esoteric hermeneutic in terms of the interior dimensions (*bāṭin*) of both scripture and the world's phenomena. This process leads the mystical aspirant to transcend visions of corporeality (*jismāniyya*) in order to witness three hidden layers of reality that closely echo philosophical conceptions of particulars and universals: the particular realities (*daqāʾiq*) that veil corporeality, the subtle realities (*raqāʾiq*) that veil the particulars, and finally the universal true realities (*ḥaqāʾiq kulliyyāt*) that veil all of the previous and that are created from light. Ibn Qasī explains that the mystical elect's perception of the universal true realities, which echoes the philosopher's cognitive grasp of the universals, leads to greater acquisition of the light of knowledge and guidance, and that ultimately it is the Sufi gnostics (*ʿārifūn*) who can witness the ultimate hidden truth of this interior knowledge: the oneness of the universal true realities as a reflection of the oneness of the Creator of these realities. This truth notably echoes Ibn Barrajān's discussion of the oneness of God's agency perceived in the world and ultimately anticipates Ibn ʿArabī's massively influential and controversial notion of the oneness of existence (*waḥdat al-wujūd*).

Critically, from a political perspective, Ibn Qasī represents people in his own lifetime who grasp this knowledge, and whom he believes preserve the light of higher knowledge and guidance following the end of prophecy, as the virtuous "strangers" (*ghurabāʾ*) mentioned in the *ḥadīth*. He describes these figures as social reformers living in his own lifetime who resist Pharaonic-scale tyranny. That is, his theory of knowledge is integrated into an explicitly articulated political model of communal leadership that, in historical practice, clashed with the Almoravids' political authority and the scholars' conception of sound communal guidance.

Ibn Qasī's *Doffing of the Sandals*

The Doffing of the Sandals offers a clear window into Ibn Qasī's presentation of the mystical knowledge of the Sufis and his characterization of them as social reformers. The text sets out to answer what the contents of this knowledge are, who claims this knowledge, and what their role in society is. In a manner that echoes Ibn Barrajān's work and that of Ibn Masarra, Ibn Qasī defines the knowledge emerging from an esoteric hermeneutic in terms of the pursuit of the true realities (*ḥaqāʾiq*) or universal true realities (*ḥaqāʾiq kulliyyāt*). These universal true realities are ultimately indicative of certain philosophical phenomena in the order of the world that, in a final analysis, make the *ḥaqāʾiq kulliyyāt* closely resemble the Peripatetic philosophers' universals (*kulliyyāt*).[10]

The elect are defined as those who can ascetically remove the sandals of their worldliness in order to grasp the unseen universal true realities and acquire the light of knowledge and guidance it reflects downward from the divine pedestal, the *kursī*. The elect, according to this theory, acquire the ability to discover that the unity or oneness of these created universal true realities reflect the unity or oneness of the Creator of these realities.

Ibn Qasī uses the scriptural story of Moses addressed by God atop Mount Sinai to frame the most fundamental theme in the treatise, namely, the acquisition of knowledge as light. As the text's title suggests, Ibn Qasī is particularly interested in the fact that Moses was instructed to remove his sandals at the start of his divine encounter as he stood before the burning bush. For Ibn Qasī, Moses' "removal of the sandals" reflects how he extended his sensory perspective beyond the immediate world around him such that the divine world and its secrets could come into clearer view.[11] Ibn Qasī understands Moses' ability to extend his perspective beyond the world in pursuit of higher knowledge as having conditioned his preparedness to receive revelation. In Ibn Qasī's representation of this scene, an ascetic broadening of perspective beyond the limits of worldly concerns and desires appears as an element of ritual that undergirds the mystical pursuit of higher knowledge.

> This [acquisition of light] was the fruit of the doffing [of the sandals] and the benefit of listening and hearing. [It was] the reward of sincerity in belief, certainty, and of thinking well [and positively] of the Lord of the Worlds. [This acquisition] continued to be his disposition (*hay'a*), raising him to the seat of truth, and it was the manner of his (blessings of God be upon him) learning the true word.... Therefore [as for] the one who longs to hear the truth and the true word from where truth manifests to him like a flash of a sparkling light from the seat of truth, let him remove the sandals of his worldliness and let him present alms quietly in silence[12] [and in silent longing for the divine], and let him know that God is the Benevolent, the Merciful, the Almighty, the Generous, the One Who guides whom He wills to the Straight Path.[13]

Ibn Barrajān is significant that Ibn Qasī does not present the removal of the sandals of worldliness as an end in itself, a point indicative of the fact that this treatise is not a work on asceticism. Rather, his comments reflect the fact that this treatise is oriented around the mystical acquisition of knowledge as light. The description of asceticism here constitutes a vehicle for reaching a certain level of knowledge that strikes the ascetic as a "flash of sparkling light." This flash of light is also an "opening" (*fatḥ*), as he will state later. What one discovers following an "opening" represents almost the entire content of Ibn Qasī's treatise, much as Ibn 'Arabī's "openings" in his famous *Meccan Openings* constitute the entire content of Ibn 'Arabī's work. *The Doffing of the Sandals* is essentially an outline of what Ibn Qasī represents as his own opening. This representation of the text as a product of his own mystical opening is illustrative of how he conceives of his own role as a mystical guide.[14]

As [this light] was an opening of knowledge and an unveiling through contemplation, it was among the gifts of the secrets and the fragrances of the abode of the lights. [This light] was the sending forth of life and the ripening of plants, and the opening of the sheaths of the light of the heavens. I do not mean by this the intent of [poetic] authors, nor the method of classification in categories of [philosophical] writers, but rather the expression of this opening as it [actually] came and the elucidation of the locus of the sparkling light whence it [truly] shined. When [this knowledge] came together, it came as unrolled parchment, and when it was arranged together, it was arranged as a penned book. It was Hebraic (*ʿibrānī*) of origination in its type and spiritual of extraction in its foundation, and I named it *The Doffing of the Sandals and the Acquisition of Light from the Pedestal.* I made it a knowledge established and a parable drawn in such a way that it would be an allusion to what [should be truly] understood, and in order that what it suggests is grasped, and in order that that the perspicacious know that [as scripture says:] houses are not entered except from their [proper] doors, and that places are not reached except by their [proper] means.[15]

Crucially, Ibn Qasī is interested in elaborating not only the content of mystical knowledge as light, but also the modality of human reception of this light and the question of who in mankind acquires the most light. The answers to these questions are built around a concept that is a central building block of many of his other mystical concepts, namely, that knowledge as light derives from the divine Pedestal of scripture, which he later characterizes as one of the levels of existence in his philosophically oriented cosmology. The treatise's title indicates that when Moses removed his sandals and suddenly encountered light, he was subsequently enlightened by light from above. Ibn Qasī presents himself as someone who was similarly able to remove the sandals of his worldliness, but he identifies the knowledge he received as an "opening" as opposed to the "revelation" of prophets. Even though he does not make a claim to new revelation or a new law, emphasizing elsewhere in the text that the legal stipulations and rituals of Islam's final prophecy are central to his path to higher knowledge, he nonetheless represents his opening as having come in the form of "unrolled parchment" that was "Hebraic in generation." That is, his representation of his own mystical knowledge is boldly evocative of scriptural representations of Moses' prophetic reception of revelation. At the same time, Ibn Qasī tempers his claims to mystical knowledge by identifying his language as only allusions and parables, even as he asks the reader to accept the validity of his mystical opening, which Ibn ʿArabī ultimately rejected.[16]

The essential points to draw from this discussion is that he places himself among the spiritual elect who are below prophets, that the light of knowledge is drawn from the Pedestal (*kursī*) as a continuing source of light, and that the attainment of the light reflected from the *kursī* is conditional on the expansion of one's perspective beyond the limits of the world through ascetic piety in controlling appetite and desire. In emphasizing the centrality of asceticism in his work, he indicates, "Let it be clear to him with two eyes that the intention of the doffing of the sandals is only that one doffs himself of the sandals of his worldliness and removes from himself the two garments of his appetite and desire."[17] Mystical knowledge, in this way, follows from this ascetic piety. In expanding on his description of the *kursī*, he says that "each heavenly unveiling is made manifest from this mirror," which he also calls a "niche" in reference to the Qur'anic light verse and in parallel with al-Ghazālī's earlier discussion in the *Niche of the Lights*.[18] In this way, an "unveiling of the heavenly dominion" (*kashf malakūtī*) and an "opening" constitute the development of new vision made possible by the light of the *kursī*. This unveiling appears not according to "traditional patterns of knowledge transmission" among people, he explains, but rather according to the direct Will of God.

> The acquisition is in accordance with what the conditions of [divine] wisdom demand and in accordance with the descent of God's favor and mercy. It [proceeds] neither according to human order nor any traditional pattern of [knowledge] transmission, but rather according to the wise decree [of God] and the descent of God's ordaining Will.[19]

Ibn Qasī offers additional information about the modality of his acquisition of mystical knowledge, distinguishing it from knowledge that is passed from teacher to student. That is, he highlights how the descent of this light as an "opening" occurs not according to the transmission of knowledge passed between two individuals, but rather according to the direct grace of God, Who wills the manifestation of light as a descending of mercy from the divine world.[20] This point implies that this mystical knowledge is transmitted outside the circles of the scholars. What follows is a closer look at what Ibn Qasī presents as the contents of this mystical knowledge and the hidden realities perceived by the mystical aspirant. These details emerge in his discussion of the three levels of reality that one must climb in the cognitive move toward the veiled world of universals, or more precisely, the universal true realities. These three levels of reality are, more specifically, the particular realities (*daqā'iq*), the subtle realities (*raqā'iq*) or the subtle particular realities (*raqā'iq juz'iyyāt*), and the true realities (*ḥaqā'iq*) or the universal true realities (*ḥaqā'iq kulliyyāt*), all three levels of reality veiled by corporeality.[21] A deeper understanding of Ibn Qasī's representation of the mystical aspirant's perception of these hidden realities will ultimately contextualize how he conceives of the mystical elect as philosophically minded mystical guides and political reformers.

The Platonizing Ascent to the Universals

In Ibn Qasī's methodology, the expansion of one's perspective beyond the limits of the world moves the mystical aspirant from ascetic regulation of worldly desire to the cognitive recognition that one's own nature is not limited to the sensory world. Ibn Qasī introduces this latter concept in terms of the scriptural notion that mankind was extracted from Adam to take a covenant, testifying to God in recognition of God as mankind's Lord and Sustainer. Ibn Qasī expands the idea of this covenant into multiple covenants corresponding to man's spirit and lesser soul, which he identifies as two distinct incorporeal elements veiled by the corporeal body.

> He created the primary spirit characteristic [of the individual] (*al-rūḥāniyya al-ūlā*), and he then created the secondary soul characteristic [of the individual] (*al-nafsāniyyā al-ukhrā*), and to each one is a covenant, pact, and custom in the establishment of a covenant and accord. It was then said to [the soul characteristic]: If you honor the covenant and remember My power in every case and situation and you descend to your lower [humble] station and do not forget your lot in this worldly life, and if you recognize and affirm [your humble place] and you humble and lower yourself, then you will join [again] the primary spirit characteristic and you will be [even] in your human form in the higher [heavenly] host's form and in the best conformation and clearest splendor and honor.[22]

Despite mankind's recognition of God's Lordship (*rubūbiyya*) during the primordial covenant, the lower self or the soul that veils the true hidden spirit is tied to the particular realities (*daqāʾiq*) of the created world, and the soul thus takes on the worldly attributes of pride and arrogance as well as other qualities shared by the least angelic among corporeal worldly created beings. The lower self or the soul is potentially tied to the veiled spirit, which is the more angelic hidden reality veiled by the soul, if the soul can take on spiritual angelic qualities like humility. In the assimilation of these qualities and in the recognition of one's place in the world as a humble servant subject to God's power or agency, one fulfills the covenant and can expand perspective beyond the limits of one's own existence in the immediate surrounding world in order to ascend to a more angelic state. He calls the spirit, which he describes as a kind of higher angelic aspiration of the embodied soul, "the reality of the soul, and [in a parallel manner] the hidden (*bāṭin*) is the [true] reality of the manifest (*ẓāhir*)."[23]

In Ibn Qasī's metaphysics, the cognitive move from a limited sensory grasp of the corporeal world to an introspective awareness of the self and one's qualities, to an awareness of one's non-worldly spiritual element, and finally to consciousness of the origins of this non-worldly spiritual element in the incorporeal world above is more simply the following: the move from contemplating corporeality to contemplating the particular realities (*daqā'iq*) and subtle realities (*raqā'iq*), and finally to contemplating the true realities (*ḥaqā'iq*), a process that takes place through this ascent of the soul. A closer look at each of these sets of realities, beginning with the first, sheds light on the philosophical overtones of his mysticism.

Ibn Qasī's representation of the particular realities (*daqā'iq*) is indicative of how philosophical cosmologies and speculative theology offered a frame of reference for writers of Sufi metaphysics who sought to articulate and systematize their mystical findings. The particular realities (*daqā'iq*) in Ibn Qasī's work are neither precisely the particular forms described in *falsafa* nor the "accidents" of Islamic theology, but they closely resemble both.[24] Like the particular forms, the particular realities (*daqā'iq*) are particular manifestations of corresponding universal realities in the corporeal world. Like the "accidents" in speculative theology, the particular realities (*daqā'iq*) define the complex characteristics of an individual corporeal thing, and are therefore not immediately visible to the senses without the help of the intellect. Like speculative theology's "accidents," these particular realities in Ibn Qasī's metaphysics only exist as part of an existing thing's corporeal existence and therefore do not survive the death of the body.[25]

As for the particular realities (*daqā'iq*), they are the particular realities of separation and the marks of composition and assembly. From the [higher] angle of universal totalities in structure and synthesis, [the particular realities] are united and joined [like] the coherence of the body. However, from the [lower] perspective of particular forms (*al-ṣuwar al-juz'iyyāt*) revealing the loci of formation and structuring, they are separate [like] the scattering of the thoughts of the soul. This [vision of the particular realities beneath corporeality] is [hidden] underneath the shroud of the senses in [this shroud's] existence [covering] human forms and the self's structure. The heavenly see this [in their] preserved angelic vision. The prophetic witness this as an exalted witnessing of the intellect. The followers uncover this as a disclosure of knowledge through contemplation.[26]

Ibn Qasī explains that from the angelic perspective of universal realities, the particular realities (*daqā'iq*) are united as one, and we will see how he expands on this point later in his identification of the universal true realities (*ḥaqā'iq kulliyyāt*) as the logical origins of the particular realities (*daqā'iq*). In contrast, from the earthly perspective of particular forms, the particular realities (*daqā'iq*) are as scattered and unrelated as individual thoughts. Thus, from this earthly perspective, the particular realities (*daqāʾiq*) are related only insofar as they are manifested together in particular existents, such as an individual person. In the case of an individual person, moreover, the particular realities (*daqāʾiq*) are only visible when one transcends corporeality and can witness one's own *nafs*, which Ibn Qasī characterizes as the lower self or soul, that is, one's multifaceted self-identity or ego that makes a person an individual human. For Ibn Qasī, the soul (*nafs*) is distinct from the more real hidden spirit (*rūḥ*), which logically precedes the soul as a reality behind it. Ultimately, Ibn Qasī indicates that in individually manifesting different aspects of an individual's self or soul, the particular realities (*daqāʾiq*) seem unrelated, connected only in that they make up the individuality or selfness or soul characteristic (*nafsāniyya*) of an individual person. At the same time, in constituting a level of reality behind or beyond one's corporeality, the particular realities are one level closer than corporeality to the incorporeal subtle realities and universal true realities discussed later. Therefore, perception of the particular realities is an essential first step toward understanding the totality of the hidden true realities of the world. This perception goes hand in hand with being able to recognize one's ego (*nafs*) for all of one's ideal and less ideal qualities. Those individuals endowed with the sharpest levels of perception that transcend most easily the "shroud of the senses" are ultimately the prophets, angels, and those among the contemplative who appear after the lifetime of prophets. In this way, contemplation and pondering (*naẓar*) constitute an essential vehicle of human perception beyond the apparent corporeal world.[27] Pondering does not only allow cognitive transcendence of one's corporeality, which veils the particular realities visible upon perception of the self or soul. Rather, pondering also allows transcendence of the particular realities (*daqāʾiq*) that veil an even deeper level of reality, namely, the level of the subtle realities (*raqāʾiq*) visible upon perception of man's own spirit.

The subtle realities (*raqāʾiq*) are spirits in the particular realities (*daqāʾiq*), akin to what can emerge of offspring from a stalk of wheat in plants in accordance with the number of what is in it of separate particular realities ... as the single stalk of wheat might end up as one thousand stalks of wheat. This follows from [both] knowledge of the salubriousness of its location ... and from maintenance by the Cultivator (Exalted is His Glory). In each stalk of wheat is a portion of what was in the first wheat stalk of particular realities (*daqāʾiq*) and subtle realities (*raqāʾiq*). Likewise in the son of Adam (peace upon him) is a portion of what is in [Adam] of the particular realities (*daqāʾiq*) and subtle realities (*raqāʾiq*), part by part, portion by portion, section by section. Thus, if the corporeal veil over the expanse of the spirit characteristic [of the individual] is raised from you, it would reveal to you from within your essence the number of sons of Adam [that exist] among creation.[28]

The subtle realities (*raqāʾiq*) constitute the person's most essential aspect that can be grasped in his individual corporeal existence, and these realities are only visible upon the cognitive grasp of the spirit (*rūḥ*), man's essential human element. It is therefore at the level of the subtle realities (*raqāʾiq*) that an individual person's connection to other individual people can be recognized as a spiritual one. It is significant in this regard that the notion that all of mankind is created from one spirit, a favorite concept of the Graeco-Arabic philosophers, runs through the entire treatise.[29] Moreover, though the subtle realities behind the particular realities are also associated with an individual in his corporeal existence, the independent existence of the subtle realities is not limited by corporeal existence in the way that the particular realities (*daqāʾiq*) are.

In other words, in the case of man, Ibn Qasī explains that death does not signify the end of the subtle realities (*raqāʾiq*) as it does for the more corporeal particular realities (*daqāʾiq*), but it rather constitutes the seizing (*qabḍ*) of the subtle realities by an angel assigned to death. This process is the return of the spirit with man's subtle realities to the spirit's otherworldly existence as it awaits reckoning. This doctrine, notably, provides a small window into why many Sufi metaphysicians were subject to criticisms of using language evocative of philosophical doctrines such as the incorporeal resurrection.[30]

Critically, Ibn Qasī explains that even prior to death, in one's living corporeal existence, one can transcend the perception of these subtle realities (*raqāʾiq*) and arrive at the universal true realities (*ḥaqāʾiq kulliyyāt*), which constitute the otherworldly origins of both the subtle realities and the particular realities (*daqāʾiq*). It is ultimately the mystical aspirant's grasp of these true realities (*ḥaqāʾiq*) that leads to the next step of grasping the true oneness of the world in all of its apparent complexity, a point he will expand later in the context of grasping the oneness of the world's Creator.

As for the true realities (*ḥaqāʾiq*), they are beings among the higher abodes, scents of the spirits of life, paths of the seekers, and the places of ascent of the gnostics (*ʿārifūn*) to the highest heavenly levels. So he who treads [the true realities'] expanse stands firm, and he who rides their heavenly steed reaches the lote-tree of the farthest limit.[31] He will be granted the meal of the fasting ones and the [illumination of the] cracking open of the sleeping ones' eyes. If you realize the true reality from that point, then the end goal is reached … and the utmost [goal] is attained from the origin of [ascetic and contemplative] striving.[32]

While the particular realities and subtle realities (*raqāʾiq*) are part of what constitutes the individuality of an existing thing, the true realities (*ḥaqā'iq*) are entirely beyond the individuality of a thing and constitute the logical origin and point of return. From man's perspective, the true realities, those realities that constitute the objects of Divine Will and that veil the divine command, are central to the perception of the totality of existence. Perception of the true realities means that one can see, from the spiritual equivalent of a bird's-eye view, that the origins of creation are as one entity that was divided into firmament, earth, and the spheres between them, all of the preceding further divided by the command of God in the creation of various levels of existence that culminate in the manifestation of the particular realities, including man's particular realities. More specifically, Ibn Qasī describes this process in terms of realms evocative of, though not identical to, emanationist philosophical cosmologies.

> A simpler explanation of this is that the firmament and the earth were one solid mass[33] before being pulled apart, and one sphere before the creation of creation. Then God Most High created the earth and the heavens, each of them, as seven [levels]. He created creation between them as seven spheres like the [former] seven. So he created the celestial realm [or angelic realm] from the light of the firmament and originated the celestial reality (*al-ḥaqīqa l-samāwiyya*) out of that from which He created the realm. He created man from the light of the earth, and He originated the earthly reality (*al-ḥaqīqa l-arḍiyya*) out of that from which He created man, and [this earthly reality] is what sustains the body and is the object of [divine] intent supported by the command. He created the aerial realm from the light of the sphere of the atmosphere and brought into existence the intermediate reality (*al-ḥaqīqa l-barzakhiyya*) out of that with which He created that [aerial] realm.[34]

Ibn Qasī indicates that from the light of the firmament, God creates the celestial realm. And from the light of the spheres, God creates the aerial realm. Likewise, from the light of earth, God creates man. Ibn Qasī explains, furthermore, that God also creates certain realities that correspond to the creation of the celestial realm, the aerial realm, and man – namely the celestial reality, the intermediate reality, and the earthly reality. What is important to note is that in Ibn Qasī's presentation, the creation of these latter three universal realities (celestial reality, the intermediate reality, and earthly reality) does not precede but rather follows the creation of the corresponding realms of particulars (celestial realm, aerial realm, and man). That these universal realities are essential to the existence of the latter realms of particulars, even while the latter realms of particulars are prior in existence to the universal realities, indicates that the latter realms of particulars (celestial realm, aerial realm, and man) exist in some kind of conceptual or prototype form prior to their association with the universal realities that sustain and complete their existence. This framework resembles the ontology of Ibn ʿArabī's *aʿyān thābita*, "immutable entities" or "immutable images" that likewise evoke Platonic universals but are not identical to them.[35]

The question of the connection of Platonic universals with Ibn Qasī's framework can be framed in the following way: In what modality do these conceptual or prototype realms of particulars exist prior to their association with the realities that give them actual existence? For example, in the case of the realm of man, the universal "earthly reality" sustains man's existence as earthly living man as a living, corporeal, embodied, particular human being. However, somehow, "earthly living man" only exists *in potentia* in a conceptual way that logically precedes the "universal earthly reality" that sustains man's existence. In what modality does earthly living man exist prior to being imbued with or endowed with created existence through association with the universal earthly reality? Like Ibn ʿArabī's *aʿyān thābita*, Ibn Qasī's realms of particular concepts *in potentia* (celestial realm, aerial realm, and man) exist as known entities. He implies that they are known by God in His knowledge before God brings them into real existence with the creative "realities" (celestial reality, the intermediate reality, and earthly reality) that are veiled beneath their corporeal realities and that point to God's omnipresent agency hidden behind Ibn Qasī's philosophically oriented cosmology. It is notable that while Ibn ʿArabī characterized the immutable entities as nonexistent known things that are part of God's knowledge before they are created, Ibn Qasī in this text characterizes these individual concepts or prototypes as "creations" even prior to their association with the created *haqāʾiq* that sustain and complete their existence. This notion of the prototypes as "creations" possibly points to certain speculative theological notions of created knowledge that Ibn Ḥazm so vehemently rejected.[36]

The important point to draw from Ibn Qasī's discussion is that when these realities (*ḥaqāʾiq*), which are ultimately the universal realities veiling divine agency, are manifested as creation, they manifest as the subtle realities, particular realities, and corporeality (*jismāniyya*). Moreover, in one's cognitive transcending of the successive levels of corporeality and the particular realities as well as the subtle realities in order to discover the deeply hidden true realities, the mystical aspirant finally grasps the foundational oneness of the world's created origins by witnessing the oneness of God's hidden agency.

Critically, Ibn Qasī believes that certain individuals are most able to grasp these universal true realities (*ḥaqāʾiq*), namely, perspicacious individuals who are gnostic-like knowers (*ʿārifūn*). They are characterized by their ability to transcend the manifest world and reach the veiled universal true realities, and they recognize ultimately that the manifest plurality of particular realities veils the hidden unity of universal realities that in turn veil what lies beyond in the farthest reaches of existence. Their grasp of the universal true realities serves as a vehicle for further ascent to knowledge of what lies beyond in the unseen. He characterizes the grasp of the highest echelons of heavenly existence (*ʿilliyyīn*) as one of the final and most important objects of the mystical knowers' (*ʿārifūn*) aspiration, one that may never be reached in life but that represents a focal point and ideal direction of spiritual and contemplative movement.

In sum, Ibn Qasī believed that the mystical knowers (*ʿārifun*) were those among non-prophets most able to remove the sandals of their worldliness in order to acquire high levels of the light of knowledge reflected from the Pedestal (*kursī*), thereby ascending cognitively and spiritually to a mystical grasp of the world's universal true realities (*ḥaqāʾiq*) and a recognition of these realities' oneness. As discussed in the next section of this chapter's analysis, Ibn Qasī believed that the mystically perceived oneness of these universal true realities reflects the oneness of the Creator. What follows is a closer look at how Ibn Qasī presents cosmologically the mystical knowers' path to grasping the universal true realities as a kind of Platonizing celestial promenade through the six spheres of existence. His unique mystical cosmology, oriented around layers of unseen spheres, Thrones, and familiar scriptural notions like the Pen and Tablet, reflects an elusive engagement with the language of Neoplatonic psychology and cosmology that was similarly oriented around a procession of intellects and the cognitive ascent toward a universal intellect. As discussed in Part I, this intersection of scriptural language and Platonizing doctrines was assimilated into Sunnī theological writing by figures such as Ibn Masarra. And while some scholarly speculative theologians initially turned away from specific doctrines in Neoplatonic psychology and cosmology against the backdrop of the Platonizing Ismāʿīlī political controversy, and although revised approaches to these doctrines ultimately found their main home in philosophical theologies, these doctrines found a very different and enduring place in the language and imagery of scholarly and non-scholarly Sufi metaphysics. Ibn Qasī's celestial promenade, discussed in the next section, offers an illustrative example of a cosmologically Platonizing Sufi metaphysics that he, in contrast with his predecessor and contemporary Ibn Barrajān, integrated into a unique model of Sufi political leadership controversially evocative of Fatimid projections of a Platonizing model of political leadership.

A Philosophical Sufi Cosmology

In the previous sections of this chapter's analysis, Ibn Qasī was seen integrating discussion of the universal true realities (*ḥaqā'iq*) into an understanding of the creation of the world. He mentioned that the firmament and the earth as one created sphere were divided with the emergence of further spheres of creation and the procession of life through them. In the more detailed representation of this separation and unfolding of existence, Ibn Qasī explains that each sphere of existence constitutes a level of existence separated and unfolded from the higher level that precedes it, and at the same time each sphere constitutes a level of potential knowledge from the perspective of the lower level that follows.[37] The ultimate goal of the mystical knowers (*'ārifun*) is to return through these levels of knowledge to the origins of creation in order to achieve mystical enlightenment.

Know that it is through these two high sanctified and manifest celestial spheres [that is, the Sphere of Life and Sphere of Mercy] that existence separates and unfolds.... This living sphere [of life], which encompasses the Sphere of Mercy that extends over everything, [together] with the Sphere of Mercy, is what carries existence, and from [the Sphere of Life] begins the [process of] separating and unfolding, and so to it does [existence] return. With the life that comes from that high sphere and living sanctified veil, the ink-filled Pens proceed with the dispensations of the Will to manifest the wisdom of separation, unfolding, and establishing the pattern of fashioning and formation according to the decrees measured out in balance and in the places decreed: perfect words and firmly established ways, with no contradictory variation in them nor alteration or misplacement nor changing [of these words].[38]

With the unfolding of life or unfolding of existence comes the fashioning of forms and formation of existing things. This process is from another angle the fashioning of ink into complete and perfect words by the Pens that write according to the dispensations or principles of God's Will. With the ink of life proceeding from the Sphere of Life and the Sphere of Mercy, further levels of creation are brought into being and emerge as six further levels of existence.

From the revelation of the separation and unfolding comes the first [unfolded] existence, which is the Sphere of Life and the Encompassing Throne ... they [only] constitute veils of the Will, unfolding existence and strengthening the holds and supports [of existence] and establishing blessed life in the earth and skies, [proceeding] likewise from the highest of the high limits of heaven to the lowest of low limits.... As for the second existence, which is the Sphere of Mercy and the Noble Throne, God created from the light of its manifest aspect, which is the light of the great Pedestal [*kursī*], the spirit of holiness, which is the world of the station of contentment and the level of mercy, and to it reaches human sense and prophetic cognizance.[39]

Ibn Qasī explains that the Sphere of Life is associated with the Encompassing Throne, while the Sphere of Mercy is associated with the Noble Throne, a throne he thus distinguishes from the former throne. His presentation reflects his belief in multiple thrones that he describes according to the multiple adjectives used in the Qur'an with the scriptural word "throne."[40] According to Ibn Qasī's cosmology, the Sphere of Life and all-encompassing Throne do not manifest any new level of existence or light from which new existence is created. Rather, they serve as a universal principle of life for further levels of existence, carrying and veiling the creative Will of God. In contrast, the Sphere of Mercy and Noble Throne are together a manifest source of unfolded existence, and the level of existence they encompass is created out of the light that they manifest. This level of existence is characterized by contentment and mercy, attributes one acquires in greater degrees the closer one reaches this higher level of reality. This level is also, critically, associated with the spirit of holiness (*rūḥ al-quds*), identified by some Qur'an-commentators as the archangel Gabriel whom Ibn Qasī introduces separately in a later level of existence.[41] The key function of the spirit of holiness is in transmitting knowledge to the next level of existence, which is a function that emerges in Ibn Qasī's discussion of the letter *nūn* found in the Qur'anic passage, "*Nūn.* By the pen and what they inscribe."[42] For Ibn Qasī, the function of the Pen, which we will see him mention later in the next level of existence, reflects implementation of the divine command in the world and the transmission of knowledge to lower levels of existence. As in the Cordovan Ibn Masarra's mysticism-influenced Platonizing theological writings, the Pen in Ibn Qasī's mystical cosmology strongly resembles the role of Intellect in the Neoplatonic psychology of the Graeco-Arabic philosophers. In discussing various meanings of "*Nūn*" in the Qur'anic passage, Ibn Qasī suggests the idea that the *Nūn* represents an angelic being that is the light and ink of the Pen, and that the interior dimension (*bāṭin*) and spiritual characteristic of the *Nūn* is the spirit of holiness (*rūḥ al-quds*).[43]

According to an isolated [Prophetic] report, the *Nūn* is among the highest of the higher angels and the nearest of [that which is in] closest proximity [to the heavens], and the lights are supplied from what [*Nūn*] pours forth, and from the expanse of what it encompasses are the books and lines supplied. In this *thaqalī* world [of the *thaqalān*: man and *jinn*] and [amidst the heavenly] host, [the *Nūn*] is a spiritual secret with which [the created beings'] ability to understand life exists, and with which their stars are illuminated.... The *Nūn* is the ink of [the Pen's] flow and the light of [the Pen's] movement and the sounding effluence of its tongue in the Tablets of its exposition. [The *Nūn*] is the ultimate limit of what is descended in the veiled hiddens (*bawāṭin*) and the celestial manifests (*ẓawāhir*), and [the limit of what is descended of] the stations and treasures of beings that are firmly established [in the world]. [*Nūn*] descends from station to station through the veils of descent, and bears from station to station upon the patterns of ordering and regulation. [The *Nūn*] brings to the Pen what [the Pen] writes and to the Tablets what [the Tablets] establish as a natural disposition [in created beings to know God].... Know that the reception of the first knowledge, the exalted invocation in the pure and great expansion, is but from the spirit of holiness as descended inspiration and witnessed unveiling.[44]

In Ibn Qasī's representation of the relationship between the spirit of holiness (*rūḥ al-quds*) and the scriptural letter *Nūn*, he asserts that the spirit of holiness is the hidden dimension of *Nūn* and also *Nūn*'s hidden spiritual characteristic. He asserts, moreover, that the scriptural letter *Nūn* functions as the ink of the Pen in the writing of the Tablets. Taken together, his discussion indicates that he ascribes to the spirit of holiness the function of transmitting knowledge to all subsequent levels of existence, which he comes to articulate unambiguously at the end of the passages just cited. It is significant that it is to this level of existence that human sense and prophetic cognizance reach, according to Ibn Qasī's theory.

The implication in psychology of this mystical framework, which echoes aspects of both philosophical theology and Graeco-Arabic philosophy, is the claim that the modalities of inspiration among prophets and non-prophetic mystical aspirants are somehow related, even as prophets have greater and more complete access to highest levels of truth. While scholars found it textually sound to claim that non-prophets received lesser forms of inspired knowledge through dreams and other means, the integration of this claim into Sufi treatises was a more contested development, as it led to the following question: Which people among non-prophets did Sufis believe had the clearest access to these higher levels of truth and higher levels of knowledge of the "realities," if not the scholars (*ʿulamāʾ*)? Ibn Qasī provides an expected answer in the next level of existence in his cosmology: the gnostic-like mystical knowers (*ʿārifūn*).

As for the third existent, which is the great Pedestal and Magnificent Throne, God created from its manifest aspect – that is, the light of the Glorious Throne – the Elevated Pen and Well-Preserved Tablet, and it is the world of the decree and implementation as well as the [world of the heavenly] host of notation, and to it reaches the observation (*mulāḥaẓa*) of the [mystical] knowers (*ʿarifun*) and the witnessing (*mukāshafa*) of the prophets and messengers.[45]

Ibn Qasī names the Pedestal (*kursī*) together with the Magnificent Throne, which is a throne he distinguishes from the first two, as constituting the third unfolded existence. From the light that the Pedestal manifests, the Well-Preserved Tablet and Exalted Pen are created. This level of existence is the world of implementation and execution of the divine command, as the reader could have surmised from what he mentioned earlier about the Pen's role. Significantly, it is to this level of existence that he believes prophetic unveiling and mystical observation reach.[46] To understand the difference between these two characterizations of knowledge at this level (prophetic unveiling and mystical observation), one can look more closely at how he describes the mystical knowers' grasp of the Pen.

> The Pen is sanctified light from the light of the Pedestal (*kursī*) and descends upon the secret of knowledge to the station of dispensation. It was the light with which He enlightened space and the principal agent of the unfolding that separates and unfolds existences, and it is to this elevated primary principle that the [mystical] knowers look in contemplation.[47]

The idea that prophetic witnessing or epistemic unveiling (*mukāshafa*) and mystical observation or perception (*mulāḥaẓa*) both reach the Pen and Tablet indicates the extent to which Ibn Qasī seeks to argue the following point: non-prophetic mystical knowers (*'arifun*) have some lesser access to an aspect of the truths that prophets grasp, even as prophetic knowledge and knowledge of the mystical elect are distinct in modality and limits. This distinction emerges more clearly from his representation of how the mystical knowers look in contemplation to the Pen.

Specifically, Ibn Qasī distinguishes between, on the one hand, a complete epistemic unveiling of a particular truth among prophets and, on the other hand, the mystical knowers' (*'arifūn*) grasp of that truth following a process of contemplation that is not necessarily accompanied by a complete unveiling (*mukāshafa*), witnessing (*mushāhada*), or angelic vision (*ru'yā malakiyya*). In this context, angelic vision (*ru'yā malakiyya*) appears to refer to one of the highest levels of perception. He associates this vision primarily with angels, who are discussed in the next level of existence, the level of the Glorious Throne.

> As for the fourth existence, which is the sphere of the Illustrious Throne, God created from its manifest aspect, which is the light of the firmament, Gabriel the faithful spirit. This is the angelic world and the spiritual secret from which the secrets of the unseens (*ghuyūb*) as well as the news and tidings are descended. It is the world of the higher firmaments and the higher host, the near and chosen group, and to it reaches the heavenly disclosure of the elect among those with certainty and the luminary prophets.[48]

The Illustrious Throne, a throne Ibn Qasī distinguishes from the three previous thrones mentioned earlier, encompasses the fourth level of existence, and it manifests a light from which the Angel Gabriel is created.

This level of existence constitutes the world of angels or the angelic world from which "secrets of the unseens" are revealed to mankind. One can recall at this juncture that in his presentation of the emanation or rather unfolding of existence, his goal was to elaborate two phenomena: levels of creation and levels of perception. In this context, it is notable that his reference to prophets in this passage leads to the conclusion that he conceives of prophetic perception in multiple ways.

Specifically, he has described prophetic perception as cognizance on one level, unveiling on another level, and heavenly disclosure in this higher angelic level, this heavenly disclosure being a type of perception that Ibn Qasī indicates is shared by the elect among those with certainty. In describing this level of existence as the world of angels, and in characterizing this level as being below the previously discussed levels of existence, Ibn Qasī does not indicate that angelic perception is lower than prophetic and gnostic perception or that angelic perception is equivalent to the perception of the elect among the certain ones. Rather, he is indicating that as angels are created at this level of existence, this level therefore constitutes a more immediate level of perception for man than the higher levels in the larger process of man transcending his corporeality toward epistemic vision.[49] The "secrets of the unseens" are revealed to mankind from this level, and thus it should not come as a surprise that mankind is created in the next level of existence.

As for the fifth existence, which is the Sphere of the Firmament, God created from its manifest aspect (*ẓāhir*), which is the light of the earth, Adam (peace be upon him). This is the human world and the divine secret to which the spiritual angelic [host] prostrated, and to which the celestial luminosity was made subject, and likewise [the world to which] the lower animalic and non-animalic [creation was made subject].[50]

The Sphere of the Firmament is the fifth unfolded level of existence. From the light that it manifests, man is created. This level of existence is the world of man to whom higher and lower levels of existence, namely the celestial bodies and earthly world, were made subject. The idea presented here that man is associated originally with the Sphere of the Firmament and not the next sphere below, Earth, reflects the extent to which Ibn Qasī presents man as not being tied down by his corporeal existence. Indeed, Ibn Qasī already described how one's self or soul, which he indicated was veiled by one's spirit, is a self that is in turn veiled by corporeality and not tied to it. Likewise, a central starting point in Ibn Qasī's path to knowledge was the introspective turn inward to perceive the incorporeal self. In contrast with a human being's otherworldly spiritual origins are the creatures of the earth.

The sixth existence is the sphere of the earth. God created from its manifest aspect inanimate creation and animals and insects. It is the world of subjection and humbling and the genus of commonness. It is the lowest of the levels of discernment and lowest stations of distinguishing, [in which] each possesses a foundation in knowledge of its Creator and knowledge of what He instituted and prescribed and what He established as its purpose. "There is neither an animal that walks on earth nor bird that flies on its two wings but [forms part of] communities like you. Nothing have we omitted from the Book, and unto their Sustainer shall they be gathered."[51] "And there is no living creature on earth except that its sustenance depends on God,"[52] [to the end of] the verse.[53]

The sphere of the earth is the sixth and final unfolded level of existence, and in fact, it manifests no light at all, as it is the last unfolded level. What is created at this level of existence is created not from light that the earth manifests, but rather from the earth itself. This level of existence is the world of plants and animals. As for the level of perception associated with this sphere, it is ultimately the lowest level of perception. Notably, Ibn Qasī is not claiming that what is created at this level has the lowest cognitive abilities.[54] Rather, the key point he makes by describing this level as the lowest level of discernment is simply that what is seen at this height constitutes the most superficial dimension of vision. That is, one's eyes are least open if all that one sees is the corporeal world of the five senses. In contrast to this state is the state of the mystical knowers (*ʿārifūn*) with their eyes wide open, grasping the higher realities on their successful and continuing effort to transcend corporeality and the plurality of particular and subtle realities in the ultimate vision of the oneness of the true universal realities.[55] At the conclusion of his presentation of the unfolding of existence in his complex Platonizing mystical cosmology, he articulates the critical element this discussion has been leading up to, the final doctrine that explains why the vision of the true universal realities is so important to him and the mystical knowers who aspire to have "openings." For Ibn Qasī, the ability to grasp the true universal realities and their oneness in the path to higher levels of perception facilitates the ultimate goal of his mystical method: cognitive grasp of the oneness of the Creator.[56]

When God carried out His Will in bringing into existence His creation and perfected His Word in causing His dominion to appear, and [when] existence was unfolded and separated out according to the [divinely ordained] pattern and was produced according to [divine] wisdom and sustained according to [divine] strength and power, He saw perfection in creation and [perfection specifically] from the expertise of [His divine creative] pattern of putting [existence] in order: [He saw] that what He created was indicative of His oneness, and was an upright witness to His singularity such that intellects affirm willingly by instinct and natural predisposition (*fiṭra*) that He is the Clear Truth and that He, Most Blessed and Most High, is the best of creators.[57]

Ibn Qasī underlines what can be grasped from a broad view of creation and what can be attained upon grasp of creation's true realities. He points to a manifest truth he believes is grasped by human sense (*iḥsās basharī*), instinct (*jibilla*), and natural predisposition (*fiṭra*), a truth veiled by man's narrow sensory vision and unbalanced indulgence in sensory desire yet grasped in total disclosure through prophet-like cognizance (*idrāk nabawī*).[58] Specifically, the mystical knower aspires to grasp from this level the knowledge that the created world is an unfolding of layers of existence separated out by God from one composite whole, with the manifest particular realities associated with man's corporeal world having ontological origins in the created universal true realities. And in grasping the oneness of the created universal true realities, the mystical knower ultimately grasps the oneness of their Creator. It is a truth that follows from an ascetic willingness both to limit one's appetite and to extend one's perspective beyond the veil of the corporeal world in order to see the light that is the fundamental creative element of existence connecting the universal true realities with the particular realities. Critically, in Ibn Qasī's analysis, it is the elect as the knowers (*ʿārifūn*) among non-prophets who come closest in their certainty to grasping the complete totality of this truth, which is grasped more fully by prophets.

With this Platonizing and pre-Akbarian (Ibn ʿArabīan) elaboration of the cognitive and spiritual ascent of the mystical knowers through multiple layers of knowledge and perception, and with his articulation of the mystical grasp of the ultimate mystical truth of the oneness of God and the oneness of the universal true realities, Ibn Qasī leaves the most significant question for the current study unanswered: How did Ibn Qasī conceive of the role of these mystical knowers in society, and more specifically, how did he understand the nature of their leadership as communal guides? The political revolution that Ibn Qasī led suggests that the answer to this question was entangled with questions of political leadership. A closer look at evidence in the text indicates that Ibn Qasī's historical projection of authority, as a political reformer and Sufi sovereign among fellow political separatists, echoed aspects of the text in which he theorized the role of the mystical knowers as both communal guides as political reformers.

Sufis in Politics

The notion of the *ghurabāʾ*, knowledgeable or virtuous figures who become "strangers" in a decadent environment, figures prominently in Andalusī intellectual history and is integrated into Ibn Qasī's allusion to contemporary politics. The concept of the *ghurabāʾ* goes back to a

Prophetic *ḥadīth* and was interpreted in different ways in al-Andalus. The scholars (*ʿulamāʾ*), the Sufis, and the philosophers all made claims to being the virtuous "strangers" of their time.[59] In the case of Ibn Barrajān, some of the scholars were themselves Sufis, a group whom Ibn Barrajān identified as true claimants to the philosophical knowledge that the Peripatetic philosophers sought. In Ibn Qasī's case, his *Doffing of the Sandals* makes few clear references to the scholars (*ʿulamāʾ*), an absence that seems to reflect the extent that Ibn Qasī conceptualized the role of the scholars and Sufis differently.[60] What follows in the last section of this chapter is a brief analysis of the political overtones of his conceptualization of the mystical knowers as political reformers.

Ibn Qasī's reference to the *ghurabāʾ* appears in the context of discussing the cyclical nature of time, during which guidance appears in the form of prophets and their communities after successive periods of moral corruption. He mentions the *ghurabāʾ* specifically in the context of the period of the Prophet Muhammad's appearance, which he reminds his reader is the last prophetic period before the end of time.

> Every saintly miracle (*karāma*) given to a prophet and saintly proximity [to God] (*wilāya*) [given] to a saint (*walī*) was brought together in [the Prophet Muhammad's] prophecy and [subsequently] appeared in what followed among the family and the strangers (*ghurabāʾ*) from his community.[61]

Interestingly, Ibn Qasī believes that saintly miracles (*karāmāt*) appeared in the family of the Prophet and in the ranks of the *ghurabāʾ* among the community. His distinguishing of the *ghurabāʾ* from the family of the Prophet is important because it narrows the definition of the *ghurabāʾ*. Who is he referring to as "strangers" (*ghurabāʾ*) who are not from the descendants of the Prophet but to whom he attributes saintly miracles (*karāmāt*) and saintly proximity [to God] (*wilāya*)? The mystical elect at the center of the text, the knowers (*ʿārifun*), appear to be the overwhelmingly obvious answer.[62] In the remainder of his discussion of the topic, he explains that there are certain periods in which these figures appear. They are "strangers (*ghurabāʾ*) and chosen individuals who are for their glorious time and resplendent period the stars of the sky and horizons elevated high, a community compared to whom nothing is better than their era and [in whose case] nothing is more radiant than the words [shared] between them."[63] What is most significant about the role he ascribes to these *ghurabāʾ* is the way he characterizes them as reformers in an era of political decadence.

> Know that [as for] the tyrants of the times and the [tyrannical] pharaohs of the Qur'an, God sent them only as a test for the strangers (*ghurabāʾ*) of the time

and for the individuals of the period in order that the prophets would come out against them....[64]

In the rest of the passage, Ibn Qasī speaks of the *ghurabā'* as they appear historically in each prophetic period, upholding the virtues taught by that prophet until the next prophet comes to rescue them from the "tyrants of time" and the "pharaohs of the Qur'an." His reference alludes specifically to the scriptural example of Moses saving his followers from the persecution of Pharaoh. In the Qur'an, Moses departs with his followers in refuge from Pharaoh's Egypt after first confronting him and making an appeal to faith and upright behavior. However, Ibn Qasī's language suggests that his reference to the "strangers" is not an abstract reflection on the followers of Moses in Pharaonic Egypt and is more specifically a reflection on the strangers of his own lifetime in the Almoravid Maghrib, which he likens to Pharaonic Egypt. His language communicates a certain urgency in the need to bring about moral reform in a complex political environment, language that closely mirrors the historical reality of his political reform movement. That is, the text indicates that he appears to have theorized at an early stage some kind of reform movement oriented around Sufi epistemology, though he may not have imagined an all-out rebellion in writing this treatise. That is, on one level, the eruption of a rebellion may have had less to do with his political theories and more to do with the fact that several concurrent rebellions occurred against the Almoravids in the dynasty's final years, when the Almohads were already advancing. On another level, his discussion of the *ghurabā'* and his reference to Pharaonic-level tyranny in a text centrally about mystical metaphysics indicates that when he did rebel, he had already formulated and articulated a doctrinal pretext to draw upon in the form of his conception of Sufis as virtuous mystical guides and legitimate political leaders. The connection of the text to the political rebellion was strong enough in the eyes of early modern critics that Ibn Khaldūn, looking back centuries later, was able to comment on the intersection of Almoravid-era Sufi conceptions of communal guidance and coterminous political models of ruling leadership, specifically the semi-messianic model of the Fatimids. What made this intersection alarming in the eyes of scholarly critics was, beyond doctrinal questions, the extent that it disrupted the seemingly functional dialectic of authority in the premodern Middle East between rulers and scholars as two types of communal leaders. In later centuries, especially in the Mamluk era and as early as the Almohad period discussed in the next chapter, ruling circles appear to have responded to these new political models by reconceptualizing their own models of political leadership and absorbing this Sufi knowledge and authority through new patterns of patronage and court culture.

In sum, at a doctrinal level and in historical practice, Ibn Qasī appears to have broken with the model of the "Ghazālī of al-Andalus" Ibn Barrajān, who fit the knowledge and leadership of the Sufi metaphysicians within the religious authority of the scholars without explicit claims to political power. In contrast, Ibn Qasī's representation of the Sufis' "openings" as the product of a Platonizing cognitive and spiritual ascent through various spheres of knowledge became part of his conceptualization of the mystical "knowers" (*ʿārifun*) as political reformers. Critically, when the Almohads began to take over Almoravid territories in twelfth-century al-Andalus, they politically allied themselves with Ibn Qasī in Mértola. That short-lived alliance foreshadowed the dramatic changes in political culture and political legitimacy that were to come in the late twelfth century. By the time the philosopher-physician and Mālikī judge Ibn Rushd (Averroes) rose to prominence, the powerful Almohads had become patrons of not only scholarly writers of philosophical theology and Graeco-Arabic philosophy in continuity with the early Abbasids, but also writers of a philosophically oriented Sufi metaphysics in a centralizing political culture that absorbed the authority associated with these new scholarly forms of knowledge.

Notes

1 An analytical study of the bibliographical sources on Ibn Qasī's life is available in several works, including the following: Maribel Fierro, "Spiritual Alienation and Political Activism: The *Ghurabāʾ* in al-Andalus during the Sixth/Twelfth Century," *Arabica* 47 (2000): 230–60; Josef Dreher, "L'Imâmat d'Ibn Qasî à Mértola (automne 1144- été 1145). Legitimité d'une domination soufie?" *Mélanges de l'Institut Dominicain d'Études du Caire* 18 (1988) 153–210; Vincent Lagardère, "La tarîqa et la revolte des Murîdûn en 539 H / 1144 en Andalus," *Revue de l'Occident musulman et de la Méditerranée* 35 (1983): 157–70.

2 For a contextualization of the revolution of Ibn Qasī in the larger context of Sufism in al-Andalus, see Claude Addas, "Andalusī Mysticism and the Rise of Ibn ʿArabī," in *The Legacy of Muslim Spain*, ed. Salma Khadra Jayyusi (Leiden: Brill, 1994), pp. 909–36; Maribel Fierro, "Opposition to Ṣūfism in Al-Andalus" in *Islamic Mysticism Contested: Thirteen Centuries of Controversy and Polemics* (Brill: Leiden, 1999) pp. 174–206; J. Katura, "al-Taṣawwuf wa-l-Sulta: Namādhij min al-Qarn al-Sādis al-Hijrī fī l-Maghrib wa-l-Andalus," *al-Ijtihad* 12 (1991): 181–212.

3 Fierro has highlighted the importance of Guichard's analysis of the lack of tribes in al-Andalus in contrast with North Africa, a point that contextualizes the way political opposition movements in al-Andalus were more likely to emerge in frontier regions rather than in the tribal contexts. See Fierro, "Spiritual Alienation and Political Activism," pp. 253–7. Pierre Guichard, *Les Musulmans de Valence et la Reconquete (XI[e]–XIII[e] Siecles)* (Damascus: Institut Francais de Damas, 1990–1), 1:106ff.

4 The following editions of Ibn Qasī's *Kitāb Khalʿ al-Naʿlayn* are available, the first of which by Amrānī will be used in this chapter. Ibn Qasī, *Kitāb Khalʿ al-Naʿlayn*, ed. Muḥammad al-Amrānī (Safi: IMBH, 1997); David R. Goodrich, "*A Ṣūfī Revolt in Portugal: Ibn Qasī and His Kitāb Khalʿ al-Naʿlayn*" (Columbia University dissertation, 1978); Josef Dreher, "Das Imamat des islamischen Mystikers AbulQasīm Aḥmad ibn al-Ḥusain ibn Qasī (gest. 1151). Eine Studie zum Selbstverständnis des Autors des 'Buchs vom Ausziehen der beiden Sandalen' (Kitāb Khalʿ an-naʿlain)," PhD dissertation, Rheinische Friedrich Wilhelms Universität Bonn (Germany), 1985.

5 Fierro, "Spiritual Alienation and Political Activism," pp. 253–7; idem, "Le *mahdi* Ibn Tumart et al-Andalus: l' élaboration de la légitimité almohade," in *Mahdisme et Millenarisme en Islam*, ed. Mercedes García-Arenal (Paris: Edisud, 2000), pp. 107–24; Mercedes García-Arenal, "La conjunction du sufisme et du sharifisme au Maroc: le Mahdi comme sauveur," *Revue des Mondes Musulmans et de la Mediterranée* 55–6 (1990): 233–56.

6 Alexander D. Knysh, *Ibn ʿArabī in the Later Islamic Tradition* (Albany: State University of New York Press, 1999), pp. 190–7.

7 al-Fāsī, *al-ʿIqd al-Thamīn fī Taʾrīkh al-Balad al-Amīn*, ed. Muḥammad Ḥāmid al-Faqī, Fuʾād Sayyid, and Maḥmūd Muḥammad Tanāhī (Cairo: Maṭbaʿat al-Sunna al-Muḥammadiyya, 1958), 2:180–1.

8 Tahrali has outlined the reception of Ibn ʿArabī's Sufi thought in the Ottoman era. Mustafa Tahrali, "A General Outline of the Influence of Ibn ʿArabī on the Ottoman Era," *Journal of the Muhyiddin Ibn 'Arabi Society* 26 (1999): 43–54. The Ottoman absorption of Sufism into Ottoman political culture and patterns of patronage echoes aspects of Nasrid court ceremony, visual culture, and book patronage. Barbara Boloix Gallardo, *De la Taifa de Arjona al Reino Nazarí de Granada (1232–1246): en torno a los orígenes de un estado y de una dinastía* (Jaen: Instituto de Estudios Giennenses, 2005), pp. 58–76.

9 Ibn ʿArabī quoted Ibn Barrajān, Ibn Qasī, and Ibn Masarra in a way that makes it appear overwhelmingly likely that Ibn Barrajān and Ibn Qasī were also familiar with Ibn Masarra's work. Ibn ʿArabī writes that Ibn Masarra was "the first in the states and stations," while Ibn Marʾa indicated that Ibn Masarra wrote on the limitlessness and unity of God's attributes. Both doctrines are connected to some of Ibn Qasī's claims in this chapter as well as those of Ibn Barrajān analyzed in the previous chapter. For Ibn ʿArabī and Ibn Marʾa's comments, see Ibn ʿArabī, *al-Futūḥāt al-Makkiyya* (Cairo: Dār al-Kutub al-ʿArabiyya al-Kubrā 1329/1911), 1:147–8; Louis Massignon, *Recueuil des texts inedits concernant l'histoire de la mystique en pays d'Islam* (Paris: Geuthner, 1929), p. 70.

10 Ibn Barrajān similarly represented the *ḥaqāʾiq* as realities evocative of philosophical definitions of the universals, which indicates the possibility of some overlap in Ibn Barrajān and Ibn Qasī's educational backgrounds. We know that Ibn Barrajān likely knew of Ibn Qasī given that Ibn al-ʿArīf, whom Nwyia argued was the student of Ibn Barrajān, made reference to Ibn Qasī in Ibn al-ʿArīf's collected and published letters. Ibn al-ʿArīf, *Miftāḥ al-Saʿāda*, ed. al-Ṭibāʿī (Beirut: Dār al-Gharb al-Islāmī); Paul Nwyia, "Notes sur quelques fragments inédits de la correspondence d'Ibn al-ʿArīf avec Ibn Barrajān,"

Hespéris: Archives Berberes et Bulletin de l'Institute des Hautes Études Marocaines 48 (1955): 217–21.

11 This image has been used previously by other Sufis, including most importantly al-Ghazālī in the *Niche of the Lights* (*Mishkāt al-Anwār*) in a parallelism that speaks to the diverse sources on which Ibn Qasī could have drawn. In al-Ghazālī's words, "The outward doffing of the sandals calls attention to the abandonment of the two engendered worlds. Hence, the similitude in the outward aspect is true, and its giving rise to the inward mystery is a reality. Those who are worthy of having their attention called through this similitude have reached the degree of the 'glass,' in the sense in which the glass will be discussed." al-Ghazālī, *Mishkāt al-Anwār, The Niche of Lights*, trans. David Buchman (Provo, UT: Brigham Young University Press), p. 34.

12 Quran 58:12.

13 *Kitāb Khalʿ al-Naʿlayn*, p. 209.

14 Ibn ʿArabī was aware that claiming an "opening" of knowledge had important implications for religious authority, particularly given his claims about his own saintliness. It is therefore notable that in his commentary on Ibn Qasī's work, Ibn ʿArabī accused Ibn Qasī of fabricating his opening and actually taking all of his doctrines from his teacher. The nature of this accusation perhaps explains why Ibn ʿArabī nonetheless explicitly drew on Ibn Qasī's work (quoting him by name) in the *Pearls of Wisdom*. Goodrich's dissertation explains this paradox of Ibn ʿArabī simultaneously criticizing Ibn Qasī's credibility and drawing on Ibn Qasī's work. *Goodrich*, "A *Ṣūfī Revolt* in Portugal," pp. 49–52.

15 *Kitāb Khalʿ al-Naʿlayn*, p. 209.

16 The fact that Ibn Qasī is not necessarily asking for his use of the Qur'anic term "unrolled parchment" to be taken literally emerges from a comparison between his writings and those of his mystical predecessors. Earlier mystics like al-Sarrāj wrote of the use of allusion (*ṭarīq al-ishāra*) in their own works, while al-Ghazālī wrote of allusions and parabolic language in the introduction of his *Mishkāt al-Anwār*. al-Ghazālī, *Mishkāt al-Anwār*, pp. 1–2. In what indicates further interest in al-Ghazālī's work on Ibn Qasī's part, Goodrich has identified a whole section of the text about attainment of higher spiritual stations that is drawn directly from al-Ghazālī's *Maʿārij al-Quds fī Madārij Maʿrifat al-Nafs* in Goodrich, "A Ṣūfī Revolt in Portugal," pp. 317–19.

17 *Kitāb Khalʿ al-Naʿlayn*, p. 213.

18 *Kitāb Khalʿ al-Naʿlayn*, p. 213.

19 *Kitāb Khalʿ al-Naʿlayn*, p. 213.

20 Earlier Sufis as well as philosophers spoke of certain modes of knowledge as inspired knowledge, which was not an inherently controversial concept given the theological acceptance of non-prophetic forms of inspiration and given how Sufis and Avicennan philosophers defended the inimitability of prophecy and scripture. Where controversy did emerge was in the question of where this non-prophetic inspired knowledge fit in larger religious epistemologies, with figures like Ibn Ḥazm appealing to tools like logic as a systematic medium for grounding theological analysis. Some philosophers like the logician *par excellence* Avicenna were willing to accept notions of inspired knowledge as part of a larger logic-oriented program of knowledge acquisition. Sufi metaphysicians went further in their interest in inspired knowledge. Ibn Barrajān, for example, described his knowledge in writing the

Commentary on the Beautiful Names of God as a kind of inspired knowledge, but was clear in highlighting the inimitability of prophecy and the importance of the scholarly sciences as central sources of theological analysis. Ibn Qasī's language echoes examples like al-Makkī's discussion in *Qūt al-Qulūb*, which speaks of pious individuals who are inspired with right guidance and sound responses to the populace's questions. As quoted by Karamustafa, and in a passage rendered into English by Renard, Makkī states in the *Qūt al-Qulūb* that "They have not acquired this knowledge through the study of books, nor received it from one another by word of mouth." Karamustafa contextualizes this discussion in terms of Makkī's challenge to the scholars to develop a wider scope of knowledge. Ahmet Karamustafa, *Sufism: The Formative Period* (Edinburgh: Edinburgh University Press, 2007), p. 88ff. Ibn Barrajān's discussion of inspired knowledge is part of the framework of his introduction in Ibn Barrajān, *Sharḥ Asmāʾ al-Ḥusnā*, ed. Purificacion de la Torre (Madrid: CSIC, 2000). See also John Renard, *Knowledge of God in Classical Sufism: Foundations of Islamic Mystical Theology*, trans. John Renard (New York: Paulist Press, 2004), pp. 127–8.

21 Ibn Ḥazm's criticism of Ibn Masarra, the Ismāʿīlīs, and the philosophers for the identification of incorporeal realities in the world is especially pertinent here in that it stands in stark contrast with Ibn Qasī's understanding of true reality being incorporeal and veiled by the corporeal world of *daqāʾiq*. Ibn Qasī's discussion essentially moves in the opposite direction of Ibn Ḥazm and al-Ghazālī's nominalist critique of universals, as Ibn Qasī argues that the particulars of the world should be assigned the least ontological value as "reality." The importance of this distinction is in its implications for not only notions of knowledge acquisition, but also eschatology and ultimately ethics, with asceticism perhaps being the cornerstone of Ibn Qasī's epistemic discovery in a way that logic is for Ibn Ḥazm. Ibn Ḥazm, *al-Fiṣal*, 5:200.

22 *Kitāb Khalʿ al-Naʿlayn*, p. 220.

23 *Kitāb Khalʿ al-Naʿlayn*, p. 221.

24 Frank provides an overview of the distinction between "accidents" in speculative theology and accidents in Graeco-Arabic philosophy in a way that further highlights the analysis here of how Ibn Qasī's "particular realities" can likewise be distinguished from the ontological categories of both traditions. Richard Frank, *The Metaphysics of Created Being According to Abû l-Hudhayl al-ʿAllâf: A Philosophical Study of the Earliest Kalâm* (Istanbul: Nederlands Historisch-Archaeologisch Instituut in het Nabije Oosten), pp. 1–53.

25 *Kitāb Khalʿ al-Naʿlayn*, p. 250. The specific point that the *daqāʾiq* do not survive the death of the body is discussed in his comments regarding death. His point calls to mind two different philosophical notions in eschatology. The first is the philosophical notion that upon the death of the body, particular souls become part of one Universal Soul. The second is the philosophical notion that upon the death of the body, only souls have continued existence. Ibn Qasī's claim that the *daqāʾiq* do not survive the death of the body recalls both notions but argues neither, and indicates the extent to which his work seems to engage philosophical language without taking clear philosophical positions. Avicenna's understanding of the soul, notably, breaks with other philosophers and argues in favor of the particular or personal immortality of the soul. This perhaps contextualizes the way Sufis like Ibn Qasī, in

anticipation of the Avicennan Illuminationists, seemed interested in broadly philosophical and Platonizing language without assimilating specific philosophical arguments and conclusions. Thérèse-Anne Druart, "The Human Soul's Individuation and Its Survival after the Body's Death: Avicenna on the Causal Relation between Body and Soul," *Arabic Sciences and Philosophy* 10 (2000): 259–74; Ibn Sina, *Kitāb al-Shifā', al-Tabīʿiyyāt, al-Nafs* in *Avicenna's De Anima (Arabic Text): Being the Psychological Part of Kitāb al-Shifā'*, ed. Fazlur Rahman (Oxford: Oxford University Press, 1959), pp. 202–69.

26 *Kitāb Khalʿ al-Naʿlayn*, p. 216.

27 Ibn Qasī's use of *naẓar* here echoes the way Ibn Masarra and Ibn Barrajān used *iʿtibār* as a form of inductive pondering into the *bāṭin* of the world while also employing language characteristic of the theologians and philosophers. Ibn Qasī's use of *naẓar* implies few of the logical or dialectical methods found in the writings of the philosophers and theologians. Van Ess has provided an overview of these methods in Josef Van Ess, "Early Development of Kalam," in *Studies in the First Century of Islamic Society*, ed. G. H. A. Junyboll (Carbondale: Southern Illinois University Press, 1982), pp. 109–24; idem, "The Logical Structure of Islamic Theology," *Logic in a Classical Islamic Culture*, ed. G. E. von Grunebaum (Wiesbaden: Otto Harrassowitz, 1970), pp. 21–50; See also idem, *The Flowering of Muslim Theology* (Cambridge, MA: Harvard University Press, 2006).

28 *Kitāb Khalʿ al-Naʿlayn*, p. 216.

29 The enduring legacy of al-Kindī within this later philosophical Sufi tradition is interesting to consider here, given his role in helping bring into the Graeco-Arabic philosophical tradition the Plotinian cosmology of One, Intellect, and Soul through the Neoplatonic pseudo-Aristotelian *Theology of Aristotle*. F. W. Zimerman, "The Origins of the So-called *Theology of Aristotle*," in *Pseudo-Aristotle in the Middle Ages*, eds. Jill Kraye, W. F. Ryan, and Charles B. Schmitt (London: The Warburg Institute, 1986), pp. 110–240; H. R. Schwyzer, "Die pseudoaristotelische *Theologie* und die Plotin-Ausgabe des Porphyrios," *Museum Helveticum* 90 (1941): 216–36.

30 As in the case of Ibn Ḥazm's eschatological analysis, the notion here that the body and soul have unique trajectories upon the death of the body does not imply a rejection of bodily resurrection. For Ibn Ḥazm, the body and the soul as a subtle body have temporarily different trajectories upon an individual's death, but are then resurrected together with the resurrection of the individual. Taken together, theories of eschatology in the writings of Ibn Ḥazm and Ibn Qasī indicate that the nature of the soul was debated and contested in part because of implications for eschatology. Perhaps for this reason, al-Ghazālī's theories about the nature of the soul seem to have been elaborated in a manner that sought deliberately to straddle the worlds of theology, philosophy, and Sufism. al-Ghazālī's conclusions continue to elude the consensus of historians. Gianotti is one historian who thinks al-Ghazālī originally understood the soul as a subtle body, which recalls Ibn Ḥazm's doctrine on the soul, but then changed his theory to an immaterial one. Marmura, in contrast, offered a different picture of al-Ghazālī's understanding of the soul and eschatology. Timothy Gianotti, *al-Ghazālī's Unspeakable Doctrine of the Soul: Unveiling the Esoteric Psychology and Eschatology of the Iḥyā'* (Leiden: Brill, 2002); Michael

Marmura, "al-Ghazāli on Bodily Resurrection and Causality in the *Tahāfut* and *Iqtiṣād*," *Aligarh Journal of Islamic Thought* 2 (1989): 46–58.

31 Qur'an 53:14.

32 *Kitāb Khalʿ al-Naʿlayn*, p. 216.

33 Qur'an 21:30.

34 *Kitāb Khalʿ al-Naʿlayn*, p. 218.

35 The prominent Andalusī Sufi of the next generation, Ibn ʿArabī, provides one possible answer to the question of these individual *in potentia* concepts' ontological value. Ibn ʿArabī less than a century later spoke of the existence of individual concepts of created things, or perhaps the images of created things, prior to their creation as immutable entities (*aʿyān thābita*) existing in God's knowledge as "nonexistent things." His discussion parallels the way Frank has explained the Muʿtazilī "nonexistent thing" (*shayʾ maʿdūm*), which is somehow more real than a square circle but less real than an "existent thing" (*shayʾ mawjūd*). As Chittick has shown, these immutable entities or images exist according to Ibn ʿArabī in God's knowledge prior to God's endowing them with existence in the created world. This concept of the immutable entities is one of many concepts in Sufi metaphysics that provide a window into ways in which philosophically oriented Sufis could attract criticism for articulating philosophical doctrines without sufficiently clarifying how they avoided the problematic baggage of those doctrines. In this case, discussion of the immutable entities calls to mind the philosophical doctrine of the pre-eternity of the world. Richard Frank, "*Al-Maʿdūm wa-l-Mawjūd*: The Non-existent, the Existent, and the Possible in the Teaching of Abū Hashim and his Followers," *MIDEO: Mélanges de l'Institut Dominicain d'Etudes Orientales* 14 (1980): 185–209. William Chittick, *The Sufi Path of Knowledge: Ibn ʿArabī's Metaphysics of Imagination* (Albany: State University of New York Press), pp. 34–6.

36 Ibn Ḥazm's arguments against theological notions of created knowledge were part of his argument against discussion of the divine attributes in Ashʿarism. For Ibn Ḥazm, the theologians' interpretation of the Names as attributes implies the same problem of pre-eternal causes and sub-divine voluntary ordering of the world in what he presented as dualism (in the doctrines of the Zoroastrians, Ibn Masarra, Ismāʿīlīs, and *falāsifa*, though he rarely criticized the last group by name). Ibn Ḥazm, *al-Fiṣal*, 2:295. Gimaret provides a picture of the position of the Ashʿarī theologians in contrast with Ibn Ḥazm's position. Daniel Gimaret, *Les noms divins en Islam* (Paris: Les Editions du Cerf, 1988).

37 The more detailed picture of his cosmology that follows resembles Neoplatonic emanationist cosmology only superficially. Ibn Qasī discusses how each level of existence unfolds from the previous level and references the agency of the Pen in a role evocative of Intellect in Neoplatonic cosmology. This procession of existence, however, describes not the philosophers' logical procession, but the theologians' created ordering of the world. It offers an example in the generation before Ibn ʿArabī of what Rustom and others have described as a kind of Sufism that draws on philosophical technical language for symbolic representation of mystical truths. This method is based on these particular Sufis' view that philosophy and mysticism described the same realities. Mohammed Rustom, "Philosophical Sufism," in *The Routledge*

Companion to Islamic Philosophy, eds. Richard C. Taylor and Luis Xavier Lopez-Farjeat (New York: Routledge, 2015), pp. 309–411.

38 *Kitāb Khalʿ al-Naʿlayn*, p. 246.

39 *Kitāb Khalʿ al-Naʿlayn*, p. 246.

40 The use of multiple thrones is found also in the *Epistles of the Brethren of Purity* in Ikhwān al-*Ṣafā'*, *Rasā'il Ikhwān al-Ṣafā'*, ed. Khayr al-Dīn Ziriklī (Cairo: al-Maktaba al-Tijāriyya al-Kubrā, 1928), 2:22ff. Anton, *Islamic Cosmology: A Study of as-Suyūṭī's al-Hay'a as-Sanīya fī l-Hay'a as-Sunnīya* (Beirut: Orient-Institut der Deutschen Morgenländischen Gesellschaft, 1982); pp. 77–81.

41 This term, *rūḥ al-quds*, was typically understood by Qur'an commentators as a reference to the archangel Gabriel in the four times it appears in the Qur'an (verses 2:87, 2:253, 5:110, 16:102). Some authors who used the term to describe the archangel Gabriel often simultaneously used it in a more philosophical way to characterize a particular level of intellectual thought in a cosmology evocative of Neoplatonic doctrines. al-Ghazālī, for example, used this term in reference to Gabriel, but as Whittingham has shown, al-Ghazālī also spoke of *al-rūḥ al-qudsī al-nabawī* as one of five types of human spirits that correspond to some extent with doctrines in Avicennan psychology. Martin Whittingham, *al-Ghazālī and the Quran: One Word, Many Meanings* (New York: Routledge 2007), pp. 101–24. *Encyclopedia of Islam*, Third Edition, s.v. "Gabriel." (by Gabriel Said Reynolds)

42 Qur'an 68:1.

43 In the role of the spirit of holiness in transmitting knowledge to lower levels, the parallels with the philosophers' doctrines in psychology and cosmology become more apparent. Avicenna, for example, used this term as well. However, it is worth noting the difference in how they use these concepts. Philosophers and Sufis both brought together philosophical meanings with scriptural language. While many of the classical *falāsifa* like Avicenna appear to have assigned Aristotelian-Neoplatonic philosophical meanings more systematically to scriptural concepts, many Sufis appear to have been more eclectic in their integration of philosophical metaphysical assumptions with early Islamic theological trends. The Sufis appear to have been in dialogue with the methodology of figures like Ibn Masarra, the Ikhwān al-Ṣafā', and al-Kindī. As mentioned, Ibn al-Khaṭīb among later commentators identified this eclecticism in Andalusī Sufism, specifically with regard to its synthesis of philosophical and theological concepts. Ibn al-Khaṭīb, *Rawḍat al-Taʿrīf bi-l-Ḥubb al-Sharīf*, ed. Muḥammad al-Kattānī (Beirut: Dār al-Thaqāfa, 1970), pp. 555–60. Knysh and Griffel have written more broadly on the question of how to locate the intersection of philosophical commitments with the philosophers' Qur'anic hermeneutics. Alexander Knysh, "Multiple Areas of Influence," in *The Cambridge Companion to the Qur'an*, ed. Jane McAuliffe (Cambridge: Cambridge University Press, 2006), pp. 211–34; Frank Griffel, "Taqlīd of the Philosophers: al-Ghazālī's Initial Accusation in the *Tahāfut*," in *Ideas, Images, and Methods of Portrayal: Insights into Classical Arabic Literature and Islam*, ed. Sebastian Günther (Leiden: Brill, 2005), pp. 273–98. *Kitāb Khalʿ al-Naʿlayn*, p. 307.

44 *Kitāb Khalʿ al-Naʿlayn*, pp. 307–8.

45 *Kitāb Khalʿ al-Naʿlayn*, p. 249.

46 There is an interesting parallelism here with al-Ghazālī's discussion of the categories of spirits. Whittingham has shown how al-Ghazālī identified the prophets and some of the saintly Sufis as having a certain type of spirit that distinguishes them from others, even as al-Ghazālī adhered to the fundamental tenet of the inimitability and finality of both prophecy and scripture. Here, Ibn Qasī seems to draw on or demonstrate agreement with Ghazālīan psychology in a way that also anticipates Ibn ʿArabī's work. However, Ibn ʿArabī took this discussion much further in a way that drew the ire of both scholars and Sufis. For Ibn ʿArabī's controversial notions such as the "seal of sainthood," see Michel Chodkiewicz, "La sainteté et les saints en islam," in *Le culte des saints dans le monde musulman*, ed. Henri Chambert-Loir and C. Guillot (Paris: École française d'Extrême Orient, 1995), pp. 13–22; Michel Chodkiewicz, *Seal of the Saints: Prophethood and Sainthood in the Doctrine of Ibn ʿArabī* (Cambridge: Islamic Texts Society, 1993), pp. 17–46.

47 *Kitāb Khalʿ al-Naʿlayn*, p. 308.

48 *Kitāb Khalʿ al-Naʿlayn*, p. 249.

49 There are parallels here with Avicenna and the philosophers' discussion of the intermediary role of the Active Intellect, which Avicenna integrated into his understanding of angels. There are also parallels with Ibn Barrajān's and Ibn Ḥazm's analyses regarding the intermediary place of the angels in agency. Taken together, these parallels indicate the extent to which Ibn Qasī as a more "speculative Sufi," as Ibn Khaldūn identified both him and other Andalusī Sufis, fits within wider philosophical and theological attempts to develop a systematic philosophically oriented cosmology that explains non-prophetic perception of higher levels of existence in terms of theories about angelic knowledge. Ibn Barrajān, *Tafsīr Ibn Barrajān*, MS Yusuf Ağa 4744 ff. 226r. Ibn Ḥazm, *al-Fiṣal*, 2:291.

50 *Kitāb Khalʿ al-Naʿlayn*, p. 249.

51 Qur'an 6:38–9.

52 Qur'an 11:6.

53 *Kitāb Khalʿ al-Naʿlayn*, p. 251.

54 This point should be obvious from the fact that his emphasis in terms of cognition is on discovering realities that lead to a higher awareness of God's existence. This higher awareness of God's existence is laid out, as he previously discussed, in the natural disposition of the world. There is likewise no indication that he believes that plants and animals are veiled from that natural disposition in the way he presents man to be. In fact, Ibn Qasī presents plants and animals as extremely intelligent throughout the treatise, a point that offers an interesting window into ways that Ibn Qasī's theories echo those of the philosophical *Epistles of the Pure Brethren*, particularly the epistle in which the animal kingdom make a case against the arrogance of mankind. Epistle 22 has been published as a critical edition with translation and commentary in Ikhwān al-Ṣafāʾ, *Epistles of the Brethren of Purity: The Case of the Animals versus Man before the King of the Jinn. An Arabic Critical Edition and English Translation of Epistle 22*, ed. and trans. Lenn E. Goodman and Richard McGregor (New York: Oxford University Press, 2012).

55 These last two sentences stand in direct contrast with Ibn Ḥazm's discussion of the importance of the senses in helping rein in knowledge of the corporeal world and helping limit that knowledge to what is necessary and possible

in contrast with what is impossible and what cannot be known (ghayb) by non-prophets. One clear window into Ibn Ḥazm's alternative picture is in his criticism of Ibn Masarra's understanding of the scriptural *ghayb* and *shahāda* as the sensory corporeal world and the immaterial world, which contrasts with Ibn Ḥazm's own interpretation of these concepts as the unknown and the known in Ibn Ḥazm, *al-Fiṣal*, 5:65.

56 Ibn Masarra, like Ibn Barrajān after him, similarly used the macrocosm-microcosm paradigm of understanding God's agency to explain the oneness of God. The fact that all three figures integrate this discussion into an analysis of the Names and Attributes (each in different ways, all interested in elaborating philosophically oriented theories of cosmology) suggests the importance of understanding Ibn ʿArabī's influential metaphysics and theory of knowledge as the product of overlooked Andalusī models of mystical metaphysics. These Andalusī models, taken together, can be interpreted as being not simply derivative of al-Ghazālī's work, but rather the culmination of the intersection of Sahl al-Tustarī's mysticism and Ibn Masarra's philosophically oriented theological writing. Miguel Asín Palacios, echoing to some extent Ibn Khaldūn's representation of Andalusī Sufis, was among the first modern scholars to make the argument for the existence of a specifically Andalusī form of Sufism, though the pseudo-Empedoclean nature of that Sufism has since been disputed among historians. Miguel Asín Palacios, *Abenmasarra y su escuela. Origenes de la filosofía hispano-musulmana* (Madrid: Imprenta Ibérica – E. Maestre, 1914); Samuel Miklós Stern, "Ibn Masarra, Follower of Pseudo-Empedocles – An Illusion," in *Acts IV Congress de studios árabes e islámicos. Coimbra-Lisboa. 1 a 8 de Setembro de 1968* (Leiden: Brill, 1971), pp. 325–37.

57 *Kitāb Khalʿ al-Naʿlayn*, p. 251.

58 Ibn Qasī had al-Ghazālī's works to draw on for this concept, which echoes al-Ghazālī's discussion of *al-rūḥ al-qudsī al-nabawī* as a category of thought and spirit associated with perception of "flashes of the unseen" and knowledge that rational spirits cannot reach. al-Ghazālī, *Mishkāt al-Anwār. Niche of the Lights*, p. 38.

59 Fierro, "Spiritual Alienation and Political Activism," pp. 230–60.

60 This dearth of references to the *ʿulamāʾ* is in notable contrast with Ibn Barrajān and Ibn al-ʿArīf's works, both Sufis having emerged from the circles of the *ʿulamāʾ* as prominent Sufi Mālikī scholars. Vincent Cornell's discussion of the intersection of Sufis and scholars, including Sufis who were not among the scholars, provides important context for understanding this point. Vincent Cornell, *Realm of the Saint* (Austin: University of Texas Press, 1998), pp. 32–62.

61 *Kitāb Khalʿ al-Naʿlayn*, p. 233

62 Goodrich was among the first modern historians to point out these political dimensions. However, one can underline the fact that the representation of the mystical knowers throughout Ibn Qasī's text, including this particular section, does not necessarily represent this group as politically activist. In contrast, the discussion of the *ghurabāʾ* and reference to Pharaonic-scale tyranny does indeed introduce these politically reformist overtones more explicitly.

63 *Kitāb Khalʿ al-Naʿlayn*, p. 235.

64 *Kitāb Khalʿ al-Naʿlayn*, p. 238.

6 The Transformation of Caliphal Politics

The Almohads' political administration accorded an important place to the patronage of philosophy and Sufism in a political culture that contrasted sharply with the Almoravid-era censure of al-Ghazālī's works. The rise of the philosopher-physician and judge Ibn Rushd (Averroes d. 595/1198) and his mentor Ibn Ṭufayl (d. 580/1185) as powerful Almohad administrators offers a multifaceted picture into some of the changes that were taking place in Andalusī political culture in the twelfth century. Ibn Ṭufayl rose to high ranks in Almohad circles first as a physician and secretary to Abū Saʿīd, the governor of Granada and son of the Almohad caliph ʿAbd al-Muʾmin (r. 1130–1163), and later as a physician and Almohad courtier in the court of the caliph Abū Yaʿqūb Yūsuf (r. 1163–1184). Ibn Ṭufayl's famous legacy in medieval Europe and the Islamic world rests not only on his status as a mentor of Ibn Rushd, but also on his authorship of a widely circulated novel he wrote in the Almohad period called *Alive the Son of Awake* (*Ḥayy ibn Yaqẓān*). The novel was one of the first of its genre. It was framed in terms of the legacies of Aristotle, Avicenna (Ibn Sīna), and al-Ghazālī, and offered an exposition of a mixed philosophical and mystical method, one that Ibn Ṭufayl identified as a synthesis of Peripatetic (Aristotelian-Neoplatonic) philosophy and Sufi metaphysics. By the mid-twelfth century, particularly following the transmission of al-Ghazālī's works, Graeco-Arabic philosophy and Sufism had become increasingly assimilated into the sciences of the scholars (*ʿulamāʾ*) from al-Andalus to Iraq. Against this backdrop, the patronage of Ibn Ṭufayl's work by the Almohad court in effect sought to assimilate into the Almohads' centralizing political culture the religious authority associated with these forms of knowledge. At the same time, the allegory included a critique of more political forms of Sufi metaphysics. The critique functioned as a caution to the Sufis, whether they were within or outside of scholarly circles, about the political dangers of emulating the recent Sufi political rebellion of Ibn Qasī (d. 536/1151) against the earlier Almoravids.

Figure 6.1. Minaret of the Mosque of the Booksellers (Jāmiʿ al-Kutubiyya), built in Almohad-era Marrakesh in the late twelfth century and one of the models for Seville's Giralda bell tower.

The Almohads' Articulation of a New Caliphal Legitimacy

By 1147, the Almohads had fully wrested control of al-Andalus from the Almoravids, moving al-Andalus's regional capital from Cordoba to Seville. By the end of the Almoravid period, the wider, less politically aligned circles of scholars had become increasingly and overwhelmingly receptive to both Graeco-Arabic philosophy and Sufism as scholarly sciences.[1] By the early decades of the Almohad period, philosophical theology (Ashʿarism), Graeco-Arabic philosophy, and Sufi metaphysics all became part of what characterized the knowledge of the powerful scholarly Sufis and their role as communal guides. These scholars included the Ashʿarī theologian and Sufi al-Shūdhī (d. 600/1203) and the later Ashʿarī theologian and Sufi Ibn Marʾa (d. 611/1214) in the years leading up to the career of the Platonizing scholarly Sufi Ibn ʿArabī (d. 638/1240).[2] The Almohads' centralizing political model sought to keep up with these wider changes in conceptions of communal guidance and leadership by becoming political patrons of writings in philosophy and Sufi metaphysics. Their reign marked a kind of political revival of Graeco-Arabic philosophy and Sufism more than 200 years after early the tenth-century Andalusī Umayyad period, when administrative circles included patrons of philosophy and followers of Ibn Masarra. Part of the way the Almohad administrators brought about this change in political culture was to cultivate a new circle of Almohad-aligned scholars (*ʿulamāʾ*), the so-called *ṭalaba*, in an attempt to sideline and coopt the authority of the earlier generations of Mālikī scholars.[3] Maribel Fierro's research suggests that the rise of Ibn Ṭufayl's student Ibn Rushd (Averroes) as both chief judge and as a Peripatetic court philosopher reflects the likelihood that Ibn Rushd himself numbered among these politically influential *ṭalaba*, even though he emerged from late Almoravid-era Mālikī scholarly circles. A political administrator, Ibn Rushd was one of the key figures who began to introduce influential scholarly forms of knowledge into the Almohads' new centralizing model of political authority.[4] The legacy of the philosopher Ibn Ṭufayl, Ibn Rushd's mentor who introduced him to the court, can likewise be understood in this political context.

Ibn Ṭufayl earned widespread fame in medieval Europe as the author of his court-sponsored philosophical novel, *Ḥayy ibn Yaqẓān* (*Alive the Son of Awake*). The novel expounded a philosophical Sufi method that he represented in the text's introduction as an integration of Ibn Sīna and al-Ghazālī's methodologies. One of the interesting implications of reading Ibn Ṭufayl's work in the context of Almohad political culture is that it highlights further dimensions of current research findings on the Almohads' political legitimacy, which rivaled that of the collapsing Fatimid Ismāʿīlī caliphate. The Fatimid caliphate finally collapsed during Ibn Ṭufayl's political career in 1171, about twenty years after the fall of Ibn Qasī's short-lived Sufi state.[5] What Almohad administrators appear to have seen in the Fatimid Ismāʿīlīs' model of political leadership, and perhaps more significantly in Ibn Qasī's Almohad-allied Sufi model of political leadership, was the fact that both models shared a centralizing intersection of political and religious authority within ruling circles in way that challenged the enduring dialectic of authority between ruling circles and scholars. Against this political backdrop, and in accordance with Fierro's research findings, Ibn Ṭufayl's student Ibn Rushd might be interpreted as an Almohad-aligned Mālikī scholar *par excellence*, simultaneously working directly for the centralizing Almohads as chief judge while producing Peripatetic philosophical works under court patronage. Likewise, Ibn Ṭufayl, Ibn Rushd's philosophical mentor who was also notably a Sufi, should be interpreted as a similar kind of ideal court philosopher and court Sufi.[6] He worked directly for the Almohads while simultaneously producing writings on philosophical and Sufi themes under court patronage. Ibn Ṭufayl and Ibn Rushd's works lent legitimacy to an Almohad dynasty that, like the Fatimid caliphate and Ibn Qasī's rebel city-state, sought in its early years to construct a model of political leadership oriented around both the founder's saintly or semi-messianic (*mahdī*) legacy and the dynasty's support of a new philosophical and mystical Ghazālian-Avicennan scholarly elect.[7] In this regard, that al-Ghazālī became something of a patron saint of the dynasty comes as no surprise. What points to the limited success of the Almohads' centralizing attempt to coopt the authority of the Mālikī scholars, however, is the famous episode in which Ibn Rushd fell afoul of both his fellow scholars and his Almohad patrons before being rehired at the end of his life. Still, the Almohads' process of centralizing authority appears to have been more effective in the long run in the way the Almohad court became a center for the patronage and production of the most influential forms of knowledge and communal guidance elaborated by the scholars' (*ʿulamāʾ*), including philosophical theology (Ghazālian neo-Ashʿarism), Graeco-Arabic philosophy, and Sufi metaphysics.

In this regard, this chapter considers more closely the possibility that Ibn Ṭufayl's *Alive the Son of Awake* represents a specific window into the Almohads' political absorption and projection of the religious authority previously associated more closely with the scholars' knowledge of Sufi metaphysics and philosophical theology. Specifically, this chapter considers the possibility that the reason Ibn Ṭufayl framed the text in terms of al-Ghazālī's and Ibn Sīna's (Avicenna) respective legacies was specifically in order to help consolidate politically the various intellectual movements associated in the twelfth century with sound Sunnī theological guidance and communal leadership. As discussed in Chapter 3, al-Ghazālī's Platonizing Sufi metaphysics saw the intersection of Graeco-Arabic philosophy and Sufism and was central to the background of Sufis like Ibn Barrajān. Ibn Ṭufayl thus named al-Ghazālī in the introduction of his text as a model for the methodology elaborated by the protagonist of his philosophical and Sufi allegory, named *Ḥayy* (Alive). Ibn Ṭufayl representation of Ibn Sīna as a mystical figure required more effort, however. In an analysis of the text, Dimitri Gutas has argued that since Sufism was not central to Ibn Sīna's writings, Ibn Ṭufayl mysticized Ibn Sīna's legacy in the text in order to bring his legacy closer to that of al-Ghazālī.[8] Ibn Ṭufayl essentially sought to represent not only al-Ghazālī, but also Ibn Sīna as a philosophical Sufi. Ibn Ṭufayl's writing, thus, echoed the example seen in Chapter 4 of near contemporary Sufis like Ibn Barrajān similarly making mystical claims on Graeco-Arabic philosophy as a Sufi science of mystical wisdom (*ḥikma*). Ibn Ṭufayl's choice of Ibn Sīna and al-Ghazālī as framing figures for his allegory, thus, served the purpose of the text as a court-sponsored treatise that was part of the Almohads' integration into Almohad political culture of not only philosophical theology, Graeco-Arabic philosophy, and Sufi metaphysics, but also the religious authority associated with these increasingly widespread forms of scholarly theological knowledge.

Much of the earliest scholarship on Ibn Ṭufayl appears to have missed the text's political engagement with historical Sufi religious authority. As far back as Pockocke's seventeenth-century study of Ibn Ṭufayl, studies including those of Gauthier and Hourani have argued or suggested that the mystical elements of the story constitute a kind of veil over the story's true philosophical or "rationalist" intentions.[9] More recent contributions have identified the interplay between philosophical and Sufi language, but have continued to argue that one mode of thought veils the other or serves as its lead-in without recognizing how the text reflects contemporary philosophical Sufi currents.[10]

This chapter reads Ibn Ṭufayl's philosophical Sufi treatise as a multifaceted window into the Almohad political establishment's explicit participation in scholarly debates about philosophical and Sufi knowledge and the scholarly religious authority associated with these forms of knowledge. This participation was part of the construction of the dynasty's new and centralizing political culture. What is particularly illustrative of the political overtones of the text is how Ibn Ṭufayl strikes a balance between an approval of the knowledge of Sufi metaphysics and a criticism of its potential to undergird a problematic model of political authority, which was seen during Ibn Ṭufayl's lifetime in the case of Ibn Qasī's rebel Sufi state in Mértola.[11]

Mysticizing Aristotle in a Platonizing Sufi Treatise

Ibn Ṭufayl's *Ḥayy ibn Yaqẓān* (*Alive the Son of Awake*) displays a curious mix of philosophical methods, mystical goals, and a familiar engagement with the typically Sufi language of esoteric hermeneutics oriented toward the mystical aspirant's intellectual and spiritual ascent to a higher level of cognition. In the introduction of the novel, Ibn Ṭufayl praises Ibn Sīna (Avicenna), whom he represents as a follower of Aristotle interested in Sufism. He likewise praises al-Ghazālī, whom he represents as a philosophically minded Sufi. Ibn Ṭufayl declares in the introduction of the text that his intention in writing *Alive the Son of Awake* is to expound allegorically the true doctrine of Ibn Sīna and to check Ibn Sīna's Peripatetic (Aristotelian-Neoplatonic) ideas against those of the more mystically oriented writings of al-Ghazālī. He claims that the doctrines of both figures can be brought together because they achieved some mystical witnessing of the divine realm in contrast with the case of other philosophers like al-Fārābī and Ibn Bājja, who only attained a limited intellectual witnessing. That is, he represents both Ibn Sīna and al-Ghazālī as saintly mystics, one a philosopher saint, and the other a Sufi saint, who were in an agreement with an ostensibly mystical side of Aristotle. The fact that he, in effect, almost renders Aristotle a proto-Sufi is illustrative of his engagement with the contemporary Sufi metaphysicians' overall claims on philosophy as part of their metaphysics of wisdom (*ḥikma*).

> As for the writings of Aristotle (*Arisṭūṭālīs*), the Master Abū ʿAlī [Ibn Sīna] undertook an exposition of their contents. [Ibn Sīna] went about it according to [Aristotle's] method and followed [Aristotle's] path of philosophy in his book *The Healing*. However, [Ibn Sīna] states at the start of the book that the truth for him is something different, that he only wrote this book according to the way of the Peripatetics (*mashshāʾiyyūn*), and that he who wants the truth without incoherence must read his writings in *The Eastern Philosophy* (*al-Ḥikma al-Mashriqiyya*). For anyone who takes the trouble to read through *The Healing* and reads the books of Aristotle, it will be clear that while in most matters they agree, there are some [additional] things in *The Healing* that did not come down to us on the authority of Aristotle. If everything that the books of Aristotle and *The Healing* offer were taken at its [manifest or] exterior level (*ẓāhir*) without its secret (*sirr*) and interior (*bāṭin*) meanings discerned, the totality [of the text] would not be reached in view of what the Master Abū ʿAlī [Avicenna] indicated in *The Healing*.[12]

Ibn Ṭufayl suggests in the introduction of his allegory that the intellectual knowledge of the Greek and Graeco-Arabic Peripatetic philosophers is limited in comparison with the experiential knowledge of the Sufis, including al-Ghazālī. He makes this point by representing Ibn Sīna as an Aristotelian philosopher whose methodology encompassed not only its familiar Peripatetic logic-oriented approach, but also a more subtle aspect that he will identify as the Sufis' mystical epistemology.[13] Shihāb al-Dīn al-Suhrawardī and other Sufis explicitly ascribed to pre-Islamic philosophers like Plato and Socrates a mystical and essentially proto-Sufi method, even representing the early mystics of Iraq as the true inheritors of the ancient philosophical tradition.[14] This mysticizing representation of figures like Plato and Socrates as proto-Sufis was part of a larger claim by Sufi metaphysicians on the truths sought by the Peripatetic philosophers. As discussed in Chapter 4, this representation appeared with an almost trope-like frequency in the writings of Sufi metaphysicians in al-Andalus who articulated Platonizing doctrines in psychology and cosmology without relying on the philosophers' Aristotelian-Avicennan logical arguments. al-Ghazālī's Sufi legacy loomed large in the writings of these Sufis, particularly in al-Andalus, and Ibn Ṭufayl's engagement as a political administrator with this Sufi aspect of al-Ghazālī's legacy is illustrative of the wider Almohad absorption of Sufi metaphysics into its multifaceted political culture.

I have no doubt that our master Abū Ḥāmid [al-Ghazālī] was among those who have had the fortune of delighting in this ultimate bliss and [eventually] reached this sublime and hallowed level.... The truth I have attained would not have reached me in my pursuit of knowledge without following [al-Ghazālī's] words as well as those of the Master Abū ʿAlī [Ibn Sīna] and checking one against the other.[15]

In his larger exposition of the unique attributes of Ibn Sīna's and al-Ghazālī's respective writings, Ibn Ṭufayl explains that while the philosophers (*falāsifa*) were successful in arriving at some understanding of divine truths through an intellectual-mystical ascent, their understanding was detached and even superficial. He compares the Graeco-Arabic philosophers more broadly with a clever blind man who has a keen but limited understanding of the world based on only four out of five senses. Ibn Sīna, in contrast, achieved the mystical experience sought by the Sufis.

[As for] these states that [Ibn Sīna] has described, he only meant by them that they are like a taste (*dhawq*), but not by way of theorizing derived by syllogistic deductions, postulating premises, and drawing inferences. If you would like an [explanatory] example to clarify for you the difference between the perception of this [mystical] group and the perception of others, then imagine the condition of one created blind yet with good instincts (*fiṭra*), strong intuition, good memory, and a sound mind. He grows up in a particular town, and he still gets to know individuals among the people in it as well as many types of animals and objects, the streets of the town and its alleys, and the houses and markets. [He manages to recognize them] through his other means of perception to the point that he can begin to walk through the town without a guide, knowing everyone he encounters and greeting them at first sight. Colors, however, he only knows by explanations of their name and some aspects that indicate [their meaning]. Then [suddenly], after he reaches this level, his vision opens for him and visual perception comes to him. He walks throughout the entire city, wandering all around it, and he finds nothing in contradiction with what he originally understood, nor does he deny [the truth of] anything in it. The colors conform to the truth of the representations that were depicted for him. Yet, in all of this, two major things occur to him, one following the other: greater clarity and vibrancy as well as profound delight.

Ibn Ṭufayl tells his reader that the mystical perception of the divine realm, achieved by Ibn Sīna and the Sufis, offers a level of color and experience unattained by the philosophers in their more exclusive reliance on syllogistic deduction. He contrasts the philosophers with both Ibn Sīna and al-Ghazālī by highlighting how the latter two figures' experiential state extended beyond the limits of the syllogistic methods and logical sciences in the achievement of a true spiritual ascent or mystical proximity to God, that is, *wilāya*.[16]

The condition of the contemplative thinkers (*ḥāl al-nāẓirīn*) who have not reached the level of spiritual proximity (*ṭawr al-wilāya*) is the first condition of the blind man. The colors in this condition, [which are] known by the explanations of their names, are those matters that Abū Bakr [Ibn Bājja] said are more majestic than what corresponds to ordinary life, that God gifts to whom He wills among his servants. The second state [of the blind man] is that of the contemplative thinkers who achieve the level of divine proximity (*wilāya*), [for whom] God (Most Great) grants something we said we can only figuratively call a faculty.[17]

In the analogy of the blind man achieving vision and in his discussion of Ibn Sīna later, he seems at first to represent mystical experience as something that should be pursued at the expense of intellectual and syllogistic methods, a claim that would resemble a common Sufi dichotomy between Peripatetic philosophy and Sufi metaphysics. However, a closer look at his analysis shows that he does not find the Sufis' mystical experience and the philosophers' contemplative methods to be mutually exclusive. On the contrary, Ibn Ṭufayl indicates that mystical experience begins where contemplative methods ends. He makes this unique point by defining the limits of logical methods and reason in terms of the experiential realm of Ibn Sīna's and al-Ghazālī's mystical achievements.

Look at what Abū Bakr Ibn al-Ṣā'igh [Ibn Bājja] said, who attained in his [own] words a description of the conjunction (*ittiṣāl*) [with the Active Intellect], for he says: If the intended meaning of [al-Ghazālī's] book was understood, it would be clear there that it cannot be known from the sciences undertaken at its rank.... They are, rather, states from among the states of the blessed (*su'adā'*), more refined than the structure of ordinary life, fit to be called divine states granted by God (Most High, praise be to Him) to whom He wills among his servants. [However, as for] this level that Abu Bakr [Ibn Bājja] indicated, he reached it by means of speculative knowledge (*al-'ilm al-naẓarī*) and contemplative study. There is no doubt that he reached it, but he did not surpass it.[18]

Ibn Ṭufayl claims, in other words, that the Graeco-Arabic philosophers achieve something close to mystical experience in the form of an intellectual conjunction (*ittiṣāl*) with one of the higher intellects. In the writings of the Graeco-Arabic philosophers, particularly according to al-Fārābī's integration of Plotinian cosmology with Ptolemaic astronomy, that higher intellect is specifically the Active Intellect that he associated with the moon and that is the source of forms (*ṣuwar*) for the contemplative human intellects of the sublunary world.[19] Ibn Ṭufayl explains that the philosophers achieve intellectual conjunction with this higher intellect, but they do not go further in their cognitive ascent. They do not reach the levels attained in the experiential realm by Ibn Sīna and al-Ghazālī, where colors and clear vision breathe life into the intellectual perception of the colorblind. Ibn Ṭufayl's use of Ibn Sīna's legacy as the foundation for his approach is, thus, oriented around those aspects of Ibn Sīna's doctrines that incline toward the Sufis' experiential union, and he sees no conflict between Ibn Sīna's Peripatetic (Aristotelian-Neoplatonic) philosophical methods and the mystical methods of the Sufis.[20]

Ibn Ṭufayl's representation of Ibn Sīna offers additional evidence of a phenomenon discussed in Chapter 3, namely, the twelfth-century bifurcation of Ibn Sīna's Peripatetic (Aristotelian-Neoplatonic) legacy into two intertwined traditions among the scholars: (1) an Aristotelian-Avicennan logic-oriented methodological tendency assimilated by the scholars into philosophical theology (Ghazālian neo-Ash'arism), and a (2) Neoplatonic-Avicennan doctrinal tendency in psychology and cosmology assimilated by scholarly Sufis into Sufi metaphysics, especially the Andalusī Sufis. Both traditions, despite appearing in different genres of writing, were often interconnected in the writings of the same polymathic scholars. From the introduction's explicit description of Ibn Sīna as the most illustrious philosopher in the tradition of Aristotle, we know that it was as clear to Ibn Ṭufayl as it is to intellectual historians today that Ibn Sīna was a Peripatetic (Aristotelian-Neoplatonic) philosopher (*faylasūf*) in the tradition of al-Fārābī, for whom the intellectual ascent and conjunction (*ittiṣāl*) was specifically the intellectual endeavor of conditioning the rational soul to become closer to the Active Intellect.[21] At the same time, as mentioned, Ibn Ṭufayl is accurate in claiming that Ibn Sīna did genuinely engage specific conceptions of mystical experience that Sufis spoke of. Ibn Ṭufayl highlights this point by choosing a quotation from Ibn Sīna's *al-Ishārāt* that used Sufi language, a passage that helps Ibn Ṭufayl emphasize or perhaps overemphasize Ibn Sīna's historical interest in Sufism. The limits of Ibn Sīna's textual engagement with Sufism can be seen in the fact that Ibn Sīna's *al-Ishārāt*, though drawing on Sufi language, does not represent the Sufis' mystical experience as something that precludes the fundamental importance of the philosophers' logical methods. Still, Ibn Ṭufayl appears to appreciate this nuance in Ibn Sīna's interest in Sufi language, and he quotes Ibn Sīna accordingly.

> This state that I mentioned, and that your question brought me to taste (*dhawq*), is one of the collection of states that the Master Abū ʿAlī [Ibn Sīna] calls attention to when he says: 'Then, when willpower (*irāda*) and exercises (*riyāḍa*) reach a certain point, delightful glimpses of the glimmer of the light of the Real strike like flashes of light shining upon [the aspirant], then dimming from him, and then these losses of consciousness increase if he devotes himself to his exercises (*irtiyāḍ*). [The aspirant] then enters [this state] more deeply until it envelopes him without the exercises, such that whenever something appears to him, he bends [away] from it towards the Holy Presence.... he can almost see the Real in everything. Then his exercises bring him to a point where his time becomes serenity (*sakīna*) ... the [glimpses of] light become a clear star, and his [experiential] knowledge (*maʿrifa*) become permanent as if they were lasting companions.[22]

Ibn Ṭufayl references Ibn Sīna on how the contemplative aspirant's intellectual training and willpower only bring the intellect to a certain point, beyond which lies a very Sufi-like realm of mystical experience. That is, this experiential vision where self-consciousness begins to diminish and become enveloped by God-consciousness is a description of not just al-Ghazālī's Sufi experience, but also the highest state that Ibn Sīna envisioned for his fellow philosophers. Ibn Ṭufayl wants the reader to understand that Ibn Sīna idealized a level of experience in which the bliss that the philosophers enjoyed in intellectual conjunction with the Active Intellect would extend into the ecstasy that the Sufis achieved through mystical experience. Passages from Ibn Sīna's *al-Ishārāt* not quoted by Ibn Ṭufayl show that Ibn Sīna was indeed interested in this connection between contemplation and mystical insight. Specifically, on the one hand and in agreement with the philosophers, Ibn Sīna understood the process of self-purification in the ascent toward intellectual conjunction with the Active Intellect as an intellectual process that occurs by conditioning of the intellect through speculative contemplation.[23] On the other hand, and in agreement with the Sufis, Ibn Sīna noted the importance of ascetic practices and mystical insight in his discussion in *al-Ishārāt* of desiring the first Truth and worshipping God.[24]

It appears, therefore, that Ibn Sīna's philosophical use of the term "*dhawq*" (taste) in the passage quoted by Ibn Ṭufayl earlier is not the same as al-Ghazālī's more mystical use of the term *dhawq*, which even in al-Ghazālī's works had strong philosophical overtones.[25] Ibn Sīna's *dhawq* did not claim to eschew philosophical methods in the way that al-Ghazālī claimed to do in representing *dhawq* as a direct mystical experience distinct from philosophy. Ibn Sīna's *dhawq* was not a method or state that could replace the philosopher's intellectual conjunction, but rather a concept that reoriented intellectual conjunction as a primer for moving beyond the Active Intellect into the realm of self-diminishing experiential ecstasy amidst God's immanence. It is this intersection between Peripatetic philosophy and Sufi metaphysics in Ibn Sīna's language that most interests Ibn Ṭufayl. Critically, and in parallel with contemporary philosophical Sufism, Ibn Ṭufayl made this peripheral doctrine of Ibn Sīna's work a central part of his own conception of mystical experience as represented in the protagonist's celestial promenade.

Ḥayy ibn Yaqẓān's Celestial Promenade

Much of Ḥayy's story leading up to its most famous passage on mystical experience reflects Ibn Ṭufayl's interest in articulating Graeco-Arabic philosophy's epistemic and ontological assumptions for a wider audience. The story demonstrates how the protagonist Ḥayy ("Alive") developed the ability to apply syllogistic and logical methods to understand universal truths about the world around him, arriving ultimately at an understanding that God exists and is the Necessary Existent. Ḥayy's methods lead him to conclusions about the ontological nature of the world that closely echo those of the Peripatetic (Aristotelian-Neoplatonic) philosophers. Like the philosophers, and in marked disagreement with Ibn Ḥazm's critique of Neoplatonic ontology, the protagonist Ḥayy concludes that the world is composed of material bodies and immaterial forms. What he understands about his own body is reminiscent of Ibn Sīna's discourse on the soul.[26] Ḥayy concludes that he himself is composed of a material body associated with an immaterial form, the soul, which represents his true essence, and whose nature is related to the immaterial nature of the super-terrestrial world.

It became clear [to Ḥayy] that this existent, the Necessary Existence, was free of the characteristics of bodies in all respects. Thus, there is no way to come to know it except by something not of the body, nor a faculty of the body, nor [something] connected to [the body] in any respect of the body.... It became clear to him that he came to know [the Necessary Existent] through his [true] self, and that this knowledge occurred to him through [this true self]. It became clear to him from this that his [true] essence, through which he came to know [the Necessary Existent], cannot be assigned the qualities of the body, and that everything he came to know outside of his [true] essence from among the corporeal things are not his true self. His true self is only that thing with which he came to know the absolute existent, the Necessary Existent.[27]

Ḥayy's identification of his true self or essence with his soul, which he understands as an incorporeal principle associated with his body, brings him to ponder the world above him. He sees planets spinning in what appears to him as a kind of celestial cognition. He seeks to emulate this spinning cognition in his quest to make his nature resemble their nature so that he can contemplate higher levels of truth beyond truths associated with corporeal matter.[28] For al-Fārābī and Ibn Bājja, such contemplation was what brought the philosophers to the joy of intellectual conjunction with the Active Intellect. Ibn Ṭufayl's stated goal in the introduction of the story was to articulate for the reader the colorful mystical experience attained by Ibn Sīna and the Sufis. In the fifth septennial of Ḥayy's life, having conditioned his own soul through both speculative reasoning and ascetic exercises, Ḥayy reaches this mystical experience. Ibn Ṭufayl portrays it as an experience full of bliss and joy in the loss of self-consciousness within the divine realm. That is, Ibn Ṭufayl bridges a description of Ḥayy's contemplation, which is evocative of the philosophers' methods, with a description of Ḥayy's mystical ecstasy, which calls to mind the Sufis' mystical experience.

From his memory and mind, the heavens and earth and everything in between disappeared, as well as all of the spiritual forms (*al-ṣuwar al-rūḥāniyya*) and the corporeal faculties (*al-quwā l-jismāniyya*), together with the faculties separate from matter that are the [true] essences that know the existent [the Necessary Existent]. His own [true] essence disappeared among all of these [disappearing] essences. Everything vanished and faded away and became [like] scattered dust. Nothing remained except the One, the Real, the existent, the Enduring Existent. He became immersed in this condition of his and witnessed what no eye has seen nor ear heard, nor struck the heart of any person.... He who asks for a description of this state asks for the impossible, for he is in the position of one who wants to taste dyed colors inasmuch as they are colors, and at the same time demands that black, for example, be sweet or sour.[29]

Ibn Ṭufayl describes Ḥayy's mystical experience in a way reminiscent of the Sufi *fanāʾ*, that is, the total loss of self-consciousness in the realm of divine witnessing. Ibn Ṭufayl highlights the ineffability of mystical experience in a way that echoes al-Ghazālī's idealization of a kind of scrupulous reticence in articulating mystical experience. The passage just cited, taken in isolation, seems to indicate that Ibn Ṭufayl uses philosophy as a primer for Sufi metaphysics, or that philosophy justifies the need for Sufism.[30] However, Ibn Ṭufayl's introduction indicated his intention to extend the results of philosophy's intellectual goals into Sufi experience, and not to replace contemplative syllogistic reasoning with mysticism. If the reader's expectations are met, one might expect to find cosmological doctrines of the Baghdad Peripatetics make an appearance in Ibn Ṭufayl's representation of Ḥayy's mystical experience. Interestingly, a closer look at the description of Ḥayy's celestial promenade reveals a key Fārābian aspect of its philosophical underpinnings that has not been noted by modern readers of the text. Specifically, Ibn Ṭufayl strings into his description of Ḥayy's mystical experience an allusion to the philosophers' conjunction with the Active Intellect associated with the moon, and a representation of the Sufis' ability to surpass it. As the next two passages indicate, Ḥayy's celestial promenade is illustrative of how Ibn Ṭufayl's Sufi metaphysics calls not for the elimination of the philosophers' intellectual conjunction in favor of the Sufis' mystical experience, but rather a synthesis of the two methods in a truly intellectual-experiential method.

If you are among those satisfied with this kind of allusion and intimation (*al-talwīḥ wa-l-ishāra*) to what is in the divine world, and you do not take words for the meanings convention carries, then I will expand for you something of what Ḥayy ibn Yaqẓān saw in the station of sincerity that his memory approached. After pure engrossment, complete diminishing [of the self], and real attainment, he witnessed the highest sphere (*al-falak al-aʿlā*) that was incorporeal (*lā jism lahū*). He saw an essence free of matter, neither being the essence of the One, the Real, nor being the sphere itself, nor other than it, as if it were the form of the sun that appears in a polished mirror, [the form] being neither the sun nor the mirror nor other than these last two. He saw that the essence of that sphere, which was distinct in its perfection, splendor, and beauty, was something too great to be described by the tongue and too subtle to be clothed in a letter or sound. He saw it at the [highest] threshold of delight, bliss, joy, and happiness, in his witnessing of the essence of the Real, glorious be His Majesty.[31]

In the beginning of this passage that describes the Ḥayy's celestial promenade, Ḥayy advances to the experiential realm of *fanāʾ* (the mystical diminishing of the self), exceeding the limits of the philosopher's intellectual consciousness and losing himself amidst the rapturous proximity to the realm of the Necessary Existent, the One. Ḥayy then descends through the various philosophical levels of emanated material spheres and immaterial intellects and souls until he reaches the level of the intellect associated with the moon. If Ibn Ṭufayl truly follows Ibn Sīna as he claims, the intellect associated with the moon should be the Active

Intellect in Ibn Sīna's Fārābian cosmology. Very notably, in a manner long overlooked by historians of the text, Ḥayy begins to regain consciousness while in the last moments of mystical union's bliss in the realm of the moon, just before fully returning to his senses in the sublunary world.[32]

> [Ḥayy] continued to see in every sphere an essence distinct and free from matter, not being of the essences that were before it nor other than them, as though it were the image of the sun reflected from a mirror to a mirror according to the arrangement of the order of the spheres. In each essence from among these essences was beauty, splendor, delight, and happiness that no eye has seen, nor ear heard, nor occurred to the heart of any person, until he arrived at the world of generation and decay, all of it being the innards of the sphere of the moon. Here he saw in it an essence free of matter, not among those essences that he saw before [the essence], nor other than them ... [then] his senses returned to him.... He became aware [of himself] following this state that resembled fainted consciousness ... the world of the senses (*al-maḥsūs*) and the divine world vanished (*ghāba*), for the conjunction [of the two worlds] cannot be in one state.[33]

As much as the passage employs "allusions and intimations" (*al-talwīḥ wa-l-ishāra*), especially in the discussion of mirrors and sunlight, it assigns an important role to the level of the moon that is reminiscent of the role of the Active Intellect. Specifically, as in the case of the Sufis, Ḥayy's mysticism reaches the level of *fanāʾ*, a loss of self-consciousness in the experiential realm. For the so-called "sober" or theologically scrupulous Sufis, including early figures like al-Junayd, this *fanāʾ* was followed by *baqāʾ*, the regaining of self-consciousness while maintaining mystical vision. Ibn Ṭufayl alludes to the Active Intellect in his representation of the *baqāʾ* of Ḥayy's mystical experience occurring at the level of the moon. In this way, Ibn Ṭufayl's allegorical representation of an intellectual-experiential mystical experience reflects a rather creative synthesis of Ibn Sīna's Peripatetic (Aristotelian-Neoplatonic) and specifically Fārābian philosophy, which is oriented around the Active Intellect and the moon, and al-Ghazālī's Sufi metaphysics, which is oriented around witnessing the divine realm. On one level, in agreement with the philosophers, Ibn Ṭufayl situates intellectual conjunction in a Peripatetic cosmological context, assigning a central role to the Active Intellect. On another level, in agreement with the Sufis, that experiential union is part of the *fanāʾ-baqāʾ* (diminishing of self – regaining of the self) paradigm of mystical experience. In departure from both, Ibn Ṭufayl's representation of mysticism comes in the form of a new intellectual-experiential union that uses mystical experience to amplify or flesh out Ibn Sīna's own intellectual-experiential goals, in a sense bringing to the center Ibn Sīna's textually peripheral interest in connecting a Peripatetic (Aristotelian-Neoplatonic) logic-oriented method and cosmology with the Sufis' saintly perception.[34] As in the case of Ibn Barrajān's and Ibn Qasī's writings of Sufi metaphysics, which appeared in the form of a scriptural commentary (*tafsīr*) and a mystical treatise respectively, Ibn Ṭufayl's articulation of Sufi metaphysics appears in the form of an allegorical celestial promenade that leaves the reader with a familiar question: What kind of social role does Ibn Ṭufayl ascribe to this simultaneously philosophical and mystical protagonist Ḥayy? His answer, offered in the form of the novel's final episode, sheds light on the political overtones of the text.

An Enduring Dialectic of Political and Religious Authority

Following the climax of Ḥayy's intellectual-experiential mysticism, represented in the form of a celestial promenade, Ḥayy decides to leave the isolated island he grew up on and explore neighboring islands. On one particular island, he discovers two interesting characters, Absāl and Salāmān, who practice revealed religion. Salāmān takes a literal approach to revelation while Absāl is inclined toward metaphorical or esoteric interpretation in the hope of discovering deeper layers of scriptural meaning. Ḥayy finds that nothing he learned using logical methods and mystical inspiration contradicts the revealed religion of Absāl. Ḥayy is even inclined to work with Absāl and study the latter's esoteric hermeneutical approach in order to transmit the knowledge Ḥayy gained of speculative reasoning and mystical vision to the wider general populace. However, Ibn Ṭufayl explains that much to Ḥayy's dismay, the populace on the island resists Absāl's esoteric scriptural hermeneutics and Ḥayy's intellectual-experiential mystical findings. By the end of the story, Ḥayy's failure to spread his intellectual-experiential knowledge to the masses encourages him to return with Absāl to his original home, where Absāl becomes Ḥayy's lone student.

A simplistic and problematic way of understanding the ending of the novel would be to conclude that Ibn Ṭufayl sought to reconcile Peripatetic (Aristotelian-Neoplatonic) philosophy and Islamic prophecy through metaphorical or esoteric interpretation of revelation. This reading of the allegory would make for a surprisingly unoriginal story.[35] According to this interpretation, Ḥayy's religion-transcending mysticism and esoteric hermeneutics would be reserved for some philosophical elect, and Ḥayy's outlook on revelation would resemble a Eurocentric stereotype of the Graeco-Arabic philosophers' perspective on scripture. However, a closer look at the conclusion of the text, together with various comments Ibn Ṭufayl makes in the introduction, indicates that the return of Ḥayy to his original island with just one student reflects Ibn

Ṭufayl's simultaneous approval of Sufi metaphysics as a sound mode of knowledge and his political critique of the Sufis' religious authority. This reading of Ibn Ṭufayl's intentions follows from a look specifically at his comments on prophecy and ritual.

In the introduction of the novel, Ibn Ṭufayl indicates quite clearly that he finds fault with key aspects of the philosophers' epistemologies and conceptions of prophecy. In agreement with Ibn Masarra and Ibn Barrajān, he writes that the philosophers neglected the importance of prophecy in their articulation of philosophical doctrines.

> As for what reached us from the books of Abū Naṣr [al-Fārābī], most are on logic (*al-manṭiq*). What came on philosophy [more broadly] is full of doubts.... This in addition to what he stated out of his misbelief (*sū' muʿtaqad*) on prophecy (*nubuwwa*), alleging that it is particular to the imaginative faculty, as well as his preference of philosophy over it [prophecy], and things that we need not mention.[36]

From the very start of the story, then, Ibn Ṭufayl announces to the reader that he intends to treat prophecy differently from al-Fārābī's Peripatetic representation of prophetic inspiration, which Ibn Sīna sought to rectify in an attempt to underline prophecy's utter inimitability. For medieval critics of aspects of Graeco-Arabic philosophy's epistemic theories, one of the problems with the philosophers' and Platonizing Ismāʿīlī theologians' use of an esoteric scriptural hermeneutic was how extensively it was applied to the scriptural text. Critics argued that in some cases, this esoteric scriptural hermeneutic destabilized the efficacy of scripture's ritual and legal injunctions, leading to concerns of antinomianism.[37] Ibn Ṭufayl's disapproving representation of al-Fārābī as someone who subsumed prophecy into Peripatetic philosophical theories of psychology indicates very clearly that the protagonist Ḥayy is likely to emerge, by the end of the story, as a figure who by contrast emphasizes the inimitability of prophecy and who is a careful adherent of the efficacy of the scriptural word and its recommended ritual practices. As expected, when Ḥayy learns that Absāl's religion does not contradict what Ḥayy learned through his intellectual-experiential method, Ḥayy adopts the religion and commits himself to all of its outward practices and rituals. This episode points to the fact that the allegory does not offer Sufi mysticism and theological language as veils for the story's ostensibly deeper philosophical commitments, but rather the allegory attempts to synthesize philosophy with Sufi metaphysics and Islamic theology in accordance with scholarly trends of the twelfth century.

> Ḥayy inquired about [Absāl's] situation and affairs, and Absāl began to describe the affairs of the island.... He described how their practice was before religion (*al-milla*) reached them, and how it is now after it reached them. He described for

> him all that appeared in the revealed law, including the description of the divine world, the paradise and the fire, the resurrection, the gathering and the reckoning [of judgment day], the scales of justice and the straight path.... Ḥayy understood all of this and saw nothing in it in contradiction with what he had witnessed himself in his noble station. He knew that the one who [originally] described [all of] this and brought it was correct in his description, truthful in his words, a messenger from God. Ḥayy believed in [this messenger] and his truthfulness and bore witness to his message. Ḥayy then began to ask [Absāl] what obligations [this messenger] brought and what acts of worship (*ʿibādāt*) he laid down. [Absāl] described for [Ḥayy] prayer, alms, fasting, the pilgrimage and so on among the outer acts (*al-aʿmāl al-ẓāhira*). [Ḥayy] accepted this and committed himself to it. He held himself responsible to practice them, obeying the command of the one whose truthfulness he did not doubt.[38]

It is significant that Ḥayy not only believes in the sincerity of the prophetic messenger of God whom Absāl speaks of, but also takes the next step of actually adopting all of the messenger's prescribed outward practices and rituals (prayer, alms, fasting, pilgrimage, and other practices) with disciplined commitment. This episode of the text indicates that Ibn Ṭufayl is interested in making a specific point about prophecy that goes beyond simply showing how the results of syllogistic reasoning do not contradict revealed religion. Ibn Ṭufayl asks the reader to consider that the reason Ḥayy adopts the practices of Absāl's prophet is because Ḥayy, in agreement with Ibn Sīna's revision of al-Fārābī's theory of prophecy, recognizes the messenger Absāl as a cognitively exceptional figure with superior access to various universal and mystical truths that Ḥayy never grasped.[39] Specifically, the messenger Absāl follows has an intellectual grasp of the wisdom behind beneficial rituals and practices that a philosopher or mystic might erroneously neglect according to an unsystematically applied esoteric scriptural hermeneutic or a mistaken inattention to the inimitability of prophecy. If Ibn Ṭufayl represents Ḥayy as a philosophical and saintly mystic, then the messenger of Absal's religion is a philosophical and saintly prophet, whose revealed wisdom and prescribed rituals Ḥayy can accept without understanding all of the dimensions of their intent. It is at this point where Ibn Ṭufayl introduces his political commentary that Ḥayy, as a philosophical saintly mystic, must scale back his originally intended social role as a communal guide for the general populace. Ibn Ṭufayl highlights Ḥayy's confusion about why various ascetic and mystical practices are not a required part of the religion, and why a more sound version of an esoteric scriptural hermeneutic and the results of a philosophically oriented mystical experience are not taught to the general populace. In this context, Ibn Ṭufayl introduces the notion of the Sufis as an elect who need to be more cautious about the problem of confusing the general populace. Ibn Ṭufayl believes that the general populace might lose their access to an understanding of eternal bliss in the afterlife if they comprehend neither the general meanings of the scriptural text nor the interior layers of meaning that the philosophers and Sufis claim to discover. Ḥayy discovers this conclusion himself.

Yet, there were two issues that concerned [Ḥayy], which made him wonder, as he did not know the purpose of their wisdom. One of them [was the following]: Why did this [messenger's scripture] employ representations (*amthāl*) for people in much of what he described on the subject of the divine world ... to the point that the people fell into anthropomorphism and believing things about the essence of the Real that He is far from and free of, and likewise with regards to [the nature of] reward and punishment? The second matter: Why did it limit itself to these [religious] requirements and ritual obligations (*waẓaʾif al-ʿibādāt*), yet it allowed the amassing of wealth and indulgence in eating, to the extent that people occupy their time with idle activity and turn away from the Real? [Ḥayy's own] opinion was that no one should take [or consume] anything except [as much as] what is called for by bare necessity for survival. As for wealth (*amwāl*), it had no meaning [or value] for [Ḥayy]. He saw what was in the law among the [legal] stipulations on the subject of money, like the alms and its division [and distribution] as well as [rules regulating] purchases and usury.... He was surprised by all of this, and he saw it as excessive. He said: If people understood things for what they really are, they would turn away from these trivialities and turn toward the Real, avoiding all of this [excessive consumption].[40]

This passage is one of the most critical parts of the entire text of *Ḥayy ibn Yaqẓān* because it overturns popular modern interpretations of Ibn Ṭufayl as a philosophical skeptic of Islamic theology and ritual. A closer look at the questions Ḥayy asks indicates that he is not asking why followers of religions adhere to ritual practices and believe in theological doctrines about God and the afterlife. Rather, Ḥayy is specifically interested in two questions. The first question is the following: Why, Ḥayy asks, does Absāl's religion call for a certain level of ritual discipline without going the extra step of restricting the amassing of wealth and indulgence in consumption as well? That is, Ḥayy does not understand why asceticism is not a ritual requirement, since he believes that the requirement of asceticism would make the other rituals oriented around self-discipline self-evident and not necessary to prescribe.[41] To understand what motivates this question, the reader of the allegory should keep in mind that the crucial element that connected the intellectual aspect of Ḥayy's method with the experiential aspect was his realization of the importance of ascetic practices. In effect, Ḥayy wonders if his intellect was flawed in its conclusions about the importance of asceticism for mystical experience. The second question Ḥayy asks is the following:

Why, Ḥayy asks, does Absāl's religion appear to use symbols and images in place of various deeper truths that Ḥayy thinks these images allude to? More specifically, his question is the following: Why are images used to describe the divine world, including corporeal images of reward and punishment (and God), when it seems to Ḥayy that the divine world is something greater and more super-worldly and incorporeal?[42] In his philosophical mysticism, Ḥayy appears to believe that beyond the enticing corporeal images of reward stands a greater reward that is the fruit of the combination of asceticism and contemplation of the divine realm: enduring and continuous mystical vision. He also appears to believe that behind the ominous corporeal images of punishments stands a more profound punishment: the deprivation of this experiential vision.[43] According to the allegory, this punishment is one whose burden is heaviest not on the souls of the masses, who are unaware of the possibility of mystical vision, but on those knowledgeable philosophers whose souls have come to a deeper understanding of the divine realm but never really grasp it. According to Ibn Ṭufayl's allegory, the philosophers are blinded by their reluctance to step past the Active Intellect through the gates of the divine realm.

Ibn Ṭufayl's answer to both of Ḥayy's questions, about why asceticism is not required and why images of the divine realm appear in the scriptural text, is the following: Ibn Ṭufayl, like the Andalusī Sufi metaphysicians, overestimates the general populace's capacity for supererogatory Sufi rituals and deeper spiritual meanings. That is, Ibn Ṭufayl believes that the general populace should not be burdened with asceticism, esoteric scriptural hermeneutics, and philosophical-mystical conclusions that can potentially mislead people from their original path to bliss in the afterlife.

> What made Ḥayy come to all of this [questioning] was [the assumption] that people are all exceptional moral instincts, sharp minds, and strong spirits. He did not know what they had of slackness, deficiency, poor thought, and weak wills.[44]

In other words, in an effort to protect the general populace's own access to knowledge of the divine realm, Ibn Ṭufayl argues in favor of delimiting the religious authority of Sufis like Ḥayy as part of a more strict delineation of the gap between the Sufis as an elect and the general populace. In this conception of an elect who must avoid confusing the general populace, Ibn Ṭufayl agrees with Ibn Rushd, who argued for a very strict delineation between an elect (*khāṣṣa*), defined by Ibn Rushd as philosopher-scholars, and the general populace. Despite similarly acknowledging the limitations of the general populace's understanding of the theologians' conclusions, the earlier reformer Ibn Ḥazm nonetheless denounced conceptions of an elect (*khāṣṣa*) and rejected the idea that religion is full of symbols and hidden meanings intended for this elect. Ibn Ḥazm argued instead that theologians should simply endeavor more systematically with the help of Aristotelian logic to decipher the exact meaning of scriptural words, and that they should follow the lead of the logic-oriented Ẓāhirī theologians.[45] While Ibn Rushd and his teacher Ibn Ṭufayl disagreed with Ibn Ḥazm and still believed in the validity of an esoteric scriptural hermeneutic associated with some philosophical or mystical elect (*khāṣṣa*), they nonetheless shared with Ibn Ḥazm an interest in the idea that some among the general populace could be confused by the complex philosophical doctrines and esoteric scriptural hermeneutics that were being taught to them by various theological groups. In other words, in recounting this episode of Ḥayy's misunderstanding of the intellectual limitations of the masses, Ibn Ṭufayl seeks to remind the reader that the Sufi elect in particular should be wary of confusing the general populace, and that neither asceticism nor philosophical and mystical conclusions should be made a burden for the masses.

This argument, which should be read as a critique of contemporary Sufi metaphysicians, constitutes the political centerpiece of Ibn Ṭufayl's allegory. While Ibn Ṭufayl's novel has been characterized simplistically as a defense of philosophy in a religious society, the story more specifically offers an official approval of contemporary forms of philosophically oriented Sufi metaphysics and a simultaneous call for placing limits on the religious authority of these Sufi metaphysicians, who numbered in large part among the scholars. Ḥayy concludes his journey, thus, as a praying and fasting philosophically minded saintly figure, who accepts and follows the outward efficacy of revelation while simultaneously engaging inward interpretation in ways that are important for his larger mystical goals. Ḥayy pursues this philosophical and mystical knowledge back on the island where he originally grew up. In Ibn Ṭufayl's political commentary in the Almohad era, this allegorical island is not intended to signify an actual physical space for Sufis that is remote and distinct from the urban space of the ruling circles and scholars. Rather, the allegorical island appears to signify a distinct intellectual world where Sufis should articulate their Sufi metaphysics in private – that is, an ivory tower of sorts for Sufi metaphysicians that disrupts neither the ruling circles' popular projection of political leadership nor the scholars' articulation of more simplistic forms of guidance in ethics and theology for the general populace. As a politically commissioned text, *Ḥayy b. Yaqẓān* offers a window into how the politically centralizing authority of the Almohads was projected in a wide variety of mediums. As the allegory illustrates in agreement with historical record, early Almohad political theory ultimately sanctioned the religious authority of the scholarly Ghazālian Sufis such as Ibn Barrajān while simultaneously rejecting Ibn Qasī's model of the political Sufi sovereign who challenged the authority of both rulers and scholars. Ibn Ṭufayl's *Ḥayy ibn Yaqẓān*, in effect, illustrated the Almohads' interest in assimilating Sufi metaphysics into the dynasty's Ghazālian-Avicennan political culture while reducing the possibilities of independent political influence among the scholarly and non-scholarly Sufis, which had previously been seen at the end of the Almoravid period in Chapters 4 and 5.

From the perspective of Almohad political culture, Ibn Ṭufayl's *Ḥayy ibn Yaqẓān* offers a window into the way the Almohads made the pivotal political choice in twelfth-century al-Andalus to break with the previous Almoravids' political polices. In contrast with the Almoravids' anti-Ghazālian book-burning campaign and clash with Ibn Barrajān, the Almohads sought to appropriate the increasingly widespread modes of philosophical and mystical knowledge that the scholars understood to be part of sound theological knowledge and communal guidance. What is most significant about the Almohads' absorption of philosophy and Sufism into their political culture is how it anticipated a similar process that occurred under several new centralizing dynasties that emerged in the Islamic world in the late medieval and early modern eras. While the post-Almohad Nasrids of Granada (r. 1232 – 1492) commissioned philosophical and Sufi court treatises and developed an increasingly Sufi-oriented court ceremonial, the Mamluks of Egypt (r. 1250–1517) became major patrons of philosophical texts and Sufi sacred spaces. Further east, the Seljuks of Anatolia (r. 1277–1308) became patrons of the Platonizing Andalusī Sufi Ibn ʿArabī's career upon his departure from Almohad al-Andalus, and ultimately the Ottomans turned the late Ibn ʿArabī into something of a patron saint in Istanbul. In this regard, Ibn Ṭufayl's court-sponsored allegory offers an important lens into the culmination of specific changes in the enduring yet fluid dialectic of political and religious authority in the medieval Islamic world. By the thirteenth century, in a development that followed changes in how the scholars (*ʿulamāʾ*) conceived of sound knowledge and communal leadership, dynasties throughout the late medieval Middle East saw the complete assimilation of Graeco-Arabic philosophy and Platonizing forms of Sufi metaphysics into patterns of political patronage following more than two centuries of political debate, which was stirred originally by the enduring rivalry between the bibliophile Hellenizing Abbasid caliphs and their Platonizing Fatimid competitors.

Notes

1 The evolution of Almohad-era political legitimacy and scholarly religious authority has been the subject of an increasingly vast body of literature, particularly in Spain. One of the key themes in this research is the changing place of philosophy in Almohad political culture, which Maribel Fierro has shown to include the patronage of philosophical works in a manner that also contextualizes Castilian political culture. Maribel Fierro, "Alfonso the Wise: The Last Almohad Caliph?" *Medieval Encounters* 15 (2009): 175–98. Emilio Tornero, "Filosofía," in *Historia de España Menéndez Pidal – El retroceso territorial de al-Andalus. Almorávides y Almohades, siglos IX–XIII*, eds. José María Jover Zamora and María Jesús Viguera Molíns (Madrid: Espasa-Calpe, 1997): 8-2:587–602; Allen J. Fromherz, *The Almohads: The Rise of an Islamic Empire* (London: I. B. Tauris, 2010).

2 Alexander Knysh has offered a multifaceted analysis of the political and scholarly debates surrounding these Sufis and the Sufis of al-Andalus more broadly. Alexander D. Knysh, *Ibn ʿArabī in the Later Islamic Tradition* (Albany: State University of New York Press, 1999).

3 On the *ṭalaba* as a new circle of Almohad-supported politically influential scholars and the construction of Almohad political and religious authority, see Ambrosio Huici Miranda, *Historia Política del Imperio Almohade*, 2 vols. (Tetuán: Editora Marroquí, 1956–7); Maribel Fierro, "Le *mahdi* Ibn Tumart et al-Andalus: l'élaboration de la légitimité almohade," in *Mahdisme et millenarisme en Islam*, ed. Mercedes García-Arenal (Paris: Edisud, 2000), pp. 107–24; Émile Fricaud, "Les ṭalaba dans la société almohade (Le temps d'Averroès)," *al-Qantara* 18 (1997): 331–88.

4 Maribel Fierro, "The Legal Policies of the Almohad Caliphs and Ibn Rushd's *Bidāyat al-Mujtahid*," *Journal of Islamic Studies* 10 (1999): 226–48. Richard Taylor, "Ibn Rushd / Averroes and 'Islamic Rationalism,'" in *Medieval Encounters: Jewish, Christian and Muslim Culture in Confluence and Dialogue* 15 (2009): 125–35.

5 Though the Fatimid caliphate had collapsed with the rise of the Ayyubids and Mamluks, their legacy endured as an intellectual counterpoint in political and scholarly writing to acceptable models of political leadership and religious authority. That this counterpoint could also have been a source of political thought for the rapidly changing Almohads is an important and recent argument illustrative of the Almohads' multifaceted political culture. Maribel Fierro "The Almohads and the Fatimids," in *Ismāʿīlī and Fatimid Studies in Honor of Paul E. Walker*, ed. Bruce D. Craig (Chicago: Middle East Documentation Center, 2010), pp. 161–75.

6 Vincent Cornell highlights the evidence that Ibn Ṭufayl was a Sufi in Vincent J. Cornell, "Ḥayy in the Land of Absāl: Ibn Ṭufayl and Ṣūfism in the Western Maghrib During the Muwaḥḥid Era," in *The World of Ibn Ṭufayl: Interdisciplinary Perspectives on Ḥayy ibn Yaqẓān*, Ed. Lawrence Conrad. (Leiden: Brill, 1997), pp. 133–65.

7 Delfina Serrano, "¿Por qué llamaron los almohades antropomorfistas a los almorávides?" in *Los almohades: problemas y perspectivas*, ed. M. Fierro,

P. Cressier, and L. Molina (Madrid: CSIC, 2005), pp. 2:815–52. Fierro, "The Legal Policies of the Almohad Caliphs and Ibn Rushd's *Bidāyat al-Mujtahid*," 226–48.

8 Dimitri Gutas, "Ibn Ṭufayl on Ibn Sīna's Eastern Philosophy," *Oriens* 34 (1994): 221–41; idem, *Avicenna and the Aristotelian Tradition: An Introduction to Reading Avicenna's Philosophical Works* (Leiden: E. J. Brill, 1988), pp. 115–30; idem, "The Study of Arabic Philosophy in the Twentieth Century: An Essay on the Historiography of Arabic Philosophy," *British Journal of Middle Eastern Studies* 29 (2002): 5–25.

9 Edward Pockocke, *Philosophus autodidactus, sive epistola Abi Jaafar, Ebn Tophail de Hai Ebn Yokdhan. In qua Ostenditur, quomodo ex Inferiorum contemplatione ad Superiorum notitiam Ratio humana ascendere possit* (Oxford: H. Hall, 1671); Leon Gauthier, *Ibn Thofail: sa vie, ses oeuvres* (Paris: Ernest Leroux, 1909); George Hourani, "The Principal Subject of Ibn Ṭufayl's *Ḥayy ibn Yaqẓān*," *Journal of Near Eastern Studies* 15 (1956).

10 Josef Puig Montada, see "Philosophy in Andalusia: Ibn Bājja and Ibn Ṭufayl," in *The Cambridge Companion to Arabic Philosophy*, eds. Peter Adamson and Richard Taylor (Cambridge: Cambridge University Press, 2005), pp. 155–79; Vincent J. Cornell, "Ḥayy in the Land of Absāl," pp. 133–65.

11 The importance of reading the treatise in the context of Almohad political culture, and with attention to the possibility that the text indicates both approval and criticism of Sufism, has been emphasized by Maribel Fierro in an analysis of Almohad politics and religion more broadly. Maribel Fierro, "La religión," in *Historia de España Menéndez Pidal – El retroceso territorial de al-Andalus. Almorávides y Almohades, siglos IX–XIII*, eds. José María Jover Zamora and María Jesús Viguera Molíns (Madrid: Espasa-Calpe, 1997), 8-2:435–546.

12 *Ḥayy ibn Yaqẓān*, p. 12.

13 While Ibn Ṭufayl is certainly mysticizing Ibn Sīna's legacy in this text, Ibn Sīna's theory of prophecy nonetheless does include an eclectic approach to understanding intuition that harmonizes with the Sufis' mystical epistemologies. For Ibn Sīna, intuition is an ordered and logical capacity shared by all men with varied abilities to grasp a syllogism's middle term from the Active Intellect. Ibn Sīna's works describe intuition as something that simultaneously extends beyond the Active Intellect and that is improved by aspects of ritual piety such as prayer. He also notably draws on Sufi language of experiential mysticism, including *dhawq* (taste). Michael Marmura, "Avicenna's Theory of Prophecy in the Light of Ashʿarite Theology," in *The Seed of Wisdom: Essays in Honour of T. J. Meek*, ed. W. S. McCullough (Toronto: Toronto University Press, 1964), pp. 159–78; Ibn Sina, *Kitāb al-Shifā', al-Nafs, Part 5: Avicenna's "De Anima" (Arabic Text): Being the Psychological Part of Kitāb al-Shifā'*, ed. Fazlur Rahman (Oxford: Oxford University Press, 1959), pp. 173, 249–50; Ibn Sīna, *Kitāb al-Najāt*, M.S. Kurdī (Cairo: 1939), pp. 166–7; Ibn Sīna, *Aḥwāl al-Nafs*, ed. F. Aḥwānī (Cairo: Dar al-Iḥyā' al-Kutub al-ʿArabiyya, 1952), pp. 123–4; *Kitāb al-Ishārāt wa-l-Tanbīhāt*, ed. J. Forget (Leiden: 1892), p. 127ff.

14 Ali Humayun Akhtar, "The Political Controversy over Graeco-Arabic Philosophy and Sufism in Nasrid Government: The Case of Ibn al-Khaṭīb in al-Andalus," *International Journal of Middle Eastern Studies* 47 (2015): 323–42.

15 *Ḥayy ibn Yaqẓān*, p. 15.

16 Ibn Ṭufayl is accurate in stating that Ibn Sīna's experiential state reaches beyond the limits of intellectual (psychological) conjunction, and his conclusion contrasts what Gardet, Finnegan, and Radtke respectively understand of Ibn Sīna's conception of union as a "psychological union." These historians seem to conflate Ibn Sīna's doctrine on intuition, associated with the Active Intellect, with his discussion of mystical experience, associated with God. While the intuitive knowledge of the Sufis is intimately related to their mystical experience, Ibn Sīna's notion of intuition is not as clearly connected with his description of the experiential state. The intuition Ibn Sīna speaks of is logically ordered, and the source of the universals in intuition is the Active Intellect, not God. In contrast, Ibn Sīna's experiential state refers to an intellectual conjunction oriented not around the Active Intellect, but beyond it, and thus, beyond ordered intuition. Historians have debated whether Ibn Sīna's experiential union is psychological or ontological, when in fact it is neither of these. Ibn Sīna's *intellectus sanctus* is the soul in union with the Active Intellect, not God, with the Active Intellect being the direct source of that logically ordered intuition communicated through the *intellectus sanctus*. Given that Ibn Sīna's intuition (associated with the Active Intellect) is not the Sufis' intuition (associated with God), one can understand how Ibn Sīna's description of mystical experience indeed lies beyond the limits of intuition associated with the Active Intellect. Ibn Ṭufayl's "mysticizing" of Ibn Sīna, therefore, is specifically an attempt to isolate and expand on Ibn Sīna's minimally articulated two-step intellectual-experiential path to the divine found in Ibn Sīna's *al-Ishārāt* and *Risālat al-ʿIshq*. For the arguments mentioned, see L. Gardet, *Pensée religieuse d'Avicenne* (Paris: J. Vrin, 1951), pp. 149–55; J. Finnegan, "Avicenna's Refutation of Porphyrius," in *Avicenna Commemoration Volume*, ed. V. Courtois (Calcutta: 1956), pp. 187–203, especially p. 189ff; B. Radtke, "How Can Man Reach the Mystical Union?: Ibn Ṭufayl and the Divine Spark," in *The World of Ibn Ṭufayl*, ed. Lawrence Conrad (Leiden: Brill, 1997), pp. 165–94, especially pp. 176–8.

17 *Ḥayy ibn Yaqẓān*, p. 6.

18 *Ḥayy ibn Yaqẓān*, p. 4.

19 Reisman offers a succinct overview and analysis of al-Fārābī's thought. David Reisman, "al-Fārābī and the Philosophical Curriculum," *The Cambridge Companion to Arabic Philosophy*, eds. Peter Adamson and Richard Taylor (Cambridge: Cambridge University Press, 2005), pp. 52–71.

20 Ibn Ṭufayl's thought parallels or perhaps anticipates what historians have identified as the Avicennan tendencies of later Sufism in the years after Ibn ʿArabī. Morris provides an analytical overview of this phenomenon. James W. Morris, "Ibn ʿArabī and His Interpreters Part II (Conclusion): Influences and Interpretations," *Journal of the American Oriental Society* 107 (1987): 101–19.

21 Herbert A. Davidson, *Alfarabi, Avicenna, and Averroes on Intellect* (New York: Oxford University Press, 1992), p. 45ff; Thérèse-Anne Druart, "Al-Fārābī's

Causation of the Heavenly Bodies," in *Islamic Philosophy and Mysticism*, ed. Parviz Morewedge (Delmar, NY: Caravan Books, 1981), pp. 35–45; idem, "Al-Fārābī and Emanationism," in *Studies in Medieval Philosophy*, ed. J. F. Wippel (Washington, DC: The Catholic University of America Press, 1987), pp. 23–43; idem "Al-Fārābī, Emanation and Metaphysics," in *Neoplatonism and Islamic Thought*, ed. Parviz Morewedge (Albany: State University of New York Press, 1992), pp. 127–48.

22 *Ḥayy ibn Yaqẓān*, p. 5.

23 Radtke provides important analysis of Ibn Sīna's representation of conditioning the intellect through speculative contemplation. Radtke, "How Can Man Reach the Mystical Union?" p. 176ff.

24 With regard to Ibn Sīna's simultaneous interest in asceticism and mystical insight, he states in his own words, "Asceticism without mystical insight is a sort of business transaction where one sells the pleasure of this world for the pleasure of the world to come … [on the other hand], the mystic only desires the first Truth for no reason except Him, and he prefers nothing more than mystical insight and worship of Him." Ibn Sīna, *al-Ishārāt wa-l-Tanbihāt*, pp. 11–13.

25 To be sure, even al-Ghazālī's notion of *dhawq* cannot be pinned down clearly. On the one hand, certain references taken in isolation, like in *al-Munqidh min al-Ḍalāl*, indicate that mystical experiential knowledge as *dhawq* is superior to reasoned verification of arguments, but on the other hand, the elaboration of mysticism in texts like the *Mishkāt al-Anwār* rely on philosophical language, as discussed in Chapter 5. al-Ghazālī, *al-Munqidh min al-Ḍalāl wa-l-Muwaṣṣil ilā dhī l-ʿIzza wa-l-Jalāl*, ed. Farid Jabre (Beirut: al-Lajna l-Duwaliyya li-Tarjamat al-Rawāʾiʿ, 1959), pp. 16–40.

26 Ḥayy's discovery of his true self or essence that lies at the core of his corporeal self is reminiscent of, and likely draws on, Ibn Sīna's flying man example. The question Ibn Sīna asks is whether man, were he floating in midair and unable to sense his extremities, could still recognize his own existence. Michael Marmura, "Avicenna's Flying Man in Context," *The Monist* 69 (1986): 383–95.

27 *Ḥayy ibn Yaqẓān*, p. 72.

28 Ibn Ṭufayl's allegory offers an interesting early example of how the typically philosophical notion that the planets' circular movement is a perfect kind of movement, which Ibn Ḥazm objects is no more perfect than irregular non-circular movement, finds overlaps with Sufi ritual. Ibn Ṭufayl's whirling in emulation of the cosmos is evocative of the practices of Jalāl al-Dīn al-Rūmī's followers. Ibn Ḥazm's argument mentioned here can be found in Ibn Ḥazm, *al-Fiṣal wa-l-Milal fil-Milal wa-l-Ahwāʾ wa-l-Niḥal*, ed. Muḥammad Ibrāhīm Naṣr and ʿAbd al-Raḥmān Umayra (Beirut: Dār al-Jayl, 1995), 5:147.

29 *Ḥayy ibn Yaqẓān*, p. 94.

30 This position is similar to the way the following otherwise multifaceted and illuminating analysis interprets Ibn Ṭufayl's text. Puig Montada, "Philosophy in Andalusia," pp. 155–79.

31 *Ḥayy ibn Yaqẓān*, pp. 97–101.

32 Historians have typically read the celestial promenade in the story as an example of *fanāʾ* while overlooking the reference to *baqāʾ*. One of several examples of this reading is the following: Puig Montada, "Philosophy in Andalusia," p. 179, n. 47.

33 *Ḥayy ibn Yaqẓān*, pp. 97–101.

34 At some point, this project's intellectual goals resemble al-Qūnawī's reading of Ibn ʿArabī's writings. As much as al-Qūnawī read Ibn ʿArabī through an Avicennan lens, he may have intended simultaneously to elaborate any mystical aspects of Ibn Sīna's work that he identifies in Ibn Sīna's explicit discussion of and interest in Sufism. This argument follows from the fact that al-Qūnawī did not simply read the various parts of Ibn ʿArabī's corpus through an Avicennan lens, but as Chittick has argued, also focused on the more philosophical aspects to the exclusion of other less philosophical ones. Chittick provides an overview of this aspect of Ibn ʿArabī's legacy in William Chittick, *The Sufi Path of Knowledge: Ibn al-ʿArabī's Metaphysics of Imagination* (Albany: State University of New York Press, 1998), pp. xvi–xx.

35 For the same conclusion derived from a study of symbolism in *Ḥayy ibn Yaqẓān*, see J. Christoph, "Symbols and Hints: Some Considerations Concerning the Meaning of Ibn Ṭufayl's *Ḥayy ibn Yaqẓān*," in *The World of Ibn Ṭufayl*, ed. Lawrence Conrad (Leiden: Brill, 1997), pp. 238–67.

36 *Ḥayy ibn Yaqẓān*, p. 16.

37 As discussed in Chapter 3, a good example of such antinomianism that was considered scandalous in doxographical writing is the reputation of Ismʿāīl b. al-Ruʿaynī, the leader of the Masarrīs (*masariyya*) of Almería in the first half of the eleventh century. Claude Addas, "Andalusi Mysticism and the Rise of Ibn ʿArabī," in *The Legacy of Muslim Spain*, ed. Salma K. Jayyusi (Leiden: Brill, 1994), pp. 909–36.

38 *Ḥayy ibn Yaqẓān*, p. 112.

39 Marmura's overview of Ibn Sīna's philosophical conception of prophecy offers a useful starting point for considering obvious parallels with Avicennan doctrines in this part of the text. Marmura, "Avicenna's Theory of Prophecy."

40 *Ḥayy ibn Yaqẓān*, p. 113.

41 Scholars from earlier periods who embodied the model of the scholar-ascetic both in Baghdad and al-Andalus debated this question about the place of ascetic practices in Islamic ritual. Richard Gramlich, *Alte Vorbilder des Sufitums* (Wiesbaden: Harrassowitz, 1997).

42 This hermeneutical question has been dealt with differently by various theological groups. As Weiss discusses, *ta'wīl* as a method in Muʿtazilī and Ashʿarī Qur'an commentary was a way to discover the intended meaning of scriptural language in Arabic by "deflecting" the apparent meaning and looking for the *majāz* meaning. As discussed in Chapter 4, Ibn Ḥazm's approach was comparable, but he simply argued that since the meanings of words always vary by context, words do not have primary or apparent meanings such that they need to be read metaphorically. His argument, in effect, claims that what the Ashʿarīs and Muʿtazilīs might call the *majāz* meaning is not the *majāz*, but should rather be called the univocal *ẓāhir* meaning that might be different in each specific occurrence of the word. Martin has shed light on some early examples of these hermeneutical approaches in Muʿtazilism, highlighting in particular the role of Naẓẓām (d. 846) on *ṣarfa* as deflection. What these theologians' methods agree on, and where they differ from Sufi hermeneutics, is in the idea that the intended meaning is intended for all readers of the text. In Sufi hermeneutics, the meanings intended for the elect and the general

populace can be two different intended meanings, and in cases when the exterior and interior meanings appeared to clash in the eyes of critics, controversy emerged. Bernard Weiss, *The Spirit of Islamic Law* (Athens: University of Georgia Press, 1998), pp. 96–103; Richard C. Martin, "The Role of the Basrah Muʿtazilah in Formulating the Doctrine of the Apologetic Miracle," *Journal of Near Eastern Studies* 39 (1980): 175–89.

43 During his celestial promenade, what Ḥayy saw at the level of the Active Intellect upon his return descent from the highest spheres appears to have led him to conceptualize rewards and punishments in terms of access to and deprivation of mystical vision. "From this height, he saw other essences like his own essence … he saw in his own essence and in those essences that were in his level goodness, splendor, and delight without end, what no eye saw nor ear heard nor occurred to the heart of any person … nor what anyone can conceive except those who have arrived [to God] and the [mystical] knowers [of God] (*al-wāṣilūn wa-l-ʿārifūn*). He saw many disembodied selves, like rusted mirrors, wickedness had taken possession of them. They were [nonetheless] turned towards the brilliant mirrors in which the image of the sun was outlined, [but] their faces turned away from it. He saw in these essences ugliness and deficiency that had never imagined. He saw them in unending agony and unextinguishing affliction…." When Ḥayy moved from the *fanāʾ* (diminishing of the self) in the otherworldly realm to the *baqāʾ* (recovery of the self) associated with the lunar Active Intellect, he saw that the incorporeal misery among these latter souls was ultimately the deprivation of mystical vision. These souls recognize and yearn for the Necessary Existent but simply do not transcend the partition separating the self-conscious discolored realm from the selfless clear experiential realm, living thus a tormented existence. The implication in Ibn Ṭufayl's representation of mysticism is that the pleasure the philosophers feel in their intellectual conjunction with the Active Intellect is fleeting and superficial, masking their deeper agony of never attaining what the philosophical Sufis sought to attain in their transcendence of the Active Intellect. Ibn Ṭufayl's allegory, therefore, cautions the Sufis about problematically bringing the general populace halfway toward mystical experience and leaving them in the state of the philosophers, with neither a general populace's access to bliss in the afterlife nor the mystic's rapturous vision. *Ḥayy ibn Yaqẓān*, p. 101.

44 *Ḥayy ibn Yaqẓān*, p. 228.

45 Ibn Rushd made this point prior to Ibn Ṭufayl in the context of philosophical meanings of scripture being unsystematically taught to the masses. Conceiving of the scholars as simultaneously philosophers and scholars according to his own legacy, and arguing in favor of a distinction between the scholars' understanding of scripture and that of the masses, Ibn Rushd asserts in one key passage that "Revelation must be affirmed on its manifest level and not be explained to the masses in a mix of [Revelation] and philosophy, because [this mixed] explanation of it is an explanation of the results of philosophy for [the masses], without there being in their possession a proof for it." Ibn Rushd, *Kashf ʿan Manāhij al-Adilla fī ʿAqāʾid al-Milla*, M. A. al-Jabrī (Beirut: Markaz Dirāsāt al-Waḥda al-ʿArabiyya, 1998), p. 154.

Conclusion

The story told in the six chapters of this book has traced the historical relationship between government and religion in the pre-modern Middle East and North Africa. At the heart of this story has been an elusive interplay of political and religious authority that involved rival ruling administrations as well as the wider scholarly networks (*'ulamā'*) of Islam. Since the seventh century C.E., these groups have debated an enduring question that has been answered differently across time and geography: in the post-prophetic era, what constituted sound models of political leadership and communal guidance of the general faithful populace?

By bridging analysis of the judiciary with an investigation of widely circulating philosophical and theological writings, this study adds the following new perspective to the historical picture of how ruling circles and the scholars (*'ulamā'*) answered this question: While the scholars indeed represented much of pre-modern Islamic religious authority through their semi-independent dominance of the judiciary and through their powerful social role as urban mediators and guides of faith and ethics, the way they conceived of their role as communal guides was significantly informed by their assessment of contemporary political models of leadership. That is, despite their dominance over ruling circles in the judiciary, the scholars' (*'ulamā'*) textual articulations of what constituted sound theological knowledge and valid forms of communal guidance in belief and ethics reflected a keen awareness of the intellectual underpinnings of contemporary political movements, especially those movements they sought to distance themselves from. What is understated in the most recent research is this historical agency of political actors that impacted, often without intention, scholarly conceptions of sound theological knowledge and valid guidance and authority.

In the case study examined in this book, eleventh- and twelfth-century scholars (*'ulamā'*) active in the Andalusī Umayyad caliphate of Cordoba and Abbasid caliphate of Baghdad disapproved of the rival Fatimid caliphate in Cairo (r. 909 – 1171) and its controversial image of the ruler as a semi-messianic (*mahdī*) and Platonic philosopher-governor endowed with a special intellect. The scholars' disapproval of the Fatimid caliph occurred despite their acceptance of the earlier Abbasid caliphs' own Hellenistic model of political culture, reflected in the politically backed translation of Greek, Aramaic, Pahlavi, and Sanskrit works of learning to Arabic beginning in the eighth century C.E. With the spread of proselytizing Fatimid theologians westward and eastward to al-Andalus and Iraq, the majority-Sunnī scholars' growing alarm over the Fatimid caliphate's political power deepened their self-scrutiny over the way some fellow scholars, such as the Cordovan Ibn Masarra (d. 331/931), played an additional role in their communities as philosophical sages (*ḥukamāʾ*). The once innocuous social and religious phenomenon of scholars as philosophical sages, guiding the spiritual and intellectual ascent of their followers, suddenly became a phenomenon that was politically and religiously contentious with the rise of the Platonizing Fatimid philosopher-caliphs and their itinerant supporters.

By the twelfth century, in an intellectual synthesis epitomized by al-Ghazālī's (d. 505/1111) embrace of early Abbasid-era philosophical writings, and likewise foreshadowed by the philosophical reputations of his Sunnī predecessors Ibn Masarra (d. 331/931) and Ibn Ḥazm (d. 456/1064), the increasingly multifaceted scholars of the Middle East and North Africa largely came to the following conclusion about how to define their own role as guides of communal belief: On one level, as Sufi metaphysicians, the scholars could soundly assimilate early Neoplatonic-Avicennan doctrines on the ascent of the soul and intellect into the language they used to articulate and instruct mystical experience, and they could do so without sanctioning the specific theory of intellectual ascent used in later Fatimid political culture. On another level, as logicians, and as nuanced critics of various Platonizing Islamic theologies such as those of Ibn Masarra and the Fatimids, the scholars could soundly assimilate Aristotelian-Avicennan logic and its syllogistic tools into their knowledge of jurisprudence and theology without uncritically accepting the entirety of logic's Platonizing and seemingly dualist conclusions about the nature of the world and the human mind. That is, in a notable reflection of their political and geographical context, and in an expansion of their early social role, the increasingly polymathic scholars (*ʿulamāʾ*) of the Middle East and North Africa after the twelfth century increasingly embraced two additional roles, often simultaneously: (1) the role of Neoplatonic-Avicennan Sufi metaphysicians, who were increasingly active in Sufi lodges (*zāwiya, tekke, khānqāh*) in the early modern period, and (2) the role of Aristotelian-Avicennan neo-Ashʿarī theologians, who were active in endowed colleges of jurisprudence (*fiqh*) and theology (*kalām*). That the nominalist critique of Plato's realism emerged in Arabic in this period in the writings of the Ẓāhirī scholar Ibn Ḥazm (d. 456/1064) and the Shāfiʿī scholar al-Ghazālī (d. 505/1111), long before its wider transmission in Latin Europe, speaks to the extent that the modern border between Western and Middle Eastern historiographies overlooks a shared geographical and intellectual context dating back to the medieval world, and even further, to the world of late antiquity.

From the perspective of sources, this book has shed new light on this fluid interplay of political and religious authority by situating legal opinions and juridical institutions in the larger context of court chronicles, biographical dictionaries, mystical treatises, doxographical works, philosophical books, and theological treatises. When brought together with the history of scholarly legal opinions, these philosophical and theological sources add certain precision to the historian's picture of a dynamic interplay between the political authority of ruling circles and the religious authority of the scholars (*ʿulamāʾ*). What this book suggests in place of modern allusions to a pre-modern scholarly "orthodoxy" or orthodoxies, then, is the identification of broad trends in the scholars' juridical practices and theological beliefs that were fluid and highly contextual according to geography, time period, and most significantly in this book, political culture.

In sum, the goal of this book has been to facilitate more sound analyses of the historical relationship between government and religion in the Middle East and North Africa. What this book offers future researchers is an illustration of a key investigative paradigm: Political and religious affairs in the Middle East and North Africa are not simply illustrative of enduring theories of communal leadership and sacred beliefs. Rather, the rapidly changing political and religious landscape of the region tells a much more complex story of how geography, geopolitics, local customs, and economics have impacted and continue to impact the way these theories and beliefs are put into practice.

Bibliography

Primary Sources

al-Andalusī, Ṣāʿid. *Kitāb Ṭabaqāt al-Umam. Livre des categories des nations*. Ed. L. Cheiko. Beirut: al-Maktaba l-Kāthūlīkiyya, 1912. Trans. Regis Blachère. Paris: Larose, 1935.

Ṭabaqāt al-Umam. Science in the Medieval World: Book of the Categories of Nations. Ed. Ḥayā al-ʿĪd Bū Alwān. Beirut: Dār al-Ṭaliʿa lil-Ṭabāʿa wa-l-Nashr, 1985. trans. Sema'an I. Salem and Alok Kumar. Austin: University of Texas Press, 1991.

al-Ashʿarī, Abū l-Ḥasan. *Maqālāt al-Islāmiyyīn wa-Khtilāf al-Muṣallīn*. Ed. H. Ritter. Wiesbaden: Franz Steiner Verlag, 1963.

al-Bīrūnī and Ibn Sīna. *al-As'ila wa-l-Ajwiba. Questions and Answers: Including the Further Answers of al-Bīrūnī and al-Maʿṣūmī's Defense of Ibn Sīna*. Ed. Seyyid Hossein Nasr, Mahdi Mohaghegh. Tehran: High Council of Culture and Art, 1975.

al-Dhahabī, Muḥammad b. Aḥmad. *Siyar Aʿlām al-Nubalāʾ*. Beirut: Muʾassasāt al-Risāla, 1985.

Tadhkirat al-Ḥuffāẓ. 4 vols. Hyderabad: Dāʾirat al-Maʿārif al-ʿUthmāniyya, 1968–70.

al-Fāsī, Muḥammad b. Aḥmad. *al-ʿIqd al-Thamīn fī Taʾrīkh al-Balad al-Amīn*. Ed. Muḥammad Ḥāmid al-Faqī, Fuʾād Sayyid and Maḥmūd Muḥammad Tanāhī. Cairo: Maṭbaʿat al-Sunna al-Muḥammadiyya, 1958–1969.

al-Ghazālī, Abū Ḥāmid Muḥammad b. Muḥammad. *al-Munqidh min al-Ḍalāl wa-l-Muwaṣṣil ilā dhī l-ʿIzza wa-l-Jalāl*. Ed. Farid Jabre. Beirut: al-Lajna l-Duwaliyya li-Tarjamat al-Rawāʾiʿ, 1959.

al-Iqtiṣād fī l-Iʿtiqād. Ed. İbrahim Agah Çubukçu and Hüseyin Atay. Ankara: Nur Matbaası, 1962.

Faḍāʾiḥ al-Bāṭiniyya wa-Faḍaʾil al-Mustaẓhiriyya, ʿAbd al-Raḥmān al-Badawī. Cairo: Dār al-Qawmiyya, 1964.

Mishkāt al-Anwār. The Niche of the Lights. Trans. D. Buchman. Provo, UT: Brigham Young University Press, 1998.

Tahāfut al-Falāsifa. Ed. Maurice Bouyges. Frankfurt: Institute for the History of Arabic-Islamic Science, 1999.

Tahāfut al-Falāsifa. The Incoherence of the Philosophers. Trans. Michael E. Marmura. Provo, UT: Brigham Young University Press, 2000.

al-Ḥumaydī, Muḥammad b. Futūḥ. *Jadhwat al-Muqtabis fī Dhikr Wulāt al-Andalus*. Ed. Muḥammad al-Ṭanjī. Cairo: Maktab Nashr al-Thaqāfa al-Islāmiyya, 1952.

al-Khushanī, Muḥammad b. al-Ḥārith. *Ṭabaqāt ʿUlamāʾ Ifrīqiya, Classes des savantes de l'Ifriqiya*. Ed. and trans. M. Ben Cheneb. Algiers: Publications de la Faculté des Lettres d'Alger, 1915–20.

al-Kindī, Abū Yūsuf Ya'qūb b. Isḥāq. *Rasā'il al-Kindī al-Falsafiyya*. 2 vols. Ed. Muḥammad 'Abd al-Hadī Abū Riḍā. Cairo: Dār al-Fikr al-'Arabī, 1950–3.

al-Maqqarī, Aḥmad b. Muḥammad. *Nafḥ al-Ṭīb min Ghuṣn al-Andalus al-Raṭīb*. Ed. Ihṣān 'Abbās. 8 vols. Beirut: Dar Ṣādir, 1968.

al-Maqrīzī, Aḥmad b. 'Alī. *Kitāb al-Sulūk li-Ma'rifat Duwal al-Mulūk*. 4 vols. Ed. Muḥammad Muṣtafa Ziyāda. Cairo: Kulliyyat al-Ādāb bi-Jāmi'at al-Qāhira, 1934–72.

al-Mas'ūdī, 'Alī b. al-Ḥusayn. *Murūj al-Dhahab wa Ma'ādin al-Jawhar*. Ed. Charles Pellat. Beirut: Manshū'āt al-Jāmi'a al-Lubnāniyya, 1965.

al-Nubāhī (= al-Bunnāhī), 'Alī b. 'Abdullāh b. al-Ḥasan. *Ta'rīkh Quḍāt al-Andalus*. Ed. E. Levi Provencal (Cairo: Dār al-Kātib al-Miṣrī, 1948).

al-Qifṭī, 'Alī b. Yūsuf. *Ikhbār al-'Ulamā' bi-Akhbār al-Ḥukamā'*. Ed. Julius Lippert and August Mueller. Leipzig: Dieterich'sche Verlagbuchhandlung, 1903.

al-Sarrāj, Abū Naṣr 'Abd Allāh b. 'Alī. *Kitāb al-Luma' fī l-Taṣawwuf*. Ed. Reynold A. Nicholson. London: Luzac & Co., 1914.

al-Suhrawardī, Shihāb al-Dīn Yaḥyā. *Kitāb al-Mashāri' wa-l-Muṭāharāt*. In *Opera Metaphysica et Mystica*. Vol. 1. Ed. Henri Corbin. Istanbul: Maarif Matbaasi, 1945.

Kitāb Ḥikmat al-Ishrāq. In *Oeuvres Philosophiques et Mystiques*. Vol. 2. Ed. Henri Corbin. Paris and Tehran: Adrien Maisonneuve, 1952.

al-Tawḥīdī, Abū Ḥayyān. *al-Imtā' wa-l-Mu'ānasa*. Ed. Aḥmad Amīn and Aḥmad al-Zayn. 3 vols. Beirut: al-Maktaba al-'Aṣriyya, 1953.

al-Tirmidhī, Muḥammad b. 'Alī al-Ḥakīm. *Thalāthat Muṣannafāt lil-Ḥakīm al-Tirmidhī: Kitāb Sīrat al-Awliyā', Jawāb Masā'il allatī Sa'alahū Ahl Sarakhs 'Anhā, Jawāb Kitāb min al-Rayy*. Ed. Bernd Radtke. Stuttgart: F. Steiner, 1992.

al-Ṭurṭūshī, Abū Bakr Muḥammad. *Risāla ilā 'Abd Allāh ibn Muẓaffar*. In Sa'd Ghurāb, "Ḥawla Iḥrāq al-Murābiṭūn li-Iḥyā' al-Ghazālī." In *Actas del IV Coloquio Hispano-Tunecino (Palma de Mallorca, 1979)*. Madrid: Instituto Hispano-Arabe de Cultura, 1983, 133–63.

al-Tustarī, Sahl b. 'Abd Allāh. *Kitāb al-Ḥurūf*. Ed. Ja'far, M. K. *Min Qaḍāya l-Fikr al-Islāmi: Dirāsa wa Nuṣūs*. Cairo: Maktabat Dar al-'Ulūm, 1976.

Tafsīr al-Tustarī. Ed. Muḥammad Bāsil 'Uyūn al-Sūd. Beirut: Dār al-Kutub al-'Ilmiyya, 2002.

Ibn al-'Abbār, Abū 'Abd Allāh Muḥammad. *al-Takmila li-Kitāb al-Ṣila*. Ed. Francisco Codera Zaidín. Madrid: Bibliotheca Arabico-Hispana, 1887–9.

Ibn al-'Aqil, Abū l-Wafā' 'Alī. *al-Wāḍiḥ fī Usūl al-Fiqh*, 4 vols. Ed. George Makdisi. Beirut and Berlin: Klaus Schwarz Verlag Berlin, 1996–2002.

Ibn al-'Arabī, Abū Bakr. *al-'Awāṣim min al-Qawāṣim*. Ed. 'Ammār Ṭālibī. Cairo: Maktabat Dār al-Turāth, 1997.

Ibn 'Arabī, Abū 'Abd Allāh Muḥammad b. 'Alī. *al-Futūḥāt al-Makkiyya*, 4 vols. Cairo: Dār al-Kutub al-'Arabiyya al-Kubrā, 1329/1911.

The Ringstones of Wisdom. Trans. Caner Dagli. Chicago: Kazi, 2004.

Ibn al-'Arīf, Abū al-'Abbās Aḥmad b. Muḥammad. *Miftāḥ al-Sa'āda*. Ed. al-Ṭibā'ī. Beirut: Dār al-Gharb al-Islāmī, 1993.

Maḥāsin al-Majālis. Ed. Miguel Asín Palacios. Paris: Paul Geuthner, 1933.

Ibn Bājja, Abū Bakr Muḥammad b. Yaḥyā. *al-Qawl fī l-Ṣuwar al-Rūḥāniyya*. In *Rasā'il ibn Bājja al-Ilāhiyya*. Ed. Mājid Fakhrī. Beirut: Dar al-Nahār, 1968.

Tadbīr al-Mutawaḥḥid. In *Rasā'il ibn Bājja al-Ilāhiyya*. Ed. Mājid Fakhrī Beirut: Dar al-Nahār, 1968.

Ibn Barrajān, Abū l-Ḥakam 'Abd al-Salām. *Sharḥ Asmā' al-Ḥusnā*. Ed. Purificación de la Torre. Madrid: CSIC, 2000.

al-Tafsīr al-Ṣūfī lil-Qur'ān aw Tanbīh al-Afhām ilā Tadabbur al-Kitāb al-Ḥakīm wa-Ta'arruf al-Āyāt wa-al-Naba' al-'Aẓīm. Ed. Muḥammad al-'Adlūnī Idrīsī. Casablanca: Dār al-Thaqāfa, al-Mu'assasa lil-Nashr wa-l-Tawzī', 2011.

Tafsīr Ibn Barrajān: Tanbīh al-Afhām ilā Tadabbur al-Kitāb al-Ḥakīm wa-Ta'arruf al-Āyāt wa-l-Naba al-'Aẓīm. Ed. Aḥmad Farīd Mazyādī. Beirut: Dār al-Kutub al-'Ilmiyya, 2013.

A Qur'an Commentary by Ibn Barrajān of Seville (D. 536/1141): Īḍāḥ Al-Ḥikma bi-Aḥkām al-'Ibra (Wisdom Deciphered, the Unseen Discovered). Ed. Gerhard Böwering and Yousef Casewit. Leiden: Brill, 2015.

Tefsir Ibn Berrecan. 3 vols. Manuscript. MS Yusuf Ağa 4744, 4745, 4746. Konya: Yusuf Ağa Library.

Ibn Bashkuwāl, Abū l-Qāsim Khalaf b. 'Abd al-Malik. *al-Ṣila fī-Akhbār A'immat al-Andalus*. Ed. Francisco Codera Zaidín. Madrid: Bibliotheca Arabico-Hispana, 1892.

Kitāb al-Ṣila. 2 vols. Ed. Ibrahim al-Abyari. Beirut: Dar al-Kitāb al-Lubnāni, 1989.

Ibn al-Faraḍī, Abū l-Walīd 'Abd Allāh. *al-Mawṣūl fī Tārīkh al-'Ulamā' wa Ruwāt al-'Ilm bi-l-Andalus (Tārīkh 'Ulamā al-Andalus)*. Ed. Francisco Codera Zaidín. 2 vols. Madrid: Bibliotheca Arabico-Hispana, 1890–2.

Ibn Ḥazm, Abū Muḥammad 'Alī b. Aḥmad. *al-Taqrīb li-Ḥadd al-Manṭiq*. Ed. Iḥsān 'Abbās. Beirut: Dār Maktabat al-Ḥayā, 1959.

Marātib al-'Ulūm. In *Rasā'il Ibn Ḥazm al-Andalusī*, 4 vols. Ed. Iḥsan 'Abbās. Beirut: al-Mu'assasa l-'Arabiyya lil-Dirāsāt wa-l-Nashr, 1980–3. 4:61–92.

al-Fiṣal wa-l-Milal fī l-Milal wa-l-Ahwā' wa-l-Niḥal. 5 vols. Ed. Muḥammad Ibrāhīm Naṣr, 'Abd al-Raḥmān Umayra. Beirut: Dār al-Jayl, 1995.

Ibn Khaldūn, Abū Zayd 'Abd al-Raḥmān. *The Muqaddimah*. 3 vols. Trans. F. Rosenthal. Princeton, NJ: Princeton University Press, 1958.

Ibn Khallikān, Abū al-'Abbās Aḥmad b. Muḥammad. *Wafayāt al-A'yān wa-Anbā' Abnā' al-Zamān*. Bullaq, 1858.

Ibn Masarra, Abū 'Abd Allāh Muḥammad b. 'Abd Allāh. *Kitāb al-Ḥurūf*. Ed. Muḥammad Kamāl Ja'far, *Min Qaḍāya l-Fikr al Islāmi: Dirāsa wa Nuṣūs*. Cairo: Maktabat Dar al-'Ulūm, 1976.

Risālat al-I'tibār. Ed. Muḥammad Kamāl Ja'far, *Min Qaḍāya l-Fikr al-Islāmī: Dirāsa wa Nuṣūs*. Cairo: Maktabat Dar al-'Ulūm, 1976.

Kitāb al-Ḥurūf. Ed. Pilar Garrido. "Edición critica de K. *Jawāṣṣ al-ḥurūf* de Ibn Masarra." *Al-Andalus Magreb: Estudios árabes e islámicos* 14 (2007): 51–89.

Risālat al-I'tibār. Ed. Pilar Garrido. "Edición crítica de la *Risālat al-i'tibār* de Ibn Masarra de Córdoba." *Miscelánea de estudios árabes y hebraicos* 56 (2007): 81–104.

Ibn Qasī, Abū l-Qāsim Aḥmad b. al-Ḥusayn. *Kitāb Khal' al-Na'layn*. Ed. Muḥammad al-Amrāni. Safi: IMBH, 1997.

Ibn Rushd, Abū l-Walīd Muḥammad b. Aḥmad. *Faṣl al-Maqāl Fī Mā Bayn al-Ḥikma wa-l-Sharī'a min al-Ittiṣāl*. Ed. M. Amara Cairo: Dār al-Ma'ārif, 1983.

Kashf 'an Manāhij al-Adilla fī 'Aqā'id al-Milla. Ed. M. A. al-Jabrī. Beirut: Markaz Dirāsāt al-Waḥda al-'Arabiyya, 1998.

Ibn Sīna, Abū Alī al-Ḥusayn b. 'Abd Allāh. *Kitāb al-Ishārāt wa-l-Tanbīhāt*. Ed. J. Forget. Leiden: Brill, 1892.

Risāla fī-l-'Ishq. Ed. A. F. Mehren. In *Traites mystiques d'Avicenna*. Leiden: Brill, 1894.

Kitāb al-Najā. Ed. M.S. Kurdī. Cairo: 1939.

Aḥwāl al-Nafs. Ed. F. Aḥwānī. Cairo: Dar al-Iḥyā' al-Kutub al-'Arabiyya, 1952.

Kitāb al-Shifā', al-Nafs, Part 5: *Avicenna's "De Anima" (Arabic Text): Being the Psychological Part of Kitab al-Shifa'*. Ed. Fazlur Rahman. Oxford: Oxford University Press, 1959.

al-Ishārāt wa-l-Tanbīhāt. Ed. Sulaymān Dunyā. Cairo: Dār al-Ma'ārif, 1960.

Ibn Sīna and al-Bīrūnī. *al-As'ila wa-l-Ajwiba. Questions and Answers: Including the Further Answers of al-Bīrunī and al-Ma'ṣūmī's Defense of Ibn Sīna*. Ed. Seyyid Hossein Nasr and Mahdi Mohaghegh. Tehran: High Council of Culture and Art, 1975.

Ibn Taghrībirdī, Jamāl al-Dīn Yūsuf b. al-Amīr. *al-Nujūm al-Ẓāhira fī Mulūk Miṣr wa-l-Qāhira*. Ed. T. W. J. Juynboll, B. F. Matthes, and H. L. Fleischer. 2 vols. Leiden: Brill, 1855–61.

Ibn Taymiyya, Abū al-'Abbās Aḥmad. *al-Radd 'alā l-Manṭiqiyyīn*. Ed. 'Abd al-Ṣamad Sharaf al-Dīn al-Kutubī Bombay: al-Maṭba'at al-Qayyima, 1949.

al-Radd 'alā al-Manṭiqiyyīn. Ed. Muḥammad 'Abd al-Sattār Naṣṣār and 'Imād Khafājī. Cairo: Maktabat al-Azhar, 1976.

al-Tafsīr al-Kabīr. Beirut: Dār al-Kutub al-'Ilmiyya, 1988.

Ibn Ṭufayl, Abū Bakr Muḥammad b. 'Abd al-Malik and Gauthier L. *Ḥayy ibn Yaqẓān: roman philosophique d'Ibn Thofail, texte arabe avec les variantes des manuscrits et de plusieurs editions et traduction francaise, 2e edition, revue, augmentee et completement remaniee*. Beirut: Imprimerie Catholique, 1936.

Ibn Waḍḍāḥ, Abū 'Abd Allāh Muḥammad. *Kitāb al-Bid'a: Tratado contra las innovaciones*. Ed. Maribel Fierro. Madrid: CSIC, 1988.

Ikhwān al-Ṣafā'. *Rasā'il Ikhwān al-Ṣafā'*. 4 vols. Ed. Khayr al-Dīn Ziriklī. Cairo: al-Maktaba al-Tijāriyya al-Kubrā, 1928.

Rasā'il Ikhwān al-Ṣafā'. 4 vols. Butrus al-Bustānī. Beirut: Dār Ṣādir, 1957.

Epistles of the Brethren of Purity: The Case of the Animals versus Man before the King of the Jinn. An Arabic Critical Edition and English Translation of Epistle 22. Ed. and trans. Lenn E. Goodman and Richard McGregor. New York: Oxford University Press, 2012.

Secondary Sources

Abun-Nasr, Jamil. *Muslim Communities of Faith: The Sufi Brotherhoods in Islamic Religious Life*. New York: Columbia University Press, 2007.

Adamson, Peter. "al-Kindī." In *Cambridge Companion to Arabic Philosophy*. Ed. Adamson and Taylor. Cambridge: Cambridge University Press, 1993. 32–51.

"al-Kindī and the Mu'tazila: Divine Attributes, Creation and Freedom." *Arabic Sciences and Philosophy* 13 (2003): 45–77.

al-Kindī. New York: Oxford University Press, 2007.

Adang, Camilla. "The Spread of Ẓāhirism in al-Andalus in the Post-caliphal Period: The Evidence from the Biographical Dictionaries." In *Ideas, Images, Methods of Portrayal: Insights into Classical Arabic Literature and Islam*. Ed. Sebastian Gunther. Leiden: Brill, 2005. 297–345.

Addas, Claude. *Ibn ʿArabī ou La quête du Soufre Rouge*. Paris: Gallimard. Trans. P. Kingsley. *Quest for Red Sulphur : The Life of Ibn ʿArabī*. Cambridge: Islamic Texts Society, 1993.

"Andalusī Mysticism and the Rise of Ibn ʿArabī." In *The Legacy of Muslim Spain*. Ed. Salma Khadra Jayyusi. Leiden: Brill, 1994. 909–36.

Akhtar, Ali Humayun. "The Controversy over Graeco-Arabic Philosophy and Mysticism in al-Andalus: The Case of Ibn al-Khaṭīb." *International Journal of Middle Eastern Studies* 47 (2015): 323–47.

al-ʿAlawī, Jamāl al-Dīn. *Muʾallafāt Ibn Bājja*. Beirut and Casablanca: Dār al-Thaqāfa and Dār al-Nashr al-Maghribiyya, 1983.

Alvarez, Lourdes M. *Abū al-Ḥasan al-Shushtarī: Songs of Love and Devotion*. Mahwah, NJ: Paulist Press, 2009.

Amir-Moezzi, Mohammad Ali. *The Divine Guide in Early Shiʾism: The Sources of Esotericism in Islam*. Trans. D. Streight. Albany: State University of New York, 1994.

Arberry, A. J. *Sufism: An Account of the Mystics of Islam*. London: Allen and Unwin, 1950.

Arnaldez, Roger. *Grammaire et théologie chez Ibn Ḥazm de Cordoue: essai sur la structure et les conditions de la pensée musulmane*. Paris: Librarie Philosophique J. Vrin, 1956.

Asín Palacios, Miguel. *Abenmasarra y su escuela. Origenes de la filosofía hispano-musulmana*. Madrid: Imprenta Ibérica – E. Maestre, 1914.

Abenházam de Córdoba y su historia crítica de las ideas religiosas. 5 vols. Madrid: Real Academia de la Historia, 1927–32.

Ayoub, Mahmoud. *The Qur'an and Its Interpreters*. Albany: State University of New York Press, 1983.

Baldick, Julian. *Mystical Islam: An Introduction to Sufism*. New York: I. B. Tauris, 2012.

Bellver, José. "al-Ghazālī of al-Andalus: Ibn Barrajān, Mahdism, and the Emergence of Learned Sufism on the Iberian Peninsula," *Journal of the American Oriental Society* 133 (2013): 659–81.

Bencherifa, Muhammad. "al-Bunnāhī la al-Nubāhī," *Académia. Revue de l'Académie du Royaume du Maroc* 8 (1998): 17–89.

Berkey, Jonathan. *The Formation of Islam: Religion and Society in the Near East, 600–1800*. New York: Cambridge University Press, 2003.

Bosch Vilá, Jacinto. "Qāsim b. Aṣbagh." *Encyclopaedia of Islam*, 2nd edition.

Bowering, Gerhard. "Early Sufism Between Persecution and Heresy." In *Islamic Mysticism Contested: Thirteen Centuries of Controversy and Polemics*. Leiden: Brill, 1999. 45–67.

The Mystical Vision of Existence in Classical Islam: The Qur'anic Hermeneutics of the Sufi Sahl al-Tustarī. Berlin-New York: Walter de Gruyter, 1980.

"Dhū'l-Nūn Miṣrī." *Encyclopaedia Iranica*, vii, 1996. 572–3.

Böwering, Gerhard and Bilal Orfali. *Sufi Treatises of Abū ʿAbd Al-Raḥmān al-Sulamī*. Beirut: Dār al-Mashriq, 2009.

Brett, Michael. *The Rise of the Fatimids: The World of the Mediterranean and the Middle East in the 10th Century CE.* Leiden: Brill, 2013.

Brockopp, Jonathan. "The Formation of Islamic Law: The Egyptian School, 750–900," *Annales Islamologiques* 45 (2011): 123-40.

Burgel, Christoper J. "Ibn Ṭufayl and His *Ḥayy ibn Yaqẓān*: A Turning Point in Arabic Philosophical Writing." In *The Legacy of Muslim Spain.* Ed. Salma Khadra Jayyusi. Leiden: E. J. Brill, 1992. 830–6.

"Symbols and Hints: Some Considerations Concerning the Meaning of Ibn Ṭufayl's *Ḥayy ibn Yaqẓān*." In *The World of Ibn Ṭufayl.* Ed. Lawrence Conrad. Leiden: Brill, 1997. 238–67.

"Zoroastrianism as Viewed in Medieval Islamic Sources." In *Muslim Perceptions of Other Religions: A Historical Survey.* Ed. Jacques Waardenburg. Oxford: Oxford University Press, 1999. 202–12.

Burnett, Charles. "Magister Iohannes Hispanus: Towards the Identity of a Toledan Translator." In *Comprendre et maîtriser la nature au Moyen Age. Mélanges d'histoire des sciences offerts à Guy Beaujouan.* Geneva/Paris: Librairie Droz/Librairie Champion, 1994. 425–36.

Calero Secall, María Isabel. "El proceso de Ibn al-Jaṭīb," *al-Qantara* 22 (2001): 421–61.

Campos, Michelle. *Muslims, Christians, and Jews in Late Ottoman Palestine.* Stanford, CA: Stanford University Press, 2007.

Chabbi, Jacquiline. "Remarques sur les développement historique des mouvements ascétiques et mystiques au Khurâsân." 46 (1977): 5–72.

Chamberlain, Michael. *Knowledge and Social Practice in Medieval Damascus, 1190-1135.* Cambridge: Cambridge University Press, 1994. 69–90, 111–76.

Chittick, William C. *The Sufi Path of Knowledge: Ibn ʿArabī's Metaphysics of Imagination.* Albany: State University of New York Press, 1989.

"Rūmī and *waḥdat al-wujūd*." In *Poetry and Mysticism in Islam: The Heritage of Rūmī.* Ed. Amin Banani, Richard Hovannisian, and George Sabagh. Cambridge: Cambridge University Press, 1994. 70–111.

Encyclopaedia of Islam. 2nd edition. s. v. "*Waḥdat al-Shuhūd.*"

Chodkiewicz, Michel. *An Ocean without a Shore: Ibn ʿArabī, the Book, and the Law.* Albany: State University of New York Press, 1993.

Seal of the Saints: Prophethood and Sainthood in the Doctrine of Ibn ʿArabī. Cambridge: Islamic Texts Society, 1993.

"La sainteté et les saints en islam." In *Le Culte des saints dans le monde musulman.* Ed. H. Chambert-Loir and C. Guillot. Paris: École Française d'Extrême Orient, 1995. 13–22.

Codera Zaidín, Francisco. "Un manuscrito árabe-español en Túnez." *Boletín de la Real Academiade la Historia* 58 (1911): 285–96.

Cole, J. R. I. "The World as Text: Cosmologies of Shaykh Aḥmad al-Aḥsāʾī." *Studia Islamica* 80 (1994): 1–23.

Conrad, Lawrence I. "Through the Thin Veil: On the Question of Communication and the Socialization of Knowledge in *Ḥayy ibn Yaqẓān*." In *The World of Ibn Ṭufayl.* Ed. Lawrence Conrad. Leiden: Brill 1997. 238–67.

Cook, Michael. "Activism and Quietism in Islam: The Case of the Early Murjiʾa." In *Islam and Power.* Ed. Alexander S. Cudsi and Ali E. H. Dessouki. London: Croom Helm, 1981. 15–23.

Commanding Right and Forbidding Wrong in Islamic Thought. Cambridge: Cambridge University Press, 2000.

Corbin, Henri. "Le livre du glorieux de Jâbir ibn Ḥayyân: alchemie et archétypes." *Eranos Jahrbuch* 18 (1950): 47–114.

"Ibn Ṭufayl." In *Encyclopedia of Philosophy*. Ed. Paul Edwards. New York: Macmillan, 1967.

Cornell, Vincent. "Ḥayy in the Land of Absāl: Ibn Ṭufayl and Sufism in the Western Maghrib During the Muwaḥḥid Era." In *The World of Ibn Ṭufayl*. Ed. Lawrence Conrad. Leiden: Brill, 1997. 133–64.

Realm of the Saint. Austin: University of Texas Press, 1998.

"Faqīh versus Faqīr in Marinid Morocco: Epistemological Dimensions of a Polemic." In *Islamic Mysticism Contested*. Ed. Frederick de Jong and Bernd Radtke. Brill: Leiden, 1999: 207–24.

Cruz Hernandez, Miguel. "La persecución anti-massarí durante el reinado de ʿAbd al-Raḥmān al-Nāṣir li-Dīn Allāh según Ibn Ḥayyān." *al-Qantara* 2 (1981): 51–67.

Historia del pensamiento en el mundo islámico, vol. 2, El pensamiento de al-Andalus (Siglos IX–XIV). Madrid: Alianza Editorial, 1996.

D'Ancona, Cristina. "La doctrine de la creation 'mediante intelligentia' dans le *Liber de Causis* et dans ses sources." *Revue des sciences philosophiques et theologiques* 76 (1992): 209–33.

"Greek into Arabic: Neoplatonism in Translation." In *The Cambridge Companion to Arabic Philosophy*. Cambridge: Cambridge University Press, 1993. 10–31.

"Porphyry, Universal Soul, and the Arabic Plotinus." *Arabic Sciences and Philosophy* 9 (1999): 47–88.

Darling, Linda T. *A History of Social Justice and Political Power in the Middle East: The Circle of Justice from Mesopotamia to Globalization*. London: Routledge, 2012. 79–80.

Daftary, Farhad. *Ismaili Literature: A Bibliography of Sources and Studies*. New York: I. B. Tauris, 2004.

Davidson, Herbert A. *Alfarabi, Avicenna and Averroes on Intellect: Their Cosmologies, Theories of the Active Intellect, and Theories of Human Intellect*. New York: Oxford University Press, 1992.

de la Puente, Cristina. "Vivre et mourir pour Dieu, oeuvre et héritage d'Abū ʿAlī al-Ṣadafī (m. 514/1120)." *Studia Islamica* 88 (1998): 77–102.

Dozy, Reinhardt. *Histoire des Musulmans d'Espagne: jusqu'à la conquete de l'Andalousie par les Almoravides (711–1110)*. 4 vols. Leiden: Brill, 1861.

Dreher, Josef. "Das Imamat des islamischen Mystikers AbulQasīm Aḥmad ibn al-Ḥusain ibn Qasī (gest. 1151). Eine Studie zum Selbstverständnis des Autors des 'Buchs vom Ausziehen der beiden Sandalen (*Kitāb Khalʿ an-naʿlain*).'" Rheinische Friedrich Wilhelms Universität Bonn (Germany) Dissertation, 1985.

"L'Imâmat d'Ibn Qasî à Mértola (automne 1144- été 1145). Legitimité d'une domination soufie?" *Mélanges de l'Institut Dominicain d'Études du Caire* 18 (1988): 153–210.

Druart, Thérèse-Anne. "Al-Fārābī's Causation of the Heavenly Bodies." In *Islamic Philosophy and Mysticism*. Ed. Parviz Morewedge. Delmar, NY: Caravan Books, 1981. 35–45.

"Al-Fārābī and Emanationism." In *Studies in Medieval Philosophy*. Ed. J. F. Wippel. Washington, DC: The Catholic University of America Press, 1987. pp. 23–43.

"Al-Fārābī, Emanation, and Metaphysics." In *Neoplatonism and Islamic Thought: Studies in Neoplatonism: Ancient and Modern 5*. Ed. Morewedge. Albany: State University of New York Press, 1992: 127–48.

"The Human Soul's Individuation and Its Survival after the Body's Death: Avicenna on the Causal Relation between Body and Soul." *Arabic Sciences and Philosophy* 10 (2000): 259–74.

Dutton, B. D. "Al-Ghazālī on Possibility and the Critique of Causality." *Medieval Philosophy and Theology* 10 (2001): 23–46.

El-Hibri, Tayeb. *Reinterpreting Islamic Historiography: Harūn al-Rashīd and the Narrative of the ʿAbbāsid Caliphate*. Cambridge: Cambridge University Press, 1999.

El-Rouayheb, Khaled. *Islamic Intellectual History in the Seventeenth Century: Scholarly Currents in the Ottoman Empire and the Maghreb*. Cambridge: Cambridge University Press, 2015.

Elias, Jamal. "Sufi *tafsīr* Reconsidered: Exploring the Development of a Genre," *Journal of Qur'anic Studies* 12 (2010): 41–55.

Endress, Gerhard. "The Debate between Grammar and Greek Logic." *Journal for the History of Arabic Sciences* 2 (1977): 106–18.

Ebstein, Michael. *Mysticism and Philosophy in al-Andalus: Ibn Masarrra, Ibn al-ʿArabī and the Ismāʿīlī Tradition*. Leiden: Brill, 2013.

Ebstein, Michael and Sara Sviri. "The So-Called *Risālat al-Ḥurūf* (Epistle on Letters) Ascribed to Sahl al-Tustarī and Letter Mysticism in al-Andalus." *Journal Asiatique* 299 (2011): 213–70.

Fakhry, Majid. *Ethical Theories in Islam*. Leiden: Brill, 1991.

A Short Introduction to Islamic Philosophy, Theology, and Mysticism. Oxford: Oneworld, 1997.

Faure, A. *Encyclopedia of Islam*. 2nd edition. s. v. "Ibn al-ʿArīf," "Ibn Barrajān," "Ibn Qasī."

Ferhat, Halima. "As-Sirr al-Maṣūn de Ṭāhir as-Ṣadafī: un itinéraire mystique au XIIe siècle." *al-Qantara* 16 (1995): 237–88.

Fierro, Maribel. "Los Mālikīes de al-Andalus y los dos arbitros (*al-ḥakamān*)." *al-Qantara* (1985): 79–102.

La heterodoxia en Al-Andalus durante el Período Omeya. Madrid: Instituto Hispano-Arabe de Cultura, 1987.

"The Introduction of *Ḥadīth* in al-Andalus (2nd/8th–3rd/9th centuries)." *Der Islam* 66 (1989): 68–93.

"El derecho Mālikī en al-Andalus, ss. II/VIII-V/XI." *al-Qantara* 12 (1991): 119–31.

"Heresy in al-Andalus." In *The Legacy of Muslim Spain*. Ed. Salma Jayyusi and Manuela Marín. Leiden: Brill, 1992. 895–908.

"The Polemic about the *karāmāt al-awliyāʾ* and the Development of Sufism in al-Andalus Fourth/Tenth–Fifth/Eleventh Centuries." *Bulletin of the School of African and Oriental Studies, University of London* 55 (1992): 236–49.

"La religión." In *Historia de España Menéndez Pidal – Los Reinos de Taifas: al-Andalus en el Siglo XI*. Ed. J. M. Jover and M. J. Viguera Molíns. Madrid: Espasa-Calpe, 1994. 8-1:399–496.

"Bāṭinism in al-Andalus: Maslama b. Qāsim al-Qurṭubī (d. 353/964), author of the *Rutbat al-ḥakīm* and the *Ghāyat al-ḥakīm* (Picatrix)." *Studia Islamica* 84 (1996): 87–112.

"La religión." In *Historia de España Menéndez Pidal – El Retroceso Territorial de al-Andalus. Almoravides y Almohades, siglos IX–XIII, Historia de Espana.* Ed. J. M. Jover and M. J. Viguera Molíns. Madrid: Espasa-Calpe, 1997. 8-2:437–550.

"The Legal Policies of the Almohad Caliphs and Ibn Rushd's *Bidāyat al-mujtahid,*." *Journal of Islamic Studies* 10 (1999): 226–48.

"Opposition to Sufism in al-Andalus." In *Islamic Mysticism Contested.* Ed. Frederick de Jong and Bernd Radtke. Brill: Leiden, 1999. 174–206.

"*Le mahdi Ibn Tumart et al-Andalus: l' élaboration de la légitimité almohade.*" Ed. Mercedes García-Arenal. Paris: Edisud, 2000: 107–24.

"Revolución y tradición: algunos aspectos del mundo del saber en época almohade." In *Estudios onomásticos-biográficos de al-Ándalus.* Ed. M. L. Ávila and M. Fierro. Madrid: CSIC, 2000. 10:131–65.

"Spiritual Alienation and Political Activism: The *ġurabāʾ* in Andalusī Spain during the Sixth/Twelfth Century." *Arabica* 47 (2000): 230–60.

"La política religiosa de ʿAbd al-Raḥmān III (r. 300/912–350/961)." *al-Qantara* 25 (2004): 119–56.

"The Movable Minbar of Cordoba: How the Umayyads of al-Andalus Claimed the Inheritance of the Prophet." *Jerusalem Studies in Arabic and Islam* 33 (2007): 149–68.

"Alfonso the Wise: The Last Almohad Caliph?" *Medieval Encounters* 15 (2009): 175–98.

"The Almohads and the Fatimids." In *Ismāʿīlī and Fatimid Studies in Honor of Paul E. Walker*, Ed. Bruce D. Craig. Chicago: Middle East Documentation Center, 2010. 161–75.

Finnegan, J. "Avicenna's Refutation of Porphyrius." In *Avicenna Commemoration Volume.* Ed. V. Courtois. Calcutta: 1956. 187–203.

Forneas, José María. "De la transmisión de algunas obras de tendencia ašʿarī en al-Andalus." *Awraq* 1 (1978): 4–11.

Frank, Richard. "The *Falsafa* of Ğahm ibn Ṣafwān." *Le Museon* 78 (1965): 395–424.

The Metaphysics of Created Being According to Abû l-Hudhayl al-ʿAllâf: A Philosophical Study of the Earliest Kalâm. Istanbul: Nederlands Historisch Archaeologisch Instituut in het Nabije Oosten, 1966.

"The Structure of Created Causality According to al-Ashʿarī: An Analysis of the *Kitāb al-Lumaʿ.*" *Studia Islamica* 25 (1966): 13–75.

"The Divine Attributes According to the Teaching of Abū l-Hudhayl al-ʿAllāf." *Le Museon* 82 (1969): 451–506.

"Abū Hāshim's Theory of 'States': Its Structure and Function," *Actas do Congressu de Estudos Arabes e Islámicos* (Leiden, 1971): 85–100.

"Several Fundamental Assumptions of the Baṣra School of the Muʿtazila." *Studia Islamica* (1971): 5–18.

"Al-Maʿdūm wa-l-Mawjūd: The Non-existent, the Existent, and the Possible in the Teaching of Abū Hāshim and His Followers," MIDEO: Mélanges de l'Institut Dominicain d'Etudes Orientales," *MIDEO* 14 (1980): 185–209.

"Elements in the Development of the Teaching of al-Ashʿarī." *Le Museon* 104 (1991): 141–90.

"Al-Ghazālī on Taqlīd: Scholars, Theologians, and Philosophers." *Zeitschrift fur die Geschichte der arabisch-islamischen Wissenschaften* 7 (1991–2): 207–52.

Creation and the Cosmic System: Al-Ghazālī and Avicenna. Heidelberg: Carl Winter-Universitätsverlag, 1992.

al-Ghazālī and the Ashʿarite School. Durham, NC: Duke University Press, 1994.

Fricaud, Émile. "Les ṭalaba dans la société almohade (Le temps d'Averroès)." *al-Qantara* 18 (1997): 331–88."

"La place des ṭalaba dans la société almohade mu'minide." In *Los Almohades: Problemas y Perspectivas*. Ed. Cressier and Fierro. Molina. Madrid: CSIC, 2005. 525–45.

Gabrieli, Francesco. "Omayyades d'Espagne et Abbasides." *Studia Islamica* 31 (1970): 93–100.

García-Arenal, Mercedes. "La conjunction du sufisme et du sharifisme au Maroc: le Mahdi comme sauveur." *Revue des Mondes Musulmans et de la Mediterranée* 55–6 (1990): 233–56.

"La práctica del precepto de *al-amr bi-l-maʿrūf wa-l-nahy ʿan al-munkar* en la hagiografía maghrebí." *al-Qantara* 13 (1992): 143–65.

Ed. *Mahdisme et millenarisme en Islam*. Paris: Edisud, 2000.

Garden, Kenneth. "Al-Ghazālī's Contested Revival: *Iḥyāʾ ʿUlūm al-Dīn* and Its Critics in Khorasan and the Maghrib." University of Chicago dissertation, 2005.

The First Islamic Reviver. New York: Oxford University Press, 2013.

Gardet, Louis. *La pensée religieuse d'Avicenne*. Paris: J. Vrin, 1951.

Gauthier, Léon. *Ibn Thofail: sa vie, ses oeuvres*. Paris: Ernest Leroux, 1909.

Gianotti, Timothy J. *al-Ghazālī's Unspeakable Doctrine of the Soul: Unveiling the Esoteric Psychology and Eschatology of the Iḥyāʾ*. Leiden: Brill, 2002.

Gimaret, Daniel. *Les Noms Divins en Islam*. Paris: Les Editions du Cerf, 1988.

La Doctrine Ashʿarīte. Paris: Les Editions du Cerf, 1990.

Gohlman, William E. *The Life of Ibn Sīna*. Albany: New York, 1974.

Goldziher, Ignaz. *Livre d'Ibn Toumert*. Algiers: P. Fontana, 1903.

Streitschrift des Gazali gegen die Bāṭinijja-Sekte. Leiden: Brill, 1916.

The Ẓāhiris: Their Doctrine and Their History. Trans. Wolfgang Behn. Leiden: Brill, 1971.

Goodrich, David R. "A Ṣūfī Revolt in Portugal: Ibn Qasī and His '*Kitāb khalʿ al-naʿlayn*." Columbia University dissertation, 1978.

Gordon, Matthew. *The Breaking of a Thousand Swords: A History of the Turkish Military of Samarra (AH 200–275/815–889 CE)*. Albany: State University of New York Press, 2001.

"The Commanders of the Samarran Turkish Military: The Shaping of a Third/Ninth-Century Imperial Elite." In *A Medieval Islamic City Reconsidered: An Interdisciplinary Approach to Samarra*. Ed. Chase Robinson. Oxford: Oxford University Press, 2001. 119–40.

Gramlich, Richard. *Alte Vorbilder des Sufitums*. Wiesbaden: Harrassowitz, 1997.

Griffel, Frank. "The Relationship Between Averroes and al-Ghazâlî as It Presents Itself in Averroes' Early Writings, Especially in His Commentary on al-Ghazâlî's al-Mustaṣfâ." In *Medieval Philosophy and the Classical Tradition in Islam, Judaism, and Christianity*. Ed. J. Inglis. Richmond: Curzon Press, 2002. 51–63.

"Al-Ghazālī's Concept of Prophecy: The Introduction of Avicennan Psychology into Ashʿarite Theology." *Arabic Sciences and Philosophy* 14 (2004): 101–44.

"Taqlīd of the Philosophers: al-Ghazālī's Initial Accusation in the *Tahāfut*." In *Ideas, Images, and Methods of Portrayal: Insights into Classical Arabic Literature and Islam*. Ed. Sebastian Gunther. Leiden: Brill, 2005. 273–98.

al-Ghazālī's Philosophical Theology. New York: Oxford University Press, 2009.
Gril, Denis. "La 'lecture supérieure' du Coran selon ibn Barrağān." *Arabica* 47 (2000): 510–22.
Guichard, Pierre. *Les Musulmans de Valence et la reconquete (XIe–XIIIe siecles)*, 2 vols. Damascus: Institut Francais de Damas, 1990–1.
Gutas, Dimitri. *Avicenna and the Aristotelian Tradition: Introduction to Reading Avicenna's Philosophical Works*. Leiden: Brill, 1988.
"Ibn Ṭufayl on Ibn Sīna's Eastern Philosophy." *Oriens* 34 (1994): 359–85.
Greek Thought, Arabic Culture: The Graeco-Arabic Translation Movement in Baghdad and Early ʿAbbāsid Society (2nd–4th/8th -10th centuries). London: Routledge, 1998.
"The Heritage of Avicenna: The Golden Age of Arabic Philosophy, 1000–ca. 1350." In *Avicenna and His Heritage. Proceedings of the International Colloquium "Avicenna and his Heritage," Leuven-Louvain-la-Neuve, 8–11 September 1999*. Ed. J. Janssens and D. De Smet. Leuven: Leuven University Press, 2002. 81–97.
"The Study of Arabic Philosophy in the Twentieth Century." *British Journal of Middle Eastern Studies* 29 (2002): 5–15.
Hallaq, Wael. *Ibn Taymiyya against the Logicians*. Oxford: Clarendon Press, 1993.
Authority, Continuity, and Change in Islamic Law. Cambridge: Cambridge University Press, 2005.
Halm, Heinz. *Kosmologie und Heilslehre der früher Ismāʿīlīyya*. Wiesbaden: Franz Steiner, 1978.
"Methoden und Formen der frühesten ismailitischen Daʿwa." *In Studien zur Geschichte und Kultur des Vorderen Orients. Festschrift für Bertold Spuler zum siebzigsten Geburtstag*. Leiden: Brill, 1981. 123–36.
The Empire of the Mahdi: The Rise of the Fatimids. Leiden: Brill, 1996.
The Fatimids and Their Traditions of Learning. London: I. B. Tauris, 1997.
Hamdani, Abbas. "The Arrangement of the *Rasāʾil Ikhwān al-Ṣafā* and the Problem of Interpolations." *Journal of Semitic Studies* 29 (1984): 97–110.
Haneda, Masashi and Toru Miura. (eds.), *Islamic Urban Studies: Historical Review and Perspectives*. London: Kegan Paul International, 1994.
Hawi, Sami S. *Islamic Naturalism and Mysticism*. Leiden: Brill, 1997.
Heath, Peter. "Knowledge." In *The Literature of al-Andalus*. Ed. Maria Rosa Menocal, Raymond P. Scheindlin, and Michael Sells. Cambridge: Cambridge University Press, 2000: pp. 96–125.
Heinen, Anton M. *Islamic Cosmology: A Study of as-Suyūṭī's al-Hayʾa as-Sanīya fī l-Hayʾa as-Sunnīya*. Beirut: Orient-Institut der Deutschen Morgenländischen Gesellschaft, 1982.
Hodgson, Marshall. *Encyclopaedia of Islam*. 2nd edition s.v. "Bāṭiniyya."
Encyclopedia of Islam. 2nd edition. s. v. "Ghulāt."
Hourani, Albert. *Reason and Tradition in Islamic Ethics*. Cambridge: Cambridge University Press, 1985.
Hourani, George F. "The Principal Subject of Ibn Tufayl's *Ḥayy ibn Yaqẓān*." *Journal of Near Eastern Studies* 15 (1956): 40–6.
"The Chronology of al-Ghazālī's Writings." *Journal of the American Oriental Society* 79 (1959): 225–33.
"A Revised Chronology of Ghazālī's Writings." *Journal of the American Oriental Society* 104 (1984): 284–302.

Huici Miranda, A. *Historia Politica del Imperio Almohade*, 2 vols. Tetuan: Editora Marroquí, 1956–7.

Idris, Roger. "Reflections on Mālikīsm under the Umayyads of Spain." In *The Formation of al-Andalus Part 2*. Ed. Maribel Fierro and Julio Samso. Aldershot: Ashgate Variorum, 1998: 2:85–101.

Jaʿfar, M. K. I. *Min Qaḍāya l-Fikr al-Islāmī: Dirāsa wa Nuṣūs*. Cairo: Maktabat Dār al-ʿUlūm, 1976.

Min al-Turāth al-Falsafī li-Ibn Masarra. Cairo: Maktabat Dār al-ʿUlūm, 1982.

Kaddouri, Samir. "Ibn Ḥazm al-Qurtubī (d. 456/1064)." In *Islamic Legal Thought: A Compendium of Muslim Jurists*. Ed. Oussama Arabi, David S. Powers, and Susan A. Spectorsky. Leiden: Brill, 2013. 211–38.

"Refutations of Ibn Ḥazm by Mālikī Authors from al-Andalus and North Africa." In *Ibn Ḥazm of Cordoba: The Life and Works of a Controversial Thinker*. Ed. Camilla Adang, Maribel Fierro, and Sabine Schmidtke. Leiden: Brill, 2013. 539–600.

Karamustafa, Ahmet. *God's Unruly Friends: Dervish Groups in the Islamic Middle Period 1200–1550*. Oxford: Oneworld, 2006.

Sufism: The Formative Period. Edinburgh: Edinburgh University Press, 2007.

Kassis, H. E. "Coinage of an Enigmatic Caliph: The Midrārid Muḥammad b. al-Fatḥ of Sijilmāsah," *Al-Qantara* 9 (1988): 489–504.

Katura, J. "al-Taṣawwuf wa-l-Ṣulta: Namādhij min al-Qarn al-Sādis al-Hijrī fī l-Maghrib wa-l-Andalus." *al-Ijtihad* 12 (1991): 181–212.

Katz, Marion H. *Prayer in Islamic Thought and Practice*. Cambridge: Cambridge University Press, 2013.

Kennedy, Hugh. "From Polis to Medina: Urban Change in Late Antique and Early Islamic Syria." *Past and Present* 106 (1985): 3–27.

The Prophet and the Age of the Caliphates: The Islamic Near East from the 6th to the 11th Century. London: Longman, 1986.

Khalek, Nancy. *Damascus after the Muslim Conquest: Text and Image in Early Islam*. Oxford: Oxford University Press, 2011.

Klein, Yaron. "Between Public and Private: An Examination of ḥisba Literature." *Harvard Middle Eastern and Islamic Review* 7 (2006): 41–62.

Knysh, Alexander. *Islamic Mysticism: A Short History*. Leiden: Brill, 2000.

"Multiple Areas of Influence." In *The Cambridge Companion to the Qur'ān*. Ed. Jane McAuliffe. Cambridge: Cambridge University Press, 2006. 211–34.

Ibn ʿArabī in the Later Islamic Tradition: The Making of a Polemical Image. Albany: State University of New York Press, 2007.

Kogan, Barry S. "Eternity and Origination: Averroes' Discourse on the Manner of the World's Existence." In *Islamic Theology and Philosophy: Studies in Honor of George F. Hourani*. Ed. Michael E. Marmura. Albany: State University of New York Press, 1984. 203–35.

Kukkonen, Taneli. "Possible Worlds in the *Tahāfut al-Falāsifa:* al-Ghazālī on Creation and Contingency." *Journal of the History of Philosophy* 38 (2000): 470–502.

Lagardere, Vincent. "La tarîqa et la revolte des Murîdûn en 539 H / 1144 en Andalus." *Revue de L'Occident musulman et de la Méditerranée* 35 (1983): 157–70.

Lagerlund, Henrik. *Rethinking the History of Skepticism: The Missing Medieval Background*. Leiden: Brill, 2010.

Landolt, Hermann. "Ghazālī and 'Religionswissenschaft': Some Notes on the *Mishkāt al-Anwār.*" *Asiatische Studien* 45-1 (1991): 19–72.

Lapidus, Ira M. "The Separation of State and Religion in the Development of Early Islamic Society." *International Journal of Middle Eastern Studies* 6 (1975): 363–85.

A History of Islamic Societies. Cambridge: Cambridge University Press, 2002.

le Gall, Dina. *A Culture of Sufism: Naqshbandīs in the Ottoman World, 1450–1700.* Albany: State University of New York Press, 2005.

Lomba Fuente, Joaquín. *Avempace*. Zaragoza: Disputacion General de Aragon, 1989.

Lowry, Joseph E. *Early Islamic Legal Theory: The Risāla of Muḥammad Ibn Idrīs Al-Shāfi'ī.* Leiden: Brill, 2007.

Lowry, Joseph, Devin J. Stewart, and Shawkat M. Toorawa (eds.), *Law and Education in Medieval Islam: Studies in Memory of Professor George Makdisi.* Cambridge: E. J. W. Gibb Memorial Trust, 2004.

Madelung, Wilferd. "Das Imamat in der fruhen ismailitischen Lehre,' *Der Islam* 37 (1961): 43–135.

Makkī, M. A. "Tashayyu' fī l-Andalus." *Revista del Instituto Egipcio de Estudios Islámicos en Madrid* 2 (1954): 93–149.

Marcotte, Roxanne D. "Reason and Direct Intuition in the Works of Shihāb al-Dīn al-Suhrawardī (d. 587/1191)." In *Reason and Inspiration in Islam.* Ed. Hermann Landolt and Todd Lawson. New York: I. B. Tauris, 2005. 221–34.

Marín, Manuela. "Baqī b. Majlad y la introducción del studio del Ḥadīt en al-Andalus." *al-Qantara* 1 (1981): 165–208.

"*Zuhhād* de al-Andalus 300/912 – 420/1029." *al-Qantara* 12 (1991): 439–69.

"*Inqibāḍ 'an al-Sulṭān*: *'Ulamā'* and Political Power in al-Andalus." In *Saber, Religioso, y Poder Politico en el Islam: Acts del Simposio Internacional (Granada, 15–18 octubre 1991)*. Madrid: Agencia Espanola de Cooperacion Internacional, 1994. 127–39.

Marmura, Michael. "The Logical Role of the Argument from Time in the *Tahāfut's* Second Proof for the World's Pre-eternity." *The Muslim World* 49 (1959): 306–14.

"Al-Kindī's Discussion of Divine Existence and Oneness." *Medieval Studies* 25 (1963): 338–54.

"The Islamic Philosophers' Conception of Islam." In *Islam's Understanding of Itself.* Ed. R. G. Hovannisian and S. Vryonis Jr. Malibu: Udena Press, 1983.

"Avicenna's Flying Man in Context." *The Monist* 69 (1986): 383–95.

"al-Ghazālī on Bodily Resurrection and Causality in the *Tahāfut* and *Iqtiṣād*." *Aligarh Journal of Islamic Thought* 2 (1989): 46–58.

"al-Ghazālī's Chapter on Divine Power in the *Iqtiṣād*." *Arabic Sciences and Philosophy* 4 (1994): 279–315.

"Ghazālian Causes and Intermediaries." *JAOS* 115 (1995): 89–100.

"Ghazālī and Ash'arism Revisited." *Arabic Sciences and Philosophy* 12 (2002): 91–110.

Probing in Islamic Philosophy: Studies in the Philosophy of Ibn Sīna. Binghamton: State University of New York at Binghamton, 2004.

"al-Ghazālī." In *The Cambridge Companion to Arabic Philosophy*, Ed. Adamson and Taylor. Cambridge: Cambridge University Press, 2008. 137–54.

Marquet, Yves. "Révélation et vision véridique chez les Ikhwān al-Ṣafā." *Revues des Etudes Islamiques* 32 (1964): 27–44.

La philosophie des Ikhwān al-Ṣafā. Algiers, Societe Nationale d'Edition et de Diffusion, 1975.

Martin, Richard C. "The Role of the Basrah Muʿtazilah in Formulating the Doctrine of the Apologetic Miracle." *Journal of Near Eastern Studies* 39 (1980): 175–89.

Massignon, Louis. *Recueuil des texts inedits concernant l'histoire de la mystique en pays d'Islam*. Paris: Geuthner. 1929.

Mayer, Toby. "Theology and Sufism." In *The Cambridge Companion to Islamic Theology*. Ed. Tim Winter. Cambridge: Cambridge University Press, 2008. 258–87.

Melchert, Christopher. "Religious Policies of the Caliphs from al-Mutawakkil to al-Muqtadir, AH 232–295/AD 847–908." *Islamic Law and Society* 3 (1996): 316–42.

"The Transition from Asceticism to Mysticism at the Middle of the Ninth Century CE." *Studia Islamica* 83 (1996): 51–70.

The Formation of the Sunni Schools of Law. Brill: Leiden, 1997.

"The Ḥanābila and the Early Sufis." *Arabica* 48 (2001): 352–67.

Michot, Yahya. "L'avicennisation de la *sunna*, du ṣabéisme au leurre de la Ḥanı ¯fiyya: À propos du Livre des religions et des sectes, II d'al-Shahrastânî." *Bulletin de Philosophie Médiévale* 35 (1993): 113–20.

"Ibn Taymiyya's Commentary on the Creed of al-Ḥallāj." In *Sufism and Theology*. Ed. Ayman Shihadeh. Edinburgh: Edinburgh University Press, 2007. 123–36.

Mones, Hussain. "Le rôle des hommes de religion dans l'histoire de l'Espagne musulmane jusqu'à la fin du califat." *Studia Islamica* 20 (1964): 47–88.

Monnot, Guy. *Encyclopedia of Islam*. 2nd edition. s. v. "Thanawiyya." Monnot, G. Penseurs musulmans et religions iraniennes: ʿAbd al-Jabbār et ses *devanciers*. Paris: Vrin, 1974.

Montada, Josep Puig. "Philosophy in Andalusia: Ibn Bājja and Ibn Ṭufayl." In *The Cambridge Companion to Classical Arabic Philosophy*. Ed. P. Adamson and R. C. Taylor. Cambridge: Cambridge University Press, 2008. 155–79.

Morris, James. "Ibn Masarra: A Reconsideration of the Primary Sources." Unpublished article, 1973. pp. 1–51.

"Ibn ʿArabī and His Interpreters Part II (Conclusion): Influences and Interpretations." *Journal of the American Oriental Society* 107 (1987): 101–19.

"Ibn ʿArabī's 'Esotericism': The Problem of Spiritual Authority." *Studia Islamica* 71 (1990): 37–64.

Morrison, Robert. *Islam and Science: The Intellectual Career of Nīẓām Al-Dīn Al-Nīsābūrī*. London: Routledge, 2007. 20–36.

Mottahedeh, Roy. *The Mantle of the Prophet: Religion and Politics in Iran*. New York: Simon and Schuster, 1985.

Loyalty and Leadership in Early Islamic Society. Princeton, NJ: Princeton University Press, 2001.

Mottahedeh, Roy and Kristin Stilt. "Public and Private as Viewed Through the Work of the *Muḥtasib*." *Social Research* 70 (2003): 735–48.

Nagel, Tilman. "Le Mahdisme d'Ibn Toumert et d'Ibn Qasī: Une analyse phénoménologique." *Revue d'Etudes du Monde Musulman et de la Mediterranée* 91–4 (2000): 125–35.

Nasr, Seyyed Hossein. *An Introduction to Islamic Cosmological Doctrines*. London: Thames and Hudson, 1978.

Nwyia, Paul. "Notes sur quelques fragments inédits de la correspondence d'Ibn al-ʿArīf avec Ibn Barrajān." *Hespéris: Archives Berberes et Bulletin de l'Institute des Hautes Études Marocaines* 48 (1955): 217–21.

Peña Martín, Salvador. *Corán, palabra y verdad: Ibn al-Sīd y el humanismo en al-Andalus*. Madrid: Consejo Superior de Investigaciones Científicas, 2007.

Peters, J. R. T. M. *God's Created Speech: A Study in the Speculative Theology of the Mutʿazilī Qādī l-Qudāt Abu l-Hasan ʿAbd al-Jabbār b. Aḥmad al-Hamadhānī*. Leiden: Brill, 1976.

Pines, Shlomo. "The Limitations of Human Knowledge According to al-Fārābī, Ibn Bājja, and Maimonides." In *Studies in Medieval Jewish History and Literature*. Ed. Isadore Twersky. Cambridge, MA: Harvard University Press, 1979. 82–109.

Pockocke, Edward. *Philosophus autodidactus, sive epistola Abi Jaafar, Ebn Tophail de Hai Ebn Yokdhan. In qua Ostenditur, quomodo ex Inferiorum contemplatione ad Superiorum notitiam Ratio humana ascendere possit*. Oxford: H. Hall, 1671.

Rabb, Intisar A. "Islamic Legal Minimalism: Legal Maxims and Lawmaking When Jurists Disappear." In *Law and Tradition in Classical Islamic Thought: Studies in Honor of Professor Hossein Modarressi*. Ed. Michael Cook, Najam Haider, Intisar Rabb, and Asma Sayeed. New York: Palgrave Macmillan, 2013. 145–66.

Radtke, Bernd. "How Can Man Reach the Mystical Union?: Ibn Ṭufayl and the Divine Spark." In *The World of Ibn Ṭufayl*. Ed. Lawrence Conrad. Leiden: Brill, 1997. 165–94.

"The Concept of *Wilāya* in Early Sufism." In *The Heritage of Sufism. Vol. 1, Classical Persian Sufism from Its Origins to Rumi (700–1300)*. Oxford: Oneworld, 1999. 483–96.

"al-Ḥakīm al-Tirmidhī on Miracles." In *Miracles et karâma: Les saints et leurs miracles à travers l'hagiographie chrétienne et islamique, ive–xve siècles*. Ed. Denise Aigle. Turnhout: Brepols, 2000. 287–99.

Radtke, Bernd and John O'Kane. *The Concept of Sainthood in Early Islamic Mysticism: Two Works by al-Ḥakīm al-Tirmidhī*. New York: Routledge, 2013.

Rahman, Fazlur. *Prophecy in Islam: Philosophy and Orthodox*. London: George Allen and Unwin, 1958.

Reinhart, A. Kevin. *Before Revelation: The Boundaries of Muslim Moral Thought*. Albany: State University of New York Press, 1995.

Reynolds, Gabriel Said. *Encyclopedia of Islam*. 3rd Edition. s.v. "Gabriel." el-Rouayheb, K. *Islamic Intellectual History in the Seventeenth Century: Scholarly Currents in the Ottoman Empire and the Maghreb*. Cambridge: Cambridge University Press, 2015.

Rowson, Everett K. "Religion and Politics in the Career of Badīʿ al-Zamān al-Ḥamadhānī." *Journal of the American Oriental Society* 107 (1987): 653–73.

A Muslim Philosopher on the Soul and Its Fate: Al-ʿĀmirī's Kitāb al-Amad ʿAlā l-Abad. New Haven, CT: American Oriental Series, 1988.

"The Theology of Aristotle and Some Other Pseudo-Aristotelian Texts Reconsidered." *Journal of the American Oriental Society* 112 (1992): 478–84.

Rustom, Mohammed. "Is Ibn ʿArabī's Ontology Pantheistic?" *Journal of Islamic Philosophy* 2 (2006): 53–67.

The Triumph of Mercy: Philosophy and Scripture in Mullā Ṣadra. Albany: State University of New York Press, 2012.

"Philosophical Sufism." In *The Routledge Companion to Islamic Philosophy.* Ed. Richard C. Taylor and Luis Xavier Lopez-Farjeat. New York: Routledge, 2015. 309–411.

Safi, Omid. *The Politics of Knowledge in Premodern Islam: Negotiating Ideology and Religious Inquiry.* Chapel Hill: University of North Carolina Press, 2006.

Safran, Janina. "The Commander of the Faithful in al-Andalus: A Study in the Articulation of Caliphal Legitimacy." *International Journal of Middle Eastern Studies* 30 (1998): 19–50.

The Second Umayyad Caliphate: The Articulation of Caliphal Legitimacy In al-Andalus. Cambridge, MA: Harvard Center for Middle Eastern Studies, 2001.

Sands, Kristen. *Sufi Commentaries on the Qur'an in Classical Islam.* London: Routledge, 2006.

Schimmel, Annemarie. *Mystical Dimensions of Islam.* Chapel Hill: University of North Carolina Press, 1975.

Schmidtke, Sabine. "Ibn Ḥazm's Sources on Ashʿarīsm and Mutʿazilīsm." In *Ibn Ḥazm of Cordoba: The Life and Works of a Controversial Thinker.* Ed. Camilla Adang, Maribel Fierro, and Sabine Schmidtke. Leiden: Brill, 2013. 375–402.

Schwyzer, Hans-Rudolf. "Die pseudoaristotelische *Theologie* und die Plotin-Ausgabe des Porphyrios." *Museum Helveticum* 90 (1941): 216–36.

Sells, Michael A. *Mystical Languages of Unsaying.* Chicago: University of Chicago Press, 1994.

Serrano, Delfina. "¿Por qué llamaron los almohades antropomorfistas a los almorávides?" In *Los almohades: problemas y perspectivas.* Ed. M. Fierro, P. Cressier, and L. Molina. Madrid: CSIC, 2005. 2:815–52.

"Why Did the Scholars of al-Andalus Distrust al-Ghazālī: Ibn Rushd al-Jadd's *Fatwā* on *Awliyā'Allāh*," *Der Islam* 83 (2006): 137–56.

Shihadeh, Ayman. *The Teleological Ethics of Fakhr al-Dīn al-Rāzī.* Leiden: Brill, 2006.

Stern, S. M. "The Early Ismāʿīlī Missionaries in North-West Persia and in Khurasan and Transoxania.' *Bulletin of the School of Oriental and African Studies* 23 (1960): 56–90.

"Ibn Masarra, Follower of Pseudo-Empedocles – An Illusion." In *Acts IV Congress de studios árabes e islámicos. Coimbra-Lisboa. 1 a 8 de Setembro de 1968.* Leiden: Brill, 1971. 325–37.

Stewart, Devin. "The Doctorate of Islamic Law in Mamlūk Egypt and Syria," in *Law and Education in Medieval Islam Studies in Memory of Professor George Makdisi*, eds. Joseph. Lowry, Devin J. Stewart, and Shawkat M. Toorawa (Cambridge: The E. J. W. Gibb Memorial Trust, 2004), pp. 45–90.

Stroumsa, Sarah. "Ibn Masarra and the Beginnings of Mystical Thought in al-Andalus." In *Mystical Approaches to God: Judaism, Christianity, and Islam.* Ed. P. Schaeffer Munich: Historisches Kolleg Oldenbourg, 2006. 97–112.

Stroumsa, Sarah and Sara Sviri. "The Beginnings of Mystical Philosophy in al-Andalus: Ibn Masarra and His Epistle on Contemplation." *Jerusalem Studies in Arabic and Islam* 36 (2009): 201–53.

Tahrali, Mustafa. "A General Outline of the Influence of Ibn ʿArabī on the Ottoman Era." *Journal of the Muhyiddin Ibn ʿArabi Society* 26 (1999): 43–54.

Taylor, Richard. "Ibn Rushd / Islamic and 'Islamic' Rationalism." *Medieval Encounters. Jewish, Christian and Muslim Culture in Confluence and Dialogue* 15 (2009): 125–35.

"Arabic / Islamic Philosophy in Thomas Acquinas's Conception of the Beatific Vision in IV Sent. D. 4 49, Q. 2. A. 1." *The Thomist* 76 (2012): 509–50.

Toorawa, Shawkat M. *Ibn Abī Ṭāhir Ṭayfūr and Arabic Writerly Culture: A Ninth-Century Bookman in Baghdad.* London: RoutledgeCurzon, 2005.

Tornero, Emilio. "Nota sobre el pensamiento de Abenmasarra." *al-Qantara* 6 (1985): 503–6.

"Noticia sobre la publicación de obras inéditas de Ibn Masarra." *al-Qantara* 14 (1993): 47–64.

"Filosofía." In *Historia de España Menéndez Pidal – El retroceso territorial de al-Andalus. Almorávides y almohades, siglos IX–XIII.* Ed. J. M. Jover and M. J. Viguera Molíns. Madrid: Espasa-Calpe, 1997. 8-2:587–602.

Treiger, Alexander. "Monism and Monotheism in al-Ghazālī's *Mishkāt al-Anwār*." *Journal of Qur'anic Studies* 9 (2007): 1–27.

Inspired Knowledge in Islamic Thought. New York: Routledge, 2011.

Turki, Abdel Magid. *Polémiques entre Ibn Ḥazm et Bāǧi sur les principes de la loi musulmane. Essai sur le littéralisme ẓāhirīte et la finalité mālikīte.* Algiers: Argel, 1973.

Urvoy, Dominique. "La pensée d'Ibn Tumart." *Bulletin d'études orientales* 27 (1974): 19–44.

Pensers d'Andalus. Paris: CNRS, 1978.

Van Bladel, Kevin. *The Arabic Hermes: From Pagan Sage to Prophet of Science.* New York: Oxford University Press, 2009.

Van Ess, Josef. "The Logical Structure of Islamic Theology." In *Logic in a Classical Islamic Culture.* Ed. G. E. von Grunebaum. Wiesbaden: Otto Harrassowitz, 1970. 21–50.

"Early Development of Kalām." In *Studies in the First Century of Islamic Society.* Ed. G. H. A. Junyboll. Carbondale: Southern Illinois University Press, 1982. 109–24.

The Flowering of Muslim Theology. Cambridge, MA: Harvard University Press, 2006.

Walbridge, John. *The Leaven of the Ancients: Suhrawardī and the Heritage of the Greeks.* Albany: State University of New York Press, 2000.

The Wisdom of the Mystic East: Suhrawardī and Platonic Orientalism. Albany: State University of New York Press, 2001.

Walker, Paul. *Early Philosophical Shiism: The Ismāʿīlī Falsafa of Abū Yaʿqūb al-Sijistānī.* Cambridge: Cambridge University Press, 1993.

Abū Yaʿqūb al-Sijistānī: Intellectual Missionary. New York: I. B. Tauris 1998.

Ḥamīd al-Dīn al-Kirmānī: Ismāʿīlī Thought in the Age of al-Ḥakīm. New York: I. B. Tauris, 1999.

Exploring an Islamic Empire: Fatimid History and Its Sources. London: I. B. Tauris, 2002.

"The Ismāʿīlīs." In *The Cambridge Companion to Arabic Philosophy*. Ed. Peter Adamson and Richard Taylor. Cambridge: Cambridge University Press, 2005. 73–92.

Watt, W. Montgomery. *Islamic Philosophy and Theology*. Edinburgh: Edinburgh University Press, 1962.

Weiss, Bernard. *The Search for God's Law: Islamic Jurisprudence in the Writings of Sayf al-Dīn al-Āmidī*. Salt Lake City: University of Utah Press, 1992.

Spirit of Islamic Law. Athens: University of Georgia Press, 1998.

Whittingham, Martin. *al-Ghazālī and the Qur'ān: One Word Many Meanings*. New York: Routledge 2007.

Wisnovsky, Robert. *Avicenna's Metaphysics in Context*. Ithaca, NY: Cornell University Press 2003.

"Some Remarks on the Nature and Scope of Arabic Philosophical Commentary in Post-classical (ca. 1100–1900 CE) Islamic Intellectual History: Some Preliminary Observations." In *Philosophy, Science and Exegesis in Greek, Arabic, and Latin Commentaries*. Ed. P. Adamson, H. Baltussen, and M. W. F. Stone. London: Institute of Classical Studies, 2004. 2:149–91.

"Avicenna and the Avicennian Tradition." In *The Cambridge Companion to Arabic Philosophy*. Ed. Adamson and Taylor. Cambridge: Cambridge University Press, 2008. 92–137.

Yanagihashi, Hiroyuki. *Encyclopaedia of Islam*, 3rd ed., s.v. "Abū Ḥanīfa."

Yazaki, Saeko. *Islamic Mysticism and Abu Ṭālib al-Makkī: The Role of Heart*. New York: Routledge, 2013.

Zaman, Muhammad Qasim. *Religion and Politics under the Early ʿAbbāsids: The Emergence of the Proto-Sunnī Elite*. Leiden: Brill, 1997.

Ziai, Hossein. "The Illuminationist Tradition." In *History of Islamic Philosophy*. Ed. Seyyed Hossein Nasr and Oliver Leaman. London: Routledge, 1996. 465–96.

Zimmerman, F. W. "The Origins of the So-Called Theology of Aristotle." In *Pseudo-Aristotle in the Middle Ages: The Theology and Other Texts*. Ed. Jill Kraye, W.F. Ryan, and Charles B. Schmitt. London: Warburg Institute, 1986. 110–24.

Index